LIVES
OF THE
LORD CHANCELLORS OF ENGLAND.

LITTLETON

LIVES

OF

THE LORD CHANCELLORS

AND

KEEPERS OF THE GREAT SEAL

OF

ENGLAND,

FROM THE EARLIEST TIMES TILL THE REIGN OF QUEEN VICTORIA.

BY
LORD CAMPBELL.

SEVENTH EDITION.

ILLUSTRATED.

VOL. III.

WILDSIDE PRESS

CONTENTS

OF

THIRD VOLUME.

CHAP.		PAGE
LIII.	Continuation of the Life of Lord Bacon to the end of the reign of Elizabeth, ...	1
LIV.	Continuation of the Life of Lord Bacon from the accession of James I. till his appointment as Lord Chancellor, ...	16
LV.	Continuation of the Life of Lord Bacon from his appointment as Chancellor till his fall, . . .	53
LVI.	Conclusion of the Life of Lord Bacon, . . .	95
LVII.	Life of Lord Keeper Williams from his birth till his installation as Lord Keeper, ...	127
LVIII.	Continuation of the Life of Lord Keeper Williams till the end of the reign of James I., . . .	147
LIX.	Continuation of the Life of Lord Keeper Williams till his appointment as Archbishop of York, . .	163
LX.	Conclusion of the Life of Lord Keeper Williams, .	178
LXI.	Life of Lord Keeper Coventry from his birth till the commencement of the proceedings respecting ship money, ...	191
LXII.	Conclusion of the Life of Lord Keeper Coventry, . .	216
LXIII.	Life of Lord Keeper Finch from his birth till the meeting of the Long Parliament, ...	230
LXIV.	Conclusion of the Life of Lord Keeper Finch, . .	251
LXV.	Life of Lord Keeper Littleton from his birth till the commencement of the civil war, ...	262
LXVI.	Conclusion of the Life of Lord Keeper Littleton, .	277

CONTENTS.

CHAP.		PAGE
LXVII.	Life of Lord Keeper Lane,	292
LXVIII.	Lords Keepers of the Parliamentary Great Seal during the Commonwealth, till the first appointment of Lord Commissioner Whitelock,	305
LXIX.	Lords Commissioners of the Great Seal from the first appointment of Whitelock till the adoption of a new Great Seal bearing the insignia of the Republic,	320
LXX.	Lords Keepers from the adoption of the Republican Great Seal till Cromwell became "Protector,"	347
LXXI.	Lords Keepers during the Protectorate of Oliver Cromwell,	356
LXXII.	Lords Commissioners of the Great Seal from the death of Cromwell till the Restoration,	370
LXXIII.	Life of Lord Keeper Herbert,	394
LXXIV.	Life of Lord Chancellor Clarendon from his birth till the execution of Lord Strafford,	408
LXXV.	Continuation of the Life of Lord Clarendon till he was sent to Bristol with the charge of Prince Charles,	424
LXXVI.	Continuation of the Life of Lord Clarendon till his return from the embassy to Madrid,	439
LXXVII.	Continuation of the Life of Clarendon till the Great Seal was delivered to him at Bruges,	455

LIVES

OF THE

LORD CHANCELLORS OF ENGLAND.

CHAPTER LIII.

CONTINUATION OF THE LIFE OF LORD BACON TO THE END OF THE REIGN OF ELIZABETH.

TRANSACTIONS now come upon us, which, though they did not seriously mar Bacon's fortunes, have affixed a greater stain upon his memory than even that judicial corruption by which he was at once precipitated from the height of power and greatness.

We have seen how Essex behaved to him with princely munificence, and with more than fraternal affection. Their intimacy continued without abatement till the ill-fated young nobleman had incurred the displeasure of his Sovereign. He steadily supported the interest of his friend at Court by his personal exertions; and when he was to be absent in his expedition to the coast of Spain, he most earnestly recommended him to the Queen, and all over whom he could expect to exercise any influence. Bacon repaid this kindness by the salutary advice he gave him, and above all by cautioning him against going as Lord-Deputy to Ireland—a service unfit for his abilities, and which, from the errors he was in danger of committing in it, and the advantage to be taken of his absence by his enemies, was likely to lead to his ruin.

In spite of Essex's unfortunate campaign and unsuccessful negotiations in Ireland, Bacon stuck by him as a defender,—believing that he retained his place in the Queen's heart, and that he would yet have the disposal of the patronage of the Crown. On his sudden return without leave from his command, and his hurrying down to Nonsuch, where the Court lay, Bacon followed him, and had the mortification to find, that, after a gleam of returning favor, the Earl had been ordered into confinement. But, to guard against exaggeration of the misconduct about to be exposed, I most eagerly admit that now, and down to the hour when the unhappy youth expiated his offenses on the scaffold, Bacon showed him as much countenance as was entirely consistent with his own safety, convenience, and hope of advancement.

In a short interview with him at Nonsuch, he said, "My Lord, *Nebecula est, cito transibit;* it is but a mist;" and he wisely advised him "to seek access to the Queen *importune, opportune,* seriously, sportingly, every way."[1]

While Essex was a prisoner in the custody of Lord Keeper Egerton, at York House, as Bacon had frequent interviews with the Queen, which, he says, were only "about causes of her revenue and law business," the rumor ran that he was incensing her against his young patron; and even Robert Cecil mentioned it to him, saying, one day, in his house at the Savoy, "Cousin, I hear it, but I believe it not, that you should do some ill office to my Lord of Essex: for my part I am merely passive, and not active, in this action; and I follow the Queen, and that heavily, and I lead her not. The same course I would wish you to take." Francis justified himself, and we believe truly, from the imputation. According to his own account he did everything in his power to induce her to restore him to favor, resorting for this purpose to *rhyme* as well as to reason. About the middle of Michaelmas term, 1600, as she intimated her intention to dine with him at Twickenham, "though he professed not to be a poet, he prepared a sonnet, directly tending and alluding to draw on her Majesty's reconcilement to my Lord,"— which he presented to her at her departure. He likewise, as he says, strongly dissuaded her from prosecuting Essex, on account of his great popularity ; and he adds, " Never was I so ambitious of anything in my lifetime as I was to have carried some token or favor from her Majesty to my Lord,—using all the art I had, both to procure her Majesty to send, and myself to be the messenger." Elizabeth mentioning to him one day at Whitehall the nomination

---

[1] Apology. Works, vol. vi. 219.

of Lord Mountjoy for Deputy in Ireland, Bacon said to her, "Surely, Madam, if you mean not to employ my Lord of Essex thither again, your Majesty can not make a better choice." "Essex!" said she; "whensoever I send Essex back again into Ireland, I will marry you;—claim it of me." Whereunto, out of zeal for the imprisoned Earl, he said, "Well, Madam, I will release that contract, if his going be for the good of your state." She was so far offended, that in Christmas, Lent, and Easter term following, when he came to her on law business, her face and manner were not so clear and open to him as usual, and she was entirely silent respecting Essex. After that, she declared that she was resolved to proceed against him— by information *ore tenus* in the Star Chamber, although it should be *ad castigationem, et non ad destructionem.* Then, to divert her entirely from this purpose, Bacon said, "Madam, if you will have me speak to you in this argument, I must speak to you as Friar Bacon's head spake, that said first *Time is,* and then *Time was,* and *Time will never be;* it is now far too late—the matter is cold, and hath taken too much wind."

We have the account of these dialogues only from himself after her death, and it is to be regarded with great suspicion, as there is reason to think that she gave a somewhat different version of them in her lifetime; for, introducing his narrative, and alluding to the stories circulated against him, he says, "I will not think that they grew any way from Majesty's own speeches, whose memory I will ever honor; if they did, she is with God, and *miserum est lædi de quibus non possis queri.*"

He takes to himself the entire merit of having the Star Chamber prosecution converted into the extra-judicial inquiry before the Lord Keeper and other Commissioners at York House,[1] by saying to her, "Why, Madam, if you will needs have a proceeding, you were best have it in some such sort as Ovid spoke of his mistress, *est aliquid luce patente minus.*"

It is quite certain, however, that he had never ventured to visit the disgraced favorite during his long captivity, or to give him any public support; and the people (to the honor of England be it spoken), ever shocked by private treachery and ingratitude, were indignant at his conduct,

---

[1] Apology, vol. vi. 200, 221.

and gave credit to "a sinister speech raised of him how he was a suitor to be used against my Lord of Essex at that time." To clear himself from this imputation, he has left us the substance of a letter which he wrote to her when he heard "that her Majesty was not yet resolved whether she would have him forborne in the business or no," and which I must say, rather betrays an apprehension that he might lose the advantage and *éclat* of holding a a brief in a case of such public expectation : " That if she would be pleased to spare me in my Lord of Essex's cause out of the consideration she took of my obligation towards him, I should reckon it for one of her greatest favors; *but, otherwise, desiring her Majesty to think that I know the degrees of duties; and that no particular obligation whatsoever to any subject could supplant or weaken that entireness of duty that I did owe and bear to her service.*" The vindication was completely satisfactory to himself, according to his own standard of honor and delicacy, for he says triumphantly, "This was the goodly suit I made, being a respect no man that had his wits could have omitted.

But in casting the parts to be taken by the different counsel, he was not satisfied with the minor one assigned to him, which was to show that Essex had given some countenance to the libelous publication stolen from Cornelius Tacitus; and he objected to the allotment,—" That it was an old matter and had no manner of coherence with the rest of the charge;" but he was answered in a manner showing that others knew better what became him than himself, "because it was considered how I stood to my Lord of Essex, therefore that part was thought fittest for me which did him the least hurt, for that, whereas all the rest was matter of charge and accusation, this only was but matter of caveat and admonition." Though "*nolens volens,* he could not avoid the part laid upon him by the Queen's pleasure," when the day came he made the most of it, and, admitting that "he did handle it not tenderly," he assures us that this seeming harshness "must be ascribed to the superior duty he owed to the Queen's fame and honor in a public proceeding, and partly to the intention he had to uphold himself in credit and strength with the Queen, the better to be able to do my Lord good offices afterwards!"

At the Queen's request he wrote out for her a report of

this trial, which he read to her in two several afternoons; and when he came to Essex's defense, he says, she was much moved, and, praising the manner in which it was given, observed, "she perceived old love could not easily be forgotten." Upon which, he tells us, he ventured to reply, "that he hoped she meant that of herself."

He really had a desire,—if not to satisfy his conscience, —for the sake of his reputation, to assist in restoring Essex to favor. With this view he composed several letters for him to be addressed to the Queen, and a letter supposed to be written by his brother to Essex,—with the answer from Essex to his brother,—which were privately shown to the Queen with a view of mollifying her.

On one occasion, mentioning to her a doctor who had for a time cured his brother of the gout, but that the patient had afterwards found himself worse, she said, " I will tell you, Bacon, the error of it; the manner of these empirics is to continue one kind of medicine, which at the first is proper, being to draw out the ill humor, but after, they have not the discretion to change the medicine." "Good Lord, Madam," said he, "how wisely and aptly can you speak and discern of physic ministered to the body, and consider not that there is the like occasion of physic ministered to the mind!" And then he went on to apply the doctrine to the case of Essex, from whom the humor had been sufficiently drawn, and who stood in need of having strength and comfort ministered to him.

Essex was now liberated from custody, but soon began to set the Court at defiance, and Bacon became very unhappy at the double game he himself had been playing; for there was little prospect of the favorite being restored to power; and in the mean time Elizabeth testified great displeasure with his old "Mentor, under whose advice she believed he was acting. For three months she would not converse with her "counsel extraordinary," even on law matters, and "she turned away from him with express and purpose-like discountenance wheresoever she saw him." At last, after new-year's-tide, he boldly demanded an audience, with the evident intention of intimating to her that he was ready to renounce all connection with Essex for ever. He tells us that he thus addressed her:—

"Madam, I see you withdraw your favor from me, and now I have lost many friends for your sake. I shall lose you, too: you have put me like one of those that the Frenchmen call *enfans perdus*, that serve on foot before horsemen; so have you put me into matters of envy, without place or without strength; and I know at chess a pawn before the King is ever much played upon. A great many love me not because they think I have been against my Lord of Essex, and you love me not because you know I have been for him; yet will I never repent me that I have dealt in simplicity of heart towards you both, without respect of cautions to myself, and, therefore, *vivus videnspue pereo*. If I do break my neck, I shall do it in a manner as Mr. Dorrington did it, which walked on the battlements of the church many days, and took a view and survey where he should fall. And so, Madam, I am not so simple but that I take a prospect of my overthrow; only I thought I would tell you so much, that you may know that it was faith, and not folly, that brought me into it, and so I will pray for you." He says, that by this speech, *uttered with some passion*, her Majesty was exceedingly moved, and said to him, *Gratia mea sufficit*, with other sensible and tender words; but as touching my Lord of Essex, *ne verbum quidem*. "Whereupon," says he, "I departed, resting then determined to meddle no more in the matter, as that, I saw, would overthrow me, and not be able to do him any good."[1]

To this selfish resolve may be ascribed the fatal catastrophe which soon followed. Essex, irritated by the Queen's refusal to renew his patent for the monopoly of sweet wines, was beginning to engage in very criminal and very foolish projects; but if Bacon, whom he was yet inclined to love and honor, had continued to keep up an intercourse with him, had visited him in Essex House, had seen the desperate companions with whom he was there associating, and had warned him of the danger to which he was exposing himself and the state, it is utterly impossible that the mad attempt to raise an insurrection in the city, and forcibly to get possession of the Queen's person, should ever have been hazarded. But the rash enthusiast, suddenly deserted by him on whose sagacity and experience he had relied ever since he had entered into public life, listened to the advice of men destitute alike of prudence and of virtue; and after committing the

[1] Apology. Works, vol. vi. 231.

clearest acts of treason and rebellion, was obliged to surrender himself to justice.

It might have been expected that now, at any rate, struck with remorse and overcome by tenderness, Bacon would have hastened to the noble prisoner's cell in the Tower to comfort and console him,—to assist him in preparing an almost hopeless defense,—to devise schemes with him for assuaging the anger of the Queen,—to teach him how he might best avail himself for his deliverance of that ring which Bacon knew had been intrusted to him, with a promise that it should bend her to mercy whenever returned to her,—which she was anxiously looking to see till the very moment of his execution, and the thought of which embittered her own end. At all events, he might have helped his fated friend to meet death, and have accompanied him to the scaffold.

Tranquilized by an assurance that he was to be employed, along with the Queen's Sergeant and the Attorney and Solicitor General, as Counsel for the Crown, on the trial of Essex before the Lord High Steward, Bacon spent the ten days which elapsed between the commitment to the Tower and the arraignment, shut up in his chambers in Gray's Inn, studying the law of treason,—looking out for parallel cases of an aggravated nature in the history of other countries,—and considering how he might paint the unpardonable guilt of the accused in even blacker colors than could be employed by the ferocious Coke, famous for insulting his victims.

The 19th of February arrived. Bacon took his place early at the bar of the Court constructed for the Peers in Westminster Hall,—his mind filled with the precedents and the tropes he had accumulated. Even *he* must have felt a temporary pang when the object of general sympathy, as yet little turned of thirty years of age,—whose courage was so exalted, whose generosity was so unbounded, whose achievements were so brilliant, who had ever testified to him a friendship not exceeded by any mentioned in history or fiction,—was conducted into the Hall by Sir Walter Raleigh and the officers of the Tower, preceded by the axe, its edge still turned from him till the certain verdict of *Guilty* should be pronounced. But if Bacon felt a little awkwardness when he first met the eye of his friend, he soon recovered his composure, and he conducted himself throughout the day with coolness, zeal, and dexterity.

Yelverton, the Queen's Sergeant, and Coke, the Attorney General, first addressed the Peers, and adduced the evidence. Essex, then, unassisted with counsel, made his defense, chiefly dwelling upon the provocation he had to right himself by force from the machinations of his enemies, who had plotted his destruction. The reply was intrusted to Bacon, although it ought to have been undertaken by Fleming, the Solicitor General. We have only a short sketch of it,—from which we learn, that, taunting Essex with having denied nothing material, he particularly addressed himself to the apology he had relied upon,—comparing him to Cain, the first murderer, who took up " an excuse by impudency," and to Pisistratus, who, doting on the affections of the citizens, and wishing to usurp supreme power, wounded his own body that it might be thought he had been in danger. He thus concluded : " And now, my Lord, all you have said or can say in answer to these matters are but shadows, and therefore methinks it were your best course to confess, and not to justify." [1]

It so happened that the topics on which Essex had relied in his defense were chiefly taken from a letter which Bacon had penned for him to Queen Elizabeth. The simple-minded Earl, unprepared for such duplicity, and unable to distinguish between his private friend and the Queen's counsel, now exclaimed, " May it please your Lordship, I must produce Mr. Bacon for a witness." He then went on to explain the contents of the letter, whereby, " it will appear what conceit he held of me, and now otherwise he here coloreth and pleadeth the contrary."

Bacon, a little abashed, thus retorted :—" My Lord, I spent more hours to make you a good subject than upon any man in the world besides; but since you have stirred upon this point, My Lord, I dare warrant you this letter will not blush; for I did but perform the part of an honest man, and ever labored to have done you good, if it might have been, and to no other end; for what I intended for your good was wished from the heart, without touch of any man's honor."

Essex made a feeling appeal to the Peers sitting on his trial against " these orators, who out of a form and

---

[1] Harl. MS. No. 6854. 1 St. Tr. 1350.

custom of speaking, would throw so much criminal odium upon him, while answering at the peril of his life a particular charge brought against him." "And," he said, in a manner that made a deep impression on all who heard him, "I protest before the ever-living God, as he may have mercy on me, that my conscience is clear from any disloyal thought or harm to her Majesty. My desire ever hath been to be free from bloodshed. If in all my thoughts and purposes I did not ever desire the good estate of my Sovereign and country as of my own soul, I beseech the Lord to set some mark upon me in this place for a just vengeance of my untruths to all the world. And God, which knoweth the secrets of all hearts, knoweth that I never sought the crown of England, nor ever wished to be a higher degree than a subject. I only sought to secure my access to the Queen, that I might speedily have unfolded my griefs unto her Majesty against my private enemies, but not to have shed one drop of their blood. For my religion it is sound, and as I live I mean to die in it."

This appeal might, from sympathy, have produced a verdict of *not guilty*, or might have softened the resentment of Elizabeth; but, to deprive him of all chance of acquittal or of mercy, Bacon, after again pointing out how slenderly he had answered the objections against him, most artfully and inhumanly compared him to the *Duke de Guise*, the leader of the league in France, who kept in tutelage the last prince of the House of Valois, and who on "the day of the Barricadoes" at Paris, intending to take forcible possession of his Sovereign's person, with the purpose of dethroning him, had such confidence in the love of the citizens, that he appeared to lead the intended insurrection in his doublet and hose, attended with only eight men,—and who, when he was obliged to yield, the King taking arms against him, pretended that he had merely contemplated a private quarrel.

Essex having been condemned, Elizabeth wavered to the last moment about carrying the sentence into execution. Once, while relenting, she sent her commands, by Sir Edward Carey, that he should not be executed;—then, remembering his perverse obstinacy,—that he scorned to ask her pardon or to send her the ring, the appointed pledge of love and reconciliation,—she from time to time recalled the reprieve. It is highly probable that, under these circumstances, Bacon might have saved the life of his friend, either by advising him or interceding for him. He went not to the Tower, and although, " between the arraignment and my Lord's suffering, he was once with the Queen, yet he durst not deal directly for my Lord, as things stood." He tells us, indeed, that " he did commend her Majesty's mercy, terming it to her as an excellent balm that did continually distil from her sovereign hands, and made an excellent odor in the senses of her people." But while he thus flattered her, he did not venture to hint that her reputation for mercy would be endangered by suffering the law to take its course against Essex, who, though technically guilty of treason, instead of "imagining and compassing her death," felt for her the sincerest loyalty and reverence, and would cheerfully have died in her defense. Why did he not throw himself on his knees before her, and pray for a pardon? Because, while it was possible that he might have melted her, it was possible that he might have offended her, and that, a vacancy in the office of Solicitor General occurring, he might be again passed over.

Worse remains behind. The execution being deeply deplored and censured by the people, and Elizabeth, when she afterwards appeared in public, being received with the coldest silence instead of the enthusiastic plaudits to which she had been accustomed for forty years, she wished a pamphlet to be written to prove that Essex was properly put to death, and she selected Francis Bacon to write it. He, without hesitation, undertook the task, pleased " that her Majesty had taken a liking of his pen," and, with his usual industry and ability, soon produced " A Declaration of the Practices and Treasons of Robert, late Earl of Essex."

No honorable man would purchase Bacon's subsequent elevation at the price of being the author of this publication. A mere report of the trial for treason would have been excusable; but, to calumniate the memory of his friend, he goes back to a period when they were living together on terms of the closest intimacy,—when Essex was entirely under his influence;—and he accuses him of crimes of which he knew that the deceased was entirely innocent. Having begun by saying that the favorite aspired to the greatness of the *Præfectus Prætorio* under the emperors of Rome, he charges him with having formed a treasonable design when he first went Deputy to Ireland. "For being a man by nature of an high imagination, and a great promiser to himself as well as to others, he was confident that if he were once the first person in a Kingdom, and a sea between the Queen's seat and his, and Wales the nearest land from Ireland, and that he had got the flower of the English forces into his hands, which he thought so to intermix with his own followers as the whole body should move by his spirit, and if he might also have absolutely into his own hands *potestatem vitæ et necis et arbitrium belli et pacis* over the rebels, he should be able to make that place of lieutenancy of Ireland as a rise or step to ascend to his desired greatness in England." Next, all his proceedings in Ireland are converted into overt acts of this treasonable design. But none knew better than Bacon that, though Essex's Irish policy had been unwise and unfortunate, he had most earnestly done his best to serve his country, and that when he returned he had been both publicly and privately absolved of all disloyalty,—the only charge maintained against him being, that he had acted in some instances contrary to his instructions. In the report of the trial, several material passages of the depositions favorable to the accused are omitted; and in the originals preserved in the State Paper Offices, and verified by the handwriting of Sir Edward Coke, there may be seen opposite these passages, in the handwriting of Bacon, the abbreviated direction—"*om.*"[1]

Bacon vainly attempts to mitigate his own infamy by saying, "Never Secretary had more particular and express directions in every point how to guide my hand in it;"—adding that, after the first draught, it was materially altered by certain councillors to whom it was propounded by her Majesty's appointment,—he himself giving only words and form of style. After the specimen I have exhibited, what shall we say of his asseveration?—"their Lordships and myself both were as religious and curious of truth as desirous of satisfaction."

The base ingratitude and the slavish meanness manifested by Bacon on this occasion called forth the general

[1] This melancholy discovery was made by my friend, Mr. Jardine. See his Criminal Trials, vol. i. 332.

indignation of his contemporaries. He afterwards tried to soften this by his "Apology addressed to Mountjoy, Earl of Devonshire,"—a tract from which I have taken most of the facts on which my censure is founded, and which seals his condemnation with posterity; as it not only admits these facts, but shows that he had before his eyes no just standard of honor, and that in the race of ambition he had lost all sense of the distinction between right and wrong.[1]

A zealous advocate, however, has sprung up, who, considering Bacon to be the *purest* as well as the "wisest and brightest of mankind," pronounces his conduct through the whole course of these transactions to be deserving of high admiration.[2] It will be necessary to do little more than notice the heads of the defense or panegyric. 1. "Bacon did well in preferring the Queen to Essex, as *she* had been so kind to him; and, instead of pampering him with good things, made him for his advantage bear the yoke in his youth." This seems to proceed on the ranting and absurd maxim in the "Apology," that "every honest man that hath his heart well planted will forsake his friend rather than forsake his King." Friendship can not justify treason or any violation of the law; but are the sacred ties of friendship to be snapped asunder by the caprice of any crowned head? Elizabeth had conferred no personal obligations on Bacon; she had refused him the professional advancement to which he was fairly entitled; and her only object was to make the most of him at the least cost. 2. "Bacon was bound to appear as counsel against Essex, according to professional etiquette." Suppose that his dearly beloved brother, Anthony, who was in the service of Essex, had taken part with him in the insurrection on the 8th of February, and had been prosecuted for high treason, must Francis have appeared as counsel against him, and racked his ingenuity that his brother might be hanged, emboweled, and quartered? Etiquette can not be opposed to the feelings of nature, or the dic-

---

[1] He begins by giving a false account of the origin of his connection with Essex: "I loved my country more than was answerable to my fortune, and I held my Lord to be the fittest instrument to do good to the state, and therefore I applied myself to him," &c. He knew well that the precocious boy was wholly unfit to be a minister of state, and he applied himself to him because he hoped for advancement from the new favorite.

[2] Montagu's Life of Bacon.

tates of morality. A dispensation might easily have been obtained, if there had been a willingness to renounce the advantage and *éclat* of the appearance. 3. "Essex had abused his friendship, and had assumed the dissembling attitude of humility and penitence, that he might more securely aim a blow at the very life of his royal benefactress." This is an utter misrepresentation of the object of Essex's insurrection; at any rate, he had not engaged in it till Bacon had selfishly thrown him off; and Essex's public crime could not cancel the claims of private friendship, which he had never violated. But, 4. "Bacon was bound not to run the risk of marring his advancement, as he meant to use power, when attained, for the benefit of mankind." Will the end justify the means? and was he not more likely to improve the world by devoting himself to the completion of the *Instauratio Magna*, than by struggling to obtain the Great Seal, which he might lose by taking a bribe.

For some time after Essex's execution, Bacon was looked upon with great aversion; and, from the natural tendency of mankind to exaggerate, he was even suspected of having actively prompted that measure. But it is marvelous to witness what men of brilliant talents, and of enterprise and energy, may accomplish, in making contemporaries forget their errors and misconduct by drawing the public attention to themselves in new situations and circumstances.

Parliament meeting a few months after the execution of Essex, that event which had so deeply interested the nation was, for a time, almost forgotten in the excitement occasioned by the Queen's fainting fit on the throne, the shutting out of the Commons from the House of Lords, when the royal speech was delivered, and the efforts made to put down the frightful grievance of monopolies. Bacon being again returned as a member of the House of Commons, we may believe that he was at first not only shunned by the friends of Essex, but looked upon very coldly by men of all parties and opinions. He was determined to regain his ascendency. In the exercise of the privilege which then belonged to the representatives of the people, and still belongs to Peers, of laying bills on the table without previously asking leave to bring them in, he immediately introduced a bill "for the better suppressing abuses in weights and measures," saying, "This, Mr. Speaker, is no bill of state, nor of novelty, like a stately gallery for pleasure, but neither to live in nor sleep in; but this bill is a bill of repose, of quiet, of profit, of true and just dealings. The fault of using false weights and measures is grown so intolerable and common, that if you would build churches you shall not need for battlements and halls, other than false weights of lead and brass. I liken this bill to that sentence of the poet who set this as a paradox in the forefront of his book: *first water, then gold*, preferring necessity before pleasure. And I am of the same opinion, that things necessary in use are better than things which are glorious in estimation." He said he would speak to every particular clause "at the passing of the bill." But he was not able to carry it, and the subject remained for legislation in the reign of William IV.

A supply being proposed greater than was ever previously granted (four subsidies and eight-fifteenths), Bacon warmly supported it, and ridiculed a motion for exempting "three-pound men," saying, "dulcis tractus pari jugo:" therefore, the poor as well as the rich should pay. This drew upon him a sarcasm from Sir Walter Raleigh, then at variance with the Court, who (without quoting Hansard) referred to Bacon's famous patriotic speech, and said, "that he was afraid our enemies, the Spaniards, would hear of our selling our pots and pans to pay subsidies. *Dulcis tractus pari jugo*, says an honorable person. Call you this *par jugum*, when a poor man pays as much as a rich, and peradventure his estate is no better than he is set at, when our estates, that be £30 or £40 in the Queen's books, are not the hundredth part of our wealth? Therefore, it is not *dulcis* nor *par*." The supply, nevertheless, was carried by a large majority.

But the great question of the session was MONOPOLY, —on which Bacon took a most discreditable part. The grievance of grants of the exclusive right to deal in commodities had become altogether insupportable, and had caused the deepest ferment throughout the kingdom. It is difficult to conceive how society could subsist at a time when almost all matters of household consumption or commercial adventure (with the exception of bread, which was expected soon to be included), were assigned over to monopolists, who were so exorbitant in their demands that they sometimes raised prices tenfold; and who, to secure themselves against encroachments, were armed with high and arbitrary powers to search everywhere for contraband, and to oppress the people at pleasure. A declaratory bill having been brought in by Mr. Lawrence Hide to put down the grievance, and to restore common-law freedom of trade, it was thus opposed by:—

Mr. Francis Bacon. "The bill is very injurious and ridiculous; *injurious*, in that it taketh, or rather sweepeth, away her Majesty's prerogative; and *ridiculous*, in that there is a proviso that the statute shall not extend to grants made to corporations; that is a gull to sweeten the bill withal; it is only to make fools fain. All men of the law know that a bill which is only expository, to expound the common-law, doth enact nothing; neither is any promise of good therein."

Mr. Secretary Cecil quoted Bracton: "Prerogativum nostrum nemo audeat disputare;" adding, "and for my own part, I like not these courses should be taken; and you, Mr. Speaker, should perform the charge her Majesty gave unto you in the beginning of this parliament, not to receive bills of this nature; for her Majesty's ears be open to all grievances, and her hand stretched out to every man's petition."[1]

Bacon made an evasive attempt to support the abuse of monopolies by pretending that the proper course was humbly to petition the Queen, that she would abstain from granting them, or leave them to the course of the common-law instead of legislating against them; but the House showed such a determined spirit, that the Queen was compelled to yield; and she wisely put an end to the discussion by sending a message, through the Speaker, that the monopolies complained of should be canceled. Secretary Cecil now observed, "there is no patent whereof the execution, as I take it, hath not been injurious. Would that there never had been any granted. I hope there shall never be more." Whereupon there were loud cheers, according to the fashion of the time: "all the House said AMEN."[2]

There is nothing more interesting in our constitutional history, than to trace the growing power and influence

[1] 1 Parl. Hist. 934.   [2] Ibid.

of the House of Commons, from the increasing wealth and intelligence of the middling classes during the reign of Elizabeth, notwithstanding the arbitrary orders which she issued to them, and her habit, hardly considered illegal, of sending members to gaol when they offended her. The abolishers of monopolies were the fathers of those patriots, who, in the next generation, passed "the Petition of Right," and assembled in the Long Parliament.—Bacon himself lived to see both Houses unanimous in putting down judicial corruption.

In this reign he did not again take part in any affairs of importance. Like the Cecils, he was turning his eyes to the north, where the rising light he was desirous to worship was to appear.

CHAPTER LIV.

CONTINUATION OF THE LIFE OF LORD BACON FROM THE ACCESSION OF JAMES I. TILL HIS APPOINTMENT AS LORD KEEPER.

BACON had not contrived to open any direct communication with James during Elizabeth's life;—but no sooner had she breathed her last at Richmond, than he took active steps to recommend himself to the new monarch. He first wrote letters to Fowlys, a confidential person at the Scottish Court, to be shown to James,—in which (among other flatteries) he says, "We all thirst after the King's coming, accounting all this but as the dawning of the day before the rising of the sun, till we have his presence."[1] He wrote similar letters to Sir Thomas Chaloner, an Englishman, who had gone down to salute James, and was made governor to Prince Henry, —to Dr. Morrison, a physician at Edinburgh, in the confidence of James,—and to Lord Kinlosse, his prime favorite, who, strangely enough, for want of a place for which he was fitter, was made Master of the Rolls. In a few days after he addressed a letter directed to James himself. Having heard of his pedantic taste, he thus tries to suit it: "It may please your most excellent Majesty,—It is

[1] Works, vol. v. 272.

observed by some upon a place in the Canticles, *Ego sum flos campi et lilium convallium*, that a *dispari*, it is not said, *Ego sum flos horti et lilium montium*, because the majesty of that person is not enclosed for a few, nor appropriated to the great." He then goes on to say, that he would not have made oblation of himself, had it not been for the liberty which he enjoyed with his late dear sovereign Mistress,—" a princess happy in all things, but most happy in such a successor."[1] Having extolled the services of old Sir Nicholas and of his brother Anthony, and modestly alluding to his own, he thus shows the measure he had taken of the discernment and taste of King James: "And therefore, most high and mighty King, my most dear and dread Sovereign Lord, since now the corner-stone is laid of the mightiest monarchy in Europe, and that God above who hath ever a hand in bridling the floods and motions both of the seas and of people's hearts, hath by the miraculous and universal consent, the more strange because it proceedeth from such diversity of causes in your coming in, given a sign and token of great happiness in the continuance of your reign, I think there is no subject of your Majesty's which loveth this island, and is not hollow and unworthy, whose heart is not set on fire not only to bring you peace-offerings to make you propitious, but to sacrifice himself a burnt-offering or holocaust to your Majesty's service."[2]

Nevertheless, by some accident, Bacon's name was omitted in the first warrant sent from Holyrood, for continuing different persons connected with the law in their offices; but on the 21st of April, when James had reached Worksop in his progress to the South, he addressed another warrant to the Lord Keeper, whereby, after reciting that he had been informed that Francis Bacon, Esq., was one of the learned counsel to the late Queen by special commandment, he says, "Therefore we do require

---

[1] This seems to have afforded a happy hint for the famous Dedication ("with a double aspect") of a law-book to Lord Eldon by a gentleman who, after obtaining permission to dedicate to him, and before the book was published, seeing his intended patron suddenly turned out of office,—after some compliments to departing greatness, says, "but your felicity is that you contemplate in your successor (Lord Erskine) a person whose judgment will enable him to appreciate your merits, and whose talents have procured him a name among the eminent lawyers of his country."—*Raithby's Edition of Vernon.*

[2] Works, vol. v. 275.

you to signify our pleasure to him and others to whom it shall appertain to be thereof certified, that our meaning is that he shall continue to be of our learned counsel in such manner as before he was to the Queen."

As James approached, Bacon sent him the draught of a proclamation which he recommended to be issued,—" giving assurance that no man's virtue should be left idle, unemployed, or unrewarded;" but it was not adopted, as greater expectations of advancement had been already excited than could possibly be gratified.

Immediately on the King's arrival at Whitehall, Bacon was presented to him, and had a promise of private access. He thus confidentially describes James to the Earl of Northumberland, who had not yet been at Court :—" His speech is swift and cursory, and in the full dialect of his country; in speech of business, short; in speech of discourse, large. He affecteth popularity by gracing such as he hath heard to be popular, and not by any fashions of his own. He is thought somewhat general in his favors, and his virtue of access is rather because he is much abroad and in press than that he giveth easy audience. He hasteneth to a mixture of both kingdoms faster than policy will well bear. I told your Lordship, once before, that methought his Majesty rather asked counsel of the time past than of the time to come;' but it is yet early to ground any settled opinion."

He pretended that he had formed a resolution to devote himself for the rest of his days to philosophy, saying, " My ambition now I shall only put upon my pen, whereby I shall be able to maintain memory and merit of the times succeeding."[2] But in reality a ludicrous anxiety had entered the mind of the great Bacon—that he might be dubbed a knight, and in creditable fashion. Under the Tudors, knighthood was a distinction reserved to grace the highest offices, and to reward the most eminent services. James, from his accession, lavished it on almost all who solicited it, and turned it into a source of profit, by compelling all who had land of the yearly value of forty pounds to submit to it on payment of high fees, or to compound for it according to their ability. Bacon, perhaps, would have been better pleased with the rare dis-

[1] Bacon immediately discovered this defect in the Stuart character, which proved fatal to the dynasty. [2] Letter to Cecil, July 3, 1603.

tinction of escaping it, but for the special reasons he assigns in the following letter to Cecil, soliciting that it might be conferred upon him: " It may please your good Lordship —for this divulged and almost prostituted title of knighthood, I could, without charge, by your honor's mean, be content to have it, both because of this late disgrace,[1] and because I have three new knights in my mess in Gray's Inn commons, and because I have found out an Alderman's daughter, a handsome maiden, to my liking. So as if your honor will find the time, I will come to the Court from Gorhambury upon any warning."[2]

A promise being obtained, he now writes to Cecil, praying that he should be knighted privately by himself.— " For my knighthood I wish the manner might be such as might grace me, since the matter will not—I mean that I might be merely gregarious in a troop. The coronation is at hand." In this desire for a solitary ceremony he was disappointed, and on the 23rd of July, the day of the coronation, he was obliged to kneel down with a mob of above 300, and to receive a stroke of a sword from James, who was almost frightened to handle it, or look at it even when so used. However, he rose Sir Francis ; he was as good as the other members of his mess at Gray's Inn, and the handsome and rich Miss Barnham speedily became Lady Bacon. I am afraid that this was a match of mere convenience, and not very auspicious.

At the commencement of the new reign Bacon experienced some embarrassment from the part he had taken against Essex,—there being a strong manifestation of affection towards the memory of that nobleman, and in favor of the party who had supported him. The Earl of Southampton, famous as the enlightened patron and generous friend of Shakespeare, had been tried for treason, and, being convicted, had been kept close prisoner in the Tower till the death of Elizabeth. His pardon was now expected, and crowds went to visit him while he still remained in confinement. Among these Bacon did not venture to show himself, but he wrote a letter to the Earl, betraying a deep consciousness of having done what was wrong. "Yet," says he (clearly reflecting on his *honored*

---

[1] I do not know what this refers to. I do not find that he complained of the re-appointment of Coke and Fleming as Attorney and Solicitor General.

[2] July 3, 1603.

mistress), " it is as true as a thing that God knoweth, that this change hath wrought in me no other change towards your Lordship than this, that I may safely be that to you now which I was truly before." [1]

This meanness excited nothing but disgust, and there was such a strong expression of resentment against him, that, instead of waiting quietly till the public should be occupied with other subjects, he very imprudently published " The Apology of Sir Francis Bacon in certain Imputations concerning the late Earl of Essex," an apology which has injured him more with posterity than all the attacks upon him by his enemies.

His first appearance in public, in the new reign, was as one of the counsel for the Crown on the trial of Sir Walter Raleigh, arising out of the conspiracy to put Lady Arabella Stuart on the throne; but he was not permitted by Coke, the Attorney General, to address the jury, or even to examine any of the witnesses; and, in his present depressed state, he was rather pleased to escape from public observation. If he had any malignity, it must have been abundantly gratified by witnessing the manner in which his browbeating rival exposed himself on this occasion.[2]

When James's first parliament met, in the spring of the following year, Bacon again raised his crest, and made

---

[1] Works, v. 281.

[2] Coke, stopping Raleigh in his defense, denounced him as an atheist, saying he had an English face but a Spanish heart. Cecil, one of the commissioners, said, " Be not so impatient, Mr. Attorney; give him leave to speak."

Coke. " If I may not be patiently heard, you will encourage traitors and discourage us. I am the King's sworn servant, and I must speak. If he be guilty, he is a traitor; if not, deliver him."

Note. Mr. Attorney sat down in a chafe, and would speak no more until the Commissioners urged and entreated him. After much ado he went on, and made a long repetition of all the evidence for the direction of the jury; and at the repeating of some things Sir Walter Raleigh interrupted him, and said *he did him wrong.*

Coke. " Thou art the most vile and execrable traitor that ever lived."

Raleigh. "You speak indiscreetly, barbarously, and uncivilly."

Coke. " I want words sufficient to express your viperous treasons."

Raleigh. " I think you want words, indeed, for you have spoken one thing half a dozen times.

Coke. " Thou art an odious fellow: Thy name is hateful to all the realm of England for thy pride."

Raleigh. " It will go near to prove a measuring cast between you and me, Mr. Attorney."

Coke. " Well, I will now make it appear to the world that there never lived a viler viper upon the face of the earth than thou."—2 St. Tr. 26.

the world forget, if not forgive, his past misconduct. Being returned to the House of Commons both for St. Alban's and Ipswich, he chose to serve for the latter borough, which certainly had a most active and able representative. During this session he spoke in every debate, he sat upon twenty-nine committees, and he contrived to make himself popular by calling out for a redress of grievances,—and a special favorite of the King, by supporting James's pet plan of a union with Scotland. He was appointed one of the Commissioners for negotiating this great measure, and did all he could to soften the prejudices of the English nation against it.

Soon after the prorogation, as a mark of royal approbation, he was re-appointed King's Counsel, with a salary of forty pounds a year,[1] and a pension of sixty pounds a year was granted to him for special services rendered to the Crown by his deceased brother Anthony and himself. By the death of this brother he had recently come into possession of Gorhambury and other landed property, but he was still occasionally obliged to borrow money by pawning his valuables.[2]

In the autumn of this year Bacon paid a visit to his friend Sir Henry Saville, Provost of Eton, and on his return addressed an interesting letter to him upon the subject of education, enclosing a tract entitled "Helps to the Intellectual Powers," which strongly inculcated improved methods of study.

Soon after he wrote a letter to Lord Chancellor Ellesmere, with proposals to write a History of England; and he prepared a work, inscribed to the King, "Of the greatness of the Kingdom of Great Britain," with the courtly motto, "Fortunatos nimium sua si bona norint."[3]

To the composition of such fugitive pieces he must have resorted as a recreation while he was elaborating his noble treatise on the "Advancement of Learning," which

---

[1] This salary of £40 a year, with an allowance of stationery, was continued to all King's Counsel down to the reign of William IV., when it was very properly withdrawn, King's counselship becoming a *grade* in the profession of the law, instead of an *office*. But the moderate salary of the Attorney General was swept away at the same time, although he was still compelled to pay the land-tax upon it.

[2] In the Egerton Papers there is a receipt under date August 21, 1604, from a money-lender, for "a jewell of Susanna sett with diamonds and rubys," on which he had advanced Sir Francis Bacon, Knt., £50.—p. 395.

[3] Works, v. 293.

appeared in 1605, and exceeded the high expectations which had been formed of it. His fame as a philosopher and a fine writer was now for ever established.

Yet, on the meeting of parliament, in November, he plunged into business with unabated ardor. When the excitement of the Gunpowder Plot had subsided, he again brought forward a project for improving the law by abolishing "Wardship," and the other grievances of "Tenure in chivalry;" he made speeches as well as wrote pamphlets in support of the Union; and he was active as ever both in debate and in committees.

But he became much soured by the reflection that he derived little reward beyond praise for all his exertions. He was so much occupied with politics while parliament was sitting, and with literature during the recess, that his private practice at the bar was extremely slender, and now in his 47th year, he could hardly bear the ill luck by which his official advancement had been so long delayed.

Coke, the Attorney General, envying the fame which Bacon had acquired in the House of Commons, and by his writings,—which he pretended to despise,—still did everything in his power to depress him, and they had an interchange of sarcasms from time to time, although they had not again forgot the rules of propriety so far as in their famous altercation in the time of Elizabeth. But Coke's insolence increasing, and the recurrence of such a scene seeming not improbable, Bacon wrote him the following letter of expostulation:

"Mr. Attorney,

"I thought best once for all to let you know in plainness what I find of you, and what you shall find of me. You take to yourself a liberty to disgrace and disable my law, my experience, my discretion. What it pleaseth you, I pray, think of me: I am one that knows both mine own wants and other men's, and it may be perchance that mine mend when others stand at a stay. And surely I may not endure in public place to be wronged without repelling the same to my best advantage to right myself. You are great, and therefore have the more enviers, which would be glad to have you paid at another's cost. Since the time I missed the Solicitor's place, the rather I think by your means, I can not expect that you and I shall ever serve as Attorney and Solicitor together; but either to serve with another upon your remove, or to step into some other course; so as I am more free than ever I was from any occasion of unworthy conforming myself to you, more than general good manners or your particular good usage shall provoke; and if you had not been short-sighted in your own fortune, as I think, you might have had more use of me. But that tide is past. I write not this to show my friends what a brave letter I have written to Mr. Attorney; I have none of those humors; but that I have written is to a good end, that is, to the more decent carriage of my Master's service, and to our particular better understanding one of another. This letter, if it shall be answered by you in deed and not in word, I suppose it will not be worse for us both; else it is but a few lines lost, which for a much smaller matter I would have adventured. So this being to yourself, I for my part rest."[1]

Soon after this letter was written, the bar was relieved from the tyrant who had ruled over it so long with a rod of iron, by the promotion of Sir Edward Coke to the office of Chief Justice of the Common Pleas on the death of Lord Chief Justice Gawdey. In contemplation of this move, Bacon had written a letter to his cousin, now Earl of Salisbury and Prime Minister, in which he says:

"It is thought Mr. Attorney shall be Chief Justice of the Common Pleas; in case the Solicitor rise, I would be glad now at last to be Solicitor; chiefly because I think it would increase my practice, wherein, God blessing me a few years, I may mend my state, and so after fall to my studies at ease; whereof one is requisite for my body, and the other serveth for my mind; wherein if I shall find your Lordship's favor, I shall be more happy than I have been, which may may make me also more wise. I have small store of means about the King, and to sue myself is not fit; and therefore I shall leave it to God, his Majesty, and your Lordship, for I must still be next the door. I thank God in these transitory things I am well resolved."[2]

Notwithstanding this affected calmness, he immediately addressed another letter to Salisbury, betraying great anxiety:

"I am not ignorant how mean a thing I stand for, in

[1] Works, v 297. [2] Ibid., v. 298.

desiring to come into the Solicitor's place; for I know well it is not the thing it hath been,—time having wrought alteration both in the profession and in the special place. Yet because I think it will increase my practice, and that it may satisfy my friends, and because I have been voiced to it, I would be glad it were done. Wherein I may say to your Lordship in the confidence of your poor kinsman, and of a man by you advanced, *Tu idem fer opem, qui spem dedisti;* for I am sure it was not possible for a man living to have received from another more significant and comfortable words of hope, your Lordship being pleased to tell me, during the course of my last service, that you would raise me, and that when you had resolved to raise a man you were more careful of him than himself; and that what you had done for me in my marriage was a benefit to me, but of no use to your Lordship, and therefore I might assure myself you would not leave me there;—with many like speeches, which I know my duty too well to take any other hold of, than the hold of a thankful remembrance. And I acknowledge, and all the world knoweth, that your Lordship is no dealer of holy water, but noble and real; and on my part I am of a sure ground that I have committed nothing that may deserve alteration. And therefore my hope is, your Lordship will finish a good work, and consider that time groweth precious with me, that I am now *in vergentibus annis*. And although I know that your fortune is not to need an hundred such as I am, yet I shall be ever ready to give you my first and best fruits, and to supply as much as in me lieth worthiness by thankfulness."[1]

Bacon was again disappointed. From some intrigue not explained to us, of which his old enemy Sir Edward Coke was the author, Sir Henry Hobart was put into the office of Attorney General, and there was no vacancy in that of Solicitor. He expressed such deep resentment, that an expedient was proposed to create a vacancy by making the Solicitor General King's Sergeant, with a promise of farther promotion. Bacon sought to quicken this job by the following letter to the Lord Chancellor:—

"It may please your good Lordship:—As I conceived it to be a resolution, both with his Majesty and among your Lordships of his Council, that I should be placed

[1] Works, v. 299.

Solicitor, and the Solicitor to be removed to be the King's Sergeant ; so I must thankfully acknowledge your Lordship's furtherance and forwardness therein ; your Lordship being the man who first devised the mean ; wherefore, my humble request to your Lordship is, that you would set in with some strength to finish this your work; which, I assure your Lordship, I desire the rather, because, being placed, I hope for many favors at last to be able to do you some little service. For as I am, your Lordship can not use me, nor scarcely indeed know me. Not that I vainly think I shall be able to do any great matters, but certainly it will frame me to use a more industrious observance and application to such as I honor so much as I do your Lordship, and not, I hope, without some good offices which may now and then deserve your thanks. And herewithal, good my Lord, I humbly pray your Lordship to consider that time groweth precious with me, and that a married man is seven years older in his thoughts the first day ; and therefore what a discomfortable thing it is for me to be unsettled still? Certainly, were it not that I think myself born to do my Sovereign service, and therefore in that station I will live and die ; otherwise for mine own private comfort, it were better for me that the King should blot me out of his book; or that I should turn my course to endeavor to serve in some other kind, than for me to stand thus at a stop ; and to have that little reputation, which, by my industry, I gather, to be scattered and taken away by continual disgraces, every new man coming above me. Sure I am I shall never have fairer promises and words from your Lordships. For I know what my services are, saving that your Lordships told me they were good, and I would believe you in a much greater matter. Were it nothing else, I hope the modesty of my suit deserveth somewhat ; for I know well the Solicitor's place is not as your Lordship left it ; time working alteration, somewhat in the profession, much more in that special place. And were it not to satisfy my wife's friends, and to get myself out of being a common gaze and a speech, I protest before God I would never speak a word for it. But to conclude, as my honorable Lady, your wife, was some mean to make me change the name of another ; so if it please you to help me to change mine own name, I can be but more and more bounden to you; and I am much deceived if your Lordship find not the King well inclined, and my Lord of Salisbury forward and affectionate."[1]

However, great difficulties were experienced from Mr. Solicitor's unwillingness to resign, and Bacon, in despair, addressed the following letter to King James:—

"How honestly ready I have been, most gracious Sovereign, to do your Majesty humble service to the best of my power, and, in a manner, beyond my power, as I now stand, I am not so unfortunate but your Majesty knoweth. For both in the Commission of Union, labor whereof, for men of my profession, rested most upon my hand; and this last parliament, in the bill of the subsidy, both body and preamble; in the matter of the purveyance; in the ecclesiastical petitions; in the grievances, and the like; as I was ever careful, and not without good success, sometimes to put forward that which was good, sometimes to keep back that which was not so good; so your Majesty was pleased kindly to accept of my services, and to say to me, such conflicts were the wars of peace, and such victories the victories of peace; and therefore such servants as obtained them were, by Kings that reign in peace, no less to be esteemed than services of commanders in the wars. In all which, nevertheless, I can challenge to myself no sufficiency, but that I was diligent and reasonably happy to execute those directions which I received either immediately from your royal mouth, or from my Lord of Salisbury: at which time it pleased your Majesty also promise and assure me, that upon the remove of the then Attorney I should not be forgotten, but brought into ordinary place. And this was after confirmed to me by many of my Lords, and towards the end of the last term the manner also in particular was spoken of: that is, that Mr. Solicitor should be made your Majesty's Serjeant, and I Solicitor; for so it was thought best to sort with both our gifts and faculties for the good of your service; and of this resolution both court and country took knowledge. Neither was this any invention or project of mine own; but moved from my Lords, and I think first from my Lord Chancellor; whereupon resting, your Majesty well knoweth I never opened my mouth for the greater place; though I am sure I had two cir-

[1] Works, v. 300.

cumstances that Mr. Attorney, that now is, could not allege: the one, nine years' service of the Crown; the other, the being cousin-germain to the Lord of Salisbury, whom your Majesty esteemeth and trusteth so much. But for the less place, I conceived it was meant me. But after that Mr. Attorney Hobart was placed, I heard no more of my preferment; but it seemed to be at a stop, to my great disgrace and discouragement. For, gracious Sovereign, if still, when the waters are stirred, another shall be put in before me, your Majesty had need work a miracle, or else I shall be still a lame man to do your Majesty service. And, therefore, my most humble suit to your Majesty is, that this, which seemed to me intended, may speedily be performed; and, I hope, my former service shall be but as beginnings to better, when I am better strengthened: for, sure I am, no man's heart is fuller. I say not but many may have greater hearts; but, I say, not fuller of love and duty towards your Majesty and your children, as I hope time will manifest against envy and detraction, if any be. To conclude, I must humbly crave pardon for my boldness, and rest, &c."[1]

All parties were joyfully relieved from this embarrassment by the opportune death of Popham, Chief Justice of the King's Bench; and in consequence of the legal promotions which then took place, on the 25th day of June, in the fifth year of the reign of King James, and in the year of grace, 1607, Francis Bacon at last became Solicitor General to the Crown! It was an infelicity in his lot that, notwithstanding his capacity and his services, he never was promoted to any office without humiliating solicitations to ministers, favorites, and sovereigns.

The new Solicitor, who had made a most elaborate speech in favor of the Union with Scotland, pressing into his service the stories of Alexander and Parmenio, of Abraham and Lot, and of Solon and Crœsus, and boldly combating the argument, that, if the measure were adopted, England would be overrun with Scots; finding that the English House of Commons would not even pass a bill for the preliminary step of naturalizing their northern fellow subjects, now resorted to the expedient of obtaining a judicial decision, that all the *Postnati* were naturalized by operation of law. He argued the case very

[1] Works, v. 302.

learnedly in the Exchequer Chamber; and, what was probably more efficacious, he labored the Judges out of Court to bring them to the King's wishes.[1] Hobart, the Attorney General, was a shy and timid man, and the chief direction of the law business of the Crown was left to Bacon.

The only prosecution of much consequence during the six years he was Solicitor General was that of Lord Sanquhar for the murder of the fencing master, who had accidentally put out one of the northern's peer's eyes in playing at rapier and dagger. This he conducted with a becoming mixture of firmness and mildness. After clearly stating the law and the facts, he thus addressed the prisoner:—"I will conclude towards you, my Lord, that though your offense hath been great, yet your confession hath been free; and this shows that, though you could not resist the tempter, yet you bear a Christian and generous mind, answerable to the noble family of which you are descended."[2] The conviction and execution of this Scotch nobleman have been justly considered as reflecting great credit on the administration of justice in the reign of James.

Bacon's practice at the bar, as he expected, did increase considerably by the *prestige* of office. The most important civil case in which he was concerned was that of Sutton's Hospital, in which the validity of the noble foundation of the Charter House was established against his strenuous and able efforts.[3]

A new court being created, called the "Court of the Verge of the Palace," he was appointed Judge of it, and he opened it with a charge to the jury, recommending a strict execution of the law against dueling.

Mr. Solicitor in the meantime steadily went on with his philosophical labors, of which he occasionally gave a taste to the world in anticipation of what was hereafter to be expected. He now published the "Cogitata et Visa," perhaps his most wonderful effort of subtle reasoning, and the "De Sapientiâ Veterum," decidedly his most successful display of imagination and wit. Of these he sent copies to his friend, Mr. Matthew, saying, "My great work[4] goeth forward, and after my manner, I alter ever when I

---

[1] 2 St. Tr. 559. Case of Postnati. Works, vol. iv. 319.
[2] 2 St. Tr. 743.　　　[3] 10 Co. I.　　　[4] Novum Organum.

add." He likewise published a new and greatly enlarged edition of his Essays.

But, after all, what was nearest his heart was his official advancement. He was impatient to be Attorney General, for the superior profit and dignity of that situation;—and to secure it to himself on the next vacancy, he wrote the following letter to the King:—

"It may please your Majesty,

"Your great and princely favors towards me, in advancing me to place; and, that which is to me of no less comfort, your Majesty's benign and gracious acceptation, from time to time, of my poor services, much above the merit and value of them; hath almost brought me to an opinion, that I may sooner, perchance, be wanting to myself in not asking, than find your Majesty wanting to me in any my reasonable and modest desires. And, therefore, perceiving how, at this time, preferments of law fly about mine ears, to some above me, and to some below me, I did conceive your Majesty may think it rather a kind of dulness, or want of faith, than modesty, if I should not come with my pitcher to Jacob's well as others do. Wherein I shall propound to your Majesty that which tendeth not so much to the raising of my fortune, as to the settling of my mind; being sometimes assailed with this cogitation, that by reason of my slowness to see and apprehend sudden occasions, keeping in one plain course of painful service, I may, *in fine dierum*, be in danger to be neglected and forgotten; and if that should be, then were it much better for me now, while I stand in your Majesty's good opinion, though unworthy, and have some little reputation in the world, to give over the course I am in, and to make proof to do you some honor by my pen, either by writing some faithful narrative of your happy, though not untraduced times; or by recompiling your laws, which I perceive your Majesty laboreth with, and hath in your head, as Jupiter had Pallas, or some other the like work, for without some endeavor to do you honor I would not live; than to spend my wits and time in this laborious place wherein I now serve; if it shall be deprived of those outward ornaments which it was wont to have, in respect of an assured succession to some place of more dignity and rest, which seemeth now to be an hope altogether casual, if not wholly intercepted. Wherefore, not to hold your Majesty long, my humble suit to your Majesty is that, than the which I can not well go lower; which is, that I may obtain your royal promise to succeed, if I live, into the Attorney's place, whensoever it shall be void; it being but the natural and immediate step and rise which the place I now hold hath ever, in sort, made claim to, and almost never failed of. In this suit I make no friends but to your Majesty, rely upon no other motive but your grace, nor any other assurance but your word; whereof I had good experience, when I came to the Solicitor's place, that it was like to the two great lights, which in their motions are never retrograde. So with my best prayers for your Majesty's happiness, I rest."[1]

James admitted him to an audience, and promised, on the word of a King, that his request should be granted. Some time after, Hobart fell dangerously ill, upon which Bacon wrote to remind his Majesty of his promise..

"It may please your most excellent Majesty,

"I do understand by some of my good friends, to my great comfort, that your Majesty hath in mind your Majesty's royal promise, which to me is *anchora spei*, touching the Attorney's place. I hope Mr. Attorney shall do well. I thank God I wish no man's death, nor much mine own life, more than to do your Majesty's service. For I account my life the accident, and my duty the substance. For this I will be bold to say, if it please God that I ever serve your Majesty in the Attorney's place, I have known an Attorney Coke, and an Attorney Hobart, both worthy men, and far above myself; but if I should not find a middle way between their two dispositions and carriages, I should not satisfy myself. But these things are far or near, as it shall please God. Meanwhile, I most humbly pray your Majesty to accept my sacrifice of thanksgiving for your gracious favor. God preserve your Majesty. I ever remain,——"[2]

If he was sincere in his hope that "Mr. Attorney should do well," he was gratified by Sir Henry's entire recovery.

Nevertheless, on the death of Fleming, the object was, with a little intriguing, accomplished. Bacon immediately wrote the following letter to the King:—

---

[1] Works, v. 322.   [2] Works, v. 323.

"It may please your most excellent Majesty,

"Having understood of the death of the Lord Chief Justice, I do ground in all humbleness as an assured hope, that your Majesty will not think of any other but your poor servants, your Attorney and your Solicitor, one of them for that place. Else we shall be like Noah's dove, not knowing where to rest our feet. For the places of rest after the extreme painful places wherein we serve have used to be either the Lord Chancellor's place, or the Mastership of the Rolls, or the places of Chief Justices; whereof for the first I could be almost loth to live to see this worthy Chancellor fail.[1] The Mastership of the Rolls is blocked with a reversion.[2] My Lord Coke is likely to outlive us both. So as, if this turn fail, I for my part know not whither to look. I have served your Majesty above a prenticehood full seven years and more as your Solicitor, which is, I think, one of the painfulest places in your kingdom, especially as my employments have been; and God hath brought mine own years to fifty-two, which I think is older than ever any Solicitor continued unpreferred. My suit is principally that you would remove Mr. Attorney to the place. If he refuse, then I hope your Majesty will seek no farther than myself, that I may at last, out of your Majesty's grace and favor, step forwards to a place either of more comfort or more ease. Besides, how necessary it is for your Majesty to strengthen your service amongst the Judges by a Chief Justice which is sure to your prerogative, your Majesty knoweth. Therefore I cease farther to trouble your Majesty, humbly craving pardon, and relying wholly on your goodness and remembrance, and resting in all true humbleness, &c."[3]

The King was ready to appoint either the Attorney or Solicitor; but Hobart was unwilling to resign his present office, thrice as profitable as that offered him and held by as good a tenure,—and Bacon himself, notwithstanding what he said about the worthy Chancellor Ellesmere, was eager for the Great Seal. He therefore resorted to a most masterly stroke of policy,—to remove Coke to the King's Bench, and to make a vacancy in the office of Chief Justice of the Common Pleas, which, from its superior profit as well as quiet, Hobart was very willing to

---

[1] Ellesmere.   [2] Lord Kinlosse to be succeeded by Sir Julius Cæsar.
[3] Works. vi. 70.

accept. With this view he drew up and submitted to the King—

"Reasons why it should be exceedingly much for his Majesty's service to remove the Lord Coke from the place he now holdeth to be Chief Justice of England, and the Attorney to succeed him, and the Solicitor the Attorney.

"First, it will strengthen the King's causes greatly amongst the Judges, for both my Lord Coke will think himself near a Privy Councillor's place, and thereupon turn obsequious, and the Attorney General, a new man and a grave person in a Judge's place, will come in well to the other, and hold him hard to it, not without emulation between them who shall please the King best.

"Secondly, the Attorney General sorteth not so well with his present place, being a man timid and scrupulous, both in parliament and other business, and one, in a word, that was made fit for the late Lord Treasurer's seat, which was to do little with much formality and protestation; whereas the *new Solicitor going more roundly to work, and being of a quicker and more earnest temper, and more effectual in that he dealeth in,* is like to recover that strength to the King's prerogative which it hath had in times past, and which is due unto it. And for that purpose there must be brought to be Solicitor some man of courage and speech, and a grounded lawyer; which done, his Majesty will speedily find a marvelous change in his business. For it is not to purpose for the Judges to stand well disposed, except the King's counsel, which is the active and moving part, put the Judges well to it; for in a weapon, what is a back without an edge?

"Thirdly, the King shall continue and add reputation to the Attorney's and Solicitor's place by this orderly advancement of them; which two places are the champions' places for his rights and prerogative, and, being stripped of their expectations and successions to great place, will wax vile, and then his Majesty's prerogative goeth down the wind. Besides this remove of my Lord Coke to a place of less profit, though it be with his will, yet will be thought abroad a kind of discipline to him for opposing himself in the King's causes, the example whereof will contain others in more awe."

[1] Works, vi. 71.

This plan was immediately adopted: Hobart, the Attorney General, became Chief Justice of the Common Pleas, and Bacon Attorney General.

Soon after, the new Chief Justice of the King's Bench, meeting the new Attorney General, said to him, "Mr. Attorney, this is all your doing: it is you that has made this stir." Mr. Attorney answered, "Ah, my Lord, your Lordship all this while has grown in breadth; you must needs now grow in height, or else you would be a monster."[1] The rivalry between them, as we shall see, went on with fresh animosity.

Bacon might now be considered the principal political adviser of the Crown. Salisbury was dead; Carr, from a raw Scotch lad to whom James taught the rudiments of the Latin tongue, had become Earl of Somerset, Lord Chamberlain, the King's prime favorite, the dispenser of patronage, and a person universally courted and flattered; but so contemptible was his understanding, and such was his incapacity for business, that in affairs of state James was obliged to resort to other councillors. Bacon, though not by any means disdaining to avail himself of the protection of a favorite (as he had shown in the time of Essex, and as he speedily again showed on the rise of Villiers,) had never much connection with Somerset,—perhaps from not being able to make himself appreciated by such a simpleton, or perhaps from foreseeing that the royal fancy for him must be fleeting. The Attorney General was in direct communication with the King, and for a considerable time had great influence in his councils. His first advice was constitutional and wise,—to discontinue the irregular expedients which had been resorted to for some years for raising money, and to ask for a supply from a new parliament. But he overrated the influence he should have in the House of Commons, and he was not sufficiently aware of the growing national discontent.

Being re-elected since his last appointment, he was about to take his seat, when a Mr. Duncombe raised the question—"Whether the Attorney General might be elected, in respect there was no precedent that such an officer of the Crown could be chosen member of the house?"[2] Bacon's friends answered, that Sir Henry Hobart had

[1] Lord Bacon's Apophthegms, or Jest Book. Works, vol. ii. 421.
[2] 1 Parl. Hist. 1159

been allowed to sit while Attorney General; but so much do opinions on such subjects vary from age to age, that the House then agreed that this case did not apply, as he was a member of the House when he was made Attorney General, and therefore could not be unseated.

Sir Roger Owen argued that no Attorney General was ever chosen, nor anciently any Privy Councillor, nor any that took livery of the King. He relied on the authority of Sir Thomas More, who, after he had been Speaker and Chancellor, said,—"that the eye of a King's courtier can endure no colors but one, the King's livery hindering their sight." He compared those holding office at the King's pleasure to "a cloud gilded by the rays of the sun, and to brass coin which the King's stamp makes current." Sir John Saville moved "that those Privy Councillors who had got seats might stay for that time, but Mr. Attorney should not serve in that House."

After a committee to search for precedents, it was resolved that "Mr. Attorney General Bacon remain in the House for this parliament, but never any Attorney General to serve in the lower House in future." The right of the Attorney General to sit as a member of the House of Commons has not since been seriously questioned. As he is summoned according to immemorial usage to advise the House of Lords, and ought to return his writ and to take his place on the woolsack, it is easy to conceive that conflicting duties might be cast upon him; but his attendance on the Lords is dispensed with, except in Peerage cases, and it has been found much more convenient that he should be allowed to act as law adviser to the House of Commons, which might otherwise be *inops concilii*.

Mr. Attorney made his first and only speech in this parliament to press for supplies. He began by observing, "that since they had been pleased to retain him there, he owed them the best offices he could, and if they had dismissed him his wishes would have been still with them." He then most elaborately pointed out the King's wants and the necessity for supplying them, ridiculing the notion that had gone abroad that a confederacy had been formed to control the free will of the House, and again bringing out his favorite and unlucky quotation,— "Dulcis tractus pari jugo."

But a majority were much more inclined to inquire into monoplies and other grievances,—and parliament was abruptly dissolved.

After the effort he had made to obtain supplies by constitutional means, Bacon seems to have thought that all expedients by which the Exchequer might be filled were justifiable.

The most productive of these was the demanding of "Benevolences." Letters were written to the sheriffs of counties and the magistrates of corporations, calling on the King's loving subjects to contribute to his necessities. The contributions were supposed to be voluntary, but were in reality compulsory, for all who refused were denounced and treated as disloyal. Oliver St. John having written a letter to the Mayor of Marlborough, representing that this "Benevolence" was contrary to law, and that the magistrates ought not to assist in collecting it, the Attorney General prosecuted him in the Star Chamber for a libel. In his speech he strenuously defended this mode of raising money; and for the reason that "it is fit to burn incense where ill odors have been cast," he delivered an elaborate panegyric on the government of King James, whom he described as a constant protector of the liberties, laws, and customs of the kingdom, maintaining religion not only with sceptre and sword, but by his pen. The defendant was sentenced to pay a fine of £5,000, to be imprisoned during the King's pleasure, and to make a written submission. Bacon's indiscriminate admirers contend that he is exempt from all blame in this proceeding, because the judges declared that the levying of "Benevolences" was not contrary to any statute, and Lord Chancellor Ellesmere solemnly expressed a wish that passing sentence on Mr. St. John might be "his last act of judicial duty;" but there could not be a doubt that raising "Benevolences," was in substance levying an aid without authority of parliament, and that the person was morally responsible for the misconduct of the Judges who put them in a position where they must either pervert the law or forfeit their offices.[1]

The blame here imputable to Bacon, however, was light indeed compared with what he incurred in a case which soon followed. Fine and imprisonment having no effect

[1] 2 St. Tr. 899.

in quelling the rising murmurs of the people, it was resolved to make a more dreadful example, and Peacham, a clergyman of Somersetshire, between sixty and seventy years of age, was selected for the victim. On breaking into his study, a sermon was there found which he had never preached, nor intended to preach, nor shown to any human being, but which contained some passages encouraging the people to resist tyranny. He was immediately arrested, and a resolution was taken to prosecute him for high treason. But Mr. Attorney, who is alone responsible for this atrocious proceeding, anticipated considerable difficulties both in law and fact before the poor old parson could be subjected to a cruel and ignominious death. He therefore first began by tampering with the Judges of the King's Bench, to fix them by an extrajudicial opinion. His plan was to assail them separately, and therefore he skillfully called in his subordinates,—assigning Justice Dodderidge to the Solicitor General, Justice Crook to Sergeant Montague, and Justice Houghton to Sergeant Crew,—and directing these emissaries that " they should not in any case make any doubt to the Judges,—as if they mistrusted they would not deliver any opinion apart, but should speak resolutely to them." The Chief Justice he reserved for his own management,—" not being wholly without hope," says he, " that my Lord Coke himself, when I have in some dark manner put him in doubt that he shall be left alone, will not continue singular." The puisnes were pliant. The Chief at first affirmed, that "such auricular taking of opinions was not according to the custom of this realm;" but at last yielded to Bacon's remonstrance, that "though Judges might make a suit to be spared for their opinion till they had spoken with their brethren, if the King upon his own princely judgment, for reason of estate, should think fit to have it otherwise, there was no declining—nay, that it touched on a violation of their oath, which was, to counsel the King whether it were jointly or separately."[1]

Still, without some further evidence, a mere sermon found in a study seemed rather a slender overt act to be submitted to a jury of compassing the King's death. To supply the deficiency, it was resolved to subject Peacham to the rack. Interrogatories were prepared to draw a

---

[1] Letters to King Works, vol. v. 338, 343.

confession from him of his object and of his accomplices in writing the sermon, and "upon these interrogatories he was examined before torture, between torture, and after torture." These are the words of Bacon; and I relate with horror that he was himself present at scenes equaling everything that we have read or can imagine of the Inquisition at Venice. The tone in which he describes some of them to the King, though he tries to talk bravely, shows that he was ashamed of the work in which he was engaged, and that he inwardly condemned what some of his admirers now defend:

"It may please your excellent Majesty.

"It grieveth me exceedingly that your Majesty should be so much troubled with this matter of Peacham, whose raging devil seemeth to be turned into a dumb devil. But although we are driven to make our way through questions, which I wish were otherwise, yet I hope well the end will be good. But then every man must put his *helping hand;*[1] for else I must say to your Majesty in this and the like cases, as St. Paul said to the centurion, when some of the mariners had an eye to the cock-boat, *Except these stay in the ship, ye can not be safe.* I find in my Lords great and worthy care of the business; and for my part, I hold my opinion, and am strengthened in it by some records that I have found. God preserve your Majesty!"

It is quite clear that several present had expressed an opinion against going further, and that Bacon himself had not much confidence in his "Records." He still persisted, however, for the King had become very earnest about it,—and thus he writes to his Majesty (after describing Peacham's refusal to answer certain points),—" I hold it fit that myself and my fellows go to the Tower, and so I purpose to examine him upon these points and some others. I think also, it were not amiss to make a false fire,[2] as if all things were ready for his going down to his trial, and that he were upon the very point of being carried down to see what will work with him."[3] To the Tower he went accordingly, but neither old nor new-invented torture could succeed: "I send," says he, "your

---

[1] Does this mean to stretch the rack, like Lord Chancellor Wriothesley?
[2] A new species of torture not to be found in his "Records."
[3] Works v. 354.

Majesty a copy of our last examination of Peacham, whereby your Majesty may perceive that this miscreant wretch goeth back from all. He never deceived me, for when others had hopes of discovery, and thought time well spent that way, I told your Majesty *percuntibus mille figuræ*, and that he did but now turn himself into divers shapes to save or delay his punishment."[1]

The old man, with dislocated joints but unbroken spirit, was brought to trial at the summer assizes at Taunton, before the Chief Baron and Sir Henry Montagu. Bacon showed some remnant of virtue by being too much ashamed to attend in person. He sent in his stead, Crew, the King's Sergeant, and Yelverton, the Solicitor General, who conducted themselves to his entire satisfaction,—for without law or fact they obtained a conviction. The case, however, was so infamous, that even the Judges who presided at the trial expressed a doubt whether the offense amounted to high treason, and there was such a feeling of indignation excited throughout the country, that the Government did not venture to carry the sentence into execution. Peacham was allowed to languish in Taunton gaol, till, in the following year, death relieved him from his sufferings.

An attempt to defend the conduct of Bacon in this affair, or to palliate its enormity, is to confound the sacred distinctions of right and wrong. He knew that Peacham's offense did not amount to high treason. He knew as well as the Judges, who so decided a few years after on the assassination of the Duke of Buckingham by Felton, that the law of England did not sanction torture to extort confession. If the law had been with him, he would have disgraced his character and his profession by the low subterfuges to which he resorted for the purpose of trepanning the Judges, and by directing himself the stretching of the rack, and administering his questions amidst the agonizing shrieks of the fainting victim. But Lord

---

[1] The single torture warrant for Peacham, now extant, is one dated 18th, and executed 19th January, which only authorizes the "Manacles," called by King James the "gentler torture." Hence it has been inferred that Peacham never was "*racked*." But it is quite clear that he had been tortured on several other occasions, for which there are no warrants forthcoming; and there can be no reasonable doubt that he had been made to undergo the severest suffering which the human frame can support.—See *Jardine's Reading on Torture*, a treatise full of curious learning.

Chancellor Ellesmere, from age and infirmity, could not much longer hold the Seals, and Bacon was resolved to be his successor.

To strengthen his interest he now assiduously cultivated George Villiers, the new favorite. Notwithstanding his own mature age and high station, he received the unideaed page into his intimacy, and condescended even to manage his private affairs. There are stronger contrasts of light and shade in the character of Bacon than probably of any other man who ever lived. Though seeming devoted exclusively to his own aggrandizement, yet, as Villiers was rising in favor,—had high honors and offices conferred upon him,—and was evidently advancing to supreme power in the state;—the selfish and sordid candidate for his patronage took infinite pains in instructing him how to govern for the glory and happiness of the country. His "advice to Sir George Villiers"[1] is a most noble composition, and may now be perused with great advantage by every English statesman. It is even written with freedom and manliness.—"You are a new-risen star, and the eyes of all men are upon you; let not your own negligence make you fall like a meteor." He divides his subject into eight heads:—1. Religion and the Church. 2. Justice and the laws. 3. The Council and the great officers of the kingdom. 4. Foreign negotiations and embassies. 5. War, the navy, and ports. 6. Trade at home. 7. Colonies. 8. The King's court.—I am naturally most struck by his observations respecting justice and the laws, which show that he himself sinned against knowledge.—" Let no arbitrary power be intruded; the people of this kingdom love the laws thereof, and nothing will oblige them more than a confidence of the free enjoying of them. What the nobles on an occasion once said in parliament, *Nolumus leges Angliæ mutare*, is imprinted in the hearts of all the people. But because the life of laws lies in the due execution and administration of them, let your eye be in the first place upon the choice of good Judges. These properties had they need to be furnished with,—to be learned in their profession, patient in hearing, prudent in governing, powerful in their elocution to persuade and satisfy both the parties and hearers, just in their judgment,—and, to sum up all, they must have

[1] Works, vol. iii. 429.

these three attributes,—they must be men of courage, fearing God and hating covetousness;—an ignorant man can not, a coward dares not, be a good Judge." "By no means be you persuaded to interpose yourself either by word or letter, in any cause depending in any court of justice. If any sue to be made a Judge, for my own part I should suspect him; but if either directly or indirectly he should bargain for a place of judicature, let him be rejected with shame:—*Vendere jure potest, emerat ille prius.*"—We shall ere long see how these maxims were observed between the preceptor and pupil.

Lord Ellesmere about this time had a severe illness, from which he was not expected to recover, and Bacon thrown into a state of deep anxiety, visited him almost daily, and sent bulletins of his condition to the King.[1] The old man lingering longer than was expected, Bacon pretty plainly intimates to the King that he ought to be superseded:—

"My Lord Chancellor's sickness falleth out *duro tempore*. I have always known him a wise man and of just elevation for monarchy, but your Majesty's service must not be mortal. And if you love him, as your Majesty hath now of late purchased many hearts by depressing the wicked, so God doth minister unto you a counterpart to do the like *by raising the honest.*"[2]

A few days after, in another letter to James, he speaks out more distinctly:—

"Your worthy Chancellor I fear goeth his last day. God hath hitherto used to weed out such servants as grew not fit for your Majesty; but now he hath gathered to himself one of the choicer plants, a true sage or *salvia* out of your garden; but your Majesty's service must not be mortal.

"Upon this heavy accident, I pray your Majesty in all humbleness and sincerity to give me leave to use a few

---

[1] Specimens:—"Because I knew your Majesty would be glad to hear how it is with my Lord Chancellor, and that it pleased him, out of his ancient and great love for me, which many times in sickness appeareth most, to admit me to a great deal of speech with him this afternoon, which during these three days he hath scarcely done to any, I thought it would be pleasing to your Majesty to be certified how I found him." Jan. 29, 1616. "I spoke to him on Sunday, at what time I found him in bed, but his spirits strong." Jan. 31, 1616. "My Lord Chancellor sent for me to speak with me this morning. I perceive he hath now that *signum sanitatis* as to feel better his former weakness." Feb. 7, 1616. [2] Feb. 9, 1616.

words. I must never forget, when I moved your Majesty for the Attorney's place, that it was your own sole act, and not my Lord of Somerset's, who, when he knew your Majesty had resolved it, thrust himself into the business to gain thanks; and therefore I have no reason to pray to saints.

"I shall now again make oblation to your Majesty,—first of my heart,—then of my service,—thirdly, of my place of Attorney, which I think is honestly worth £6,000 per annum,[1]—and, fourthly, of my place in the Star Cham-

[1] Almost the whole of this income must have arisen from fees. The following were the salaries of the law officers of the Crown at this time:—

	£	s.	d.
Attorney-General	81	6	8
Solicitor-General	70	0	0
King's Sergeant	41	9	10
King's Advocate	20	0	0

The salaries of the Judges show that they must have depended a good deal on fees:—

	£	s.	d.
Sir E. Coke, Ld. C. J. of England	224	19	9
Circuits	33	6	8
	258	6	5
Puisne Judges of K. B. and C. P.	188	6	8
Besides circuits	33	6	8
	221	13	4
C. J. of C. P.	194	19	9
Chief Baron	188	6	0
Puisne Barons	133	6	8
Judge on Norfolk Circuit	12	6	8*

The usual amount of *honoraries* to counsel in this reign, I have not been able to ascertain. From an entry in the parish books of St. Margaret's, Westminster, it appears that in the reign of Edward IV. they paid "Roger Fylpott, learned in the law, for his counsel, 3s. 8d., with 4d. for his dinner."

In the reign of Henry VII. Sergeant Yaxley was at the head of the bar, and used to go special on different circuits. From the following very curious retainer it appears that he was to attend the assizes at York, Nottingham, and Derby, and plead as many causes as he should be required by his client Sir Robert Plompton at each place, for all which he was to receive only 40 marks, besides his charges in the assize towns.

"This bill indented at London the 18th day of July, the 16th yeare of the reigne of King Henry the 7th, witnesseth that John Yaxley, Sergent at the Law, shall be at the next Assizes to be holden at York, Nottin. and Derb. if they be holden and kept, and their to be of council with Sir Robert Plompton, knight, such assises and actions as the said Sir Robert shall require the said John Yaxley, for the which premisses as, well for his costs and his labour,

* From Abstract of Revenue, Temp. Jac. I.

ber, which is worth £1,600 per annum, *and, with the favor and countenance of a Chancellor, much more.*"

He then urges his father's merits, and reminds the King that the Chancellor's place was ever conferred on some law officer, and never on a Judge,—instancing *Audley*, from King's Sergeant; his own father, from Attorney of the Wards; *Bromley*, from Solicitor General; *Puckering*, from Queen's Sergeant; *Egerton*, from Master of the Rolls, having lately been Attorney General. Now he comes to disparage his rivals:—

" If you like my Lord Coke, this will follow,—first, your Majesty shall put an overruling nature into an overruling place, which may breed an extreme;—next, you shall blunt his industries in matter of your finances, which seemeth to aim at another place;—and, lastly, popular men are no sure mounters for your Majesty's saddle. If you take my Lord Hobart, you shall have a Judge at the upper end of your Council Board and another at the lower end, whereby your Majesty will find your prerogative pent; for though there should be emulation between them, yet, as legists, they will agree in magnifying that wherein they are best: he is no statesman, but an economist wholly for himself, so as your Majesty, more than an outward form, will find little help in him for the business. If you will take my Lord of Canterbury, I will say no more but the Chancellor's place requires a whole man;

John Pulan, Gentlman, bindeth him by thease presents to content and pay to the said John Yaxley 40 marks† sterling at the feast of the Nativetie of our Lady next coming, or within eight days next following, wth 5^{li} paid aforehand, parcell of paiment of the said 40 marcks. Provided alway that if the said John Yaxley have knowledg and warning only to cum to Nott. and Derby, then the said John Yaxley is agread by these presents to take onely xv^{li} besides the said 5^{li} aforesaid. Provided alwaies that if the said John Yaxley have knowledg and warning to take no labor in this matter, then he to reteine and hold the said 5^{li} resaived for his good will and labor. In witnesse herof the said John Yaxley, seriant, to the part of this indenture remaining with the said John Pulan have put his seale the day and yeare abovewritten. Provided also that the said Sir Robert Plumpton shall beare the charges of the said John Yaxley, as well at York as Nottingham and Derby, and also to content and pay the said money to the sayd John Yaxley comed to the said Assizes att Nott. Derb. and York.

"JOHN YAXLEY."

—*Plumpton Correspondence,* by Camden Society, 152. See also pp. 53, 93, 150.

Formerly the usual fee for a barrister in Westminster Hall was an angel. Whence the saying, " a barrister is like Balaam's ass—only speaking when he sees the angel."

† 26*li*. 13*s*. 4*d*.

and to have both jurisdictions, spiritual and temporal, in that height is fit but for a King.—For myself, I can only present your Majesty with *gloria in obsequio*. Yet I dare promise, that if I sit in that place, your business shall not make such short turns upon you as it doth; but when a direction is once given, it shall be pursued and performed, and your Majesty shall only be troubled with the true care of a King, which is to think what you would have done in chief, and not how, for the passages.—I do presume also, in respect of my father's memory, and that I have been always gracious in the Lower House, I have some interest in the gentlemen of England, and shall be able to do some effect in rectifying that body of parliament men, which is *cardo rerum*. For let me tell your Majesty, that that part of the Chancellor's place which is to judge in Equity between party and party, that same *regnum judiciale*, which since my father's time is but too much enlarged, concerneth your Majesty least, more than the acquitting of your conscience for justice; but it is the other parts of a moderator amongst your Council, of an overseer of your Judges, of a planter of fit justices and governors in the country, that importeth your affairs and these times most.—To conclude, if I were the man I would be, I should hope that, as your Majesty hath of late won hearts by depressing, you should in this lose no hearts by advancing; for I see your people can better skill of *concretum* than *abstractum*, and that the waves of their affections flow rather after persons than things; so that acts of this nature, if this were one, do more good than twenty bills of grace. If God call my Lord, the warrants and commissions which are requisite for the taking of the Seal, and for the working with it, and for the reviving of warrants under his hand which die with him, and the like, shall be in readiness. And in this, time presseth more because it is the end of a term, and almost the beginning of the circuits; so that the Seal can not stand still; but this may be done as heretofore by commission, till your Majesty hath resolved of an officer. God ever preserve your Majesty."[1]

Is not this something very much like " suing to be made a Judge, and bargaining for a place of judicature?" MEANEST OF MANKIND!!! A touch of *vanity* even is to

[1] Feb. 12, 1616. Works, v. 371.

be found in this composition,—a quality he hardly ever betrays elsewhere, although he had an inward consciousness of his extraordinary powers. Boasting of his great influence in the Lower House, little did he think that, when parliament should next meet, both Houses would unanimously agree in prosecuting and punishing him.

But, alas! Ellesmere rallied, and in three days Bacon was obliged hypocritically to write,—

"I do find, *God be thanked,* a sensible amendment in my Lord Chancellor. I was with him yesterday in private conference about half an hour, and this day again at such time as he did seal, which he endured well almost the space of an hour, though the vapor of wax be offensive to him. But whoever thinketh his disease is but melancholy, he maketh no true judgment of it; for it is plainly a formed and deep cough, with a pectoral surcharge; so that at times he doth almost *animam agere.* I forbear to advertise your Majesty of the care I took to have commissions in readiness, because Mr. Secretary Luke hath let me understand he signified as much to your Majesty; but *I hope there shall be no use for them at this time.*"[1]

He next seems to have tried to prevail upon the old Chancellor to resign in his favor. But James would put no constraint on the inclinations of Ellesmere; and Bacon, to secure his succession when a vacancy should happen, now resorted to the expedient of being made a Privy Councillor,—which was pretty much the same as, in modern speech, being admitted to a seat in the Cabinet. He writes to Villiers,—

"My Lord Chancellor's health growing with the days, and his resignation being an uncertainty, I would be glad you went on with my first motion, my swearing Privy Councillor. Tho' I desire not so much to make myself more sure of the other, and to put it past competition, for herein I rest wholly upon the King and your excellent self, but because I find hourly that I need this strength in his Majesty's service, both for my better warrant and satisfaction of my conscience that I deal not in things above my vocation, and for my better countenance and prevailing where his Majesty's service is under any pretext opposed, I would it were dispatched. . . . . I sent a pretty while since a paper to Mr. John Murray, which

[1] Feb. 15, 1616. Works, v. 374.

was indeed a little remembrance of some things past concerning my honest and faithful services to his Majesty; not by way of boasting,—from which I am far,—but as tokens of my studying his service uprightly and carefully. If you be pleased to call for the paper which is with Mr. John Murray, and to find a fit time that his Majesty may cast an eye upon it, I think it will do no hurt; and I have written to Mr. Murray to deliver the paper if you call for it."[1]

To such minute artifices did he descend for effecting his object.—After some interval, and renewed solicitations, the King gave him his choice, either that he should have an express promise to succeed to the Great Seal, or that he should forthwith be sworn of the Privy Council. The bare promise, he thought, would not much improve his chance, while a seat at the council-table could not fail to place him above competition. *More suo*, he makes his election in a letter to Villiers to be shown to James:—

"The King giveth me a noble choice, and you are the man my heart ever told me you were. Ambition would draw me to the latter part of the choice; but in respect *my hearty wishes that my Lord Chancellor may live long,* and the small hopes I have that I shall live long myself, and, above all, because I see his Majesty's service daily and instantly bleedeth; towards which I persuade myself (vainly, perhaps, but yet in mine own thoughts firmly and constantly) that I shall give, when I am of the table, some effectual furtherance,—I do accept of the former, to be Councillor for the present, and to give over pleading at the bar; let other matter rest upon my proof and his Majesty's pleasure, and the accidents of time."[2]

In consequence of Villiers's representation the King consented; and on the 9th of June, Bacon was sworn of the Privy Council, and took his place at the table,—it having been, at his own request, previously arranged that with permission to give advice at chambers to those who might consult him, he should cease to plead as an advocate at the bar in private causes,—unless some weighty matter might arise in which he was to be allowed to be engaged under the King's express license.

Having thus got rid of his private practice, he applied his leisure to a most noble account, dedicating himself by

[1] Feb. 21, 1616. Works, v. 377.   [2] June 3, 1616. Works, v. 420.

turns to the prosecution of his philosphical pursuits, and to the improvement of the institutions of his country. The NOVUM ORGANUM made great progress, though it was not ready to see the light for some years; and he actually published " A Proposition to his Majesty touching the Compiling and Amendment of the Laws of England."[1] He commences this treatise with the following dignified address:—

"Your Majesty, of your favor, having made me Privy Councillor, and continuing me in the place of your Attorney General, which is more than was three hundred years before, I do not understand it to be that, by putting off the dealing in causes between party and party, I should keep holiday the more, but that I should dedicate my time to your service with less distraction. Wherefore, in this plentiful accession of time which I have now gained, I take it to be my duty, not only to speed your commandments and the business of my place, but to meditate and excogitate of myself wherein I may best by my travels derive your virtues to the good of your people, and return their thanks and increase of love to you again. And after I had thought of many things, I could find in my judgment none more proper for your Majesty as a master, nor for me as a workman, than the reducing and recompiling of the laws of England."

In this scheme he displays great caution and wisdom; not venturing to codify the common law, but contenting himself with reforming the statute-book, and extracting from the jumble of Reports a series of sound and consistent decisions.[2] It is curious to reflect that his exhortations in favor of law reform produced no fruit till the Republic was established under Cromwell, and that the subject was entirely neglected from the Restoration to our own times. Much has been done in the spirit which he recommends; and in what remains to be done he will be found our safest guide.

Bacon was called away from all such speculations to conduct the prosecutions which arose out of the murder

[1] Works, iv. 366.
[2] In this address Bacon displays his great anxiety about his reputation as a lawyer. "And I do assure your Majesty I am in good hope that when Sir Edward Coke's 'Reports' and my 'Rules and Decisions' shall come to posterity, there will be, whatsoever is now thought, question who was the greater lawyer"

of Sir Thomas Overbury. An attempt was made to satisfy the public by the punishment of the inferior agents in this black transaction; but the guilt of the Somersets became so notorious, and the cry for justice was so loud against them, that the King found it necessary to have these noble culprits arrested, and brought to trial before the Court of the Lord High Steward.

I am sorry to say that Bacon shared in the disgrace incurred by James and all his ministers in that mysterious affair. He prepared the questions to be put to the Judges prior to the trial, and arranged the course to be adopted " If Somerset should break forth in any speech taxing the King;" and it is quite clear that, though the inferior agents employed in the murder were to be sacrificed, he was in collusion with the King to spare the two great offenders who had planned it, notwithstanding James's celebrated imprecation on himself and his posterity if he should impede the course of justice. Bacon has been praised for the mild manner in which he stated the case against Somerset; but this was in performance of his promise: " It shall be my care so to moderate the manner of charging him as it might make him not odious beyond the extent of mercy."[1] The disgraceful pardon Bacon himself, as Attorney General, prepared.

Coke, the Chief Justice, had now rendered himself very obnoxious to the Court by his activity in detecting and prosecuting the murderers of Overbury, and by the part he had taken in the dispute about Injunctions and the affair of Commendams, or staying suits *Rege inconsulto*, which will be found circumstantially detailed in the Life of Lord Ellesmere.[2] Bacon, having at last gained an as-

---

[1] April 28, 1616. Works, v. 395.

[2] How zealously Bacon labored in the affair, and how he did his best permanently to pervert the due administration of justice in this country, by establishing the power of the Sovereign to interfere in private causes, strikingly appears from his letter to James, giving an account of the manner in which he had tried to mislead the Judges by his argument before them in support of this pretended prerogative. " I do perceive that I have not only stopped, but almost turned the stream, and I see how things cool by this, that the Judges, who were wont to call so hotly upon the business, when they had heard, of themselves took a fortnight to advise what they will do. Yet because the times are as they are, I could wish in all humbleness that your Majesty would remember and renew your former commandment, which you gave my Lord Chief Justice in Michaelmas Term, which was, that after he had heard your Attorney, he should forbear further proceeding till he had spoke with your Majesty. This writ (viz. a letter from the King forbidding the Court to

cendency over him, was determined to show him no quarter. Little was to be apprehended from his rivalry in the competition for the Great Seal, but there still rested in Bacon's mind a rankling recollection of unavenged insults. After the conviction of Somerset, all manner of titles and offices were conferred on the new favorite, who was ostensibly the King's servant, but really ruled the King and the kingdom. Bacon was on the best possible footing with him, and they cordially entered into the schemes of each other.[1]

About this time Villiers had a personal quarrel with Coke about the appointment to a lucrative office in the Court of King's Bench, which he wished to obtain for a dependent. Bacon, of course, did all he could to assist in this job.[2] Coke, after some hesitation, at last peremptorily resisted the encroachment on his patronage,—and his dismissal was resolved upon. The difficulty was to find a pretext for removing him. Although the judges all held during pleasure, the power of cashiering them had hitherto been very sparingly exercised, and never except upon some charge of misconduct. Coke was the greatest master of the Common Law that ever had ap-

proceed *Rege inconsulto*) is a mean provided by the ancient law of England to bring any cause that may concern your Majesty in profit or power from the ordinary benches, to be tried and judged before your Chancellor of England by the ordinary and legal part of his power; and your Majesty knoweth your Chancellor is ever a principal councillor and instrument of monarchy, of immediate dependence upon the King, and therefore like to be a safe and tender guardian of the royal rights."—Jan. 27, 1616. Works, v. 366. Bacon knew that he was misstating the law—to please the King—and to show that, by appointing himself Chancellor, prerogative might be exercised without control.

[1] "Your Majesty certainly hath found out and chosen a safe nature, a capable man, an honest will, generous and noble affections, and a courage well lodged, and one that I know loveth your Majesty unfeignedly, and admireth you as much as is in a man to admire his Sovereign upon earth."—*Bacon to James*. Yet no human being ever more thoroughly despised another than Buckingham his "Dad."

[2] Bacon gives Villiers an amusing account of a conversation on this subject with Coke "As I was sitting by my Lord Chief Justice, one of the judges asked him, '*Whether Roper* were dead?*' He said, '*He for his part knew not.*' Another of the Judges answered, '*It should concern you, my Lord, to know it.*' Whereupon he turned his speech to me, and said, '*No, Mr. Attorney, I will not wrestle now in my latter times.*' '*My Lord,*' said I, '*you speak like a wise man.*' '*Well,*' saith he, '*they have had no luck with it that have had it.*' I said again, '*Those days are past.*' Here you have the dialogue to make you merry."—Jan. 22, 1616.

---

* The person who then held the office.

peared in England. Notwithstanding the arrogance with which he was chargeable when at the bar he had given the highest satisfaction to the profession and the public since his elevation to the Bench. His opposition to the equitable jurisdiction of the Lord Chancellor, though unjustifiable, was generally popular, and all mankind (with the exception of the King and the most slavish of the ministers) approved of the noble stand he had made for judicial independence in Peacham's case and the affair of the "Commendams," and he had been rapturously applauded for his energy, on the discovery of the murder of Sir Thomas Overbury, in posting off to Theobald's to arrest Somerset with his own hands. The expedient to which Bacon resorted shows that it is no more possible "to *hate*"—than "to *love*,—and be wise." The frivolous, unfounded, preposterous, ludicrous charge brought against Coke was, that in his Reports of decided cases he had introduced several things in derogation of the royal prerogative.[1] On no better ground, in the month of June, 1616, though not formally superseded, and still allowed to do duty at chambers, he was suspended from the public execution of his office and from the council-table, and, instead of appearing in Court at Westminster, or going his circuit, it was most insultingly ordered that, during the long vacation, he should enter into a view and retractation of such novelties and errors and offensive conceits as were dispersed in his Reports."

Bacon having laid his enemy prostrate on the ground, trampled on his body. He now addressed an "Expostulation to the Lord Chief Justice Coke," in which, after some profane applications of Scripture, and pointing out how in his fallen state he ought to rejoice in the humiliation which God had inflicted upon him, he thus pithily proceeds:—

"Not only knowledge, but also every other gift which we call the gifts of fortune, have power to puff up earth; afflictions only level these mole-hills of pride, plough the heart, and make it fit for wisdom to sow her seed, and for

[1] Of these very Reports Bacon himself had deliberately written, "To give every man his due—had it not been for Sir Edward Coke's Reports, which, though they may have errors, and some peremptory and extra judicial resolutions more than are warranted, yet they contain infinite good decisions and rulings over cases—the law by this time had been almost like a ship without ballast."

grace to bring forth her increase. Happy is that man, therefore, both in regard of heavenly and earthly wisdom, that is thus wounded to be cured, thus broken to be made straight, thus made acquainted with his own imperfections that he may be perfected.

"Supposing this to be the time of your affliction, that which I have propounded to myself is by taking this seasonable advantage, *like a true friend*, though far unworthy to be counted so, to show you your true shape in a glass, and that not in a false one to flatter you, nor yet in one that should make you seem worse than you are, and so offend you, but in one made by the reflection of your own words and actions, from whose light proceeds the voice of the people, which is often, not unfitly, called the voice of God. It proceedeth from love, and a true desire to do you good. All men can see their own profit; that part of the wallet hangs before. A true friend (whose worthy office I would perform, since I fear both yourself and all great men want such) is to show the other, and which is from your eyes.

"First, therefore, behold your errors. In discourse you delight to speak too much, not to hear other men; this some say becomes a pleader, not a judge. While you speak in your own element, the law, no man ordinarily equals you; but when you wander, as you often delight to do, you wander indeed, and give never such satisfaction as the curious time requires.

"Secondly, you clog your auditory when you would be observed; speech must be either sweet or short.

"Thirdly, you converse with books, not men, and books especially human; and have no excellent choice with men, who are the best books; for a man of action and employment you seldom converse with, and then but with your underlings; not freely, but as a schoolmaster with his scholars, ever to teach, never to learn. But if sometimes you would in your familiar discourse hear others and make election of such as know what they speak, you should know many of these tales you tell to be but ordinary, and many other things which you delight to repeat and serve out for novelties to be but stale. As in your pleadings you were wont to insult over misery, and to inveigh bitterly at the persons, which bred you many enemies, whose poison yet smelleth, so are you still wont

to be a little careless in this point, to praise and disgrace
upon slight grounds, and that sometimes untruly; so that
your reproofs and commendations are for the most part
neglected and condemned; where the censure of a Judge
coming slow but sure, should be a brand to the guilty, and
a crown to the virtuous. You will jest at any man in
public, without respect to the person's dignity or your
own; this disgraceth your gravity more than it can advance the opinion of your wit; and so do all actions
which we see you do directly with a touch of vain-glory,
having no respect to the true end. You make the law to
lean too much to your opinion, whereby you show yourself to be a legal tyrant, striking with that weapon where
you please, since you are able to turn the edge any way.
Your too much love of the world is too much seen, where
having the living of a thousand you relieve few or none.
The hand that hath taken so much, can it give so little?
Herein you show no bowels of compassion, as if you
thought all too little for yourself. We desire you to
amend this, and let your poor tenants in Norfolk find
some comfort; where nothing of your estate is spent towards their relief, but all brought up hither to the im-
poverishing of your country.

"But now, since the case so standeth, we desire you to
give way to power, and so to fight that you be not utterly
broken, but reserved entirely to serve the commonwealth
again, and to do what good you can, since you can not do
all the good you would; and since you are fallen upon
this rock, cast out the goods to save the bottom; stop
the leaks, and make towards land; learn of the steward to
make friends of the unrighteous Mammon. You can not
but have much of your estate (pardon my plainness) ill
got. Think how much of that you never spake for, how
much by speaking unjustly or in unjust causes. Account
it then a blessing of God if thus it may be laid out for
your good, and not left for your heir.

"Do not, if you be restored, as some others do, fly
from the service of virtue to serve the time, but rather let
this cross make you zealous in God's cause, sensible in
ours, and more sensible in all."

After much more reproof and admonition, he jeeringly
advises him not to be too much cast down. "To humble
ourselves before God is the part of a Christian; but

for the world and our enemies the counsel of the poet is apt,

> 'Tu ne cede malis, sed contrà audentior ito.' "[1]

In no composition that I have met with is there a greater display of vengeful malignity. Under pretense of acting a Christian part, he pours oil of vitriol into the wounds he had inflicted. There seems to have been an intention to make Coke disgorge some of his ill-gotten gains, by a heavy fine in the Star Chamber. That was abandoned, but the dismissal was consummated. After the long vacation, the Chief Justice was summoned by Bacon before the Privy Council, to give an account of what he had done in the way of correcting his Reports. He declared that in his eleven volumes, containing 500 cases, there were only four errors, and that there were as many in the much-esteemed Plowden, which the wisdom of time had discovered, and later judgments controlled. The order, prompted by Bacon, and pronounced by the Lord Chancellor, was "that the Chief Justice should still forbear his sitting at Westminster, &c., not restraining, nevertheless, any other exercise of his place in private."

Bacon, having made a report of this proceeding to the King with a view of hastening the final blow, says,—" If upon this probation added to former matters, your Majesty think him not fit for your service, we must in all humbleness subscribe to your Majesty, and acknowledge that neither his displacing, considering he holdeth his place but during your will and pleasure, nor the choice of a fit man to put in his room, are council-table matters, but are to proceed wholly from your Majesty's great wisdom and pleasure. So that in this course it is but the signification of your pleasure, and the business is at an end as to him."

At length Bacon had the exquisite delight of making out Coke's "*supersedeas*," and a warrant to the Lord Chancellor for a writ to create a new Chief Justice.[2]

To add to his satisfaction, he contrived to get himself into the good graces of Prince Charles, and was appointed Chancellor of the Duchy of Cornwall.

---

[1] Works, v. 403.
[2] Sir E. Coke was removed Nov. 15, 1616, and Sir Henry Montagu was sworn in as his successor the following day.

The office of Chief Justice of the King's Bench he declined, on account of the moribund condition of Lord Ellesmere.

CHAPTER LV.

CONTINUATION OF THE LIFE OF LORD BACON FROM HIS APPOINTMENT AS CHANCELLOR TILL HIS FALL.

THERE was nothing now wanting to the earthly felicity of Bacon except the actual possession of the Great Seal of England. He continued from time to time to remind the King of his pretensions; and he induced the Prince to say a good word for his further advancement. He pretended that the King's service was his great object, adding, "Were your Majesty mounted and seated without difficulties and distastes in your business as I desire to see you, I should *ex animo* desire to spend the decline of my years in my studies; wherein, also, I should not forget to do him honor, who, besides his active and politic virtues, is the best pen of Kings, much more, the best subject of a pen."

On the 7th of March, 1617, his wish was accomplished. The Great Seal, having been surrendered by Lord Ellesmere, was, between the hours of eleven and twelve on that day, in the Palace at Whitehall, delivered to Sir FRANCIS BACON by the King, who, at the same time, in a speech, graciously commemorated his services as Solicitor General, Attorney General, and Privy Councillor, and gave him four admonitions for his guidance as Lord Keeper.—1. To restrain the jurisdiction of the Court within its true and due limits. 2. Not to put the Great Seal to letters patent without due consideration. *Quod dubites ne feceris.* 3. To retrench all unnecessary delays. *Bis dat qui cito dat.* 4. That justice might pass with as easy charge as might be.[1] Sir Francis, on bended knees, humbly, and with a most grateful mind, acknowledged the constant and never-tiring kindness of the King, who had conducted

---

[1] "Predictus Franciscus Bacon flexis genibus humiliter gratiosissimo animo agnovit constantem Dni Regis et prennem beneficor, cursum utpote qui per tot gradus eum manu quasi duxerit ad sum, honoris fastigium," &c.—Cl. R. 16 Jac. 1.

him, step by step, to the highest pinnacle of honor,—professing dutifully his determination to preserve all the rights and prerogatives of the Crown,—equally to administer the law to all in the Courts in which he himself should preside, and to exercise a general superintendence over the administration of justice throughout the realm.

As soon as Bacon had got home—the Great Seal, in its silken purse, lying on the table before him—his eye glancing from the paper to the long-courted bauble, and his heart overflowing with gratitude—he wrote the following letter to Villiers, now Earl of Buckingham, who had witnessed the ceremony at Whitehall:—

"My dearest Lord,—It is both in cares and kindness that small ones float up to the tongue, and great ones sink down into the heart in silence. Therefore, I could speak little to your Lordship to-day, neither had I fit a time; but I must profess thus much, that, in this day's work, you are the truest and perfectest mirror and example of firm and generous friendship that ever was in Court. And I shall count every day lost wherein I shall not either study your well-doing in thought, or do your name honor in speech, or perform your service in deed. Good my Lord, account and accept me

"Your most bounden and devoted Friend,
"and Servant of all men living,
"FR. BACON, C. S."[1]

With what rapture he must have written the letters C. S., which he added to his name for the first time! It has been supposed by some of his blind admirers that he reluctantly submitted to his elevation, and that, inwardly desirous of retirement and contemplation, he would have shut himself up for the rest of his days in his library at Gorhambury, had it not been for the importunities of his family and dependents, joined to his hope of being able to do more good to mankind by sacrificing his inclinations, and showing to the world what could be effected by a philosopher in high office and in the exercise of great power. For this opinion no better reason can be given than an extract of an Essay written by him while a student in Gray's Inn:—"Men in great place are thrice servants; servants of the Sovereign or state; servants of fame; and servants of business: so as they have no freedom, neither

[1] Works, vol. v. 463.

in their persons, nor in their actions, nor in their times. It is a strange desire to seek power and to lose liberty, or to seek power over others and to lose power over a man's self." [1] It may as well be said that he despised money, because in his writings he calls riches "the baggage of virtue." In seasons of reflection and remorse he must often have said to himself—

———"Video meliora proboque ;
Deteriora sequor."

His first act was graceful and becoming ; he went next day to York House to pay his respects to his predecessor —to thank him for that kindness which had contributed to his advancement—and, in the King's name, to offer him an Earldom.

The Court was now in the bustle of preparation for James's visit to Scotland. On his accession to the throne of England, he had promised his countrymen to pay them at least a triennial visit ; but during fourteen long years the halls of Holyrood had been empty—and the progress to the North, at last about to take place, attracted the attention of both nations. Buckingham was to accompany the King, that he might direct his proceedings, and take care that no fresh favorite should engage his affections. The new Lord Keeper was to be left at the head of the government in London. In the contemplation of this journey, he had prepared, while Attorney General, "Remembrances for the King before his going into Scotland ;" and he now sketched out the "Council business" to be done in his Majesty's absence, the great object of which was to preserve the public tranquillity during Easter term, when the town was expected to be very full of company.[2] The King took his departure from Whitehall on the 14th of March, exactly a week after Bacon had received the Great Seal.

It was luckily vacation time, and the Lord Keeper had full leisure to prepare for entering on the discharge of his judicial duties. His promotion had given general satis-

---

[1] Essay, "Of Great Place."
[2] These papers show that the attendance of persons in London from the country, now depending on the meeting of parliament, was then regulated by the law terms, and this seems to have continued to the reign of Queen Anne :

"Rhymes ere he wakes, and prints *before term ends*,
Obliged by hunger and request of friends."

faction; he was congratulated upon it not only by his Alma Mater, but by the University of Oxford,[1] and the universal expectation was, that the *beau idéal* of a perfect Judge, which he had so admirably imaged in his Essay "Of Judicature," was really to be exemplified to the admiring gaze of mankind.

At the commencement of his judicial career there was no disappointment. On the 7th of May, the first day of Easter Term, he took his seat in the Court of Chancery. The splendor of the ceremony was little impaired by the absence of the grandees who were attending the King,—their place being supplied by the general eagerness to do honor to the new Lord Keeper. The procession was formed at his "lodging" in Gray's Inn, and marched by Holborn, Chancery Lane, the Strand, Charing, Whitehall, and King Street, to Westminster Hall, in the following order:—1. Clerks and officers in Chancery. 2. Students of Law. 3. Sergeant-at-arms, purse-bearer, and gentlemen servants of the Lord Keeper. 4. The Lord Keeper, in a gown of purple satin, riding between the Lord Treasurer and the Keeper of the Privy Seal. 5. Earls and Barons. 6. Privy Councillors. 7. The Judges. 8. Knights and Esquires;—all of whom followed the Lord Keeper, mounted on caparisoned steeds. Alighting in Palace Yard, and entering Westminster Hall, the Lord Keeper was received by the Sergeants at Law and the Benchers and Readers of the Inns of Court, and conducted into the Court of Chancery, now filled with those who had composed the cavalcade.

The oaths being administered to him, he delivered an address on which he had bestowed much pains, and which shows his intimate familiarity with the duties he had to perform. He thus began:—"Before I enter into the business of the Court, I shall take advantage of so many honorable witnesses to publish and make known summarily what charge the King's most excellent Majesty gave me

---

[1] To Cambridge he replied, "Your gratulations shall be no more welcome to me than your business or occasions, which I will attend; and yet not so but that I shall endeavour to prevent them by my care of your good." To Oxford: "I shall, by the grace of God, as far as may concern me, hold the balance as equally between the two Universities as I shall hold the balance of other justice between party and party. And yet in both cases I must meet with some inclinations of affection, which nevertheless shall not carry me aside."—April 12, 1617.

when I received the Seal, and what orders and resolutions I myself have taken in conformity to that charge, that the King may have the honor of direction, and I the part of obedience." After some pardonable flattery of his royal Master, he proceeds to lay down most excellent practical rules, which he undertook to observe. "I am resolved that my decree shall come speedily, if not instantly, after the hearing, and my signed decree speedily upon my decree pronounced. For it hath been a manner much used of late in my Lord's time, of whom I learn much to imitate, and somewhat to avoid, that upon the solemn and full hearing of a cause nothing is pronounced in Court, but breviates are required to be made, which I do not dislike in itself in causes perplexed. But yet I find, when such breviates were taken, the cause was sometimes forgotten a term or two, and then set down for a new hearing. I will promise regularly to pronounce my decree within a few days after my hearing, and to sign my decree, at the least, in the vacation after the pronouncing. For fresh justice is sweetest.

"Again, because justice is a sacred thing, and the end for which I am called to this place, and therefore is my way to heaven (and if it be shorter, it is never a whit the worse), I shall, by the grace of God, as far as God will give me strength, add the afternoon to the forenoon, and some fortnight of the vacation to the term, for the expediting and clearing of the causes of the Court ; only the depth of the three long vacations I would reserve, in some measure, free from business of estate, and for studies, arts, and sciences, to which, in my own nature, I am most induced.[1]

"There is another point of true expedition which resteth much in itself, and that is in my manner of giving orders. For I have seen an affectation of dispatch turn utterly to delay at length. But I mean not to purchase the praise of expedition in that kind. My endeavor shall be to hear patiently, and to cast my order into such a mold as may soonest bring the subject to the end of his journey.

"I will maintain strictly and with severity the former orders which I find my Lord Chancellor hath taken for the immoderate and needless prolixity and length of bills

---

[1] He here beautifully pays homage to philosophy.

and answers, as well in punishing the party as fining the counsel whose hand I shall find at such bills and answers.

"I shall be careful there be no exaction of any new fees, but according as they have been heretofore set and tabled. As for lawyers' fees, I must leave that to the conscience and merit of the lawyer, and estimation and gratitude of the client."

After touching on other topics rather of temporary interest, he intimates his intention, for the sake of the junior barristers who could not be heard above once or twice in a term, to hear motions every Tuesday between nine and eleven,—and he proceeds to announce to their Lordships what he truly calls "a fancy"—which would cause a mutiny at the bar in our times. "It falleth out that there be three of us the King's servants, in great places, that are lawyers by descent, Mr. Attorney, son of a Judge, Mr. Solicitor, likewise son of a Judge, and myself, a Chancellor's son. Now, because the law roots so well in my time, I will water it at the root thus far, as besides these great ones I will hear any Judge's son before a Sergeant, and any Sergeant's son before a reader, if there be not many of them."

He announced that he was preparing "new orders" to regulate the practice of the Court,—and again proclaimed his loyalty by saying,—"It is my comfort to serve such a Master, that I shall need to be but a conduit only for the conveying of his goodness to his people,"—not omitting a pious compliment to his father,—"*optimus magistratus præstat optimæ legi;* for myself I doubt I shall not attain it; yet I have a domestic example to follow."[1]

Next morning he wrote an account of the ceremony to Buckingham:—

"Yesterday I took my place in Chancery, which I hold only for the King's grace and favor, and your constant friendship. There was much ado and a great deal of world: but this matter of pomp, which is heaven to some men, is hell to me (?) or purgatory at least. It is true I was glad to see that the King's choice was so generally approved, and that I had so much interest in men's good will and good opinions, because it maketh me a fitter instrument to do my Master service, and my friend also. After I was set in Chancery, I published his Majesty's

[1] Works, iv. 486.

charge which he gave me when he gave me the Seal, and what rules and resolutions I had taken for the fulfilling his commandments. I send your Lordship a copy of what I said. Men tell me it hath done the King a great deal of honor, insomuch that some of my friends, that are wise and no vain ones, did not stick to say to me that there was not this seven years such a preparation for a parliament,—which was a commendation which I confess pleased me well. I pray take some fit time to show it his Majesty, because, if I misunderstood him in anything, I may amend it. because I know his judgment is higher and deeper than mine."[1]

He was greatly delighted with the following answer:—

"I have acquainted his Majesty with your letter and the papers that came enclosed, who is exceedingly well satisfied—especially with the speech you made at the taking of your place in the Chancery. Whereby his Maesty perceiveth that you have not only given proof how well you understand the place of a Chancellor, but done him much right also in giving notice to those that were present, that you have received such instructions from his Majesty, whose honor will be so much the greater in that all men will acknowledge the sufficiency and worthiness of his Majesty's choice in preferring a man of such abilities to that place, which besides can not but be a great advancement and furtherance to his service; and I can assure your Lordship that his Majesty was never so well pleased as he is with this account you have given him of this passage."[2]

The Lord Keeper resolved to show what could be effected by vigor and perseverance. He sat forenoon and afternoon,—coming punctually into Court and staying a little beyond his time to finish a matter, which if postponed might have taken another day,—most patiently listening to everything that could assist him in arriving at a right conclusion, but giving a broad hint to counsel by a question, a shrug, or a look, when they were wandering from the subject,—not baulking the hopes of the suitors by breaking up to attend a Cabinet or the House of Lords, —not encouraging lengthiness at the bar to save the trouble of thought, not postponing judgment till the

[1] Works, v. 469. Bacon no doubt expected that the letter, as well as the address, would be laid before the King.   [2] Works, v. 475.

argument was forgotten,—not seeking to allay the discontent of the bar by "nods, and becks, and wreathed smiles."

At the end of one month he had satisfactorily cleared off the whole arrear, and on the 8th of June he thus exultingly writes to Buckingham:—

"My very good Lord,—This day I have made even with the business of the kingdom for common justice; not one cause unheard · the lawyers drawn dry of all the motions they were to make; not one petition unanswered. And this I think could not be said in our age before. This I speak not out of ostentation, but out of gladness when I have done my duty. I know men think I can not continue if I should thus oppress myself with business; but that account is made. The duties of life are more than life, and if I die now, I shall die before the world will be weary of me, which in our times is somewhat rare."[1]

He then goes on to mention a slight attack of the gout in his foot, which he ascribed to "changing from a field air to a Thames air," that is, from Gray's Inn to York House, of which he had now taken possession with great delight, as his father had so long occupied it, and it was the place of his own birth.[2]

To gain the good will of the profession, he wisely revived a practice which, having succeeded well with Lord Chancellor Hatton, had fallen into desuetude, and which all prudent Chancellors follow,—to give dinners to the Judges and the leaders of the bar.[3] He sends the follow-

[1] Works, vi. 149.
[2] York House having been the residence of so many Chancellors and Lord Keepers, and being so often mentioned, some further account of it may please the curious reader. The see of York being deprived of its ancient inn by Wolsey's cession of Whitehall to Henry VIII., Heath, Archbishop of York and Chancellor, purchased a piece of land and certain old buildings between the river Thames and the Strand, near where Villiers Street now stands; there he erected York House, in which he resided, and which, under leases from successive Archbishops of York, was occupied by almost all the holders of the Great Seal who succeeded him down to Lord Bacon. The hall was fitted as a court for business in the afternoons and out of term, and it contained various accommodations for the Chancellor's officers. Coming by exchange to the Crown, after the fall of Bacon, it was granted to Buckingham. Being seized as forfeited by the Long Parliament, it was granted to Lord Fairfax, but reverting to the second Duke of Buckingham, he sold it for building, and there were erected upon it "George Street," "Villiers Street," "Duke Street," and "Buckingham Street," which, with "Of Alley," still preserve his name and title—the lines of Pope being a lasting record of his infamy.
[3] The complaints of Lord Eldon's delays were much aggravated by his

ing account in a letter to Buckingham of his first banquet:—

"Yesterday, which was my weary day, I bid all the Judges to dinner, which was not used to be, and entertained them in a private withdrawing chamber with the learned counsel. When the feast was past, I came amongst them and sat me down at the end of the table, and prayed them to think I was one of them and but a foreman.[1] I told them I was weary, and therefore must be short, and would now speak to them upon two points." The first was about injunctions:—" I plainly told them that, for my part, as I would not suffer any the least diminution or derogation from the ancient and due power of the Chancery, so if anything should be brought to them at any time touching the proceedings of the Chancery, which did seem to them exorbitant or inordinate, that they should freely and friendly acquaint me with it, and we should soon agree; or if not, we had a Master that could easily both discern and rule. At which speech of mine, besides a great deal of thanks and acknowledgment, I did see cheer and comfort in their faces, as if it were a new world." The second point was, requiring from each of them a written account of what they had done and observed on circuits, to be sent to the King.

What was not so laudable,—he already began to tamper privately with the Judges, and soliciting such of them as were most apt for his purpose, prosecuted a scheme for extending still farther the usurped jurisdiction of the *High Commission Court*.

He continued regularly to correspond on all matters of State with the King and Buckingham, who were holding a parliament in Scotland, in the vain hope of establishing episcopacy in that country. Having at first ventured to oppose the projected matrimonial alliance between Prince

---

non-feasance in this respect. During a course of professional dinners by Sir Thomas Plomer, Romilly observed, that "the Master of the Rolls was very properly clearing off the arrears of the Lord Chancellor."

[1] I do not exactly understand how my Lord Keeper Bacon comported himself on this occasion. Are we to understand that he could not be at table during dinner from indisposition? or that he was too great to eat with his company, and condescendingly asked them to "think he was one of them," when he came in to harangue them? Whoever has had the good fortune to be present when Lord Chancellor Lyndhurst presides at similar dinners, will form a better opinion of the manners of the man and the times.

Charles and the Infanta of Spain, he yielded to the King's wishes, and did all in his power to promote it.

He was thus in the highest possible favor, when suddenly his inextinguishable enmity to Sir E. Coke had nearly accomplished his ruin. Not satisfied with turning him out of his office of Chief Justice, and erasing his name from the list of Privy Councillors, Bacon still went on with the absurd charge against him about his Reports, and hoped to "make a Star Chamber business of it."[1]

The Ex-Chief Justice counteracted this scheme by a most masterly stroke of policy. His second wife, Lady Hatton, had brought him one child, a daughter, who was to succeed to all her mother's immense property. This heiress he offered in marriage to Sir John Villiers, the brother of the favorite, who was eager for the aggrandizement of his family. The proposal was highly agreeable to both brothers and their mother who ruled them, —but most highly alarming to Bacon. He was delighted to hear that Lady Hatton disliked the match as much as himself, and forgetting the scornful usage he had experienced from her in former days, when he sought her hand in marriage,—he opened a correspondence with her, and strenuously abetted her resistance. Without duly considering what were likely to be the feelings of Buckingham on the occasion, he wrote to him:—"The mother's consent is not had, nor the young gentlewoman's, who expecteth a great fortune from her mother, which, without her consent, is endangered. This match, out of my faith and freedom towards your Lordship, I hold very inconvenient both for your brother and yourself. First, he shall marry into a disgraced house, which in reason of state is never held good. Next, he shall marry into a troubled house of man and wife, which in religion and Christian discretion is disliked. Thirdly, your Lordship will go near to lose all such your friends as are adverse to Sir Edward Coke, myself only except, who, out of a pure love and thankfulness shall ever be firm to you. And, lastly and chiefly, it will greatly weaken and distract the King's service." He therefore strongly advises that the match shall be broken off, "or not proceeded in without

---

[1] "I did call upon the committees also for the proceeding in their purging of Sir Edward Coke's Reports, which I see they go on with seriously."— *Bacon to Buckingham*, May, 1617.

the consent of both parents, required by religion and the law of God."[1]

Bacon wrote still more strongly to the King, pointing out the public mischief which would arise from the notion that Coke was about to be restored to favor. " Now, then, I reasonably doubt that, if there be but an opinion of his coming in with the strength of such an alliance, it will give a turn and relapse in men's mind's into the former state of things hardly to be helpen, to the great weakening of your Majesty's service." Having dwelt upon the dangerous influence which Coke might thus acquire if a parliament were called, he contrasts himself with the dangerous rival—whose coming patriotism seems to have cast its shadow before: I am *omnibus omnia* for your Majesty's service; but he is by nature unsociable, and by habit popular, and too old now to take a new ply. And men begin already to collect, yea, and to conclude, that he that raiseth such a smoke to get in, will set all on fire when he is in."[2] Bacon's head was so turned by his elevation, that in this letter he madly went so far as to throw out some sarcasms upon the favorite himself. To him, as might have been expected, it was immediately communicated. Buckingham was thrown in an ecstacy of rage, and he easily contrived to make the King, if possible, more indignant at the presumption and impertinence of the Lord Keeper.

Meanwhile the plot thickened in England. Lady Hatton, with the concurrence of her present adviser, carried off her daughter, and concealed her in a country house near Hampton Court. The Ex-Chief Justice, tracing the young lady to her hiding place, demanded a warrant from the Lord Keeper to recover her, and this being refused, he went thither at the head of a band of armed men, and forcibly rescued her. For this alleged outrage he was summoned, and several times examined before the Council,—and, by the Lord Keeper's directions, Yelverton, the Attorney General, filed an information against him in the Star Chamber.

Intelligence of these events being brought to Edinburgh, the King and Buckingham put an end to the sullen silence they had for some time observed towards

---

[1] Bacon's works, v. 477.   [2] Ibid., v. 478.

the Lord Keeper,[1] and wrote him letters filled with bitter complaints, invectives, and threats. Bacon suddenly awoke as from a dream, and all at once saw his imprudence and his danger. In an agony of terror, he ordered the Attorney General to discontinue the prosecution in the Star Chamber; he sent for Lady Hatton, and tried to reconcile her to the match, and he made the most abject submission to Buckingham's mother, who had complained of having been insulted by him. He then sent dispatches by a special messenger to Edinburgh, to relate his altered conduct.

There never was a more striking instance of "kissing the rod" then is exhibited in his answer to the King. "I do very much thank your Majesty for your letter, and I think myself much honored by it. For though it contains some matter of dislike, in which respect it hath grieved me more than any event which hath fallen out in my life, yet I know reprehensions from the first masters to the best servants are necessary, and chastisement, though not pleasant for the time, worketh good effects." But the great difficulty was to explain away the disparaging expressions he had so unguardedly used about Buckingham. "I know him to be naturally a wise man, of a sound and staid wit, as I ever said unto your Majesty. And again, I know he hath the best tutor in Europe. But yet I was afraid that the height of his fortune might make him too secure, and, as the proverb is, *a looker on seeth more than a gamester.*" With respect to his treatment of Sir Edward Coke, he says, "I was sometimes sharp, it may be too much, but it was with end to have your Majesty's will performed, or else when methought he was more peremptory then became him, in respect of the honor of the table.[2] It is true, also, that I disliked the riot of violence whereof we of the Council gave your Majesty advertisement, and I disliked it the more because he justified it by law, which was his old song. Now that your Majesty hath been pleased to open yourself to me, I shall be willing to further the match by anything that shall be desired of me, or that is in my power."[3]

---

[1] Bacon had complained of this silence. "I do think long to hear from your Lordship touching my last letter, wherein I gave you my opinion touching your brother's match."—July 25, 1617.
[2] Privy Council.
[3] Works, vi. 157.

James, now on his return to the South,—by order of Buckingham, wrote back an answer, showing an unappeased resentment:[1] "Was not the theftous stealing away of the daughter from her own father the first ground whereupon all this great noise hath since proceeded? We never took upon us such a patrocinying of Sir Edward Coke, as if he were a man not to be meddled withal in any case. *De bonis operibus non lapidamus vos.* But whereas you talk of the riot and violence committed by him, we wonder you make no mention of the riot and violence of them that stole away his daughter." After repeating Bacon's explanation about the favorite, he proceeds, "Now we know not how to interpret this in plain English, otherwise than that you were afraid that the height of his fortune might make him misknow himself. We find him farthest from that vice of any courtier that ever we had so near about us; so do we fear you shall prove the only Phœnix in that jealously of all the kingdom. We can not conceal that we think it was least your part of any to enter into that jealously of him, *of whom we have often heard you speak in a contrary style.* We will not speak of obligation, for surely we think, even in good manners, you had reason not to have crossed anything wherein you had heard his name used till you had heard from him."[2]

Bacon, with the most painful anxiety, awaited the return of the Court to Whitehall, and he made another desperate effort, by a letter to the King, to apologize for his words about Buckingham. "My meaning was plain and simple, that his Lordship might, through his great fortune, be the less apt to cast and forsee the unfaithfulness of friends, and the malignity of enemies, and accidents of time. Therefore I beseech your Majesty to deliver me in this from any the least imputation upon my dear and noble Lord and friend."

The time at length arrived when Bacon's fate was to be decided. As soon as he heard of Buckingham's return, he hastened to his house, but was denied an audience. For two successive days was he suffered to remain in an antechamber, among lacqueys, seated on an old wooden box, with the purse holding the Great Seal in his own

---

[1] It is superscribed "James R.," and coldly begins, "Right trusty and well-beloved Councillor, we greet you well." [2] Works, vi. 161.

being witnessed by the Prince of Wales and many of the first nobility.

But he was now under considerable apprehension from the violence of Lord Clifton, against whom he had very justly pronounced a decree in the Court of Chancery. The noble defendant being defeated in his wicked attempt, when he had left the Court, declared publicly that " he was sorry he had not stabbed the Lord Chancellor in his chair the moment the judgment was given." He was sent to the Tower, where he manifested complete derangement of mind, and finally destroyed himself. While he was in confinement, Bacon thus wrote to Buckingham, intimating an opinion that maniacs should be made amenable to the criminal law, although it may not be proper to carry the sentence against them into full effect : " I little fear the Lord Clifton, but I much fear the example—that it will animate ruffians and *rodomonti* against all authority, if this pass without censure. The punishment it may please his Majesty to remit; and I shall not formally, but heartily, intercede for him ; but an example (setting myself aside) I wish for terror of persons that may be more dangerous than he towards the first Judge of the kingdom."

The Lord Chancellor now acted rather a conspicuous part in an affair which reflected lasting disgrace on the King and his Councillors. Sir Walter Raleigh, after having been imprisoned many years in the Tower since his conviction for treason, had been released upon a representation of the glory and riches he could secure to the nation by an expedition to America, and having met with discomfiture, was in custody on a charge of burning a Spanish town, and making war against Spain contrary to his orders. There being much difficulty as to the mode of proceeding against him, the Lord Chancellor assembled all the Judges at York House, and concurred with them in an opinion " that Sir Walter Raleigh, being attainted of high treason, which is the highest and last work of law, he can not be drawn in question judicially for any crime or offense since committed"—recommending " either that a warrant should be immediately sent to the Lieutenant of the Tower for his immediate execution under the former sentence, or that he should be brought before the Council and principal Judges, some of the nobility and

James, now on his return to the South,—by order of Buckingham, wrote back an answer, showing an unappeased resentment:[1] "Was not the theftcous stealing away of the daughter from her own father the first ground whereupon all this great noise hath since proceeded? We never took upon us such a patrocinying of Sir Edward Coke, as if he were a man not to be meddled withal in any case. *De bonis operibus non lapidamus vos.* But whereas you talk of the riot and violence committed by him, we wonder you make no mention of the riot and violence of them that stole away his daughter." After repeating Bacon's explanation about the favorite, he proceeds, "Now we know not how to interpret this in plain English, otherwise than that you were afraid that the height of his fortune might make him misknow himself. We find him farthest from that vice of any courtier that ever we had so near about us; so do we fear you shall prove the only Phœnix in that jealously of all the kingdom. We can not conceal that we think it was least your part of any to enter into that jealously of him, *of whom we have often heard you speak in a contrary style.* We will not speak of obligation, for surely we think, even in good manners, you had reason not to have crossed anything wherein you had heard his name used till you had heard from him."[2]

Bacon, with the most painful anxiety, awaited the return of the Court to Whitehall, and he made another desperate effort, by a letter to the King, to apologize for his words about Buckingham. "My meaning was plain and simple, that his Lordship might, through his great fortune, be the less apt to cast and forsee the unfaithfulness of friends, and the malignity of enemies, and accidents of time. Therefore I beseech your Majesty to deliver me in this from any the least imputation upon my dear and noble Lord and friend."

The time at length arrived when Bacon's fate was to be decided. As soon as he heard of Buckingham's return, he hastened to his house, but was denied an audience. For two successive days was he suffered to remain in an antechamber, among lacqueys, seated on an old wooden box, with the purse holding the Great Seal in his own

---

[1] It is superscribed "James R.," and coldly begins, "Right trusty and well-beloved Councillor, we greet you well." [2] Works, vi. 161.

hand, as if prepared to go in the presence of the Sovereign, or to receive a message from the Commons at the bar of the Upper House. When, at length he was admitted, he flung himself on the floor kissed the favorite's feet, and vowed never to rise till he was forgiven.[1]

Buckingham, having effectually frightened him out of any future resistance to his will,—being convinced that he himself could not find elsewhere so pliant and useful an instrument of his government,—accepted his submission, and agreed to a reconciliation. The marriage was celebrated,—Bacon retained the Great Seal,—and Coke was restored to the Privy Council.

The Lord Keeper was soon made sensible of the bondage into which he had fallen. He was well aware of the evils of monopolies, which had excited such complaints in the late and in the present reign, and he had promised to stay such grants when they came to the Great Seal: but Buckingham found them the readiest means of enriching his own family, and providing for dependents. He therefore multiplied them with reckless prodigality, and without any control. The most famous, from the proceedings to which they afterwards gave rise, were the patents to Sir Giles Mompesson, the original of Massinger's "Sir Giles Overreach," and to Sir Francis Michell, his "Justice Greedy," for licensing alehouses and taverns, and for the exclusive manufacture of gold and silver lace,—with authority to arrest interlopers, and other powers as great as have ever been given to farmers of the revenue in the worst governed states. These not only leading to gross frauds by the patentees, but their agents abusing the enormous powers conferred upon them to the wreaking of old grudges, and even the corruption of female chastity,—the public clamor was so great that a reference was made by the King to the Lord Keeper respecting the legality of such proceedings. Having taken down Sir Giles with him to Kew, where he went to recreate himself for a few days after long application to business, he reports "that though there were some things he would set by, he found some things that he liked very well,"—and he afterwards gave a deliberate opinion (in which he made the Attorney and Solicitor concur) in favor of the validity of the gold and silver wire patent, as "a means of setting

[1] See Sir Anthony Weldon's account of this scene.

many of his Majesty's poor subjects on work;"—with an intimation that "it were good the dispute were settled with all convenient speed,"—which is supposed to mean, it were good "that certain of the house of Villiers should go shares with Overreach and Greedy in the plunder of the public." Sir Edward, a half brother of the favorite, was admitted into the patent, and then the Lord Keeper committed to prison all who infringed it.

Buckingham's interference with the Lord Keeper in his judicial capacity was still more reprehensible. Few causes of any importance were about to come to a hearing in the Court of Chancery, in which he did not write to the Judge for favor to either of the parties. He at times used the transparent qualification, "so far as may stand with justice and equity,"—or "so far as your Lordship may see him grounded upon equity and reason,"—and in a charity suit he would pledge himself that the defendants charged with breach of trust "desired only the honor of their ancestor's gift"—but he often entirely omitted these decent forms, and pretty plainly hinted that he was to dictate the decree. While Bacon held the Great Seal, I do not find one remonstrance against these applications, and Buckingham, and those who paid for them must have believed that they were effectual. Such was the result of the advice of the instructor to the pupil: " By no means be you persuaded to interpose yourself, either by word or letter, in any cause depending in any court of justice!"

As a reward for his subserviency, the Lord Keeper, on the 4th of January, 1618, had the higher title of Lord Chancellor conferred upon him,[1] and a few months after, he was raised to the Peerage by the title of Baron Verulam—the preamble reciting that the King was "moved by the grateful sense he had of the many faithful services rendered him by this worthy person"—and the patent

---

[1] The ceremony took place in the palace at Whitehall, at four in the afternoon, when "in presencia excellentissimi Principis Caroli Principis Wallie, &c., predictus Dns Rex prm Mag. Sigill. a custodia dci Dni Custodis Francisci Bacon requirens et recipiens et penes se paulisper restinens atque grata obsequia et fidelia servia dci Dni Custodis non solum in administratione justicie sed eciam in conciliis assidue Dno Regi prestita comemorans et intendens ill. ad locum et officium Dni Cancellarii Angl. ulterius erigere et transferre Regia Majestas eidem Francisco Bacon Dno Cust. tanquam Cancellar. suo Angl. Mag. Sig. Angl. reddidit et deliberavit," &c.—Cl. R. 15 Jac. 1

being witnessed by the Prince of Wales and many of the first nobility.

But he was now under considerable apprehension from the violence of Lord Clifton, against whom he had very justly pronounced a decree in the Court of Chancery. The noble defendant being defeated in his wicked attempt, when he had left the Court, declared publicly that " he was sorry he had not stabbed the Lord Chancellor in his chair the moment the judgment was given." He was sent to the Tower, where he manifested complete derangement of mind, and finally destroyed himself. While he was in confinement, Bacon thus wrote to Buckingham, intimating an opinion that maniacs should be made amenable to the criminal law, although it may not be proper to carry the sentence against them into full effect : " I little fear the Lord Clifton, but I much fear the example—that it will animate ruffians and *rodomonti* against all authority, if this pass without censure. The punishment it may please his Majesty to remit; and I shall not formally, but heartily, intercede for him ; but an example (setting myself aside) I wish for terror of persons that may be more dangerous than he towards the first Judge of the kingdom."

The Lord Chancellor now acted rather a conspicuous part in an affair which reflected lasting disgrace on the King and his Councillors. Sir Walter Raleigh, after having been imprisoned many years in the Tower since his conviction for treason, had been released upon a representation of the glory and riches he could secure to the nation by an expedition to America, and having met with discomfiture, was in custody on a charge of burning a Spanish town, and making war against Spain contrary to his orders. There being much difficulty as to the mode of proceeding against him, the Lord Chancellor assembled all the Judges at York House, and concurred with them in an opinion " that Sir Walter Raleigh, being attainted of high treason, which is the highest and last work of law, he can not be drawn in question judicially for any crime or offense since committed"—recommending " either that a warrant should be immediately sent to the Lieutenant of the Tower for his immediate execution under the former sentence, or that he should be brought before the Council and principal Judges, some of the nobility and gentlemen of quality being admitted to be present, and there being a recital of all his recent offenses, and then he being heard and withdrawn—without any fresh sentence, the Lords of the Council and Judges should give their advice openly, whether in respect of these offenses the King might not with justice and honor give warrant for his execution on his attainder?" The course adopted was to bring Raleigh to the King's Bench bar, where execution was awarded against him—and the Lord Chancellor made out writs for it, addressed to the Lieutenant of the Tower and the Sheriff of Middlesex.

Did Bacon feel any satisfaction from the recollection that Raleigh had been instrumental in ruining Essex, and had guarded him with savage exultation at his trial? No! Bacon had not even the merit of being "a good hater," and his enmities as well as his friendships being short-lived, he would have been better pleased if, without any inconvenience to himself, this victim could have been spared. When Raleigh was going on his expedition to Guiana, and was desirous to have a formal pardon, Bacon had said to him, "Sir, the knee-timber of your voyage is money; spare your purse in this particular, for, upon my life, you have a sufficient pardon for all that is passed already, the King having, under his Broad Seal, made you admiral of his fleet, and given you power of life and death over the soldiers and officers you command."[1] It must have been disagreeable for him now to declare the law, "that nothing short of an express pardon could purge the penalties of treason, and that Raleigh, being *civiliter mortuus* ought *naturally* to be put to death."

The end of this great man, notwithstanding his faults, was deplored and condemned. Bacon was not suspected of prompting it, but he was severely censured by his contemporaries for acquiescing in it: and surely, if he had been the upright and constant character we are now desired to consider him, he would, as the head of the law, and superintending the administration of justice,—even at the risk of offending the King or the favorite,—have resisted the outrage of executing a man under a sentence pronounced near sixteen years before, who, in the mean time, having gained universal applause by his literary

[1] 2 St. Tr. 37.

productions, had been intrusted with supreme power over the lives of others. His alleged recent offences, if proved, could not have been legally visited with capital punishment.

Bacon was engaged in other juridical proceedings about this time, which, though of less consequence, ought not to be passed over unnoticed. In the first case I shall mention, he was no more to blame than that he was not in advance of his age in the science of political economy, and that he entertained notions respecting the use of the precious metals which are not yet entirely exploded. It was found that certain Dutch merchants had clandestinely exported bullion and coin from London to a large amount, in payment of commodities imported, and a cry was raised that the country was robbed. To make certain that the alleged delinquents should be amenable to justice, the Chancellor issued writs against them of "ne exeant regno," and he appointed a commission to investigate the matter, consisting of himself, Sir E. Coke, the Chancellor of the Exchequer, and the Lord Chief Justice of the King's Bench. On their advice 180 informations were filed, and 20 of the principal merchants being tried and convicted, were fined to the amount of £100,000.

Then came a strange prosecution in the Star Chamber, which seems to have been instituted by Buckingham, and Bacon to get rid of the Lord Treasurer, the Earl of Suffolk. He and his wife were accused of "trafficking with the public money,"—and being convicted, they were ordered to be imprisoned and fined £30,000. Sir E. Coke having proposed that the fine should be £100,000. The ex-Chief Justice on this occasion extorted praise from the Chancellor, who, in a letter giving an account of the proceeding to the King, says, "Sir Edward Coke did his part—I have not heard him do better—and began with a fine of £100,000, but the Judges first and most of the rest reduced it."[1] Buckingham compromised the matter with Suffolk for £7,000, and for £20,000 sold the Treasurer's place to Lord Chief Justice Montagu, with a Peerage into the bargain.

Strong complaints began to be made against the Chancellor's decisions in his own Court. He selected as a subject of prosecution a libel upon himself,—not the most

[1] Letter, Nov. 13, 1619.

severe then circulated,—but which luckily happened to be unfounded. He had pronounced a decree against one Wraynham rather hastily, not corruptly,—and an epistle to the King, representing it as unjust contained these words: "He that judgeth unjustly must, to maintain it, speak untruly, and the height of authority maketh man to presume." The sentence on the libeler was the mildest I read of in the records of the Star Chamber— merely "that the defendant should be censured." It may probably be accounted for by the grudge against the prosecutor still harbored by Sir Edward Coke, by whom it was proposed.[1]

The Chancellor, on the prompting of Buckingham, was himself prosecutor and judge in the next case of importance which came forward. Sir Henry Yelverton had been appointed his successor as Attorney General. "When the business was done, he went privately to the King, and told him he did acknowlege how like a good Master and worthy Prince he had dealt with him and although there was never mention, speech, or expectation of anything to be had for his place, yet out of his duty he would give him £4,000 ready money. The King took him in his arms, thanked him, and commended him much for it, and told him he had need of it, for it must serve even to buy him dishes."[2] Buckingham was chagrined that no part of this donation came to his private purse, and Yelverton was afterwards so indiscreet as to behave disrespectfully to the Chancellor, who thus complains of him:—"Mr. Attorney groweth pretty pert with me of late; and I see well who they are that maintain him. But be they flies or be they wasps, I neither care for buzzing nor stings." Yelverton now gave great offense to both by refusing to pass some illegal patents, and they vowed his destruction. The pretext was, his having introduced into a charter granted to the city of London, certain clauses alleged not to be agreeable to the King's warrant, and derogatory to his honor. For this supposed offense the Chancellor ordered an information to be filed against him in the Star Chamber, and resolved to preside

---

[1] 2 St. Tr. 1059.—But it has been suggested to me this could hardly mean a mere reprimand; for "censure," in the language of the Star Chamber, is *adjudge*. Thus Prynne was "*censured* to lose his ears," &c.
[2] Diary of Whitelock, p 63.

himself at the trial. There is a curious paper preserved to us with the notes he had made for his speech in passing sentence: "Sorry for the person, being a gentleman that I lived with in Gray's Inn,—served with him when I was Attorney,—joined with him in many services,—and one that ever gave me more attributes in public than I deserved,—and, besides, a man of very good parts,—which, with me, is friendship at first sight,—much more joined with so ancient an acquaintance. But, as Judge, hold the offense very great," &c.[1]

The following is Bacon's boastful account to Buckingham of the conclusion of the trial:—"Yesternight we made an end of Sir Henry Yelverton's cause. I have almost killed myself by sitting almost eight hours. He is sentenced to imprisonment in the Tower during the King's pleasure, the fine of £4,000, and discharge of his place, by way of opinion of the Court,—referring it to the King's pleasure. How I stirred the Court I leave it to others to speak; but things passed to his Majesty's great honor. I would not for anything but he had made his defense for many deep parts of the charge were deeper printed by the defense." Yelverton having been suspended from his office of Attorney General during the prosecution, was now turned out, and was farther punished on the meeting of parliament for his conduct in the granting of monopolies; but he was made a Judge of the Common Pleas at the commencement of the next reign.[2]

Amidst all these low, groveling, and disgraceful occupations, Bacon was indefatigably employed upon his immortal work, the "NOVUM ORGANUM," which had engaged his thoughts for thirty years, and which he had twelve times transcribed with his own hand,—as often enlarging and amending it.[3] He still considered it defective in itself, and it was only a part of his "INSTAURATIO MAGNA," which he once hoped to have completed. But "numbering his days," he thought he should best consult his own fame and the good of mankind by now giving it to the world. It was published in October, 1620, when he was in his sixtieth year, the preceding long va-

[1] Works, vi. 258. [2] 2 St. Tr. 1141. Works, vi. 259.
[3] "Ipse reperi in archivis dominationis suæ autographa plus minus duodecim ORGANI NOVI de anno in annum elaborati, et ad incudem revocati ; et singulis annis, ulteriore lima subinde politi et castigati ; donec in illud tandem corpus adoleverat, quo in lucem editum fuit."—*Rawley.*

cation having been spent in again retouching it and getting it through the press.

In addition to the public Dedication to James, the author accompanied the copy which he sent to him with a private letter, giving this beautiful and comprehensive view of his undertaking:—" The work, in what color soever it may be set forth, is no more but a new logic teaching to invent and judge by induction, as finding syllogism incompetent for sciences of nature ; and thereby to make philosophy and sciences both more true and more active." The compliment which follows may be excused:—" This tending to enlarge the bounds of reason, and to endow man's estate with new value, was no improper oblation to your Majesty, who of men is the greatest master of reason and author of beneficence."

James's many failings are to a certain degree redeemed by his love of learning and respect for those who had gained intellectual distinction. With his own hand he wrote the answer:—

"MY LORD,

" I have received your letter and your book, than the which you could not have sent a more acceptable present unto me. How thankful I am for it, can not better be expressed by me than by a firm resolution I have taken— first, to read it through with care and attention, though I should steal some hours from my sleep,—having otherwise as little spare time to read it as you had to write it. And then to use the liberty of a true friend in not sparing to ask you the question in any point whereof I shall stand in doubt,—*nam ejus est explicare cujus est condere;* as on the other part I will willingly give a due commendation to such places as in my opinion shall deserve it. . . . . . And so, praying God to give your work as good success as your heart can wish and your labors deserve, I bid you heartily farewell.

" JAMES R." [1]

Bacon replied, eagerly soliciting his Majesty's criticism : —" For though this work as by position and principle doth disclaim to be tried by anything but by experience and the results of experience in a true way, yet the sharpness and profoundness of your Majesty's judgment ought

[1] Works, v. 535.

to be an exception to this general rule; and your questions, observations, and admonishments may do infinite good :

> "'*Astrum quo segetes gauderent frugibus et quo
> Duceret apricis in collibus uva colorem ?*'"

Even Buckingham, who was not without generous tastes and feelings, forgot his intrigues,—for once ceased to consider Bacon as the instrument of his power,—and although incapable of fully appreciating the work, wrote a kind of seemingly sincere congratulation to him as a philosopher.

Bacon and Coke were now living together on terms of decent courtesy, and frequently met at the council-table. A presentation-copy of the NOVUM ORGANUM was therefore sent by the Chancellor to the Ex-Chief Justice. This copy is still preserved at Holkham, showing, by the inscription upon the title-page in Sir Edward's handwriting, in what spirit it was received :—

> "*Edw. C. ex dono auctoris.*"
> "AUCTORI CONSILIUM.
> " Instaurare paras veterum documenta sophorum
> Instaura Leges Justitiamque prius." [1]

This edition contains the device of a ship passing through the pillars of Hercules, over which Sir Edward, driven by indignation against his nature to make verses, has written :—

> "It deserves not to be read in schooles,
> But to be freighted in the *ship of Fools*."

Notwithstanding the envious snarlings of a legal pedant, the work was received with the highest applause by all capable of understanding it,—and raised the fame of Bacon, and of the nation to which he belonged, all over the civilized world.

Now was his worldly prosperity at its height, and he seemed in the full enjoyment of almost everything that man can desire. He was courted and flattered by all classes of the community. The multitude, dazzled by the splendor of his reputation as a statesman, an orator, a judge, a fine writer, a philosopher,—for a time were blind to the faults in his character, and overlooked the evil arts by which he had risen. Bystanders, who were not interested in the cases before him (a large class com-

---

[1] Alluding to Sebastian Brand's famous "Shyp of Folys."

pared to the suffering suitors[1]), were struck with the eloquence and apparent equity of his decisions, and the murmurs of those whom he had wronged were drowned by the plaudits of his admirers. He was on the best terms both with the King and the favorite; and it was generally expected that, like his father, he would keep his office while he lived. Foreigners visiting this country were more eager to see him as author of the NOVUM ORGANUM than as Lord High Chancellor.

We have a specimen of the magnificent mode in which he lived, from the description of the grand banquet he gave at York House on entering his 60th year. Ben Jonson, who was present, celebrates "the fare, the wine, the the men;" and breaks out in enthusiastic praise of the illustrious host:

> "England's high Chancellor, the destin'd heir,
> In his soft cradle to his father's chair;
> Whose even thread the Fates spin round and full
> Out of their choicest and their whitest wool."

He had a villa at Kew, to which he could retire for a day in seasons of business; and his vacations he spent at Gorhambury, "in studies, arts, and sciences, to which, in his own nature, he was most inclined,"—and in gardening, "the purest of human pleasures." Here, at a cost of £10,000, he erected a private retreat, furnished with every intelligent luxury,—to which he repaired when he wished to avoid all visitors, except a few choice spirits, whom he occasionally selected as the companions of his retirement and his lucubrations.

Thence, in January, 1621, he was drawn, not unwillingly to the King's Court, at Theobald's, for there he was raised in the peerage by the title of Viscount St. Albans, his patent being expressed in the most flattering language, particularly celebrating his integrity in the administration of justice; and he was invested by the King with his new dignity, Buckingham supporting his robe of state, while his coronet was borne by the Lord Wenworth.[2] In answer to a complimentary address from the King, he delivered a

---

[1] Sir Samuel Romilly once observed to me, "The number of suitors in Chancery is nothing compared to the community—or this Court would long ago have been abolished as a nuisance."

[2] A question had arisen immediately after his appointment as Lord Keeper whether an Earl could be created without the investiture.—Works, vol. v. 465, 474.

studied oration, enumerating the successive favors he had received from the Crown, and shadowing forth the fresh services he was to render, in his future career, as evidence of his gratitude.

In little more than three months from this day he was a prisoner in the Tower,—stripped of his office for confessed corruption,—and condemned to spend the remainder of his days in disgrace and penury.

It is a remarkable circumstance, and affords a striking instance of a really great man being very ignorant of the state of public opinion, that Bacon had strongly recommended the calling of a parliament, and confidently expected, not only that there would be a grant of liberal supplies, but that no difficulty would be experienced in stifling inquiry into grievances, and in carrying through all the measures of the government. He had penned a reasoned proclamation for calling parliament, with a view to influence the elections; and he had prepared a plan of operations, which had been approved of by the King and Buckingham, for the conduct of the session.

On the 30th of January, a day inauspicious to the Stuarts, the two houses assembled. James, having made a long speech from the throne in his rambling, familiar, shrewd style,[1] the Lord Chancellor thus addressed him: "May it please your Majesty, I am struck with admiration in respect of your profound discourses,—with reference of your royal precepts,—and contentment in a number of gracious passages which have fallen from your Majesty. For myself, I hold it as great commendation in a Chancellor to be silent when such a King is by, who can so well deliver the oracles of his mind. Only, Sir, give me leave to give my advice to the Upper and Lower House briefly in two words, *Nosce teipsum.* I would have the parliament know itself: 1st, in a modest carriage to so gracious a Sovereign: 2ndly, in valuing themselves thus far as to know now it is in them, by their careful dealing, to procure an infinite good to themselves in substance, and reputation at home or abroad."[2]

[1] He now complains that his eloquence on former occasions had not been properly appreciated, and he says with much *naïveté*, "So it may be it pleased God (seeing some vanity in me) to send back my words as wind spit into my own face. So as I may truly say, '*I have often piped unto you, but you have not danced; I have often mourned, but you have not lamented.*'"—1 Parl. Hist. 1176.

[2] 1 Parl. Hist. 1168.

As soon as a Speaker had been chosen and approved, the Commons set to work in a manner which showed that they knew their duty, and were resolved to fulfill it. They first voted an adequate supply, that there might be no ground for saying that the Crown was driven to unconstitutional modes of raising money. They then proceeded to the redress of grievances,—and here they were headed by Sir Edward Coke, become member for Liskeard, and a flaming patriot. He had for several years been contented with assisting in the judicial business of the Privy Council without office or emolument. Finding this rather dull work,—presuming that the intention was to make use of his services without promoting him, and having the sagacity to discover that the time had arrived when he might gratify the envy and malignity with which he had viewed the ascendency of his rival, he entirely broke with the Court, and he was gladly hailed as leader of the opposition.

He struck a decisive blow by moving for a committee to inquire into the grievance of monopolies, which the ministers found they could not attempt to resist. A report was speedily presented, showing the dreadful oppression which the monopolies were producing,—and it was resolved to demand a conference on the subject with the Lords. The message to demand the conference was sent up by Sir Edward Coke.

It must have been curious to have witnessed the following scene at the bar of the House of Peers on this occasion, when the two rivals came into such close contact. *Gentleman Usher of the Black Rod.*—" My Lords, a message from the House of Commons." *Bacon.*—" Is it your Lordships' pleasure that the messengers be called in? Call in the messengers." (The Chancellor leaves the woolsack, with the purse holding the Great Seal in his hand, and marches towards the bar, where he sees Sir Edward Coke. Their eyes encounter, but all indecorous looks and gestures are suppressed. Coke makes his *congés*, delivers in his paper, and retires.) *Bacon from the woolsack.*—"The message from the Commons by Sir Edward Coke

[1] Bacon, in yielding to the Speaker's prayer for liberty of speech, added this caution: "That liberty of speech turn not into license, but be joined with that gravity and discretion as may taste of duty and love to your Sovereign, reverence to your own assembly, and respect to the matters ye handle."

and others is this, that the Commons, having entered into a due consideration of divers heavy grievances, touching patents and monopolies, do desire a conference with your Lordships thereupon, leaving the time and place and numbers to your Lordship's appointment." (The messengers being again called in), *Bacon sitting on the woolsack, covered.*—" I am desired by their Lordships to inform the Commons that their Lordships agree to the conference, and appoint it to be held on the 5th of March, at two of the clock in the afternoon in the Painted Chamber, where, in respect of the importance of the subject, the whole House will attend." *Sir Edward Coke.*—" My Lords, I crave liberty to explain my message a little further. The Commons will scantly be prepared to meet your Lordships so soon, and their wish was, that, if your Lordships should yield to a conference, they would prepare the business, so as to give least interruption to your Lordship's greater affairs; and when they are ready, I will return and inform your Lordships therewith." *Bacon.*—" Gentlemen of the House of Commons, their Lordships will suspend the time till they have notice that the Commons are ready for the conference."[1]

Buckingham and the King were now fully aware of the impending danger. Another committee of the House of Commons was sitting to inquire into "the abuses of Courts of Justice,"—the proceedings of which were directed by the indefatigable and vindictive Sir Edward Coke, although, out of decency, he had declined to be its chairman. The object of this inquiry was known to be to establish certain charges of bribery and corruption against the Lord Chancellor, and to effect his ruin.

This was the crisis in the fate of the man whose life we shall next have to relate, Williams, then Dean of Westminster, afterwards Lord Keeper of the Great Seal, Bishop of Lincoln, and Archbishop of York. Hitherto he had only been known to Buckingham as a divine, having been employed by him to convert from the errors of popery the Lady Catherine Manners, a great heiress, whom he wished to marry,—and to smooth the difficulties which stood in his way in that enterprise. But Williams being noted for his shrewdness and dexterity in business, his advice was asked in the present extremity, and he de-

[1] 1 Parl. Hist. 119). Journal of Lords, 18 Jac. I.

clared that the storm was too violent to be resisted, and that Buckingham himself would be in danger if some great concession were not speedily made to public opinion. He recommended that Sir Edward Villiers, implicated with Mompesson and Mitchell in the most obnoxious monopolies, should be sent abroad on an embassy; that the other two "should be thrown overboard as wares that might be spared;" and that the power of the Crown should not be exerted to screen the Chancellor from any charges which might be established against him. "Swim with the tide," said he, "and you can not be drowned."[1] Buckingham, pleased with his insinuating manner and plausible advice, immediately carried him to the King, and from that moment the Dean of Westminster directed the measures of the Court, although it was a considerable time before the public, or even Bacon, became aware of his influence.

Sir Edward Villiers was sent on his embassy. Mompesson and Mitchell were impeached, and in due time sentence was pronounced upon them of fine, imprisonment, and perpetual infamy.

At a conference on this subject between the two Houses, at which the Lord Chancellor was one of the managers for the Peers, he took the opportunity,—very irregularly, though dexterously,—to make a long speech to the Commons, vindicating the whole of his conduct, which had recently been brought in question before them. He might have been forewarned of his approaching fall by the proceeding which took place on the return of the managers of the House. The Lord Chamberlain then complained, "that the Lord Chancellor, at the conference, had spoken in his own defense, not being allowed so to do, the said conference being directed and limited by this House, which was against the ancient orders thereof," and moved "that an order may now be entered to prevent the like hereafter, and that the Lord Chancellor should give the House satisfaction by an acknowledgement of his error herein." The Lord Chancellor had the mortification to put the question upon this motion, and to declare "the CONTENTS have it,"—no one venturing to dissent. "Whereupon the Lord Chancellor removing from the woolsack to his seat as a Peer, did

[1] Hacket's Life of Williams, Part I. 50.

acknowledge that, contrary to the orders of this House, he had spoken at the last conference more than he had direction from the House to do, and owned that he had erred therein."[1]

In three days more the public exposure of the Lord Chancellor began—by the Report of the committee on the abuses in Courts of Justice being presented to the House. It expressly charged him with corruption on the complaint of parties against whom he had given judgment. One Aubrey stated, "that having a suit pending in the Court of Chancery, and being worn out by delays, he had been advised by his counsel to present £100 to the Chancellor, that his cause might, by more than ordinary means, be expedited, and that in consequence he had delivered the money to Sir George Hastings and Mr. Jenkins, of Gray's Inn, by whom it was presented to his Lordship; but notwithstanding this offering, the Chancellor had pronounced a *killing decree* against him." Egerton was the other petitioner, who averred that, "to procure my Lord's favor, he had been persuaded by Sir George Hastings and Sir Richard Young to make some present to the Chancellor, and that he accordingly delivered to them £400, which they presented to the Chancellor as a gratuity, under color that my Lord when Attorney General had befriended him—which was in addition to a former gratuity of a piece of plate worth fifty guineas—but that, notwithstanding these presents, the Lord Chancellor, assisted by Lord Chief Justice Hobart, decided for his opponent." Various witnesses had been examined in support of these charges, and the committee had passed a resolution that they ought to be made the subject of an impeachment of the Lord Chancellor.

Bacon reckoning on the support of the Crown, and thinking that the worst that could happen would be a sudden dissolution of the parliament—at first had talked with scorn and defiance of these accusations—but he became alarmed by the increased roar of public disapprobation, and the diminished courtesy of the hangers-on about the Court.

On the 17th of March he presided in the House of Lords—for the last time. He had a fright on that day by the spectre that had so often crossed his path, and was

[1] Lords' Journals, 18 Jac. I. 1 Parl. Hist. 1202.

now ever present to his imagination. "A message from the Commons" was announced—and the Chancellor marching down to the bar perceived that it was brought by Sir Edward Coke. He suspected that the message might have been to exhibit articles of impeachment against himself for bribery and corruption. He was relieved when Coke declared the message to be, "that the Commons, for the furtherance of justice, waived an objection they had at first made to members of their House being sworn at the bar of the House of Lords as witnesses against Mompesson and Mitchell." [1]

Notwithstanding this respite, Bacon's courage now failed him—he hurried the adjournment of the House as much as possible, lest another message might come up of a more serious nature, which it would have been very awkward for him to have announced from the woolsack—and as soon as he got home, he took to his bed, pretending a sudden and serious illness. From an interview he had had with Buckingham and the King, he discovered that they were not to be relied upon, and he heard of the declarations they were now making to gain popularity, "that monopolies should be put down, and that guilt in high places deserved severer punishment."

At Bacon's own request a commission passed the Great Seal, reciting that, by reason of illness, he was unable to attend in the House of Lords, and authorizing Sir James Ley, Knight and Baronet, Chief Justice of the King's Bench, to act as Speaker in his absence.[2]

On the 19th of March the Chief Justice took his place on the woolsack under this commission, and immediately a conference was demanded by Sir Robert Phillips and others, on the part of the Commons, respecting "abuses in the Courts of Justice." A present conference being granted, "they commended the incomparable good parts of the Lord Chancellor; they magnified the place he holds, from whence bounty, justice, and mercy were to be distributed to the subjects; but they were obliged to declare that the Lord Chancellor was accused of bribery and

---

[1] Coke himself had long battled this point of privilege, contending that the members of the House of Commons were *quasi* Judges in parliament, and that Judges were not to be sworn in their own Court.—1 Parl. Hist. 1206.

[2] The Chief Justice has now a standing commission to act as Speaker of the House of Lords in the absence of the Chancellor.

corruption in this his eminent place." They proceeded to detail the particulars and proofs of the charge.

Next day Buckingham, affecting to act a friendly part to the Chancellor, declared in the House of Lords "that he had been twice to see him, being sent to him by the King—that the first time his Lordship was very sick and heavy, but the second time he found him better, and much comforted with the thought that the complaint against him was come into this House, where he assured himself to find honorable justice, in confidence whereof his Lordship had written a letter to the House." The letter was delivered into the hands of the Chief Justice, and read by him from the woolsack:—

"To the Right Honourable his very good Lords, the Lords Spiritual and Temporal in the Upper House of Parliament assembled:

"My very good Lords,—I humbly pray your Lordships all to make a favorable and true construction of my absence. It is no feigning or fainting, but sickness both of my heart and of my back, though joined with that comfort of mind which persuadeth me that I am not far from heaven, whereof I feel the first fruits. And because, whether I live or die, I would be glad to preserve my honor and fame so far as I am worthy, hearing that some complaints of base bribery are before your Lordships, my requests to your Lordships are:—

"First, That you will maintain me in your good opinion, without prejudice, until my cause be heard.

"Secondly, That in regard I have sequestered my mind at this time in great part from wordly matters, thinking of my account and answers in a higher Court, your Lordships will give me convenient time, according to the course of other Courts, to advise with my counsel, and to make my answer; wherein, nevertheless, my counsel's part will be the least, for I shall not, by the grace of God, trick up an innocency by cavillations, but plainly and ingenuously (as your Lordships know my manner is) declare what I know or remember.

"Thirdly, That according to the course of justice I may be allowed to except to the witnesses brought against me, and to move questions to your Lordships for their cross-examinations; and likewise to produce my own witnesses for the discovery of the truth.

"And, lastly, That if there be any more petitions of like nature, that your Lordships would be pleased not to take any prejudice or apprehension of any number or muster of them, especially against a Judge that makes 2,000 orders and decrees in a year (not to speak of the courses that have been taken for hunting out complaints against me), but that I may answer them according to the rules of justice severally and respectively.

"These requests I hope appear to your Lordships no other than just. And so thinking myself happy to have so noble peers and reverend prelates to discern of my cause; and desiring no privilege of greatness for subterfuge of guiltiness, but meaning, as I said, to deal fairly and plainly with your Lordships, and to put myself upon your honors and favors, I pray God to bless your counsels and persons, and rest your Lordships' humble servant,
"FR. ST. ALBAN, Canc."

A courteous answer was returned to him, "that it was the wish of the House that his Lordship should clear his honor from all the aspersions cast upon it, and that they prayed he would provide for his defense."

The King was startled at these prosecutions, which he considered dangerous to prerogative, and, in the hope of diverting the Commons from their purpose without offending them, he sent them a message,—"that he was very sorry a person so much advanced by him, and sitting in so high a place, should be suspected; that he can not answer for all others under him, though his care in the choice of Judges had been great; but if this accusation could be proved, his Majesty would punish him to the full; that the King would, if it be thought fitting, here grant a commission under the Great Seal of England to examine all upon oath that can speak in this business."

This message was most gratefully welcomed by the Commons, and had nearly gained its object,—when Sir Edward Coke rose and begged "they would take heed this commission did not hinder the manner of their parliamentary proceeding against a great public delinquent." Thereupon a general address of thanks to the King was voted, and they resolved to prosecute the case before the Lords.[1]

A vast number of fresh charges of bribery and corrup-

[1] 1 Parl. Hist. 1223.

tion now poured in against the Chancellor, and the Commons were preparing regular articles of impeachment on which he might be brought to trial, when, on the approach of Easter, the two Houses were adjourned by royal mandate till the 17th of April,—in the hope that during the recess the clamor might subside, or some expedient might be devised to defeat or delay the investigation. Before the adjournment his Majesty, rather in an unusual manner, came to the House of Lords, and in the absence of the Commons made a long speech in which he alluded to the Chancellor's case, and expressed his readiness at all times, without the assistance of parliament, to do justice to his subjects. The Lords affected to be so much pleased with his condescension, that they made an order that ever after a sermon should be preached on the anniversary of the day, and that in all future parliaments the Lords should on that day sit in their robes, *in perpetuam rei memoriam ;* [1] —but nevertheless they saw through James's kingcraft, and were resolved to defeat it.

The state of Bacon's mind during this interval is differently represented. One acquaintance of his wrote to a correspondent, "Your good friend the Lord Chancellor hath so many grievous accusations brought against him, that his enemies do pittie him, and his most judicious friends have alreadie given him for gon. Notwithstanding, himself is merrie, and doubteth not that he shall be able to calme al the tempests raysed against him." Another describes him as "sick in bed and swoln in his body, and suffering none to come at him;" and adds, "some say he desired his gentleman not to take any notice of him, but altogether, to forget him, and not hereafter to speak of him, or to remember there ever was such a man in the world."[2] His servants rising as he passed through the hall, "Sit down, my friends," he said; "your rise has been my fall." When one of his friends, to comfort him, observed, "You must look around you;" he answered, with an air of piety, which he knew how to assume with great effect, "I look *above* me." He declared, "If this be to be a Chancellor, I think, if the Great Seal lay upon Hounslow Heath, nobody would take it up."

Meantime he tried to soften the hearts of Buckingham

---

[1] 1 Parl. Hist. 1228.   [2] See Montagu's Life of Bacon, cccxxviii.

and the King. The former he denominated "his anchor in these floods."—He thus addressed the latter:

"Time hath been when I have brought unto you '*gemitum columbæ*' from others, now I bring it from myself. I fly unto your Majesty with the wings of a dove, which, once within these seven days, I thought would have carried me a higher flight. When I enter into myself, I find not the materials of such a tempest as is come upon me. I have been (as your Majesty knoweth best) never author of any immoderate counsel, but always desired to have things carried *suavibus modis*. I have been no avaricious oppressor of the people. I have been no haughty, or intolerable, or hateful man in my conversation or carriage. I have inherited no hatred from my father, but am a good patriot born. Whence should this be? for these are the things which are to raise dislikes abroad.

"For the House of Commons, I began my credit there, and now it must be the place of the sepulture thereof.

"For the Upper House, even within these days,—before these troubles,—they seemed as to take me into their arms, finding in me ingenuity, which they took to be the true straight line of nobleness, without crooks or angles.

"And for the briberies and gifts wherewith I am charged, when the books of hearts shall be opened, I hope I shall not be found to have the troubled fountain of a corrupt heart in a depraved habit of taking rewards to pervert justice; howsoever I may be frail, and partake of the abuses of the times.

"And therefore I am resolved, when I come to my answer, not to trick my innocency (as I went to the Lords) by cavillations or ordinances, but to speak to them the language that my heart speaketh to me, inexcusing, extenuating, or ingenuous confessing, praying God to give me the grace to see the bottom of my faults, and that no hardness of heart steal upon me, under show of more neatness of conscience than is cause."

After many apologies and compliments, he concludes by saying, "I rest as clay in your Majesty's gracious hands."[1]

Having no answer, and there being no reaction in his favor,—before the Houses met again he had a private interview with the King. Preparatory to this he made some notes, which are preserved, of the topics he was to

[1] Works, v. 549.

use: "The law of nature teaches me to speak in my own defense: With respect to this charge of bribery, I am as innocent as any born upon St. Innocent's day: I never had bribe or reward in my eye or thought when pronouncing sentence or order.[1] If, however, it is absolutely necessary, the King's will shall be obeyed. I am ready to make an oblation of myself to the King, in whose hands I am as clay, to be made a vessel of honor or dishonor." At the interview, Bacon recommended an immediate dissolution of the parliament, but James advised him to submit himself to the House of Peers, promising to restore him again if they should not be sensible of his merits. Bacon exclaimed, "I see my approaching ruin: there is no hope of mercy in a multitude. When my enemies are to give fire, am I to make no resistance, and is there to be none to shield me? Those who strike at your Chancellor will strike at your Crown. I am the first, I wish I may be the last sacrifice."

James was greatly shaken, and inclined to dissolve the parliament, even if thereby the subsidy voted him should be lost. He was kept steady, however, by his new adviser, the Dean of Westminster, who said, "there is no color to quarrel at this general assembly of the kingdom for tracing delinquents to their form. If you break up this Parliament while in pursuit of justice, only to save some cormorants who have devoured that which they must disgorge, you will pluck up a sluice which will overwhelm you all."[2]

Accordingly, parliament was again permitted to assemble on the 17th of April; and the members of the Lower House returned keener for the attack from their intercourse with their constituents,—the cry for justice having been raised all over England. The Lords vigorously resumed their inquiries into the charges against the Chancellor, which were now reduced into form, and were twenty-three in number. He was about to be regularly put upon his trial; but on the 24th of April, the Prince of Wales was the bearer from him of the following paper, which Buckingham and the King had previously approved

[1] A clear "negative pregnant," admitting that the bribes had been received, although he was not influenced by them in giving judgment. It would puzzle a casuist to say whether disregard of the bribe when received be an extenuation or aggravation of the offense.
[2] Hacket's Life of Williams, Part i. 50.

and intrusted to the heir apparent as a messenger, that it might be more favorably received.

"To the Right Honorable the Lords of Parliament in the Upper House assembled.

"The humble submission and supplication of the Lord Chancellor.

"It may please your Lordships,—I shall crave, at your Lordship's hands, a benign interpretation of that which I shall now write. For words that come from wasted spirits, and an oppressed mind, are more safe in being deposited in a noble construction than in being circled with any reserved caution.

"This being moved, and as I hope obtained in the nature of a protection to all that I shall say, I shall now make into the rest of that wherewith I shall, at this time, trouble your Lordships, a very strange entrance. For in the midst of a state of as great affliction as I think a mortal man can endure (honor being above life), I shall begin with the professing of gladness in some things."

[He artfully suggests, that from what has already taken place, it will be remembered hereafter that greatness is no protection to guiltiness, and that Judges will fly from anything like corruption.]

"But to pass from the motions of my heart, whereof God is only Judge, to the merits of my cause, whereof your Lordships are Judges, under God and his Lieutenant,—I understand there hath been heretofore expected from me some justification; and, therefore, I have chosen one only justification, instead of all other,—out of the justifications of Job. "For, after the clear submission and confession which I shall now make unto your Lordships, I hope I may say and justify with Job in these words: *I have not hid my sin as did Adam, nor concealed my faults in my bosom.* This is the only justification which I will use.

"It resteth, therefore, that, without fig-leaves, I do ingenuously confess and acknowledge, that, having understood the particulars of the charge, not formally from the House, but enough to inform my conscience and memory, I find matter sufficient and full in both to move me to desert the defense, and to move your Lordships to condemn and censure me. Neither will I trouble your Lordships by singling those particulars which I think may fall off.

"'Quid te exempta juvat spinis de pluribus una.'

"Neither will I prompt your Lordships to observe upon the proofs where they come not home, or the scruples touching the credits of the witnesses; neither will I represent unto your Lordships how far a defense might, in divers things, extenuate the offense, in respect of the time or manner of the gift, or the like circumstances, but only leave these things to spring out of your own noble thoughts and observations of the evidence and examinations themselves, and charitably to wind about the particulars of the charge, here and there, as God shall put into your mind, and so submit myself wholly to your piety and grace."

[He then reminds their Lordships, that they are not tied down, like ordinary Courts, by precedents; and points out to them how mercy, in one case, may do as much good as severity in another, from the example of Quintus Maximus; who, after being sentenced, was pardoned for fighting without orders; the same offense for which Tit. Manlius was put to death. *Neque minus firmata est disciplina militaris periculo Quinti Maximi quam miserabili supplicio Titi Manlii.*]

"But my case standeth not there. For my humble desire is, that his Majesty would take the Seal into his hands, which is a great downfall, and may serve, I hope, in itself, for an expiation of my faults. Therefore, if mercy and mitigation be in your power, and do no way cross your ends, why should I not hope of your Lordships' favor and commiseration?"

[Having introduced elaborate compliments to the King, the Prince, and the Peers, reminding them that there are *vitia temporis*, as well as *vitia hominis*, he thus concludes:]

"And therefore, my humble suit to your Lordships is, that my penitent submission may be my sentence, and the loss of the Seal my punishment; and that your Lordships will spare any further sentence, but recommend me to his Majesty's grace and pardon for all that is past. God's holy Spirit be amongst you.

"Your Lordships' humble servant and suppliant,

"FR. ST. ALBAN, Canc."

This was a very dexterous move; for although the submission had the appearance of a confession to be followed by punishment,—as no specific charges had been communicated to him, its generalities might easily afterwards have been explained away, and the Great Seal, after being a little while in commission, might have been restored to him.

The Lords, though by no means disposed to treat him with unnecessary harshness, and ever bearing in mind his high qualities which rendered his prosecution so painful a duty to all concerned in it,[1] resolved "that the Lord Chancellor's submission gave not satisfaction to their Lordships; that he should be charged particularly with the briberies and corruptions alleged against him, and that he should make a particular answer thereunto with all convenient expedition."

The formal articles of charge were now communicated to him, with the proofs in support of each. On the 30th of April, the Lord Chief Justice signified that he had received from the Lord Chancellor a paper-roll sealed up. Being opened and read by the Clerk, it was found entitled "The *Confession* and humble submission of me, the Lord Chancellor." It begins: "Upon advised consideration of the charge, descending into my conscience and calling my memory to account so far as I am able, I do plainly and ingenuously confess that I am guilty of corruption, and do renounce all defense, and put myself upon the grace and mercy of your Lordships." He then goes over the different charges articulately, confessing in every instance the receipt of the money, and valuable things from the suitors in his Court, though with qualification in some instances, that it was after judgment, or understood by him to be as new-year's gifts, or for prior services.

The confession being read, it was resolved "that certain Lords do go unto the Lord Chancellor, and show him the said Confession, and tell him that the Lords do conceive it to be an ingenuous and full confession, and demand whether it be his own hand that is subscribed to the same?" Nine temporal and three spiritual Lords being appointed a committee for this purpose, repaired to York House, and were received by him in the hall where he had been accustomed to sit as Judge. After mutual salutations, they with great delicacy asked him merely if the signature to

---

[1] Except Sir Edward Coke.

the paper which they showed him was genuine? He passionately exclaimed,—" My Lords, it is my act, my hand, my heart. I beseech your Lordships to be merciful to a broken reed." Shocked at witnessing the agonies of such a mind, and the degradation of such a name, they instantly withdrew, and he again retired to his chamber in the deepest dejection.

Still a difficulty remained in proceeding farther while he retained the Great Seal, for by the rules and customs of the House of Lords, a defendant prosecuted before them is to receive sentence on his knees at the bar, and the Lord Chancellor, if present, must preside on the woolsack and pass the sentence. This embarrassment was removed on the first of May, when the King, finding all further resistance hopeless, sent the Lord Treasurer, the Duke of Lennox, the Earl of Pembroke, and the Earl of Arundel to demand the Great Seal.[1] They found Bacon confined to his bed by illness; and when they had explained the object of their mission,—hiding his face with one hand, with the other he delivered to them that bauble for which "he had sullied his integrity, had resigned his independence, had violated the most sacred obligations of friendship and gratitude, had flattered the worthless, had persecuted the innocent, had tampered with Judges, had tortured prisoners, and had wasted on paltry intrigues all the powers of the most exquisitely constructed intellect that has ever been bestowed on any of the children of men."[2]

On the 2nd of May, the House of Lords resolved to

[1] " Dns Thesaurarius, &c., ad illustrissimum Franciscum Vicecomt. Sanct. A'ban' Cancellar. Angl. in Ed. Ebor. morbo laborantem et ad lectum suum decumben em accesser. ubi postea jam mentem et propositum Regie majestas de Magno Sigillo Angl. resumen lo paucis explicassent Dns Cancellarius cum sigillum, &c., Dno Thesaurario &c., omni qua decuit reverencia in manus exhibuit," &c.—Cl. R. 19. Jac. 1, which tells us that the messengers, having put the Seal into its silk purse, carried it to the King at Whitehall, where three commissions were sealed with it by the King's order: 1. To the Master of the Rolls and others to hear causes in Chancery; 2. To the Chief Justice to preside in the House of Lords; and, 3. To the Lord Treasurer and others to seal writs and patents.

[2] Macaulay's Essays, vol. ii. 349. What a contrast between Bacon's feelings now, and those with which he surveyed the Great Seal when he carried it home to Gray's Inn, and wrote his first letter signed " F. Bacon, C. S. !" There might be a very instructive set of prints referring to those remote times, entitled " The Lawyer's Progress"—the two most remarkable of which would be his "selling himself to the Devil;" and " Mephistopheles coming to enforce the terms of the bargain."

proceed to judgment next day, "wherefore the gentleman usher and the sergeant-at-arms were commanded to go and summon the Viscount St. Alban to appear here in person to-morrow morning by nine of the clock." They reported that, having repaired to York House, they found him sick in bed, and that he had declared he feigned not this for an excuse, for that if able he would willingly have obeyed the summons, but that it was wholly impossible for him to attend. The Lords readily sustained the excuse, and resolved to proceed to sentence in his absence. He was thrown into great consternation when he heard of this, and made a last effort to obtain the interposition of the King in his favor, that so, "the cup might pass from him." He thus concludes his letter, perhaps not in the best taste:—"But because he that hath taken bribes is apt to give bribes, I will go further and present your Majesty with a bribe; for if your Majesty give me peace and leisure, and God give me life, I will present you with a good History of England and a better Digest of your Laws."

The King could not interpose, and on the 3rd of May, final judgment was pronounced. The proceeding began by the Attorney General reading the articles, and the confession. The question was then put, "whether the Viscount St. Alban was guilty of the matters wherewith he was charged?" and it was agreed that he was guilty, *nemine dissentiente.* The punishment was then considered, and there being a majority, by means of the Bishops, against suspending him from all his titles of nobility during life, there was unanimity as to the rest of the sentence, and a message was sent to the Commons "that they were ready to give judgment against the Lord Viscount St. Alban if the Commons should come to demand it." In the mean time the Peers robed, and the Speaker, soon after coming to the bar, "demanded judgment against the Lord Chancellor as his offenses required."

The Lord Chief Justice declared the sentence to be, "1. That the Lord Viscount St. Alban should pay a fine of £40,000; 2. That he should be imprisoned in the Tower during the King's pleasure; 3. That he should be for ever incapable of holding any public office, place, or employment; 4. That he should never sit in parliament, nor come within the verge of the Court." Thus was deservedly fixed the ineffaceable brand of public infamy upon the character of this most extraordinary man.

Although there were none bold or weak enough to defend these transactions in the times when they could be best examined and appreciated, we are told by some of his amiable admirers in the nineteenth century, that he was made a sacrifice to the crimes of others, and that he was free from all legal and moral blame. While I can easily forgive such well-meant efforts produced by a sincere admiration of genius, I can not but lament them,—and the slightest attention to fact must show them to be futile.

It is affirmed that there is an undisclosed mystery in the course which Bacon adopted of making no defense. But he pleaded *guilty* for this plain reason, that he had no defense to make. Whoever will submit to the trouble of comparing the charges and the evidence, will see that they are all fully substantiated.[1] Instead of questioning the veracity of the witnesses, he circumstantially admits their statements; and the qualified denials to which he at first resorted, when accurately examined, will be found quite consistent with his final confession. He knew that he had no contradictory evidence to offer, and further investigation would only have made his delinquency more aggravated and more notorious. We must believe then that repeatedly and systematically he received money and articles of value from the parties in causes depending before him, which he was aware they presented to him with a view to influence his judgment in their favor. I presume it is not disputed that this in point of law amounts to judicial bribery, subjecting the Judge to be prosecuted

---

[1] It may be said that his decree in Egerton *v*. Egerton was confirmed by Lord Coventry, but this was on the express ground that both parties had acquiesced in the decree; and it was then found as a fact, that "the matter alleged in the parliament against the said Lord Viscount St. Alban's, that he the said Viscount St. Alban's had received from the said Edward Egerton (plaintiff), and after from the said Sir Rowland Egerton (defendant), several sums of money before making the said decree, appeareth to be true."—Reg. Lib. 19 Nov. 1627. 3 Car. I.—Lord Hale accounts for the introduction of appeals to the House of Lords in equity cases from the notorious misconduct of Bacon as a judge: "The Lord Verulam being Chancellor, made many decrees upon most gross bribery and corruption, for which he was deeply censured in the parliament of 18 *Jac.* And this gave such a discredit and brand to the decrees thus obtained, that they were easily set aside; and made a way in the parliament of 3 *Car.* for the like attempts against decrees made by other Chancellors."—Hale's Jurisdictions, ch. xxxiii.

for a high misdemeanor; and the only question that can be made is, whether it implies moral turpitude?

There can be no doubt that men are to be judged by the standard of their own age. It would be very unjust to blame persons who were engaged in the sixteenth century in burning witches or heretics, as if these *acts of faith* had occurred in the reign of Queen Victoria: and if it can be shown that judicial bribery was considered an innocent practice in Bacon's time, he is to be pitied, and not condemned. But the House of Commons who prosecuted him, the House of Lords who tried him, and the public who ratified the sentence, with one voice pronounced the practice most culpable and disgraceful. He had no private enemies; he had not, like Strafford, in the next age, strong party prejudices to encounter; he was a favorite at Court, and popular with the nation, who were pleased with the flowing courtesy of his manners, and proud of his literary glory. Yet there was a national cry for his punishment, and no solitary individual stood forward to vindicate his innocence, or to palliate the enormity of his guilt. Look back to the time when similar charges were unjustly brought against the virtuous Sir Thomas More. He demonstrated that they were all unfounded in fact, but he allowed that he might have been properly punished if they could have been established by evidence.

As a proof of the public feeling upon the subject, it might be enough to give an extract from an energetic sermon of Hugh Latimer, who continued to be much read in the reign of James, and who, preaching against bribery, says, "I am sure this is *sacala inferni*, the right way to hell, to be covetous, to take bribes, and pervert justice. If a Judge should ask me the way to hell, I would show him this way. First, let him be a covetous man; let his heart be poisoned with covetousness. Then let him go a little farther, and take bribes; and, lastly, pervert judgment. Lo, there is the mother, and the daughter, and the daughter's daughter. Avarice is the mother; she brings forth bribe-taking, and bribe-taking perverting of judgment. There lacks a fourth thing to make up the mess, which, so help me God, if I were a Judge, should be *hangum tuum*, a Tyburn tippet to take with him; and it were the Judge of the King's Bench, my Lord Chief Justice of England, yea, an it were my Lord Chancellor himself, *to Tyburn with him!* He that took the silver basin and ewer for a bribe, thinketh that it will never come out. But he may now know that I know it. Oh, briber and bribery! He was never a good man that will so take bribes. It will never be merry in England till we have the skins of such."

But from his own mouth let us judge him. *Sic cogitavit Franciscus de Verulamio:* "For corruption; do not only bind thine own hands or thy servant's hands from taking, but bind the hands of suitors also from offering. For integrity used doth the one; but integrity professed, and with a manifest detestation of bribery, doth the other: and avoid not only the fault, but the suspicion."[1]

The crime of judicial bribery had been practiced like perjury and theft, but it was evidently held in abhorrence;—and there never has been a period in our history, when, the suitors in a court of justice and the Judge being the parties spoken of, an historian could have said, "*Corrumpere et corrumpi seculum vocatur.*"

Bacon, doubtless, sometimes decided against those who had bribed him: but this was inevitable where, as occasionally happened, he had received bribes from both sides, or where the bribing party was flagrantly in the wrong, or a common-law Judge had been called in to assist, or where, from the long list of bribes, they could not be all borne in recollection at the moment when the decision was to be pronounced. We are told, indeed, that the offense could not by possibility be committed by him, on account of the purity of his character; but ought we not rather to judge of his character from his actions, than of his actions from his character? Evidence of "habit and repute," I fear, would not be in favor of this defendant. Notwithstanding his gigantic intellect, his moral perceptions were blunt, and he was ever ready to yield to the temptation of present interest. When he received the Great Seal he was still harassed by debts which he had imprudently contracted, and, instead of then trying to discharge them, his love of splendor involved him in increased difficulties. His secretaries and servants found a ready resource in the offers made by the suitors, and when it was once understood that money was available,—till the

[1] Essay, "Of Great Place."

catastrophe occurred, the system was carried to such a pitch that even eminent counsel, at their consultations, recommended a bribe to the Chancellor.¹ His confession ought to be received as sincere, even out of regard to his reputation; for, although the taking of bribes by a Judge be bad, there would be still greater infamy in a man acknowledging himself to be guilty of a series of disgraceful offenses which he had never committed, merely to humor the caprice of a King or a minister. But it is absurd to suppose that James and Buckingham would not cordially have supported him if he could have been successfully defended;—for, setting aside friendship and personal regard, which, in courts, are not much to be calculated upon,—they had no object whatever to gain by his ruin, – and it would have been most desirable in their eyes, if possible, to have repulsed the first assault of the Commons on a great officer of the Crown, and to have prevented a precedent which they distinctly foresaw would be dangerous to the royal prerogative,—which was soon actually directed against Buckingham himself, though ineffectually,—which was successfully pursued in the impeachment of Strafford,—and which materially assisted in the ultimate ruin of the Stuart dynasty.

I have thought it becoming to make these observations in vindication of the great principles of right and justice. But I now have a more pleasing task,—to record the composure, the industry, the energy displayed by Bacon after his fall, and the benefits he continued to confer by his philosophical and literary labors on his country,—though I must again be pained by pointing out instances of weakness and meanness by which he still tarnished his fame.

CHAPTER LVI.

CONCLUSION OF THE LIFE OF LORD BACON.

IF Bacon's illness had been feigned when proceedings were pending against him,—after his sentence it was real and alarming. For some time he could not have been removed from York House without hazard of his

¹ See Aubrey's case in the impeachment. 2 St. Tr. 1101.

life. But the first burst of mental agony having expended itself, he recovered his composure, and his health improved. There was a disposition, creditable to all parties, to show him the utmost consideration and forbearance consistent with the substantial interests of justice. Still the sentence of the House of Peers could not be treated as a nullity, although it might be mitigated by the prerogative of mercy in the Crown.

On the last day of May he was carried a prisoner to the Tower. To save him the humiliation of marching through the Strand and the principal streets of the city in custody of tipstaves,—a procession contrasting sadly with that which he headed when he proudly rode from Gray's Inn, attended by the nobility and Judges to be installed as Lord Keeper in Westminster Hall,—a barge was privately ordered to the stairs of York House, and, the tide suiting early in the morning so that London Bridge might be conveniently shot, he was quietly conducted by the Sheriff of Middlesex to the Traitors' Gate, and there, with the warrant for his imprisonment, delivered to the Lieutenant of the Tower. A comfortable apartment had been prepared for him; but he was overcome by the sense of his disgrace. He might have had some compunctious visitings when he recognized the scene of Peacham's tortures, and we certainly know that he could not bear the thought of spending even a single night near those cells—

"With many a foul and midnight murder fed."

He instantly sat down and wrote the following letter to Buckingham:

"Good my Lord,—Procure the warrant for my discharge this day. Death, I thank God, is so far from being unwelcome to me, as I have called for it (as Christian resolution would permit) any time these two months. But to die before the time of his Majesty's grace, and in this disgraceful place, is even the worst that could be; and when I am dead, he is gone that was always in one tenor a true and perfect servant to his Master, and one that was never author of any immoderate, no, nor unsafe, no (I will say it), nor unfortunate counsel, and one that no temptation could ever make other than a trusty, and honest, and Christ-loving friend to your Lordship; and (howsoever I acknowledge the sentence just, and for reformation sake fit) the justest Chancellor that hath been in the five changes since Sir Nicholas Bacon's time.[1] God bless and prosper your Lordship, whatsoever becomes of me.

"Your Lordship's true friend, living and dying,
"FRANCIS ST. ALBAN.

"*Tower, 31st May, 1621.*"

At the same time he wrote a letter to the King which is not preserved, but which we may believe was very touching, from his own representation, that it was "*de profundis.*"

Prince Charles, in a manner for which he has not been sufficiently praised, hearing of the deplorable condition of the prostrate Ex-Chancellor, took a more lively interest in procuring his liberation than older councillors, who were afraid of giving offense to the parliament. Nothing effectual could be done that day; but on the 1st of June, a warrant under the sign-manual was made out for the noble prisoner's discharge. It was arranged that Sir John Vaughan, who held an office in the Prince's household, and lived in a beautiful villa at Parson's Green, should receive him, and that he should continue in retirement there till parliament was prorogued.[2] The very same day he returned his warmest thanks to the Prince:—"I am much beholden to your Highness's worthy servant, Sir John Vaughan, the sweet air and loving usage of whose house hath already much revived my languishing spirits. I beseech your Highness thank him for me. God ever preserve and prosper your Highness."[3]

The buoyancy of his spirit immediately returned, and in three days after he thus writes to Buckingham. "I heartily thank you for getting me out of prison; and now my body is out, my mind nevertheless will be still in prison, till I may be on my feet to do his Majesty and your Lordship faithful service. Wherein your Lordship, by the grace of God, shall find that my adversity hath neither spent nor pent my spirits."[4]

But his creditors, finding out where he was, became very troublesome to him. He wished to have been al-

---

[1] He tries to delude himself into some sort of self-complacency from the thought that his decrees were sound in spite of all the bribes he had accepted, and that he sold justice, not injustice.

[2] Camden says, "Ex-cancellarius in arcem traditur; post *biduum* deliberatus;" but he must reckon time according to the manner of the Jews.

[3] Works, v. 552.   [4] Works, v. 554.

lowed to return to York House, and to remain there till he had made some settlement of his affairs; and he sent his faithful secretary, Meautys, who served him in his adversity, with fresh zeal, to obtain this favor; but, although the Prince joined in the solicitations, it was refused—on the ground that he had been condemned "not to come within the verge of the Court." He was ordered immediately to take up his residence at Gorhambury, and not to move elsewhere till his Majesty's pleasure should be further notified to him.

Thither he accordingly repaired; but the place had a very different aspect to him from what it had presented when accompanied by the great and the witty, he retreated to its shades after the splendid fatigues of office. He found this solitude,—without cheering retrospect or anticipation,—most painful,—and he prepared a petition to the House of Lords, that he might be released from it. To move their compassion he says,—" I am old, weak, ruined, in want, a very subject of pity. My only suit to your Lordships is to show me your noble favor towards the release of my confinement—to me, I protest, worse than the Tower. There I could have company, physicians, conference with my creditors and friends about my debts, and the necessities of my estate, helps for my studies and the writings I have in hand. Here I live upon the sword point of a sharp air, endangered if I go abroad, dulled if I stay within, solitary and comfortless, without company, banished from all opportunities to treat with any to do myself good and to help out any wrecks; and that which is one of my greatest griefs, my wife, that hath been no partaker of my offending, must be partaker of this misery of my restraint." After imploring them to intercede for him, he thus concludes:—" Herein your Lordships shall do a work of charity and nobility; you shall do me good; you shall do my creditors good, and it may be you shall do posterity good, if, out of the carcass of dead and rotten greatness, as out of Samson's lion, there may be honey gathered for the use of future times." But the public indignation had not yet sufficiently subsided to permit his restoration to society, and he was obliged to shut himself up at Gorhambury till the spring of the following year.[1]

For some time he was most irksomely occupied with

---

[1] Buckingham, in the King's name, sent him a refusal to reside in London

his pecuniary accounts; and he found it difficult to provide for the day that was passing over him. To Buckingham he writes,—" I have lived hitherto upon the scraps of my former fortune; and I shall not be able to hold out longer." To the King,—" The honors which your Majesty hath done me have put me above the means to get my living, and the misery I have fallen into hath put me below the means to subsist as I am."

These representations produced such an impression that an arrangement was made, which, with common prudence, might have enabled him to live in comfort during the rest of his days. The fine of £40,000 was in truth remitted; but, to protect his property from his more importunate creditors, it was assigned to trustees for his benefit. A pension was granted to him of £1,200 a year: he drew £600 from the Alienation Office, and the rents of his estate amounted to a further sum of £700 a year, making altogether an income equal, probably, to that of many of the hereditary nobility.

The nation would not yet have endured an entire remission of his sentence, whereby he would have been entitled to sit in parliament, and to hold office under the Crown; but the King signed a warrant for a qualified pardon to be made out for him. This was opposed by the new Lord Keeper, who began to be alarmed lest his predecessor might ere long be his successor, and wrote him a letter, proposing to suspend the sealing of the pardon till after the close of the ensuing session of parliament. Williams, at the same time, strongly remonstrated with Buckingham against it—suggesting that the two Houses would consider themselves mocked and derided by such a proceeding. He likewise attempted to do Bacon a permanent injury, by representing that he had been guilty of a gross fraud in the manner in which the fine had been kept alive and assigned for his benefit.'

This malicious attempt was defeated; a peremptory order

—" which being but a small advantage to you, would be a great and general distaste, as you can not but easily conceive, to the whole state."

¹ " The pardoning of his fine is much spoken against, not for the matter (for no man objects to that), but for the manner, which is full of knavery, and a wicked precedent. For by this assignation of his fine he is protected from all his creditors, which I dare say was neither his Majesty's nor your lordship's meaning. His lordship was too cunning for me. He passed his fine (whereby he hath deceived his creditors) ten days before he presented his pardon to the seal."—*Williams to Buckingham.*

from the King came to speed the pardon, and on the 17th of October, it passed the Great Seal. Williams's fears were very natural; for Bacon certainly had now hopes of recovering his ascendency. When he wrote to the King —counting a little upon royal ignorance—with this view he did not scruple slightly to pervert history, that he might quote parallel cases of reintegration: "Demosthenes was banished for bribery of the highest nature, yet was recalled with honor. Marcus Lucius was condemned for exactions, yet afterwards made consul and censor. Seneca was banished for divers corruptions, yet was afterwards restored, and an instrument in that memorable *Quinquennium Neronis.*"[1]

Although he still cast a longing, lingering look behind at the splendors of office, and the blandishments of power, he now magnanimously and vigorously resumed his literary labors, inspired by the nobler ambition of extending the boundaries of human knowledge, and enlarging the stores of material and intellectual enjoyment.

Great expectation was excited, both at home and on the Continent, by the announcement that he was engaged upon an historical work, "The Life and Reign of Henry VII."[2] He finished it at Gorhambury, and was allowed to come to London to superintend the printing of it in the beginning of 1622. It was dedicated to the Prince as a mark of gratitude for the generous interest Charles had taken in his misfortunes. He sent a copy to the Queen of Bohemia, with a letter strongly showing the feelings of a disgraced minister; "Time was, I had honor without leisure; and now I have leisure without honor."

Of all his works this gave the least satisfaction to the public; and after recently again perusing it, I must confess that it is hardly equal to Sir Thomas More's History of Richard III., or to Camden's of Queen Elizabeth,— leaving the reproach upon our literature of being lamentably deficient in historical composition till the days of Hume, Robertson, and Gibbon. Some have accounted for Bacon's failure by supposing a decline in his faculties;

---

[1] Works, v. 559.
[2] A learned Italian, writing to the Earl of Devonshire, says, "he should impatiently look for the promised history of Lord Chancellor Bacon, as a thing that would be singularly perfect, as the character of Henry VII. would exercise the talent of his divine understanding."—*Rawley's Life of Bacon.*

but he afterwards showed that they remained in their pristine vigor to the very close of his career. The true solution probably is, that he undertook the subject to please the King, with a view of doing honor to the ancestor of the reigning family, who had united the Roses by his own marriage, and had united the kingdoms by the marriage of his daughter. The manuscript was, from time to time, submitted to James, and he condescended to correct it. Bacon was therefore obliged by anticipation to consider what would be agreeable to the royal censor, and could neither use much freedom with the character of his hero, nor introduce any reflections inconsistent with the maxims of government now inculcated from the throne.[1] He gives us, therefore, a tame, chronological narrative, filled up with proclamations and long speeches, descending to such minute facts as a call of sergeants, and though interspersed with some passages of deep thought, by no means abounding in the delineations of men and manners which might have been expected from so great an artist.[2]

This task being performed, he returned to philosophy, and was "himself again." It is most consolatory to think of the intervals of pleasure and contentment which he now enjoyed. He was compared to a mariner, who, being wrecked on an island, with a rocky and savage shore, on going into the interior finds it covered with beautiful verdure, watered with clear streams, and abounding with all sorts of delicious fruits.

In the following year he gave to the world his celebrated treatise, "De Augmentis Scientiarum," which not only further raised his reputation among his countrymen, but was immediately republished on the Continent, and translated into French and Italian. His "Advancement of Learning" was the basis of this work; but he recast it, and enriched and improved it to such a degree, that he again made a sensation among the learned, as if a new prodigy had suddenly appeared in the world.

He soon followed this up with his "Historia Vitæ et Mortis,"—with several of his minor publications,—and with another edition of his Essays, adding several new

[1] His letters, accompanying the copies he sent to the King, Buckingham, and the Lord Keeper, are still preserved; but they contain nothing beyond commonplace compliments.

[2] James even made him expunge a legal axiom, "that on the reversal of an attainder, the party attained is restored to all his rights."

ones, which gave striking proof of his incessant industry and the fertility of his genius. As far as his literary fame is concerned, his political misfortunes are not to be regretted. More than any man who ever lived he could mix refined speculation with groveling occupations: but if he had continued to preside at the Council Board, in the Star Chamber, in the Court of Chancery, and on the Woolsack, till carried off by disease, we should have had but a small portion of those lucubrations which illustrated the five last years of his life. In his happier mood, no one could make a juster estimate of the superiority, both for present enjoyment and lasting fame,—of success in literature and science, over the glittering rewards of vulgar ambition.[1]

But he was now struggling with penury. Though his income was large, his old debts were very heavy; and one of his weaknesses was a love of show. He had been obliged to sell York House, with all its splendid furniture,—very much to reduce his establishment at Gorhambury, and to confine himself chiefly to his "lodgings" in Gray's Inn. Yet when he came into public, or made a journey into the country, he still insisted on appearing in a handsome equipage, attended with a numerous retinue. About this time, Prince Charles, falling in with him on the road, exclaimed with surprise, "Well! do what we can, this man scorns to go out in snuff." The consequence was, that his embarrassments multiplied upon him, instead of being cleared off. He was obliged to write (very irregularly) to the Lord Keeper, praying him not to issue an extent on a security he had given to a goldsmith for a shop debt twelve years before.[2] He often wanted funds for his most pressing necessities; and was obliged to borrow small sums from his friends. The steadiest of these was

---

[1] Several Englishmen owe their distinction as authors to their crosses as politicians. If my "Lives of the Chancellors" gain any celebrity, my humble name may be added to the class adorned by Clarendon and Bolingbroke. I shall then be highly contented with my lot. I do not undervalue great judicial reputation, but I would rather have written Hyde's character of Falkland, than have pronounced the most celebrated judgments of Lord Hardwicke or Lord Eldon.*   [2] May 30, 1622.

* Written in 1845, when I was Ex-Chancellor of Ireland, without prospect of ever again being in office. My success as a Biographer makes me cordially rejoice that for near seven years I remained without office, profession, salary, or pension.—*Note to 3rd Edition.*

Sir Julius Cæsar, the Master of the Rolls, who had married his niece,—and now not only lent him money, but occasionally received him into his house in Chancery Lane. There is even a tradition, that not liking the beer of Gray's Inn, and not having credit with the publicans of Holborn, the Ex-Chancellor sent to borrow a bottle of beer from Greville, Lord Brooke, who lived in the neighborhood, and that, having done this often, the butler had at last orders to deny him.[1] Yet he would not allow his woods to be cut down at Gorhambury, from which he might have had a handsome supply;—exclaiming, "I will not be stripped of my feathers."[2]

The provostship of Eton becoming vacant, he pressingly applied for the situation, in terms which should have insured his success. "It were a pretty cell for my fortune. The college and school, I do not doubt but I shall make to flourish."[3] Every one must wish that he had succeeded; not only from a kindly feeling towards him, but for the benefit of this great seminary, and the cause of good education in England. The Lord Keeper spitefully interposed with his wise saws: "It is somewhat necessary to be a good scholar; but more that he be a good husband, and a careful manager, and a stayed man; which no man can be that is so much indebted as the Lord St. Alban."[4] A prior promise to Sir William Beecher was the first excuse; but the place was finally jobbed to Sir Henry Wottom, on his releasing a reversionary grant of the Mastership of the Rolls, to be conferred on a rapacious dependent of Buckingham, who could still do him service. Bacon received the news of this appointment while he was dictating to Rawley, his chaplain and secretary; and when the messenger was gone, he said calmly, "Well, Sir, yon business won't go on; let us go on with this, *for this is in our power;*"—and then he dictated to him afresh for some hours without the least hesitation of speech, or interruption of thought.

When fresh grievances and conflicts had made the people forget the Ex-Chancellor's offenses and his punishment, the part of his sentence, "that he should not come within the verge of the Court," was disregarded; and at

---
[1] Wilson's Hist. James I. Kennet, vol. ii. 736.
[2] Ibid. [3] Ibid.
[4] Williams to Buckingham, 11 April, 1623.

his earnest entreaty, the King agreed to see him privately at Whitehall. We have an account of what passed at this interview by Bacon himself, which he drew up and sent to the King, that the impression might be more lasting. Amidst a great deal of flattery heaped upon his Majesty, he seems not to have overlooked his own merits and services; dwelling as he was often wont to do on the assertion, that "no measure he had ever brought forward had miscarried, and that though unfortunate for himself he had always been successful for the Crown." He then strongly pressed that he might be again employed; promising, that in that case, " he would so live and spend his time, as neither discontinuance should disable him, nor adversity discourage him, nor anything he did should bring any scandal or envy upon him." If he can not have public employment, he begs that his opinion may be taken, or that propositions may be required of him privately, as he should be glad even to be a laborer or pioneer in the service. Lastly, he prayed that he might serve *calamo* if not *consilio;* and that the King, an universal scholar, would appoint him some new task or literary province, to which he might devote himself for his Majesty's honor. Upon this occasion he seems to have aimed several blows at the more prosperous courtiers, who were still basking in the sunshine of royal favor: " There be mountebanks as well in the civil body as in the natural. I ever served his Majesty with modesty; no shouldering, no undertaking. Of my offenses, far be it from me to say, *dat veniam corvis vexat censura columbas;* but I will say that I have good warrant for, *they were not the greatest offenders in Israel upon whom the tower of Siloam fell.*" He contended that his recall to office would rather be well received by the public: " For it is an almanac of the last year, and, as a friend of mine said, the parliament died penitent towards me." To the objection, that a miracle only could restore him, he answers, " Your Majesty has power: I have faith; therefore a miracle may soon be wrought." His last observation, which affects to be merry, is full of melancholy. " I would live to study, and not study to live; yet I am prepared for *date obolum Belisario;* and I that have borne a bag,[1] can bear a wallet." But Buckingham had found

[1] The bag or purse containing the Great Seal.

agents whom he considered more useful, and Bacon remained in disgrace.

During the romantic expedition of "Baby Charles," and "the dog Steenie," to Madrid to hasten the match with the Infanta, he renewed his instances with the King, but even with less prospect of success, for the royal word had been passed that no change should be made till their return.

On this event Bacon sent a letter of congratulation to Buckingham, concluding with the prayer, "My Lord, do some good work upon me that I may end my days in comfort, which nevertheless can not be complete, except you put me in some way to do your noble self service."[1]

Still, while the nation was agitated by the discussion between the King and the Commons, by the sudden dissolution of parliament, by the unhappy fate of the Palatinate, by the intrigues about the Spanish match, by the struggle between Buckingham and Bristol, by the new alliance with France, and by the impeachment, in a new parliament, of the Lord Treasurer Middlesex,—Bacon was condemned to look on as an idle spectator, or to shut himself up in Gray's Inn like a cloistered friar.

What he felt most severely was his exclusion from parliament. During his long career in the House of Commons, and during the short time he had sat in the House of Peers, he had enjoyed the consequence of being the best debater of his time, and he was confident that, if the disqualification imposed by his sentence were removed, he not only would have an agreeable and creditable occupation in again taking a part in parliamentary business, but that the weight and importance he should soon acquire would force him back into high office. This speculation was very reasonable. Never sat so formidable an Ex-Chancellor. In the first encounter he must have utterly extinguished the Right Reverend the Lord Keeper Williams, the present occupant of the woolsack. For a season, he might have thought that he observed a little shyness and coldness in the manner of old associates; and there might have been a few awkward allusions to the cause of his long absence from the House; but from the amenity of his manners, his unrivaled eloquence, and his power of sarcasm, he would soon have been courted,

[1] Works, v. 577.

feared, and flattered. The past being forgotten by general consent, he would have swayed the deliberations of the assembly, and the government must have secured his support on his own terms.

Perhaps some such contemplations mixed themselves up with his affected humility, when he thus wrote to the King: " I prostrate myself at your Majesty's feet, I, your ancient servant, now sixty-four years old in age, and three years five months old in misery. I desire not from your Majesty means, nor place, nor employment, but only, after so long a time of expiation, a complete and total remission of the sentence of the Upper House, to the end that blot of ignominy may be removed from me, and from my memory with posterity; that I die not a condemned man, but may be to your Majesty, as I am to God, *nova creatura*. Look down, dear Sovereign, upon me in pity. This, my most humble request granted, may make me live a year or two happily; and denied, will kill me quickly." [1]

This appeal was effectual, and the King directed a warrant to the Attorney General, which, after reciting the sentence upon the late Lord Chancellor, his former services, *how well and profitably he had spent his time since his trouble,* and his Majesty's desire to remove from him that blot of ignominy which yet remained upon him of incapacity and disablement, required a pardon to be made out in due form of the whole sentence.

This was accordingly done, and Bacon was once more entitled to appear in his robes on the Viscounts' bench, and to enjoy all the rights of the Peerage. But parliament did not again assemble during the remainder of this reign; and although he was summoned to the parliament which met on the accession of Charles I., he was then so broken down by age and sickness, that he was unable to take his seat, and all his visions of power and greatness had for ever fled.

Surmounting the feebleness of frame which had prevented him from partaking in school-boy sports, his constitution never was robust; from severe study the marks of age were early impressed upon him, and his mental sufferings had greatly assisted the attacks of disease by which he was periodically visited. He continued, how-

[1] Works, v. 583.

ever, to carry on a noble struggle against all his ills and infirmities. He published new editions of his works, and, with assistance, translated those in English into Latin,—from the mistaken notion that this would for ever continue the familiar dialect of all men of education, and that only fleeting fame could be acquired by composing in any modern tongue. His English Essays and Treatises will be read and admired by the Anglo-Saxon race all over the world, to the most distant generations; while since the age which immediately succeeded his own, only a few recondite scholars have penetrated and relished the admirable good sense enveloped in his crabbed Latinity.

To show the versatility of his powers,—in imitation of Julius Cæsar, he wrote a "Collection of Apophthegms," or a "Jest Book." This is said "to have been dictated by him in one rainy day, and to be the best extant." That it was begun in a rainy day is very probable, but it is evidently the result of much labor, and of repeated efforts of recollection. He himself, after praising these *mucrones verborum*, says, "I have for my own recreation, amongst more serious studies, collected some few of them."—language not at all applicable to one continuous dictation. As to its "excellence," the world is certainly much indebted to it, for it contains many most excellent *mots* of the author and his contemporaries, which otherwise would have perished; but they are mixed up with not a few platitudes, which do not give us a high notion of the relish for true wit among the lawyers and statesmen of Elizabeth and James.

In performance of his promise to the King, he actually began the stupendous undertaking of framing a "Digest of the Laws of England;" but finding "it was a work of assistance, and that which he could not master by his own forces and pen, he soon laid it aside."[1] He seems to have been conscious that he did not excel in historical composition; for, having been urged to write a "History of Great Britain," and a "History of the Reign of Henry VIII.," he never got beyond the first chapter of either His last publications in James's reign were his "Dialogue touching an Holy War,"—an abstract speculation upon the grounds of justifiable warfare among Christians,—and "Considerations touching a War with Spain, inscribed to

[1] Preface to Holy War.

Prince Charles,"—palliating the perfidy with which the Duke of Buckingham had broken off negotiations with the Spanish government, and the folly with which he was involving the country in useless hostilities. This help was much wanted, for the adherents of Bristol and Pembroke were multiplying rapidly, and bitter discontent was spreading among all ranks of society.

While Bacon looked for his reward, the scene suddenly shifted. The Sovereign whom he had so long despised and flattered was no more, and a new reign had commenced.

Bacon no doubt was in hopes that Charles, who had shown such attachment to him, and whom he had so seduously cultivated by letters, dedications, and messages, being on the throne, Buckingham, who had kept the prince in a state of great thralldom, would be dismissed, and he himself might be placed at the helm of affairs. Even if Buckingham retained his ascendency, a hope remained to the Ex-Chancellor from a growing coldness between him and Lord Keeper Williams. But what was Bacon's mortification to see the despotism of Buckingham still more absolute, if possible, under the son than it had ever been under the father, and the Great Seal restored to the keeping of the Welshman, whom he invariably condemned, and whom he had such reason to dislike!

He felt the deepest disappointment;[1] a severe attack of illness followed, and he resolved to renounce politics—in which he bitterly regretted that he had ever engaged, uttering this lamentation,—"The talent which God has given me I have misspent in things for which I was least fit." He published no more pamphlets; he wrote no more letters of solicitation to Buckingham; he did not seek to disturb by any memorial of himself the festivities of the young Sovereign on his marriage with a French bride; he declined attending the coronation as a Peer, which he was entitled to do, taking precedence of all the ancient Barons: and when the writ of summons to the parliament requiring him to be present to counsel the King *circa ardua regni* was delivered to him, he said,— " I have done with such vanities." While squabbles were

---

[1] Even in his last will he can not conceal his sense of the inconstancy of Charles, whom he thus describes: " My most gracious Sovereign, *who ever when he was Prince* was my patron."

going on in parliament, first at Westminster and then at Oxford,—and the nation was in a flame by the abrupt dissolution,—he remained in retirement at Gorhambury, and, as far as his exhausted frame would permit, dedicated himself to those studies which he regretted had been so often interrupted by pursuits neither calculated to confer internal peace nor solid glory.

He even heard without emotion, in the following November, that, preparatory to the summoning of another parliament, Lord Keeper Williams had been dismissed, and that, without any application or communication to himself, the Great Seal had been transferred to Sir Thomas Coventry. He foresaw that his earthly career was drawing to a close, and he prepared to meet his end with decency and courage. He was reconciled to Bishop Williams, whom he forgave the various evil turns he had formerly so bitterly complained of, and whom he even now admitted into his confidence.

On the 19th of December, 1625, with his own hand, he wrote his last will,—which contains touches of true pathos and sublimity. After some introductory words, he thus proceeds: "For my burial, I desire it may be in St. Michael's Church, near St. Alban's: there was my mother buried, and it is the parish church of my mansion-house at Gorhambury, and it is the only Christian church within the walls of old Verulam. For my name and memory, I leave it to men's charitable speeches, and to foreign nations, and the next ages." He then gives directions respecting his published works, and leaves two volumes of his Speeches and Letters, which he had collected, to the Bishop of Lincoln and the Chancellor of the Duchy of Lancaster, to be dealt with as they should think fit. He bequeaths many legacies to his friends, and directs the surplus of his property, after payment of debts and legacies, to be laid out in founding lectureships in the Universities.

Laudably anxious about his future fame, while he was making Christian preparation for the great change which approached, he wrote a few days after to the Bishop of Lincoln, to inform him of the trust he wished him to undertake:—"I find that the ancients, as Cicero, Demosthenes, Plinius, Secundus, and others, have preserved both their orations and their epistles. In imitation of whom I have done the like to my own, which nevertheless I will not publish while I live; but I have been bold to bequeath them to your Lordship and Mr. Chancellor of the Duchy. My speeches perhaps you will think fit to publish: the letters, many of them, touch too much upon late matters of state to be published; yet I was willing they should not be lost." The Bishop said in his answer, —"I do embrace the honor with all thankfulness, and the trust imposed upon me with all religion and devotion." At the same time, while he does justice to Bacon's oratorical powers, he pretty plainly intimates that his fame would not be raised by the publication of his letters,—a criticism in which I entirely concur; in general they are written in a stiff, formal, ungraceful style,—and when the writer tries to be light and airy, we have such a botch as might have been expected if Horace Walpole had been condemned to write the NOVUM ORGANUM. The felicitous epistolary tone had not yet been caught from the French; and it was not till near half a century afterwards that there were any good letters in our language.

Though his body was now much enfeebled, his mental activity never left him. He wrote some religious tracts, and he employed himself in a metrical translation, into English, of some of the Psalms of David,—showing by this effort, it must be confessed, more piety than poetry. His ear had not been formed, nor his fancy fed, by a perusal of the divine productions of Surrey, Wyat, Spenser, and Shakespeare, or he could not have produced rhymes so rugged, and turns of expression so mean. Few poets deal in finer imagery than is to be found in the writings of Bacon; but if his prose is sometimes poetical, his poetry is always prosaic.

This, the last of his works which he lived to finish, he dedicated to a much valued private friend, who was a divine, and himself a writer of sacred poetry; thus addressing him:—" It being my manner for dedications to choose those that I hold most fit for the argument, I thought that in respect of divinity and poesy met, whereof the one is the matter, the other the style of this little writing, I could not make better choice."[1]

" By means of the sweet air of the country he had ob-

---

[1] Mr. George Herbert. Works, ii. 552.

tained some degree of health"[1] in the autumn of 1625; but a dreadfully severe winter followed, which aggravated his complaints and brought him very low.

In the beginning of the following year he was removed, for the benefit of medical advice, to his lodging in Gray's Inn, and his strength and spirits revived; but he confined himself to those noble studies which he had long sacrificed to professional drudgery and courtly intrigue. Summoned as a Peer to Charles's second parliament, which met in February, he declined to take his seat, or to interest himself in the struggles going on between the King and the Commons, and between Bristol and Buckingham. But the firmness and magnanimity which he displayed gave to this last sad stage of his life a dignity beyond what office and power could bestow. His friends affectionately gathered round him, showing him every mark of attachment and respect; the public, forgetting his errors, anticipated what was due to his " name and memory;" and the learned in foreign countries eagerly inquired after the great English Philosopher, who was hardly known to them as a Judge or a Minister.

Many distinguished foreigners came to England for the express purpose of seeing and conversing with him.[2] Gondomar, the Spanish ambassador, having returned to his own country, kept up a close correspondence with him till the time of his death.

The Marquis d'Effiat, who brought over the Princess Henrietta Maria, distinguished for his elegant accomplishments no less than his high rank, went to Gray's Inn to pay his respects to the man whose writings he had studied and admired. Bacon, sick in bed, did not like to turn him away, but received him with the curtains drawn. "You resemble the angels," said the Ambassador; "we hear those beings continually talked of; we believe them superior to mankind; and we never have the consolation to see them."

In reference to the noble close of his career Ben Jonson exclaimed, " My conceit towards his person was never increased by his place or honors; but I have and do rev-

---

[1] Letter to Mr. Palmer, Oct. 29, 1625.
[2] " Viri primarii aliquot, dum adhuc in vivis fuit, nullam aliam ob causam huc in Angliam transfretarunt, quam ut eum conspicirent et cum eo coram loquendi opportunitatem captarent."—*Rawley.*

erence him for the greatness that was only proper to himself, in that he seemed to me ever by his works one of the greatest men, and most worthy of admiration, that had been in many ages: in his adversity I ever prayed that God would give him strength,—for greatness he could not want;—neither could I condole in a word or syllable for him, as knowing no accident could do harm to virtue, but rather help to make it manifest."

His love of science never was more eager and unwearied than now, amidst the evils which surrounded him, and which he knew he could not overcome. In contemplation of a new edition of his "Natural History," he was keenly examining the subject of antiseptics, or the best means of preventing putrefaction in animal substances. "The great apostle of experimental philosophy, was destined to become its martyr." It struck him suddenly, that flesh might as well be preserved by snow as by salt. From the length and severity of the winter, he expected that snow might still, in shaded situations, be discovered on the ground. Dr. Wetherborne, the King's physician, agreed to accompany and assist him in a little experimental excursion. At Highgate they found snow lying behind a hedge in great abundance, and, entering a cottage, they purchased a fowl lately killed, which was to be the subject of the experiment. The philosopher insisted on cramming the snow into the body of the fowl with his own hands. Soon after this operation, the cold and the damp struck him with a chill, and he began to shiver. He was carried to his coach, but was so seriously indisposed that he could not travel back to Gray's Inn, and he was conveyed to the house of his friend, the Earl of Arundel, at Highgate. There he was kindly received, and, out of ceremony, placed in the state bed. But it was damp, not having been slept in for a year before, and he became worse. A messenger was dispatched for his old friend and connection, Sir Julius Cæsar, who immediately came to him. Next day he was rather better, and was able to dictate the following letter to the Earl of Arundel, which proved his dying effort:—

"My very good Lord,

"I was likely to have had the fortune of Cajus Plinius the elder, who lost his life by trying an experiment about the burning of the Mount Vesuvius. For I was also desirous to try an experiment or two, touching the conservation and induration of bodies. As for the experiment itself, it succeeded excellently well; but in the journey between London and Highgate I was taken with such a fit of casting as I knew not whether it were the stone, or some surfeit of cold, or indeed a touch of them all three. But when I came to your Lordship's house I was not able to go back, and therefore was forced to take up my lodging here, where your housekeeper is very careful and diligent about me, which I assure myself your Lordship will not only pardon toward him,[1] but think the better of him[1] for it. For indeed your Lordship's house was happy to me; and I kiss your noble hands for the welcome which I am sure you give me to it.

"I know how unfit it is for me to write to your Lordship with any other hand than my own; but, by my troth, my fingers are so disjointed with this fit of sickness that I can not steadily hold a pen."

A like fortune to that of the elder Pliny actually did abide him; for a violent attack of fever supervened, with a defluxion on his breast; and early in the morning of Easter Sunday, the 9th of April, 1626, he expired in the arms of Sir Julius Cæsar. He had not in his last moments the soothing consolations of female tenderness. Although his wife had brought him no children, and she had never been a companion to him, they had lived together on decent terms till within the last few months,—when they had separated, and he, "for just and great causes," had revoked all the testamentary dispositions he had made in her favor.[2]

Thus died, in the 66th year of his age, Francis Bacon, not merely the most distinguished man who ever held

---

[1] *Sic.* Housekeepers then were of the male sex.—"To be said an honest man and a good housekeeper."—*Shakespeare.* The word had changed its gender in the reign of Queen Anne:

"Call the old housekeeper, and get *her*
To fill a place for want of better."—*Swift.*

[2] Rawley, in terms which shake our confidence in him as a biographer, celebrates their uninterrupted connubial love and happiness. "Neque vero liberorum defectus ullo pacto amorem ejus erga nuptam imminuit, quam summa semper dilectione conjugali et amoris indiciis prosecutus est; supellectili lauta, monilibus variis et fundis insuper donavit." Whereas, the irritated husband says by his codicil, "Whatsoever I have given, granted, confirmed, or appointed to my wife, I do now, for just and great causes, utterly revoke and make void, and leave her to her right only."

the Great Seal of England, but, notwithstanding all his faults, one of the greatest ornaments and benefactors of the human race.

The plan of the present work has justified me in giving this circumstantial account of his life, but prevents me from dwelling at any length upon his character, or attempting an analysis of his writings.

Unfortunately, hardly any of his judgments on questions of law or equity have come down to us; but we need not doubt that, when unbiased by mandates from Buckingham, or gifts from the parties, they were uniformly sound. No one ever sat in Westminster Hall with a finer judicial understanding; no one ever more thoroughly understood the duties of a judge,[1] and his professional acquirements and experience were sufficient to enable him satisfactorily to dispose of all the variety of business which came before him. I attach little weight to the assertion that "none of his decrees were reversed," as there was then no appeal from the Court of Chancery, and there is no authentic account of what was done when some of the cases he had decided were reheard by his successor.

The "Orders" which he promised when he took his seat he soon issued to the number of one hundred, and they remain a monument of his fame as a great Judge. They are wisely conceived, and expressed with the greatest precision and perspicuity. They are the foundation of the practice of the Court of Chancery, and are still cited as authority.[2]

King James, being told by Lord Coke that he could only dispense justice in the Courts of law by his Judges, had a mind to try his hand in Chancery, believing, according to the vulgar notion, that the only thing to be done there was to temper rigid rules according to the justice of the particular case, which he thought was peculiarly the

---

[1] See particularly his Essays, "Of Great Place," "Of Seeming Wise," and "Of Judicature," which ought to be frequently read and pondered by all Judges.

[2] Although they have been varied in detail, I only find in them one principle which would not now be recognized. No. 6. "No decrees shall be made upon pretense of equity against the express provision of an act of parliament" (So far so well.) "Nevertheless, if the construction of such act of parliament hath for a time gone one way in general opinion and reputation, and after by a later judgment hath been controlled, *then relief may be given upon matter of equity for cases arising before the said judgment*, because the subject was in no default."—See *Beames's Orders*.

province of the Sovereign. Bacon, however, soon disgusted him with equity, by making him understand that he must hear both sides before he determined. The modern Solomon declared that he could make up his mind without difficulty when he had only heard the plaintiff's case, but that the conflict between the counsel on opposite sides so puzzled and perplexed him, that, if he must hear both, he would thereafter hear neither;—and he went off to join in the safer amusement of hunting at Royston.[1]

While Bacon was Chancellor he regularly twice a year —before the commencement of each of the two circuits— assembled all the Judges and all the Justices of Peace that happened to be in London in the Exchequer Chamber, and lectured them upon their duties—above all admonishing them to uphold the prerogative—"the twelve Judges of the realm being the twelve lions under Solomon's throne, stoutly to bear it up, and Judges going circuit being like planets, revolving round the Sovereign as their sun." He warned them against hunting for popularity, saying, "A popular Judge is a deformed thing, and *plaudites* are fitter for players than magistrates." The Justices he roundly threatened with dismissal if they did not effectually repress faction, "of which ensue infinite inconveniences and perturbations of all good order, and crossing of all good service in court and country." And he told them he should follow a fine remedy devised by Cicero when consul, a mild one but an apt one: *Eos qui otium perturbant reddam otiosos.*[2]

In swearing in new Judges, he delivered most excellent advice to them, which should be kept in remembrance by

[1] But James, in the early part of his reign, actually heard to the end a long trial in the Star Chamber, presiding and giving judgment. *Countess of Exeter* v. *Sir Thomas Lake*. On this occasion he was celebrated by the courtiers for having even exceeded the best performances of the ancient Solomon. "His most excellent Majesty, *with more than Solomon's wisdom*, heard the cause for five days, and pronounced a sentence more accurately eloquent, judiciously grave, and honorably just, to the satisfaction of all hearers and of all the lovers of justice, than all the records extant in this kingdom can declare to have been at any former time done by any of his royal progenitors."—*Hudson*, p. 9. The Star Chamber being in reality only the Privy Council, over which the King continued personally to preside, James was probably here acting according to law, if it was his taste to play the Judge, however wrong he might be in contending that he had a right to decide causes in the King's Bench, although they are said to be "*coram Rege ipso.*"

[2] Bacon's Works, vol. vi. 141, 194, 244, iv. 497.

all their successors. Thus he counsels JUSTICE HUTTON, when called to be a Judge of the Common Pleas:—

"Draw your learning out of your books, not out of your brain.

"Mix well the freedom of your own opinion with the reverence of the opinion of your fellows.

"Continue the studying of your books, and do not spend on upon the old stock.

"Fear no man's face, yet turn not stoutness into bravery.

"Be a light to jurors to open their eyes, not a guide to lead them by the noses.

"*Affect not the opinion of pregnancy and expedition by an impatient and catching hearing of the counsellors at the bar.*

"Let your speech be with gravity, as one of the sages of the law, and *not talkative*, nor with impertinent flying out to show learning.[1]

"Contain the jurisdiction of your Court within the ancient merestones, without removing the mark."

Bacon, although without any natural taste for legal studies, felt that he must ascribe the elevation which he prized so much to his profession, and he had a sincere desire to repay the debt of gratitude which he was ever ready to acknowledge that he owed it. He wrote valuable treatises to explain and improve the laws of England,—he was eager to assist in digesting them,—and he induced the King to appoint reporters with adequate salaries, who should authoritatively print such decisions of the Courts, and such only, as would be useful—guarding against the publication of crude, trifling, contradictory cases, which had then become alarming, and by which we are now overwhelmed.[2]

Viewed as a statesman,—as far as right principles and inclinations are concerned, Bacon deserves high commendation. He was for governing constitutionally by parlia-

---

[1] "An overspeaking Judge is no well-timed cymbal. It is no grace to a Judge first to find that which he might have heard in due time from the bar, or to show quickness of conceit in cutting off evidence or counsel too short, or to prevent [anticipate] information by questions, though pertinent."—*Essay of Judicature.*

[2] Rymer's Fœd., vol. xvii. p. 27. "Ordinatio qua constituantur les Reporters de lege." After stating the King's anxiety to preserve the ancient law, and to prevent innovations, he declares that he has thought it good to revive the custom of appointing some grave and learned lawyers as reporters, &c.; their stipend was fixed at £100, but there were only two for all the Courts.

ments; he never counseled violent measures; and, though he labored under the common error about the balance of trade and the necessity for laws to prevent the exportation of coin, he had generally just views both of domestic and foreign policy. He was a reformer, yet he saw the danger of rash innovation; and he says, "it is not good to try experiments in states except the necessity be urgent, or the utility evident, and well to beware that it is the reformation that draweth on the change, and not the desire of change that pretendeth the reformation."[1]

The advice he gave respecting Ireland is beyond all praise, and never having been steadily acted upon, it is unfortunately highly applicable to our own times. On new-year's day, 1606, he presented to the King, as a "Gift," a "Discourse touching the Plantation in Ireland," saying to him, "I assure myself that England, Scotland, and Ireland, *well united*, in such a trefoil as no Prince, except yourself, who are the worthiest, weareth in his crown;"—and points out to him how, by liberality and kindness, the union might be accomplished. He displays a most intimate knowledge of the miseries of Ireland, their causes and cure. "This desolate and neglected country is blessed with almost all the dowries of nature—with rivers, havens, woods, quarries, good soil, temperate climate, and a race and generation of men, valiant, hard, and active, as it is not easy to find such confluence of commodities,—if the hand of man did join with the hand of nature; but they are severed,—the harp of Ireland is not strung or attuned to concord."

We must not suppose that he was either insincere or unenlightened in his political theories by merely regarding his practice; for he had no moral courage, and no power of self-sacrifice or self-denial. Hence we account for his clinging to every minister who could advance him, —for his sealing patents to create a monopoly in all articles of necessity and luxury,—and for his writing in defense of a Spanish war, for which he knew there was no just cause, and which he knew could promote no national object.

His published speeches (which he evidently thought

---

[1] If misled by no personal interest he would have supported the Bill of Rights in 1689, and the Reform Bill in 1832—and by going so far and no further, would have assisted in saving the constitution.

might be compared to the choice specimens of ancient eloquence) do not support his fame as an orator. They are superior to those of his contemporaries, and even to those of the leaders of the Long Parliament, who, as boys, were studying under him, but who suffered the effect of their masculine thinking to be weakened by endless heads and subdivisions, and to be counteracted by courtly ribaldry or by puritanical cant. Nevertheless, no speech of his, at the bar or in parliament, even approaches the standard of pure and sustained eloquence set us by Erskine and Burke,—and to get his weighty, rich, and pathetic passages we must pass over much that is quaint, pedantic and dull.[1]

But it was as a philosopher that Bacon conquered immortality, and here he stands superior to all who went before, and to all who have followed him. If he be not entitled to a place in the interior of the splendid temple which he imagined for those who, by inventing arts, have embellished life, his statue ought to appear in the more honorable position of the portico, as the great master who has taught how arts are to be invented—with this inscription on its pedestal,—

"O tenebris tantis tam clarum extollere lumen
Qui primus potuisti, illustrans commoda vitæ."

However, I must limit myself to declaring my humble but hearty concurrence in the highest praises that have been bestowed upon him for what he did for science. No one is so absurd as to suppose that he was the first to render experience available in the search after truth; but he it was that first systematically showed the true object of philosophical inquiry, and the true means by which that object was to be attained. Before and during his time discoveries were accidentally made; but they were retarded and perverted by fantastical *à priori theories*, which they were supposed to illustrate. He taught as one inspired, that the labor of all who think ought to be to multiply human enjoyments and to mitigate human sufferings, and that for this purpose they must observe and

---

[1] In his own time he seems to have been considered equally eminent as an orator and as an author. Raleigh, no mean judge, declared that "Lord Salisbury was a great speaker but a bad writer, and Lord Northampton was a great writer but a bad speaker, while Lord Bacon was equally excellent in speaking and writing."

reason only from what they see. All who have studied the history of ancient or modern science, must be aware of the host of established errors he had to encounter, which were supposed to be sanctioned by names of no meaner note than those of Plato and Aristotle. But with what courage, steadiness, and perseverance did he proceed with his undertaking! Luckily he was in no danger of losing the place of Solicitor or Attorney General, or Lord Chancellor, by exposing the *idola tribus*, the *idola sp. cus*, the *idola fori*, or the *idola theatri*.

His plan was left unfinished; but in spite of all the distractions of professional drudgery and groveling ambition,—although, in the language of Sir Thomas Bodley, "he wasted many years on such study as was not worthy of such a student,"—he accomplished more for the real advancement of knowledge than any of those who spent their lives in calm meditation under sequestered porticoes or amidst academic groves.

With all his boldness he is entirely free from dogmatism and intolerance,—unlike the religious reformers of his day, who, assailing an ancient superstition, wished to burn all who doubted the new system which they set up in its place. Having put down tyranny, he did not himself assume the sceptre, but proclaimed freedom to mankind.

I deny the recent assertion, that little practical benefit arose from his writings—which is founded on the false statement that they were little read in England, and were hardly known abroad till analyzed in the Preface to the French Encyclopædia by D'Alembert and Diderot. They were eagerly read and studied in this country from the time they were respectively published; and as soon as they appeared here, they were all reprinted and translated on the Continent. Attacked by obscure men, they were defended by Gassendi, Puffendorff, and Leibnitz. They made a deep impression on the public mind of Europe, which has never been effaced; and to their direct and indirect influence may be ascribed many of the brilliant discoveries which illustrated the latter half the seventeenth century.[1]

---

[1] It is not very creditable to England that Bacon's philosophical works have fallen into comparative neglect in his own country. Aristotle excludes them at Oxford, and they are not the subject of any lectures or examinations at Cambridge—while at most foreign universities " the Baconian system " is

I must likewise indignantly repel the charge brought against him, that he is a mere "*utilitarian*"—in the contracted and bad sense of the word—having regard only to our physical wants. He always remembered that man is a social and reasonable and accountable being, and never erred by supposing that his true welfare could be promoted without ample provision for cultivating his affections, enlightening his understanding, and teaching him his duties to his Maker. A most perfect body of ethics might be made out from the writings of Bacon; and though he deals chiefly, in his examples, with natural philosophy, his method is equally well adapted to examine and classify the phenomena of mind.

I may not enter into any minute criticisms on the style of his philosophical works, whether English or Latin; yet I can not refrain from remarking, that while he instructs he is exact, perspicuous, and forcible,—charming his reader with a felicity of illustration peculiar to himself, —even seconded by the commanding powers of a bold and figurative eloquence. To beginners, the "Advancement of Learning" is certainly the most captivating performance,—but let them proceed, and they will soon be familiar with the "De Augmentis,"—and the most abstract aphorisms in the "NOVUM ORGANUM" will yield them delight.

Bacon's miscellanous literary productions would of themselves place him high as an author. Many of the observations on life and manners in his "Essays" have passed into maxims or proverbs, and are familiar to us from infancy. Of all the compositions in any language I am acquainted with, these will bear to be the oftenest perused and reperused, and after every perusal they still present some new meaning and some new beauty. He was himself conscious of his power in this department of literature, and of the "luster and reputation these *recreations of his other studies* would yield to his name."[1]

His "New Atlantis" he seems to have intended as a rival to the "Utopia" of Sir Thomas More, although his object was less to satirize existing institutions and man-

regularly taught—and it is to Scotch professors, Reid, Dugald Stewart, Robison, and Playfair, that it owes its best illustrations.

[1] Letter to Bishop of Winchester. Again, he resembles his short Essays to the reformed coin, "where the pieces are small, but the silver is good."

ners than to point out the unbounded progress that might be made in discovery and improvement.[1] Some of his suggestions which must have appeared the most extravagant to his contemporaries have been realized in the present age.

His tract "On Church Controversies" is admirably written,—to inculcate the salutary precept that Christians should contend "not as the brier with the thistle, which can wound deepest; but as the vine with the olive, which bears best fruit."

His derivation of all physical and moral truth from mythological fables in his "Wisdom of the Ancients," is often forced and far-fetched; but nowhere do we trace more striking proofs of his imagination, and his power of discovering resemblances and differences,—in which consist wit and wisdom.

His Latin style, though pointed and forcible, is not sweet nor pure; but he has left us some of the best specimens of genuine Anglicism, and the few antiquated words and turns of expression which we find in his writing, as in the contemporary translation of the Bible, only give additional weight and solemnity to the sentiments which he expresses. Addison, who knew what good composition was, talks with rapture of his "beautiful lights, graces, and embellishments."

In considering his private character, we must begin with the formidable admission that he was without steady attachments as well as aversions, and that, regardless of friendship or gratitude, he was governed by a selfish view of his own interest. But he was perfectly free from malignity; he was good-natured and obliging; when friends stood between him and his object—sacrificing them to the necessary extent—he did them as little further damage as possible—and instead of hating those whom he had injured, he was rather disposed to be reconciled to them, and to make them amends by courtesy, if he could not render them real service.

I find no impeachment of his morals deserving of attention—and he certainly must have been a man of very

[1] This work seems to have been deeply studied by Swift, who has happily ridiculed some parts of it in Gulliver's Travels, particularly in the voyage to Laputa. Another Lord Chancellor has attempted a philosophical romance, but Lord Erskine's "Armata" does not encourage his successors to venture again upon this mode of addressing the public.

great temperance, for the business and studies through which he went would be enough to fill up the lives of ten men who spend their evenings over their wine, and awake crapulous in the morning. "Nullum momentum aut temporis segmentum perire et intercidere passus est"[1]— knowing that if he took good care of sections of an hour, entire days would take care of themselves.

All accounts represent him as a most delightful companion, adapting himself to company of every degree, calling, and humor—not engrossing the conversation—but trying to get all to talk in turn on the subject they best understood—and not disdaining to light his own candle at the lamp of any other.[2] He was generally merry and playful, bringing out with great effect his unexhausted store of jests, new and old, and remembering that " to be free-minded and cheerfully disposed at hours of meat, and of sleep, and of exercise, is one of the best precepts of long lasting."[3]

If he was not very steady in his friendships, where disturbed by ambition or rivalry, it should be recollected that he was ever kind to his servants and dependents ; and the attachment of Meautys, who remained devotedly true to him in all his fortunes, is equally honorable to both parties.

He was rather fanciful about his health, preferring meats which bred "juices substantial and less dissipable" —taking three grains of niter daily in warm broth, and an infusion of rhubarb into white wine and beer once in six or seven days, immediately before his meal, " that it might dry the body less."

To show something supernatural about such a man, for the purpose of raising our wonder and admiration—Rawley, his chaplain and secretary, asserts—and his subsequent

---

[1] Rawley.
[2] "Convivantium neminem aut alias colloquentium pudore suffundere gloriæ sibi duxit, sicut nonnulli gestiunt ; sed facultates eorum qualescunque fovere et provehere paratus erat. Quin et sermonis licentiam sibi soli arripere in more non erat ; sed et aliis simul considentibus libertatem et vicissitudinem loquendi permittere : hoc etiam addendo, quod in arte unumquemque propria lubentissime audiret, et ad ejusmodi dissertationem pellicere et provocare consueverit. Ipse autem nullius observationes contempsit ; sed ad candelam cujuslibet lampada suam accendere non erubuit."—*Rawley.* This passage seems to have escaped the attention of two illustrious writers who have drawn his character—Hallam and Macaulay.
[3] Rawley. Oh ! for a Boswell to have recorded the conversation when he had Raleigh, Ben Jonson, Selden, and Gondomar for guests !

biographers have repeated—that at every change or any eclipse of the moon, he invariably fainted, although he was not aware that such an event was to take place, but that he recovered as soon as the sun's rays again illumined her disc.[1] As no instance is recorded of his ever having fainted in public, or put off the hearing of a cause on account of the change of the moon, or of any approaching eclipse, visible or invisible—and neither himself nor any of his other contemporaries refer to any such infirmity, and such a "delicacy of temperament" is somewhat incredible—we must set down the story to the invention or easy credulity of the man who thought that it might be explained by his hero's "lunar horoscope at the moment of his birth."

A more serious matter is the charge brought against him of infidelity. At one time in his youth he seems not only to have been sceptical, but to have been disposed openly to insult the religion of others. Notwithstanding the stout denial that he was the author of the "Paradoxes," I can not doubt that the publication is from his pen, and I can not characterize it otherwise than as a profane attempt to ridicule the Christian faith. But I suspect that he is describing the history of his own mind when he says, "It is an assured truth, and a conclusion of experience, that a little or superficial knowledge of philosophy may incline the mind of man to atheism, but a further proceeding therein doth bring the mind back again to religion; for in the entrance of philosophy, when the second causes, which are next unto the senses, do offer themselves to the mind of man, if it dwell and stay there, it may induce some oblivion of the highest cause; but when a man passeth on further, and seeth the dependence of causes and the works of Providence—then, according to the allegory of the poets, he will easily believe that the highest link of Nature's chain must needs be tied to the foot of Jupiter's chair."[2]

[1] "Verisimile est lunam in themate ejus natalitio præcipuum aliquem locum (veluti in horoscopo aut medio cœli) tenuisse. Quoties enim luna defecit aut eclipsim passa est, repentino animi deliquio correptus fuit: idque etiam si nullam defectionis lunaris notitiam præviam habuisset. Quamprimum autem luna lumini priori restituta fuisset, confestim refocillatus est et convaluit "—*Rawley.*

[2] "Advancement of Learning". See the Essay "Of Atheism," which was added in the later editions.

He certainly received a most pious education; and if his early religious impressions were for a time weakened or effaced by his intercourse with French philosophers, or his own first rash examination of the reasons of his belief, I am fully convinced that they were restored and deepened by subsequent study and reflection. I rely not merely on his "Confession of Faith," or the other direct declarations of his belief in the great truths of our religion (although I know not what right we have to question his sincerity), but I am swayed more by the devotional feelings which from time to time, without premeditation or design, break out in his writings, and the incidental indications he gives of his full conviction of the being and providence of God, and the Divine mission of our blessed Savior. His lapses from the path of honor afford no argument against the genuineness of his speculative belief. Upon the whole, we may be well assured that the difficulties which at one time perplexed him had been completely dissipated; his keen perception saw as clearly as it is ever given to man in this state to discover—the hand of the Creator, Preserver, and Governor of the universe;—and his gigantic intellect must have been satisfied with the consideration, that assuming the truth of natural and revealed religion, it is utterly inconsistent with the system of human affairs, and with the condition of man in this world, that they should have been more clearly disclosed to us.

Among his good qualities it ought to be mentioned, that he had no mean jealousy of others, and he was always disposed to patronize merit. Feeling how long he himself had been unjustly depressed from unworthy motives, he never would inflict similar injustice on others, and he repeatedly cautions statesmen to guard against this propensity. "He that plots to be a figure among ciphers is the decay of a whole age."

He retained through life his passion for planting and gardening, and when Chancellor, he ornamented Lincoln's Inn Fields with walks and groves, and gave the first example of an umbrageous square in a great metropolis.[1]

Little remains except to give some account of his person. He was of a middling stature,—his limbs well formed, though not robust,—his forehead high, spacious, and open,—his eye lively and penetrating;—there were

[1] Letter to Buckingham, Nov. 12, 1618.

deep lines of thinking in his face;—his smile was both intellectual and benevolent;—the marks of age were prematurely impressed upon him;—in advanced life, his whole appearance was venerably pleasing, so that a stranger was insensibly drawn to love before knowing how much reason there was to admire him.

It is with great pain that I have found myself obliged to take an impartial view of his character and conduct;—

"A fairer person lost not heaven ; he seem'd
For dignity composed and high exploits ;"

but to suppress or pervert facts,—to confound, for the purpose of holding him up as a pefect being, moral distinctions which should be kept well defined and far apart, —would be a vain attempt to do honor to his genius,— would not be creditable to the biographer who perceives his faults,—and would tend to demoralize as far as it might be effectual. Others who really believe Bacon to be immaculate, are fully justified in proclaiming him to the world to be so. This was by no means the opinion he entertained of himself. He acknowledges to Sir Thomas Bodley his many errors, and among the rest, says he, "this great one which led the rest, that knowing myself by inward calling to be fitter to hold a book than play a part, I have led my life in civil causes, for which I was not very fit by nature, and more unfit by pre-occupation of mind."

When young, he had "vast contemplative ends and moderate civil ends." If he had inherited the patrimony intended for him by his father, if he had obtained the provision which he solicited from the minister on his father's death, it is possible that he might have sunk into indolence and obscurity; but from his native energy, and from the consciousness with which he seems to have been very early inspired of his high calling to be "the great reformer of philosophy," the probability is, that he would have left the *Instauratio Magna* complete, preserving a spotless reputation. Then, indeed, we should have justly honored him beyond any of his species, to whom miraculous gifts have not been directly imparted by Heaven. But without incurring any blame in the first instance, he was driven to betake himself to the profession of the law for a subsistence; hence, he was involved in the vortex of politics; intellectual glory became his secondary object; and his nature being changed and debased,—to gain professional advancement, official station, and political power, there was no baseness to which he was not ready to submit, and hardly any crime which he would not have been willing to perpetrate. I still readily acknowledge him to be a great man; but can only wish he had been a good man. Transposing the words applied by Tacitus to Agricola, I may truly say, "Magnum virum facile crederes, bonum libenter."

According to the directions in his will, his remains were interred in St. Michael's Church, near St. Alban's. No account has reached us of his funeral, and there is reason to fear that, on this occasion, as his connection with the Court had entirely ceased, and a party squabble was engrossing the attention of the public, the great and the noble did not attend to do honor to his memory. But then and there, no doubt, appeared as a mourner, and wept tenderly, Meautys, his faithful secretary, who, at his own expense, erected to him, in the church where he lies buried, a handsome and characteristic monument, representing him in a sitting posture with his hand supporting his head, and absorbed in contemplation—with this inscription:—

> Franciscus Bacon Baro de Verula S^d Alba₁ Vic^{ms}
> Sive notioribus titulis
> Scientiarum Lumen Facundiæ Lex
> Sic sedebat.
>
> Qui postquam omnia naturalis sapientiæ
> Et civilis arcana evolvisset
> Naturæ decretum explevit
> Composita solvantur
>
> An₀ Dni MDCXXVI.
> Ætat LXVI.
>
> Tanti viri
> Mem.
> Thomas Meautys
> Superstitis cultor
> Defuncti admirator.
> H. P.

Notwithstanding all the money he had received, duly and unduly,—such was his love of expense, and his neglect of his affairs, that upon his death his estate appears to have been found insolvent. All the six executors whom he named in his will refused to act, and on the 13th of July, 1627, administration with the will annexed was granted to Sir Thomas Meautys and Sir Robert Rich, a Master in Chancery, as two of his creditors.—No funds were forthcoming for the foundation of his lectureships.[1]

His wife survived him twenty years, but lived in retirement.

Bacon perhaps comforted himself for his want of offspring, by recollecting the instances from which he drew his saying, that "Great men have no continuance;" but he seems at times to have felt a pang at the thought that he was to leave no children to close his eyes, or to weep over his grave: "They increase the cares of life, *but they mitigate the remembrance of death.*"[2]

CHAPTER LVII.

LIFE OF LORD KEEPER WILLIAMS FROM HIS BIRTH TILL HIS INSTALLATION AS LORD KEEPER.

THE Great Seal, having been delivered up by Lord Bacon at York House previous to sentence being pronounced upon him, was brought to the King at Whitehall,—and there he immediately ordered three

[1] Since the publication of the first edition of this Life, by the assistance of my friend, Mr. C. Monro, I have ascertained beyond all question that Bacon died insolvent. It appears by the Registrar's Book that a creditors' suit was instituted for the administration of his estate. His servants were, by consent, to be paid their wages in full, and the fund arising from the sale of his property was to be divided ratably among the other creditors. A report to the Lord Chancellor, on the state of the debts and assets, contains these very curious passages: "That concerning the several debts demanded by Sir Peter Van Lord, Mr. Peacock, and Philip Holman, it is alleged that the testator was sentenced for them in parliament as bribes, and therefore not conceived reasonable that they should come in as creditors. Nevertheless, further time is given them to produce their proofs, and to hear what can be said on either side touching their said demands." Then with respect to a bond for £1,000 to secure that amount lent to him when he was Attorney-General, the report, after stating the objection by the creditors, says, "I have thought fit to set down the testator's own words touching the said debt, and so leave the same to your lordship's consideration: 'A note of such debts as either in respect of length of tyme or the nature of the first borrowing or agreement since, need not be thought upon for repayment: viz. The farmers of the Customs £1,000, lent long since, when I was Attorney, and without interest, *upon great and many pleasures don to the said farmers*, and whereas I was wont to have of them yearly a new yeares guift of £100 at least—upon this money lent it was discontinued, and soe the principall worne out, for interest was never intended.'"—Reg. Lib. 19 Feb. 1626.

[2] Essay, "Of Parents and Children."

commissions to be sealed with it in his presence,—one addressed to Sir Julius Cæsar, Master of the Rolls, and certain common-law Judges, to hear causes in the Court of Chancery,—another to Sir James Ley, Chief Justice of the King's Bench, to preside as Speaker in the House of Lords,—and the third to Viscount Mandeville, the Lord Treasurer, the Duke of Lennox, the Earl of Pembroke, and the Earl of Arundel, to keep the Great Seal, and to affix it to all writs and letters patent requiring to be sealed.[1]

This arrangement continued above two months following,—when, for reasons which we shall hereafter explain, the Clavis Regni, after having been held during a period of sixty-three years by six successive laymen bred to the law, was, to the dismay of Westminster Hall and the astonishment of the public, delivered to an ecclesiastical Lord Keeper, JOHN WILLIAMS, Dean of Westminster and Bishop of Lincoln elect,—a man of sharp natural intellect, of unwearied industry, of great scholastic acquirements, free from considerable vices, but not distinguished for any very high qualities of head or heart,—who, by a sort of frolic of fortune, was suddenly placed in the very situation for which Bacon, singularly well able to perform all its duties, and with many advantages from birth and connection, had so long plotted, before he could reach its slippery eminence.

The principality of Wales boasts of Williams as one of the most illustrious of her children. He was of the true Cambrian race, being the son of Edmund Williams and Anne Wynne, daughter of Owen Wynne, Esquire, with genealogies reaching through Llewellyn, King Arthur, and Caractacus, to Adam. He was really of a respectable gentleman's family, who bore upon their shield three Saxons' heads, which, when he was made chief of the law, gave rise to the following distich:—

> "Qui sublime fori potuit conscendere tignum,
> Par fuit hunc capitum robur habere trium."

He was born at Aberconway, in the county of Carnarvon, on the 25th day of March, 1582. He was educated at a grammar school lately established in the town of Ruthin, and is said to have there made great proficiency

---

[1] Rot. Cl. 19 Jac. 1. p. 13.

in Greek and Latin, although as yet he had very little acquaintance with *Sassenach*.

In his sixteenth year he was sent to St. John's College, Cambridge, and put under the care of a countryman, Owen Gwynne, one of the College tutors; and all the Welshmen at the Universty are said to have been proud of his learning. "One thing put him to the blush and a little shame, that such as had giggling spleens would laugh at him for his Welsh tone. For those who knew him at his admission into St. John's society would often say, that he brought more Latin and Greek than good English with him This also plucked advantage after it; for it made him a very retired student by shunning company and conference, as far as he could, till he had lost the rudeness of his native dialect."[1]

He studied four years before he took his bachelor's degree, during which time, with intervals for attending chapel, hall, and lectures, he is said to have read daily from six o'clock in the morning till three the following morning; for, "from his youth to his old age he asked but three hours' sleep in twenty-four to keep him in good plight of health."[2] He was very temperate in his diet, keeping, like all good Protestants, long after the Reformation, Lent and fish days as rigorously as the Roman Catholics. Having taken his Bachelor's degree with great applause, he was soon after elected a fellow of St. John's, a royal dispensation of some statutes, which stood in his way, having been obtained at the request of the College.

His diligence continued unabated during the three years "while he was running his course to the degree of Master, a time of loitering with too many. He surrendered up his whole time to dive into the immense well of knowledge that hath no bottom. He read the best, he heard the best, he conferred with the best, exscribed, committed to memory, disputed; he had some work continually upon the loom. And though he never did so much in this unwearied industry as himself desired, he did far more than all who did highly value him could expect. All perceived that a fellowship was a garland too little for

---

[1] Hacket, 7. "There are few of our Welsh youth but at their first coming abroad would move almost any man to laughter with the native tone of their voice, and by pronouncing all their English as if they spoke it in a passion; and thus it was with our youngster."—*Phillips.*   [2] Ibid.

his head, and that in that merit his pace would quickly go farther than St. John's Walks."[1]

Having taken orders, he accepted a small living in Norfolk, which he exchanged for another in Northamptonshire—still residing at Cambridge, and being deputed to manage all the important affairs of his college. In prosecuting an application for a license to hold lands in mortmain, he attracted the notice of Lord Chancellor Ellesmere, who, hearing of his University reputation, observing his shrewdness, and having heard him preach, took him into his service as one of his domestic chaplains.

There is a story of his having made his fortune by pleading a cause before the King, respecting the right of his parishioners in Northamptonshire to dance round a Maypole; when he is supposed to have pleased James so much by his learning and eloquence, that he was made a royal chaplain, and placed in the career of preferment which conducted him to the woolsack. But Hacket is silent respecting this introduction to greatness; and as it is even inconsistent with the authentic narrative of the friend and biographer of Williams, it can only be noticed to be rejected as spurious.

Before taking up his residence at York House, the Chancellor's chaplain was allowed to complete the year for which he was serving the office of Proctor in the University of Cambridge; and he added to his reputation by his energy in enforcing discipline, and his learning in conducting disputations. Being transferred to London, " he was now in a nest for an eagle."[2] He had an excellent opportunity to advance himself, and he made the most of it. Not only did he say prayers and preach before the worthy old Chancellor, but he constantly attended him wherever he went, and insinuated himself into his most intimate confidence. He even sat by him in the Court of Chancery, as well as in the Star Chamber; and "to climb $\text{Εις κολπον της ψυχης}$, into the bosom of his master's soul, he picked up, in a short space, *some gleanings*, in his own modest words, in the knowledge of the common laws of the realm; but, indeed, *full sheaves*, if his acquaintance might be believed—having read ' Littleton's Tenures,' 'the Doctor and Student,' and somewhat else like unto them, at hours of relaxation, he furnished himself with no

[1] Hacket, 8.   [2] Ibid.

little quantity of that learning, by discourse and conference, and inquiring after some cases how they sped in the Courts of Justice. When he was at a nonplus, he respited that difficulty till he met with Sir John Walter, (afterward Lord Chief Baron), whose judgment was most agreeable to his genius."[1]

Hacket thus concludes a long vindication of his hero, illustrated by examples of ecclesiastics who had gained renown by their skill in the civil and canon law. "Why might not Mr. Williams examine the cases, reports, and maxims of our municipal laws to be expert in them? Both being egged on to it by the happiness of his attendance in the Pretorian Court, where he might learn much and labor little for it, and making it the recreation, not the intermission, of his proper studies. The Lord Chancellor did highly countenance him in it, and was so taken with his pregnancy, that at his leisure times, both for his own solace and his chaplain's furtherance, he would impart to him the narrative of some famous causes that had been debated in Chancery or Star Chamber. What could not such a master teach? what could not such a scholar learn. Socrates says in Plato—of Alcibiades—that he gloried in nothing so much as that he was ward to Pericles, and brought up under him. Neither had this chaplain a more graceful ornament to show in the eyes of the world than that he was disciple to the Lord Egerton."[2]

By degrees, he was employed by the Chancellor to read weighty petitions, and to assist him in extracting the material facts from voluminous depositions. At first there was great jealousy of him among the secretaries; but in a little while they did their utmost to put him forward, and "none of his fellows had cause to repent that he rode upon the fore horse; for he was courteous and ready to mediate in any cause, and he left all fees and vails of profit to those to whom they did belong. The lookers-on did mark, that his Lord did not only use him in his most principal employments, but delighted to confer with him."[3]

The ecclesiastical patronage of the Lord Chancellor was placed very much at his disposal. "They were godly men whom he obliged, and such as had waited long in the Universities, and fit to be called forth to use their

[1] Hacket, 20, 23, 27 [2] Ibid. 28. [3] Ibid.

talents."[1] Meanwhile, he by no means neglected his own interest. He obtained the fine living of Waldegrave in Northamptonshire, in addition to Grafton, with stalls at Lincoln, Peterborough, Hereford, and St. David's. His panegyrist defends his pluralities by the quotation, *Quomodo liberalis esse potest, qui nihil plus acquireret quam quod sibi ad victum necessarium sufficere queat?* [2]

He likewise took his turn in preaching before the Court, pleasing James by his adhesion to the courtly doctrine now so much in vogue,—that subjects hold their liberties and their property at the will of the Sovereign, whom they are bound, in every extremity, passively to obey.

What is more to his credit than pleasing James,—he is said to have given high satisfaction to the admirer of Raleigh,—Prince Henry,—who, having heard him preach at Newmarket, "took great notice of him as an honor to Wales, and gave him his princely word that he would reward him after the weight of his worth."[3] This Prince, likely, if he had survived, to have advanced the glory rather than the happiness of his subjects, was soon after mysteriously cut off. Williams, however, reaped the reward of his pliancy and dexterity more rapidly than he himself, in his most sanguine moments, could have anticipated, although, from the growing infirmities of the Lord Chancellor, all hope of higher preferment seemed to be at an end. Ellesmere was made a Viscount; "but who did ever see that the sand in an hour-glass did run the slower because the case in which it was put was gilded? He delighted not in any talk unless his chaplain spoke to him. All his business with his great and royal master, the King, he sent by him to be delivered with trust and prudence. Upon which messages the King took great notice, that the chaplain was principled by his master to be a statesman and a pillar of the kingdom."[4] The impression now

---
[1] Hacket, 28.   [2] Ibid. 30.
[3] Ibid. 30. I have been favored by a kinsman of Lord Keeper Williams with the following copy of a letter, written by him from Cambridge a few days after, addressed to Sir John Wynn, to whose sons he had been tutor at St. John's College. "I have with my proctorship light upon a most loving and respectful lord—my Lord Chancellor—who hath a fatherly care of my estate, as I have by many immediate favors lately tasted. It was likewise my good fortune to give his Majesty and the Prince some extraordinary contentment at Newmarket upon Tuesday last, when by appointment I preached before them. I had a great deal of court holy water, if I can make myself any good thereby."—Cambridge, 22 Nov. 1611.   [4] Ibid. 30.

made on James certainly had a most favorable influence, when, four years afterwards, it was proposed that the Chancellor's chaplain should himself be Lord Keeper of the Great Seal.

In the prospect of his patron's death, Williams seemed destined to pass the remainder of his life as a parish priest, with an occasional "residence" in a cathedral town. Yet, either from some hint thrown out to him by James, who always thought the prerogative would be strengthened by the promotion of churchmen, or from the suggestions of vanity, he looked to rise high in the state, and being offered by Egerton on his death-bed any pecuniary provision he should choose to ask in recompense of his faithful services, he said, "Sir, I kiss your hands; you have filled my cup full; I am far from want unless it be of your Lordship's directions how to live in the world, if I survive you."—" Well," said the Chancellor, " I know you are an expert workman; take these tools to work with,—they are the best I have;" and he gave him the four treatises written by himself as to the mode of conducting business in Parliament, in the Court of Chancery, in the Star Chamber, and at the Council Board. The originals of these Williams presented to the King; but he made copies of them, and he diligently studied them in the retirement to which he thought it for his advantage for some time to submit.

When Bacon had got possession of the Great Seal, he proposed to continue Williams in his present situation of Chancellor's chaplain; but the acceptance of this offer was inconsistent with the ambitious projects which were springing up in the mind of the young Welshman. He declined it with many professions of gratitude, and, being resolved to settle himself on his living of Waldegrave, he was contented for the present with being made a Justice of Peace for the county of Northampton, and being put into the list of King's chaplains, whereby he would once a year be brought to Court.

He was now stationed, as in a watch-tower, to mark passing events, and to meditate future projects. He saw that all favors passed through the hands of Buckingham; but he was shy of cultivating him; first, because he apprehended that he would probably soon be supplanted in the King's affections by some other minion; and, secondly, because Buckingham himself was notorious for casting off his subordinate agents as soon as they had served his turn.¹ Meanwhile he addicted himself to study, and to the exemplary discharge of his parochial and magisterial duties. He kept up a splendid hospitality, and though he distinguished himself at his table by carving and conversation, he contrived to retain his own abstemious habits. He still occasionally visited Whitehall, when he was called upon to officiate as one of the royal chaplains, and he was surprised to find Buckingham's ascendency over the King more completely established than ever, and Lord Chancellor Bacon submissively obeying his orders.

No longer hesitating about the right channel of preferment, he was much at a loss to contrive a favorable introduction to the dispenser of the patronage of the Crown, who cared little about sermons, however eloquently the divine right of Kings might be expounded in them, and who was better pleased with active, useful service, than gross, personal flattery. While in a desponding mood, pure good luck offered him such an opening as no wisdom could have planned, and no soothsayer could have foretold. Buckingham, the handsomest man of his time, was still a bachelor, after having been engaged in many amours. He at last wished to marry the Lady Catherine Manners, the only child of the Earl of Rutland,—high born, beautiful, and the heiress of immense possessions. But he was much disliked by her family as an upstart, and she herself, having been educated as a Roman Catholic, had great scruples about being united to a Protestant. Williams, having a living in the neighborhood, had frequently visited at Belvoir, and, enjoying a great reputation for sanctity, he stood high in the good graces both of the father and daughter.

Buckingham applied to the rector of Waldegrave to become a mediator for him in this affair. He readily undertook the mission, and sped so well that the old Earl consented to take Buckingham for his son-in-law, and the young lady, swayed by the cogent theological arguments submitted to her, and the softened accounts of the gallantries of her lover now hinted to her, renounced the errors of Popery, and agreed to be married to him accord-

¹ Hacket, 34, 35, 36.

ing to the rites of the Church of England. So complete was the negotiator's success, that he was allowed himself to draw the marriage-settlement, and to perform the marriage ceremony. He used to say "that this negotiation was the key-stone in the arch of his preferment."[1]

He now considered himself regularly enlisted among Buckingham's retainers; and, that he might be constantly near the spot where intrigues were to be successfully carried on, he immediately applied to his patron to be made Dean of Westminster, saying, "I am an humble suitor, first, to be acknowledged your servant, and, that I may be nearer, and better able to perform my desires, to be by your happy hand transplanted to Westminster. If your Honor be not bent upon an ancienter servant, I beseech you think upon me. I am true, and so reputed by my former, and, by the grace of God, will prove no otherwise to my second, master."[2]

The application succeeded, and Williams, taking up his abode at the Deanery,—while he bestowed much labor upon the financial concerns of the Chapter, which he found in sad disorder, frequently attended the Court at Whitehall, and was ready to avail himself of any chance which might happen for his further advancement.

On the 30th of January, 1621, the parliament met, from which James and his ministers expected nothing but supplies and submission, but which Williams, from having mixed with the lower and middling ranks, and being aware of the discontents which had been long accumulating, early perceived would make an irresistible attack on certain political abuses which even Court preachers could not defend. He saw the Commons begin with Sir Giles Mompesson and Monopolies, but knew they would not stop there, and, well pleased—not surprised,—he heard of the committee appointed to inquire into the corrupt practices prevailing in the Court of Chancery, and of the charges of bribery against Lord Chancellor Bacon.

But he was surprised as well as pleased when, the day after Sir R. Philips, chairman of the committee, had presented a report which declared these charges to be true and the fit subject of impeachment, he was sent for by Buckingham, and confidently consulted as to the measures to be adopted by the Court for quelling the storm.

[1] Hacket, 42.   [2] Ibid. 44.

Whether Williams at this moment dimly discovered any shadow of his coming greatness it is impossible to say Though the advice he gave coincided with his own interest, it must be allowed to have been sound. The vote of the House of Commons against the Lord Chancellor having been nearly unanimous, and the evidence against him being conclusive, he was already condemned by the public voice, and he must have been found guilty by the Lords.

To stifle the prosecution, while parliament was allowed to continue sitting, was impossible. An abrupt dissolution might have been resorted to. This was the favorite expedient of the Stuarts; but, producing a temporary respite, it fatally increased their difficulties. On the present occasion, Williams truly urged "that the House of Commons as yet had given no just cause of complaint; that if the abuses complained of existed, the whole nation would say they ought to be removed; that the government could not long be carried on without parliamentary aids, and that another parliament would only be more formidable to the prerogatives and to the ministers of the Crown." We have already related how Buckingham and the King, convinced that this was the safest course, put themselves under the guidance of the Dean of Westminster, who was supposed by the public, and even by Bacon, to be only occupied in saying prayers in the Abbey; how Sir Edward Villiers was sent on his embassy,—how Mompesson and Michell were surrendered up as victims to the public indignation,—and how the impeachment of the Chancellor was allowed to proceed, with every disposition to save him or to soften his fall.[1]

A long adjournment at Easter having been found ineffectual to divert the Commons from their purpose, Bacon, as the most expedient step for himself and the government, confessed the truth of all the charges brought against him.—Sentence being pronounced upon him, the difficult question arose, who was to be his successor?

The bold and wise step would have been to have at once offered the Great Seal to Sir Edward Coke, who would have eagerly accepted it, and whose formidable patriotism would thus have been forever extinguished, instead of blazing through the remainder of this reign, and

[1] Ante, p. 78 *et seq.*

causing a conflagration in the beginning of the next; but he had rendered himself personally so obnoxious to the King, that his promotion could not be proposed without making James threaten to abdicate the English throne and to return to his own country. Buckingham, likewise, though now connected with him by marriage, was afraid of his occasional fits of independence and his ungovernable temper.

There was more deliberation about Ley, the Chief Justice, who had very creditably performed the duties of Speaker of the House of Lords since Bacon's retirement; but it was thought that his subserviency might prove more valuable by retaining him to preside in the Court of King's Bench. Hobart, Chief Justice of the Common Pleas, had great hopes from the favor of the Prince, to whom he was Chancellor; but Buckingham had a particular antipathy to him, from his resistance to some illegal patents when he was Attorney General. The competitor who had the best chance was Sir Lionel Cranfield, Master of the Court of Wards, who, though slenderly educated, having been a merchant's clerk, had considerable natural abilities, was related to Buckingham, and was his slave. The other aspirant was Williams. Having insinuated himself into the confidence of the King and his ministers,—"out of this bud the Dean's advancement very shortly spread out into a blown flower."[1] For some reasons, he would have been greatly preferred to all the rest, but there were obvious objections to the appointment, which kept it for some time a measuring cast between him and Sir Lionel Cranfield.

Under these circumstances he was desired to draw up a statement of the profits of the office, from the information he had derived in the situation he had held under Ellesmere. His panegyrist says, with true simplicity, that, "he returned an answer on the 10th of May, with the best advantage he could foresee to the promotion of the Master of the Wards;"[2] but it seems quite clear to me, that his object was to undervalue and disparage the office that it might come to himself:—

"My most noble Lord,

"Although the more I examine myself the more unable I am made to my own judgment to wade through any

[1] Hacket, 51.   [2] Ibid. 52.

part of that great employment which your Honor vouchsafed to confer with me about, yet because I was bred under the place, and that I am credibly informed my true and noble friend, the Master of the Wards, is willing to accept it (and if be so, I hope your Lordship will incline that way), I do crave leave to inform your honor, by way of prevention, with secret underminings, which will utterly overthrow all that office, and make it beggarly and contemptible. The lawful revenue of the office stands thus, or not much above it at any time. In fines certain, £1,300 per annum, or thereabout. In fines casual £1,250, or thereabout. In greater writs, £140. For impost of wine, £100—in all £2,790—and these are all the true means of that great office."[1] He then proceeds to state how it was likely to become still poorer by the Lord Treasurer claiming a certain part of the fines, and the under officers petitioning "to have some collops out of the Lord Chancellor's fees;"[2]—thus concluding: "Now, I hope when your Lordship shall use this information to let the King see it, that you will excuse me for the boldness that I am put upon by your commands."[3]

According to Hacket, Buckingham carried this letter, "the ink scarce dry," to the King,—when the following dialogue took place between them.—*King.* "You name divers to me to be my Chancellor. Queen Elizabeth, after the death of Sir Christopher Hatton, was inclined, in her own judgment, that the good man, Archbishop Whitgift, should take the place, who modestly refused it because of his great age, and the whole multitude of ecclesiastical affairs lying upon his shoulders. Yet Whitgift knew not the half that this man doth in reference to this office." —*Buckingham.* "Sir, I am a suitor for none but for him that is so capable of the place in your great judgment."— *King.* "Be you satisfied then; I think I shall look no fur-

---

[1] This must be a most extravagant understatement of the profits of the office. I say nothing of bribes and presents, said in Lord Bacon's four years to have amounted to £100,000; but the regular legitimate fees and perquisites enabled the Lord Chancellor to maintain a princely establishment, and with common prudence to amass a great fortune. In a MS. treatise on the Court of Chancery by Sir Robert Cotton, which I have seen, it is said, "the Lord Chancellor hath for his allowance, and of the Masters of the Chancery, £542 15s., and £300 for his attendance in the Star Chamber—£200 for wine, £64 for wax, and £6 yearly for the casual fines—*communibus annis*, £300— Item £2 of every patent, and the fines of all extents." But this beggarly account can not be at all relied upon.   [2] Hacket, 51.   [3] Ibid.

ther."—Buckingham instantly sent a message to Williams, that the King had a preferment in store for him; he, not thinking of the Great Seal, conjectured it must be the Bishopric of London, then vacant, for which he had been a suitor; so it happened to him as is related of Scipio Æmilianus: "*Ædilitatem petens Consul creatus est.*"[1] The friendly biographer admits that when the appointment was announced to the public it caused great astonishment. "It was much and decidedly spoken of as a paradox of honor. Some could not believe it. Some said it was no new way, but an old one renewed; and God give him joy of it. The best professors of our laws took it sadly, without doubt, that one did never run in their race had got their garland."[2]

This appointment has not been sufficiently censured by historians. It affords a striking proof of the arbitrary principles on which the government was conducted, and the total disregard of the public interest and of public opinion which was manifested in furtherance of any scheme or whim of the King or the minister. Equity had become a branch of jurisprudence, applicable to a great portion of the property of the kingdom, and (as Lord Bacon's Or-

---

[1] Hackett, 59.
[2] Hacket, though he vouches his credit for the truth of this story, admits that a different report was spread abroad as to the manner in which the appointment was finally settled, and I must confess my belief that Sir Lionel Cranfield was induced by the letter to prefer the snug place he then held to one attended with so much envy and danger, and seemingly so little profit— whereupon Buckingham resolved that Williams should have it, on a promise to dispose of its patronage as directed—and that his Dad immediately acquiesced in the proposal made to him. Williams himself, I doubt not, gave his biographer the narrative in the text; but Clarendon has shewn that where his personal honor was concerned, his testimony is of no value.—*Hist. Reb.* vol, i. 345. See Hacket, 52.

A piece of legal preferment is said to have been still more unexpectedly conferred in the time of Lord Thurlow. A briefless barrister, the height of whose ambition was to be a commissioner of bankrupts—an office then worth not more than £100 a year—asked the Duke of Gloucester to apply for it to the Chancellor, and the following dialogue took place between them : *D. of G.* "I am very desirous to obtain for a friend of mine at the bar an office in your Lordship's Court, but unfortunately I have forgot the name of it."—*Thurlow.* "There is a Mastership in Chancery now vacant ; * perhaps that is what your Royal Highness means."—*D. of G.* "I think, my Lord, that must be the very thing."—*Thurlow.* "Sir, I can not refuse any application from your Royal Highness which it is in my power to comply with, and your friend shall be appointed." Appointed he was, and held the office very creditably many years.

* Worth £3,000 or £4,000 a year.

ders demonstrate) the practice and doctrines of the Court of Chancery had assumed a systematic form, no one was fit to preside there till after legal lucubrations of twenty years—and a Cambridge scholastic divine, although when chaplain to a Lord Chancellor he had affected to read and talk a little law, must have been as ignorant of the questions coming before him as the doorkeepers of his Court. *He* was to superintend the general administration of justice through out the realm, who had never acted as a Judge, except at the Waldegrave Petty Sessions, in making an order of bastardy, or allowing a rate for the relief of the parish poor. The case bore no resemblance to the elevation of such men as Warham, Morton, or Wolsey, who had regularly studied the civil and canon law, and who lived in times when the Chancellor was expected to act according to his own notions of justice, without regard to rule or precedent.

A story was afterwards circulated, that when the Great Seal was brought from Lord Bacon to King James, he exclaimed: " Now, by my soul, I am pained at the heart where to bestow this; for as to my lawyers, I think they be all knaves."[1] But this saying is quite apocryphal, and, if genuine, would equally have justified the appointment of the Dean of Westminster to be Chief Justice of the King's Bench or Common Pleas. We may rest assured that James was very little consulted upon the occasion, and that Buckingham, in this outrageous act, considered only what would best suit his own arbitrary schemes for governing the country.

A serious difficulty immediately arose about the installation of the new Lord Keeper. It was now Easter Term, and he ought forthwith to have taken his place in the Court of Chancery; but an apprehension was entertained that, from his gross ignorance of all that was to be done there, he might make some ludicrous blunders, so as to stir the indignation not only of the suitors and the lawyers, but of the House of Commons,—a body now regarded with considerable awe. After much deliberation it was resolved, on Williams's own suggestion, that the Great Seal should remain in commission till the commencement of the long vacation. " Thus popular discourse, inclining much to descant upon this matter, would spend

[1] Parkes on Court of Ch. p. 93.

itself away in two or three months, and, as it were, boiled from a pint to a spoonful. It was further looked into that he might have respite to study the weight and trust of the office, whereby to supply it with that skill as might in candor be expected from a beginner."[1]

The Lord Keeper elect actually began with immense vigor the study of the law. He had for preceptor Sir Harry Finch, whom he kept in his lodgings for six months following, working with him night and day. In the meanwhile, to add to his dignity, he was made a Privy Councillor, and appointed to the see of Lincoln.

Parliament being prorogued,—Trinity Term being over, —and all the causes which stood for hearing being disposed of by the Commissioners,—on the 10th of July the King ordered the Great Seal to be brought to him at Whitehall, and a document being sealed with it merely by his own order, to assert a right to use it without the intervention of any responsible officer,[2] he seated himself on his throne. The Prince of Wales and the great officers of state being present, his Majesty then called the Dean of Westminster, who knelt down, and he delivered the Great Seal to him as Lord Keeper,—with an eloquent oration on the integrity, industry and zeal requisite for duly discharging the duties of the office.[3]

When Williams had received the Great Seal into his hands, still remaining on his bended knees, he delivered this address, ascribing his promotion to the miraculous interposition of Heaven.

"Most dreaded and mighty Sovereign, if I should think myself any way worthy or sufficient for this great place wherein your Majesty is pleased to make probation of me, I were the most unworthy and insufficient wretch in all the world. But, in good faith, I do not: But as conscious of mine own weakness, as I am quite astonished at your favor and goodness, I do not therefore trouble my head to find out the reason of this advancement; because I take it for no ordinary effect, but an extraordinary miracle. *Deus et qui Deo proximus, tacito munera dispertit arbitrario, et beneficiorum suorum indignatus per homines*

---

[1] Hacket, 59, 60.
[2] The Cl. R. says, "Mos enim iste venit in consuetudinem."
[3] "Et postquam elegantissimam, gravissimam, prudentissimam, et plane Nestoream oracionem de officio, integritate, sedulitate, et industria in custode sigilli requirenda," &c.—Cl. R. 19 Jac. 1.

stare judicium, mavult de subditis dedisse Miraculum. I must only lift up mine eyes unto Heaven, and beseech that God, who, some ten years since, brought me, like Elisha, to be servant only unto that Elias, who under God and your Majesty was the chariot and horsemen of our Israel, that now he would be pleased to double the spirit of Elias upon his servant Elisha, whom your Majesty hath thus invested with his robe and mantle." After twaddling at considerable length about his being "only a probationer"—"not a keeper, but a suitor only for the Great Seal"—he proceeds, "*Non ut me consulem, sed ut consulatus candidatum putem.* And if I feel the burden too heavy (which I mightily fear and suspect), I will choose rather *desinere quam deficere*, to slip it off willingly to some stronger shoulder than to be crushed in pieces with the poise. I will say unto your Majesty, as Jacob said unto Pharaoh, *Pastor ovium est servus tuus.* I am but a keeper of sheep: in that calling your Majesty found me, and to that calling I shall ever be ready to appropriate myself again. In the mean time, I beseech your Majesty to protect this Court of Justice wherein you have placed me, that the strength and power of the body be nothing impaired through the weakness of the head. *Nemo adolescentiam meam contemnat.* And so I end with my prayer unto God that your Majesty may live long, and myself no longer than I may be serviceable to your Majesty."[1]

His Majesty graciously replied that he was as well satisfied with this appointment as any he had ever made, and he was persuaded that his judgment would not be deceived.[2]

Ever with a keen eye to his own interest, the Lord Keeper in addition to his new ecclesiastical dignity, retained *in commendam* his living of Waldegrave, his differ-

---

[1] Hacket, 61, 62. The Cl. R. thus describes this part of the ceremony: "Dns Custos pred. sig. a regiis manibus plane augustissimis mirabundus accipiens brevem et humilissimam orationem huic regiam benignitatem obstupescens extulit propriam tenuitatem et infanciam agnovit se a strepitu forensi abhorrentem et in civilibus hisce occupationibus plane peregrim professus est nec abstinere posse se dixit quin illud augustissimo Regi in mentem revocet quod Jacob olim Pharaoni Pastor ovium est servus tuus. Postremo hoc voto et observacione sermonem finivit Quod si onus hoc (alii honorem vocant) suis humeris (quod valde veritus est) impar usu expiret veniam daret serenissima Majestas ut hoc officio se sponte abdicaret et desinere pocius quam deficere eligeret."   [2] Hacket, 62.

ent prebends, and the Deanery of Westminster. For this last piece of preferment there were many applicants, and he had a hard struggle for it; but he prevailed by representing that "if he were deprived of it, he must be provided with an official house at the public expense; that he had supplies to his housekeeping from the College, in bread, beer, corn, and fuel, of which, if he should be deprived, he must be forced to call for a diet which would cost the King £1,600 *per annum*, or crave for some addition in lieu thereof out of the King's own means, as all his foregoers in the office had done; and it was but a step from thence into Westminster Hall, where his business lay, and it was a lodging which afforded him marvelous quietness to turn over his papers and to serve the King."

Succeeding in keeping all his preferments, a jest was circulated against him, "that he was a perfect diocese in his own person, being at once Bishop, Dean, Prebendary, and Parson.

To soften envy, he gave out that he was *bonâ fide* likely to resign the Great Seal very soon, and that, at all events, he could not possibly hold it more than three years, as, upon his suggestion, the King had laid down an inflexible rule that in all time coming, no one should ever be permitted to be Lord Keeper or Lord Chancellor for a more extended period.

The long vacation being spent in severe study, the first day of Michaelmas term arrived, and he was to take his seat in the Court of Chancery. According to ancient custom, he ought to have rode to Westminster Hall in grand procession. Out of affected humility he declined this pomp, perhaps having a certain misgiving that the lawyers from the Inns of Court would not very eagerly join it, and that the nobility might not very willingly follow in the train of a *parvenu* as yet so little distinguished. Some supposed that, from being so severe a student, he was not an expert horsemen, and that he had apprehensions of being spilt by the way. He summoned the Judges, who were under his control, to meet him at an early hour in the morning at the deanery,—saying that he declined all other attendance. With them he passed through the cloisters into the Abbey, and so on to Henry VII.'s chapel.[1] There he fell down on his knees, and re-

[1] "Cumque ibi in celeberrimo Hen sept. sacello preces et crationes publi

mained in secret devotion for a quarter of an hour, praying for enlightenment to perform the duties of his new office. Then rising up cheerfully, as if he had received a favorable answer to his petition, he walked at the head of the twelve Judges, and with no other train, across Palace Yard and entered at the North Gate of Westminster Hall, where curiosity had collected a great multitude of all degrees.

After the oaths had been administered to him he delivered a very long oration, of which I can only afford to give some of the more remarkable passages: "My Lords and Gentlemen all, I would to God my former course of life had so qualified me for this great place, (wherein, by the will of God and the special favor of the King, I am for a time to bestow myself), that I might have fallen to my business without any further preface or salutation. For my own part, I am as far from affecting this speech as I was from the ambition of this place. But having found by private experience that sudden and unexpected eruptions put all the world into a gaze and wonderment, I thought it most convenient to break the ice with this short deliberation which I will limit to these two heads, my calling and my carriage in this place of judicature." He goes on to explain how he came to be appointed, in a manner not very flattering to his legal auditors:—"A resolution was formed to change or reduce the Governor of this Court from a professor of our municipal laws to some one of the nobility, gentry, or clergy of this kingdom. Of such a conclusion of state *(Quæ aliquando incognita semper justa)* as I dare not take upon me to discover the cause, so I hope I shall not endure the envy."

cas et privatas effudisset Aulam Westm., &c., propriis tantum famulis stipatus ingressus est. Ibi autem Dno custode circa horam nonam ante meridianam in Cur. Canc. sellam et tribunal conscenso [he takes the oaths]. Et cum pre consuetudine et more loci illustrissimum Dam Presidentem Mag. Rot. reliquosque prime forme clericos sive cancel. magros salutasset proprio loco considit. Et cum de Curiæ istius scitis et plitis ad prescriptum Regni emendandis et corrigendis et aliis rebus haud dissimilibus oraeoem bene longam huisset Dno Presidenti humanissime valedixit officiariis ut sigillarent mandavit et se interim ad jurisconsultorum quesit. audiend. simul et terminand. placide composuit."—Cl. R. 19 Jac. This is the last specimen of Close Roll Latinity in the history of the Great Seal—all the subsequent entries being in English.

[1] On this passage Coleridge in a note passes the following just censure: "This perversion of words respecting the decrees of Providence to the caprices of James and his beslobbered minion, the Duke of Buckingham, is somewhat nearer to blasphemy than even the euphuism of the age can excuse."

He suggests that "the just management of a Court of Equity might be impeded equally by too much as too little law, and that the most distinguished of his predecessors, excepting always the mirror of the age and glory of the profession, his reverend Master (Egerton), had the commendation of the completest men, but not of the deepest lawyers." He becomes bolder as he advances:[1]—"Again, it may be—the continual practice of the strict law, without a special mixture of other knowledge, makes a man unapt and indisposed for a Court of Equity. *Jurisconsultus ipse per se nihil nisi leguleius qui dam, cautus et acuctus,*—as much used to defend the wrong as to protect and maintain the most upright cause. And if any of them should prove corrupt, he carries about him *armatam neguitiam,*—that skill and cunning to palliate the same, so that the missentence which, pronounced by a plain and understanding man, would appear most gross and palpable, by their colors, quotations, and wrenches of the law, would be made to pass for current and specious. He points out the disadvantage of a Chancellor having to decide the causes of his former clients, "who to-day have for their Judge him who yesterday was their hired advocate," and he plainly insinuates (though he professes to disclaim) the imputation, "that a proneness to take bribes may be generated from the habit of taking fees." He concludes this head with a clumsy attempt at palliation:—" These reasons, though they please some men, yet, God be praised, if we do but right to this noble profession, they are in our commonwealth no way concluding or demonstrative. For I make no question but there are many scores which profess our laws, who, beside their skill and practice in this kind, are so richly enabled in all moral and intellectual endowments, *ut omnia tanquam singula perficiant,* that there is no Court of Equity in the world but might be most safely committed unto them. With respect to himself he affects a mixture of humility and confidence:— " Surely if a sincere, upright, and well-meaning heart doth not cover thousands of other imperfections, I am the unfittest man in the kingdom to supply the place; and

[1] If Sir E. Coke was present, his feelings must have been mixed—his hatred of Bacon being at last satiated, but his regard for the honor of the profession cruelly wounded.

therefore must say of my creation as the poet said of the creation of the world,—*Materiam noli quærere, nulla fuit.* Trouble not your head to find out the cause. I confess there was none at all. It was without the least inclination or thought of mine own (?)—the immediate work of God and the King, and *their* actions are no ordinary *effects*, but extraordinary *miracles.*"[1] From this miraculous touch he becomes as courageous as a lion:— "What then? Should I beyond the limits and duty of obedience despond and refuse to make some few years' trial in this place? *Non habeo ingenium, Cæsar sed jussit, habebo. Cur me posse negem, posse quod ille putet?* I am no way fit for this great place, but because God and the King will have it so, I will endeavor as much as I can to make myself fit, and place my whole confidence in his grace and mercy,—*Qui neminem dignum eligit, sed eligendo dignum facit.*" He then goes on with better taste to confess his disadvantage in coming after two such men as Egerton and Bacon,—" one of them excelling in most things,—the other in all things,—both of them so bred in this course of life, *ut illis plurimarum rerum agitatio frequens nihil esse ignotum patiebatur;*" adding rather felicitously, "My comfort is this, that arriving here as a stranger, I may say, as Archimedes did when he found geometrical lines and angles drawn every where in the sands of Egypt, *Video vestigia humana,* I see in this Court the footsteps of wise men, many excellent rules and orders which though I might want learning and knowledge to invent, I hope I shall not want honesty to act upon." He next lays down certain principles by which he is to be governed, professing great respect for the common law, and laughing at the equitable doctrine, " that sureties are to be favored;" for, says he, " When the money is to be borrowed, the surety is the first in the intention, and therefore if it be not paid let him a God's name be the first in the execution." He thus not ungracefully concluded:—" I will propound my old master for my pattern and precedent in all things— beseeching Almighty God so to direct me that while I hold this place I may follow him by a true and constant imitation; and if I prove unfit, that I may not play the

[1] There can be nothing more revolting than the language of English divines during the seventeenth century, who frequently put the King nearly, if not altogether, on a footing with Almighty God.

mountebank so in this place as to abuse the King and the state, but follow the same most worthy Lord in his cheerful and voluntary resignation, *Sic mihi contingat vivere, sicque mori.*" [1]

CHAPTER LVIII.

CONTINUATION OF THE LIFE OF LORD KEEPER WILLIAMS TILL THE END OF THE REIGN OF JAMES I.

THE Lord Keeper now set to work with stupendous energy and with consummate discretion. By incessant reading and conversation with Finch and the officers of the Court, he had got some little insight into its rules and practice; he never sat in public without the assistance of the Master of the Rolls, or some of the Common-law Judges supposed to be most familiar with equity; and although he ostensibly delivered the judgment, he took care to be decorously prompted by those on whom he could rely.

In spite of his great caution he could not avoid sometimes misapplying technical terms, and causing a titter among the lawyers, who viewed him with no favor.[2] One morning, when his Honor, the Master of the Rolls, who had been expected, was by sudden illness detained at home, a wag at the bar had the impudence to attempt a practical joke upon the Right Reverend the Lord Keeper. When called to, the wicked counsellor rose demurely, and pretending to look at his brief, made a sham motion,— which seems to have been somewhat like that mentioned in the Life of Lord Eldon, for a writ,—" *Quare adhæsit pavimento.*" The exact terms of this motion are not mentioned by any Reporter, but we are told on undoubted authority that it was " crammed like a grenade with obsolete words, coins of far-fetched antiquity, which had been long disused, worse than Sir Thomas More's " *An averia carucæ capta in withernam sint irreplegiabilia.*"

---

[1] Hacket. 71-74.
[2] Hacket explains their dislike of him into envy, comparing them to " Joseph's brethren, who hated the very dream of a sheaf to which they must do obeysance."—p. 60.

With these misty and recondite phrases he thought to leave the new Judge groping about in the dark." Williams discovered the trick, and, notwithstanding his Welsh blood, he preserved his temper. "With a serious face the Lord Keeper answered him in a cluster of most crabbed notions picked out of metaphysics and logic, as "*categorematical*" and "*syncategorematical*," and a deal of such drumming stuff, that the motioner, being foiled at his own weapon, and well laughed at in the Court, went home with this new lesson—*that he that tempts a wise man in jest shall make himself a fool in earnest*."[1]

The account we have of his industry shames the most industrious men of this degenerate age. He entered the Court of Chancery in the winter time by candle-light between six and seven o'clock in the morning. Having sat there two hours, he went to the House of Lords between eight and nine, where the Prince and the Peers were assembled, expecting him to take his place on the woolsack. There he continued propounding and discussing the questions which arose till twelve at noon, every day, and when there was a late debate, till past one in the afternoon. Going to the Deanery, he refreshed himself with a short repast, and then returned to the Court of Chancery to hear petitions and causes which he had not been able to dispatch in the morning. Coming home about eight in the evening he perused such letters and papers as his secretaries had prepared for him,—and after that, far in the night, he prepared himself for so much as concerned him to have in readiness for the Lords' House in the morning. His attendances in the Star Chamber and at the council-table did not interfere with the business of the Court of Chancery,—where he always attended two hours early in the morning before going elsewhere. He is said to have decided five or six causes in a morning, according to the quality and measure of the points that came to be debated in them, and that he might make others industrious and punctual like himself, two or three afternoons in every week he had a peremptory paper consisting of cases that had been long depending, and that he himself appointed to be heard at all events, and, if possible, finally disposed of. He is a striking instance of what may be accomplished without genius by industry. "Industry, I think," says

[1] Hacket, 75.

his secretary, " was his recreation,—for certain he had not a drop of lazy blood in his veins. He filled up every hour of the day, and a good part of the night with the dispatch of some public and necessary business."[1]

Thus energetic and thus assisted, notwithstanding his inexperience and ignorance as a Judge, he got on marvelously well, and all the causes, petitions, and motions were disposed of without any public clamor. As yet the proceedings in Chancery were not reported, precedent not being considered binding there, as in other Courts, and none of his decisions have been preserved to us. But as there were several sessions of parliament while he held the Great Seal, and there does not appear to have been any complaint against him except in one instance, which was without foundation,[2] we are bound to believe that, in spite of all the objections reasonably made to his appointment, he gave satisfaction to the public.[3]

At all events he satisfied himself. On the 10th of July, 1622, the anniversary of his receiving the Seal, he thus wrote to Buckingham. " In this place I have now served his Majesty one whole year diligently and honestly. But to my heart's grief, by reason of my rawness and inexperience, very unprofitably. Yet, if his Majesty will examine the registers, there will be found more causes finally ended this one year than in all the seven years preceding. How well ended, I ingenuously confess, I know not. His Majesty and your Lordship (who, no doubt, have received some complaints, though in your love you conceal them from me) are in that the most competent judges."

He and his friends suggested that it was by some sort of miraculous influence that he performed so well; but the miracle is solved in his judiciously availing himself of the knowledge and skill of others. His assessors may truly be considered the Lords Commissioners of the Great Seal while he held it; and his great merit was, that he steadily kept them to their work.

He seems from his own resources to have done his duty creditably in the House of Lords. Parliament met in November, 1621. He had then to address the two Houses, in the absence of the King, who was indisposed. This

---

[1] Hacket, 76.   [2] Sir John Bouchier's case, post.
[3] *Quod nemo noverit bene non fit.*

speech was well seasoned with divine right and passive obedience, and we have this account of it in a letter written to him next day by Buckingham. "I know not how the Upper House of Parliament approve your Lordship's speech. But I am sure he that called them together, and as I think can best judge of it, is so taken with it, that he saith it is the best that ever he heard in Parliament, and the nearest to his Majesty's meaning; which, beside the contentment it hath given to his Majesty, hath much comforted me in his choice of your Lordship, which in all things doth so well answer his expectation."[1]

But the speech excited violent murmurs against the speaker and the whole order to which he belonged. A few days after, during a protracted debate respecting oaths, an aged Bishop, very infirm in health, begged permission to withdraw,—which then seems to have been necessary before a member could be absent from the division. Thereupon several Lords, who are said to have "borne a grudge to that apostolic order," cried out, that "they might all go home if they would;" and the Earl of Essex, the future leader of the parliamentary army,—then a hot-headed young man who had just taken his seat,— make a formal motion, which he required to be put from the woolsack and entered on the journals, "that their Lordships were content to open their doors wide to let out all Bishops." The Lord Keeper, who perceived that this blow was aimed at himself, "replied with a *prudent animosity*, that he would not put the question even if commanded by the House, for their Lordships, as well spiritual as temporal, were called by the King's writ to sit and abide there till the same power dissolved them, and for my Lords temporal, they had no power to license themselves, much less to authorize others to depart from the Parliament." This spirited conduct quelled the disturbance, and the debate was allowed quietly to proceed; but Williams lived to see the day when he ineffectually opposed a bill for preventing the Bishops from sitting in the House of Lords, and he had the mortification to find that this bill, after passing both Houses, received the royal assent.

The only other proceeding in which he was personally

[1] 1 Parl. Hist. 1295.

concerned during this session, was upon a petition presented to the House of Lords by Sir John Bouchier, complaining that he had given judgment against the petitioner in the Court of Chancery without allowing his counsel to speak. The case was heard for several days at the bar,—when it turned out that the complaint was entirely unfounded, as, after ample discussion, the decree had been pronounced on the advice of the Master of the Rolls, Mr. Justice Hutton, and Mr. Justice Chamberlayne.

The Lords determined that, for this false charge against the Lord Keeper, Sir John Bouchier should be imprisoned, and that he should make an acknowledgment in their House, and in Chancery, of his faults. But the Lord Keeper saying that Sir John had behaved temperately in Chancery, besought a remission of the acknowledgment of his fault in that Court, and also of his imprisonment. The Lords highly commended the Lord Keeper's clemency, and remitted both. Then Sir John being brought to the bar, and his acknowledgment, ready drawn up, being delivered to him, he kneeling, said, " My Lords, in obedience to the judgment of this House, I humbly submit myself. Whereas by the honorable sentence of the Lords spiritual and temporal, I stand convicted of a great misdemeanor, for taxing and laying an imputation on the Lord Keeper of the Great Seal of England, I do in all humbleness acknowledge the justice of their sentence, and also my own fault and offense, and am heartily sorry therefor, and do crave pardon both of your Lordships in general, and of the Lord Keeper in particular."[1]—On account of a quarrel with the House of Commons this parliament was soon after dissolved by proclamation; and by an order of Council, in which the Lord Keeper concurred, Sir Edward Coke, Sir Robert Phillips, Mr. Selden, Mr. Prynne, and several other leaders of the opposition party were committed to prison.

About this time he was instrumental in the promotion of a man who afterwards turned out to be his greatest enemy. Buckingham wished to appoint Laud, one of the King's chaplains, whom he had found very useful on several occasions, to the Bishopric of St. David's; but most unexpectedly James demurred, on account of some

---

[1] 1 Parl. Hist. 1364.

trouble caused to him from the ultra high church principles of this divine, in attempting to introduce episcopacy into Scotland. The Lord Keeper seeking to remove these scruples, the King said to him : " I perceive whose messenger you are; *Stenny* hath set you on. The plain truth is, that I keep Laud back from all place of rule and authority, because I find he hath a restless spirit, and can not see when matters are well, but loves to toss and change, and to bring things to a pitch of reformation floating in his own brain. I speak not at random; he hath made himself known to me to be such a one." The Lord Keeper allowed that this was a great fault, which might make *Laud* to be lightened to *Caius Gracchus qui nihil immotum, nihil tranquillum, nihil quietum, nihil denique in eodem statu relinquebat;*—but undertook that it should be cured in time to come. " Then take him," said the King, " but on my *saul*, you will repent it."

We now come to an affair in which Williams acted an exceedingly ungenerous part. Abbot, Archbishop of Canterbury, when shooting at a deer with a cross-bow, had accidently killed a keeper in Lord Zouch's park. Williams, on hearing of this calamity, instead of eagerly assisting in averting its consequences, and comforting the afflicted metropolitan, thought it an opportunity of raising himself to the highest ecclesiastical as well as civil dignity, and wrote the following mean and cunning letter to be laid before the King:

" My Lord's Grace, upon this accident, is, by the common law of England, to forfeit all his estate to his Majesty, and by the canon law, which is in force with us, ' *irregular*' *ipso facto*, and so suspended from all ecclesiastical function, until he be again restored by his superior, which, I take it, is the King's Majesty in this rank and order of ecclesiastical jurisdiction. I wish with all my heart, his Majesty would be as merciful as ever he was in all his life. But yet I hold it my duty to let his Majesty know, that his Majesty is fallen upon a matter of great advice and deliberation. To add affliction to the afflicted, as no doubt he is in mind, is against the King's nature. To leave a man of blood, Primate and Patriarch of all his churches, is a thing that sounds very harsh in the old councils and canons of the Church. The Papists will not spare to descant upon the one and the other. I leave the knot to his Majesty's deep wisdom to advise and resolve upon."

The Archbishop's friends quoted the maxims, "*Actus non facit reum, nisi mens sit rea,*" and "*omne peccatum in tantum est peccatum in quantum est voluntarium ;*" and it being argued against him, that if one acting *in indebitâ materiâ* kills a man involuntarily, it is to be gathered that God gave him up to that mischance, that he might be disciplined by the censure of the church,—they replied, that hunting was no unpriestly sport by the laws of England,—for every Peer in the higher House of Parliament, as well Lords spiritual and temporal, hath permission by the *Charta de Foresta,* when, after summons, he is on his journey to parliament, and travels through the King's forests, to cause a horn to be sounded, and to kill a brace of bucks for his sustentation.

To decide this knotty point, a commission was directed to ten Bishops, common-law Judges, and civilians—the Lord Keeper being chief commissioner. They were equally divided on the question, " whether the Archbishop was '*irregular*' by the fact of involuntary homicide?" But a majority held that " the act might tend to a scandal in a churchman," the Lord Keeper on both questions, voting against the Archbishop.

This intrigue was counteracted by the general sympathy in favor of the Archbishop,—and the King in due form, " assoiled him from all *irregularity*, scandal, or infamation, pronouncing him to be capable to use all metropolitical authority as if that sinistrous contingency of spilling blood had never happened."

The Lord Keeper's consecration as Bishop of Lincoln had been delayed by these proceedings,—and now, from disappointment and spleen, under pretense that the efficacy of the Archbishop's ministration might still be questioned, he obtained a license from the King that he might still be consecrated by the Bishops of London, Worcester, Ely, Oxford, and Llandaff.[1]

The following year was memorable by the romantic journey of the Prince and Buckingham to Spain. While at Madrid, Charles, to please his mistress and the Spanish Court, wrote a letter to the Lord Keeper, praying that he would do all in his power to mitigate the execution of the

[1] 2 St. Tr. 1160.

penal laws against Roman Catholics, to which the following courtly answer was returned:—

"I would I had any abilities to serve your Highness in this place wherein you have set me, and your grace and favor have countenanced and encouraged me. To observe your Highness's commands, I am sure the Spanish ambassador resiant must testify, that since your Highness's departure he hath been denied no one request for expedition of justice or care of Catholics, although I usually hear from him twice or thrice a week; which I observe the more superstitiously, that he might take knowledge how sensible we are of any honor done to your Highness. And yet, in the relaxation of the Roman Catholic penalties, I keep off the King from appearing in it as much as I can, and take all upon myself, as I believe every servant of his ought to do in such negotiations, the events whereof be hazardous and uncertain."[1]

The town was meanwhile amused by a call of Sergeants, a memorable event in those days. No fewer than thirteen jointly received the honor of the coif, and the Lord Keeper addressed them in a very long and tedious speech, which he thus sought to enliven: "Your great and sumptuous feast is like that of a King's coronation, at which you entertain the ambassadors of foreign Kings now resident about the city, and the prime officers and nobility of this realm. King Henry VII., in his own person, did grace the Sergeants' feast, held then at Ely Place, in Holborn, I should be too long if I should speak of the ornament

---

[1] The high church party afterwards invented a story that at this time the Lord Keeper wished to be reconciled to the Church of Rome, and through Buckingham's interest at the Court of Spain, to be made a cardinal. In the autograph MS. of Robert, Earl of Leicester, preserved in the British Museum, there is the following entry: "Att Yorke, 29th April, 1639. Being at dinner, at Sir John Melton's, where I lay, L.d Chamberlain, the Earle of Holland present (but I thinke he heard it not), Mr. Endymion Porter, Groome of y.e Bedchamber, told me that he knewe the Bp. of Lincolne, Williams, since Archb.p of Yorke (then in trouble), when he was in favor, and L.d Keeper w.d have bin a Cardinall, and made all the meanes he could to attaine unto it, by my Lorde of Buckingham's power, during the treaty of the match with Spaine; at which time Porter was the D. of Buckingham's servant, and in greate favor with him. 'This,' sayd Porter, 'is true upon my knowledge, or else God refuse me! and I wish this piece of bread may choke me, which I hope you believe I would not say if I did not know it!' One may see by this what an excellent conscience that Byshop hath who w.d have bin a Cardinall; while he was in favor nothing els would satisfie his ambition; and, being in disgrace, he betakes himself to the Puritan party."—Blencowe's Sydney Papers, p. 261.

of your head, your pure linen coif, which evidences that you are candidates of higher honor. So likewise your *librata magna*, your abundance of cloth and liveries, your *purple habits* belonging anciently to great senators, yea, to emperors ; all these and more are but as so many flags and ensigns to call up those young students that fight in the valleys to those hills and mountains of honor which you by your merits have now achieved.

———" 'Neque enim virtutem amplectimur ipsam,
Præmia si tollas.'"

But more serious scenes were at hand. On Buckingham's return from Spain, he found that the Lord Keeper and Cranfield, the Lord Treasurer, created Earl of Middlesex, had been intriguing against him in his absence, and had been trying to supplant him in the King's favor. Having re-established his ascendency he vowed revenge, and trusting to the popularity he contrived to gather from breaking off the Spanish match, he resolved to call a parliament, and he managed to get a number of petitions ready to be presented to the two Houses, charging the Treasurer and the Lord Keeper respectively with malversation in their offices. Williams, excessively alarmed, eagerly sought for a reconciliation with Buckingham, solicited the intercession of the Prince before parliament actually assembled, made his submission in person to the haughty chief, and received this cold yet consolatory answer, "I will not seek your ruin, though I shall cease to study your fortune."

The meeting of parliament was postponed for a week by the sudden death of the Duke of Lennox, the Lord Steward. As the royal procession was about to move from Whitehall to the House of Peers, "The King looked round and missed him," says Bishop Hacket; "he was absent indeed; absent from the body and present with God." The Lord Keeper preached his funeral sermon to the admiration of the Court, from the text, "Zabud, the son of Nathan, was principal officer, and the King's friend."[2]

[1] On which Jekyll made the following epigram :—
"The sergeants are a grateful race,
  Their dress and speeches show it,
Their purple robes *from Tyre* we trace
  Their arguments go *to it*."

[2] 1 Kings, iv. 5. This union of duties reminds me of a question put to

At last, on the 19th of February, 1624, the King, seated on his throne, delivered a long speech to the two Houses, explaining to them what had happened during the two years when there had been no parliament, particularly respecting the Palatinate and his son's marriage,—desiring them in the words of St. Paul, to "beware of genealogies and curious questions, and not to let any stir them up to law questions, debates, quirks, tricks, and jerks."[1]

According to the usage of the age, the Lord Keeper ought to have followed in the same strain; but he thus excused himself: "A Lacedemonian being invited to hear a man that could counterfeit very well the notes of a nightingale, put him off with these words, αυτης ηκουσα, I have heard the nightingale herself. And why should you be troubled with the croaking of a Chancellor that have heard the loving expressions of a most eloquent King? And indeed, for me to gloss upon his Majesty's speech were nothing else than it is in the Satyr, *Annulum aureum ferreis stellis ferruminare,* to enamel a ring of pure gold with stars of iron. I know his Majesty's grave and weighty sentences have left, as Æschines's orations were wont to do, το κεντρον, a kind of freck or sting in the hearts and minds of all the hearers. It is not fit that, with my rude fumbling, I should unsettle or discompose his elegancies. For, as Pliny observes of Nerva, that when he had adopted the Emperor Trajan, he was taken away forthwith, and never did any public act after it, *ne post illud divinum et immortale factum aliquid mortale faceret,* lest, after so transcendent and divine an act, he should commit any thing might relish of mortality; so it is fit that the judicious ears of these noble hearers be no further troubled this day, *nequid post illud divinum et immortale dictum mortale audirent.*" He therefore confined himself to desiring the Commons to retire and choose a Speaker.[2]

Sergeant Crewe being presented as Speaker on a subsequent day, and having disqualified himself, the Lord Keeper said "His Majesty doth observe that in you,

---

Mr. Justice Buller, who used often to sit for Lord Chancellor Thurlow:—"When do you preach for the Archbishop of Canterbury?" Thurlow used to say: "Buller knows no more of equity than a horse, but he gets through the causes, and I hear no more of them."

[1] 1 Parl. Hist. 1373.   [2] 1 Parl. Hist. 1378. Hacket, i. 175.

which Gorgias the philosopher did in Plato, *quod in oratoribus irridendis ipse esse orator summus videbatur.*"[1]

The Speaker then delivered a very long speech to the King, and the Lord Keeper, after having conferred a quarter of an hour with his Majesty, answered it at equal length, saying, among many things equally fine, "You have heard his Majesty's similie touching a skillful horseman, which in Zechariah is God's similie. Kings are like riders; the commonwealth is the horse, and the law is the bridle, which must be held always with a sure hand, not always with a hard hand; but *aliquando remittit ferire eques non amittat habenas.* Yet if Hagar grow insolent, 'cast out the bondswoman and her son;' his Majesty's resolution is. 'that the son of the bondswoman shall never inherit with the son of the free.'" He concludes with a compliment to Buckingham, the Lord High Admiral, whom he feared much more than him he so profanely likened to the Divinity. "The wooden walls of this kingdom, the navy, are truly his Majesty's special care; and as the carver who beautified Diana's temple, though it was at the cost of other men, yet was allowed in divers places to stamp his own name, so it can not be denied but that noble Lord who has now spent seven years' study, and has become a master in that art, may grave his name upon his works, yet a fitting distance from his master's."[2]

The petitions against the Lord Keeper as well as against the Lord Treasurer were presented; but the former by the great zeal he displayed both in a committee and in the full House in supporting Buckingham about the negotiations with Spain, earned and received forgiveness,—although a suspicion of his fidelity remained which led to his dismissal early in the next reign. Middlesex being more stubborn, and foolishly trusting in his own innocence, was made a present victim to the resentment of the favorite.

He was impeached on charges of peculation and corruption,[3] which were imperfectly established, and he was not allowed the benefit of counsel, although several eminent lawyers, members of the House of Commons,

---

[1] "Swift for the ANCIENTS has reason'd so well,
'Tis apparent from hence that the MODERNS excel."
[2] 1 Parl Hist. 1379.   [3] 2 St. Tr. 1184, 1245.

conducted the prosecution against him. Being found guilty, the Lord Keeper, the associate in his real offense, pronounced sentence against him, "that he should lose all his offices, should thereafter be incapable to hold any office, place or employment, should be imprisoned in the Tower during the King's pleasure, should pay a fine of £50,000., should be disqualified to sit in parliament, and should never come within the verge of the Court."[1]

But the Lord Keeper, not quite sure when his own turn might come,—under color of compassionating the hardships of which Middlesex had complained in his trial, prevailed on the Lords to pass a resolution, that in all subsequent impeachments for misdemeanor the accused should be furnished with copies of the depositions, and should be allowed the aid of counsel.[2]

The petitions against the Lord Keeper were suffered to lie dormant till the end of the session, when the Committee to whom they were referred reported, "that of those which had been examined some were groundless in fact, and the others furnished no matter for a criminal charge." Morley, one of the petitoners, who had complained of the Lord Keeper for some indirect practice against him in the Star Chamber, and had printed and circulated his petition, was committed to the Fleet, fined £1,000, ordered to stand in the pillory with a copy of the petition on his head, and to make acknowledgment of his fault to the Lord Keeper at the bar of the House and in the Court of Chancery.[3]

Williams regained, to a certain degree, the good graces of Buckingham, by skillfully discovering and counteracting a plot against him. Ynoiosa and Coloma, the Spanish ambassadors, having been long carefully prevented from having any personal communication with the King, at last contrived to deliver to him privately a letter, describing him as a prisoner in his own palace, and offering to communicate important information to him. In consequence, Carendolet, the secretary of legation, was admitted to a secret interview with James, and stated

---

[1] When this sentence was exultingly reported to the King by Buckingham and the Prince, who had procured it, he prophetically said to the one, "You are making a rod for your own breech;" and to the other, "You will yet live to have your bellyful of impeachments."

[2] Lords' Journals.   [3] 1 Parl. Hist. 1399.

several things which made so deep an impression on his mind, that his manner to Buckingham was visibly altered. The Prince, at Buckingham's suggestion, came early one morning from Windsor to the House of Lords before prayers, and taking the Lord Keeper aside, acknowledged his past services, and said, "You may receive greater thanks of us both, if you will spread open that black contrivance which hath lost him the good opinion of my father, and myself am in little better condition." "The curtain of privacy," answered the Lord Keeper, "is drawn before the picture that I can not guess at the colors." "Well, my Lord," said the Prince, "I expected better service from you; for if that be the picture drawer's shop, no councilor in this kingdom is better acquainted than yourself with the works and the workmen." "I might have been," says the Keeper; "and I am panged like a woman in travail till I know what misshapen creature they are drawing." He then intimated that he knew so much, that the Spanish secretary of legation had had a private interview with the King; and being pressed by the Prince to state how he came by this information, he observed: "Another, perhaps, would blush when I tell you *with what heifer I plow;* but knowing mine innocency, the worst that can happen is to expose myself to be laughed at. Don Francisco Carendolet loves me because he is a scholar: he is Archdeacon of Cambray. Sometimes we are pleasant together. I have discovered him to be a wanton, and a servant to some of our English beauties, but, above all, to one of that gentle craft in Mark Lane. A wit she is, and one that must be courted with news and occurrences at home and abroad, as well as with gifts. I have a friend that hath bribed her in my name to send me a faithful conveyance of such tidings as her paramour Carendolet brings to her. And she hath well earned a piece of plate or two from me, and shall not be unrecompensed for this service about which your Highness doth use me, if the drab can help me in it. Truly, Sir, this is my dark-lantern, and I am not ashamed to inquire of a Delilah to resolve a riddle; for in my studies of divinity I have gleaned up this maxim, *Licet uti alieno peccato.* Though the devil make her a sinner, I may make good use of her sin." "You!" says the Prince merrily, "do you deal in such ware?" "In good faith," exclaimed the Bishop, (and we are bound to believe him,) "I never saw her face."[1]

As soon as the House rose he set about gaining further information, but doubting whether more could be drawn from the lady, he resorted to the expedient of arresting a mass priest in Drury Lane, a particular friend of Carendolet, for whom it was certain he would interest himself. Accordingly the Secretary came to the Lord Keeper to sue for his friend's liberation, and was prevailed upon to disclose everything that had passed between him and the King. All this Williams communicated to Buckingham, who immediately went to the King, and with the Prince's assistance obtained a promise from him never more to confer with the Spanish ambassadors, and if they should attempt to renew their secret correspondence with him, to send them out of the kingdom.[2] Thus James was kept in subjection till his death.

The last time of his appearing on the throne was at the close of this session, when he delivered a very learned and elaborate answer to the address of the Speaker; and the Lord Keeper forgetting all he had said about "the true nightingale and the croaking of a Chancellor," delivered another equally learned and elaborate,—the chief object of which was to justify the King's refusal to pass certain bills. "Indeed," said he, "it is best for the people that this royal assent is in his Majesty, and not in themselves; for many times it falls out with the assent of Kings as it doth with God, for Almighty God many times does not grant those petitions we do ask. Now God and the King do imitate the physician, who knoweth how to fit his patients better than they do desire." He then gives the instances of Solomon refusing the petition of Bathsheba for Adonijah, and God refusing the petition of St. Paul to remove the prick of the flesh that was a hindrance to him in the performance of good things, but gave him grace —a better gift.[3]

After some compliments from James on the harmonious

---

[1] The Lord Keeper, who thus acted the part of Cicero in discovering Catiline's conspiracy, was famous for having a great number of spies and informers in his employment, from whom he gained much useful information, both domestic and foreign, and whom he is said to have paid very handsomely from his large ecclesiastical revenues

[2] Hardwicke Papers, vol. i. 460.

[3] 1 Parl. Hist. 1498.

close of the session, the Lord Keeper prorogued the Parliament, and it never met again under this Sovereign.

In the next Michaelmas term Williams had a fresh difference with Buckingham, who wished to turn him out, and tried to persuade Lord Chief Justice Hobart either to deliver to the King with his own mouth, or to set it under his hand, "that *Lord Williams*[1] was not fit for the Keeper's place because of his inabilites and ignorance,"— undertaking that Hobart should succeed him. But this great lawyer, either disinterested or sincere, or preferring to continue his repose on "the cushion of the Common Pleas," answered,—" My Lord, somewhat might have been said at the first, but he should do the Lord Williams great wrong that said so now."

In the following spring James was attacked by the ague, which, in spite of the adage with which the courtiers tried to comfort him,[2] carried him to his grave. The account of the closing scene by Hacket is creditable to all the parties he introduces. "After the Lord Keeper had presented himself before his Lord, the King, he moved him unto cheerful discourse, but it would not be. He continued till midnight at his bedside, and received no comfort; but was out of all comfort upon the consultation that the physicians held together in the morning. Presently he besought the Prince that he might acquaint his father with his feeble estate, and, like a faithful chaplain, mind him both of his mortality and immortality, which was allowed and committed to him as the principal instrument of that holy necessary service. So he went into the chamber of the King again upon that commission, and kneeling at his pallet told his Majesty, *he knew he should neither displease him nor discourage him if he brought Isaiah's message to Hezekiah to set his house in order, for he thought his days to come would be but few in this world, but the best remained for the next world.—I am satisfied, says the sick King, and I pray you assist me to make me ready to go away hence to Christ, whose mercies I call for and I hope to find them."*[3]

Williams, being soon after admitted, was constantly

---

[1] So he seems always to have been called while he held the Great Seal, as if he had been a layman.—*Hacket.*

[2] "An ague in the spring
Is physic for a King."

[3] Hacket, 223.

with him to the last,—administered the Holy communion to him—and when he expired closed his eyes with his own hand. He likewise preached his funeral sermon from the text, "Now the rest of the acts of Solomon, first and last, are they not written in the book of Nathan the prophet, and in the prophecy of Ahijah the Shilonite, and in the visions of Iddo the seer against Jeroboam the son of Nebat? And Solomon reigned in Jerusalem over all Israel forty years. And Solomon slept with his fathers, and he was buried in the city of David his father."[1] It would be unjust to judge this performance by the standard of the present age, and the parallel between the two Solomons is rather a proof of the bad taste in pulpit oratory prevailing in England in the beginning of the seventeenth century than of any peculiar servility or fulsomeness in Lord Keeper Williams.[2]

I ought now to take a retrospect of the changes in the law during the reign of James I.,—but under this head there is little to relate. His first parliament chiefly occupied itself in legislating against papists and witches, and regulating licenses to eat flesh in lent. No memorable law was introduced till the twenty-first year of his reign,—when monopolies were for ever put down, reserving the right, now so frequently exercised by the Crown, of granting patents for useful inventions,[3]—and the statute was passed which regulated prescriptions and the limitation of actions down to our own time.[4] The courts of common law were filled by very able Judges, many of whose decisions are still quoted as authority. Equity made some progress; but it was not yet regarded as a system of jurisprudence, and so little were decisions in Chancery considered binding as precedents, that they were very rarely reported, however important the question or learned the Judge.

We have seen how, after a violent struggle between Lord Coke and Lord Ellesmere, the Jurisdiction of the Court of Chancery to stay by injunction execution on judgments at law was finally established. In this reign the Court made another attempt,—which was speedily abandoned,—to determine upon the validity of wills,—

---

[1] 2 Chron. ix. 29–31.
[2] He printed the sermon under the title, "Great Britain's Solomon."
[3] 21 Jac. I, c. 3.   [4] 21 Jac. I, c. 16.

and it has been long settled that the validity of wills of real property shall be referred to courts of law, and the validity of wills of personal property to the Ecclesiastical Courts,—equity only putting a construction upon them when their validity has been established.[1]

We have the first instance in the reign of James I., of the exercise of a jurisdiction by the Court of Chancery, which has since been beneficially continued of granting writs *ne exeat regno*, by which debtors about to go abroad are obliged to give security to their creditors.[2]

Barrington says there must have been much business in the Court of Chancery while Lord Keeper Williams presided there, because fifteen Sergeants or Barristers of great eminence attended when he was invested with his high office; and Sir Edward Coke asserts in the debates in the House of Commons during the session of 1621, that in the time of Henry VI. no more than four hundred subpœnas issued one year with another out of the Chancery, whereas in the reign of James I. the number was not less than thirty-five thousand.[3]

CHAPTER LIX.

CONTINUATION OF LIFE OF LORD KEEPER WILLIAMS TILL HIS APPOINTMENT AS ARCHBISHOP OF YORK.

CHARLES having returned from Theobald's the evening of his father's death, next morning sent for the Lord Keeper Williams to St. James's, continued him in his office, employed him to swear in the Privy Councillors, and desired him to prepare two sermons, one for the funeral of the late King, and another for the coming coronation.[4] But Williams soon saw that his downfall was at hand, and before the coronation of Charles it was accomplished. The power of Buckingham was now, if possible, greater than it had been in the

[1] Toth. 286. Allen *v.* Macpherson, Dom. Proc. 1845.
[2] Toth. 233. [3] See Barr. on Stat. 404, 405.
[4] On this occasion the Seal was surrendered to Charles and delivered back by him to Williams as Lord Keeper, and a formal letter was written to him in the name of the new King, desiring him to use the old Seal till the new Seal was engraved.—Rot. Pat. 1 Car. n. 13.

late reign, and he was resolved to have a new Lord Keeper. He therefore took every opportunity of slighting and trying to disgust the present holder of the Seal, with a view to induce him to resign it; for it was then a very unusual thing forcibly to turn a man out of an office which he held, even during pleasure, without a charge of misconduct being judicially substantiated against him. The courtiers were quick-sighted enough to anticipate William's disgrace. "Laud, as soon as he saw that his advancer was under the anger of the Duke, would never acknowledge him more, but shunned him as the old Romans in their superstition walked aloof from that soil which was blasted with thunder."[1] However, as cold looks and rebuffs were preferred to voluntary resignation, it was necessary to wait till a decent pretext could be found for the change,—particularly after the *éclat* which the funeral sermon on the late King had conferred upon the preacher. Some thought that he would have objected to a proclamation for suspending the penal laws against Papists, but he put the Great Seal to it without remonstrance.

So impatient was Charles to have a supply, and so unconscious of what he was to suffer from popular assemblies, that he wished to continue the sitting of the last parliament, but he was told by the Lord Keeper that it was *ipso facto* dissolved by his father's death.

A new parliament summoned by him met on the 18th of June. Prayers were said in the presence of both Houses, while the King, uncovered, knelt at the throne. He then delivered a short speech, which has the appearance of being his own extempore composition.[2] But a labored oration followed from the Lord Keeper, urging a supply from the state of affairs in the Palatinate, in the Low Countries, and in Ireland, and inculcating loyalty on the maxim "*amor civium regis munimentum.*"

There was a much greater inclination in the Commons to inquire into grievances than to grant liberal supplies; and the plague breaking out in London,—at a council called to consider what ought to be done, a prorogation

---

[1] Hacket, part ii. 23.
[2] He begins by thanking God that the business to be treated requires no eloquence to set it forth: "for," says he, "I am neither able to do it, nor doth it stand with my nature to spend much time in words."

was proposed to Oxford, where it was thought the malcontents might be more manageable. This was strongly opposed by the Lord Keeper, who urged that when they came together there, they would vote out of discontent and displeasure, and that his Majesty was ill-counselled to give offense in the bud of his reign,—" quæ nulli magis evitandæ sunt quam juveni et principi, cujus gratia cum ætate debet adolescere." Buckingham grinned at him while he spoke.

At Oxford the Commons were more refractory, and the attempt ended in an abrupt dissolution.[1] The Lord Keeper was now most unjustly accused by Buckingham of having intrigued with Sir Edward Coke and the popular leaders, and having stirred them up to oppose the Court; and, to justify himself, he drew up and privately put into the King's hand a paper entitled—" Reasons to satisfy your most excellent Majesty concerning my carriage all this last parliament." This made a favorable impression on the King, and the young Queen Henrietta was disposed to protect him,—pleased by his forbearance to the Roman Catholics, and by a speech he had addressed to her in French, when he presented the Bishops to her on her arrival in England.

But Buckingham was not to be diverted from his purpose. He revived the charge of intriguing with the discontented parliamentary leaders at Oxford, and he reminded the King that when Williams was first made Lord Keeper, he himself had proposed the rule that " the Great Seal ought never to be held by the same person more than three years."

Charles yielded; and Lord Conway, deputed by him, came to the Lord Keeper's lodgings at Salisbury, and said —" that his Majesty understanding that his father, who is with God, had taken a resolution that the Keepers of the Great Seal of England should continue but from three years to three years, and approving very well thereof, and resolved to observe the order during his own reign, he expects that you should surrender up the Seal by All Hallowtide next,—alleging no other cause thereof,—and withal, that having so done, you should retire yourself to your bishopric of Lincoln." Williams respectfully professed his submission to the royal mandate, thanking God

[1] 2 Parl. Hist. 36.

that the Seal was not demanded on any other ground. He said the late King had continued it to him after the expiration of the three years, and the present King had restored it to him without condition or limitation of time, —" yet it is his Majesty's, and I will be ready to deliver it up to any man that his Majesty shall send with his warrant to require it." He strongly remonstrated against the order that he should be restrained to his diocese, or any place else. Lord Conway tried to soothe him by saying, " he understood this was merely meant, that he should not, after parting with the Seal, be obliged to attend the council-table, but that he should be free to go to his bishopric."

The Lord Keeper afterwards addressed a valedictory epistle to the King, and had an audience of leave preparatory to his formal surrender of the Seal. Charles, on this occasion, behaved to him with courtesy, and promised to comply with several requests which he made,—amongst others, that he might have leave to retire from Salisbury, where the Court then lay, to a little lodge lent to him by the Lord Sandys, and there my Lord Conway might receive the Seal, when his Majesty commanded it, in his journey towards Windsor. He immediately went to this retreat, finding " those suddenly strangers to him who were lately in his bosom, and that a cashiered courtier is an almanack of the last year, remembered by nothing but the great eclipse." [1]

At last, on the 25th of October the following warrant was produced to him:—

" CHARLES, R.

" Trusty and well-beloved Councillor, we greet you well. You are to deliver, upon the receipt hereof, our Great Seal of England, whereof you are our Keeper, unto our trusty and well-beloved Councillor Sir John Suckling, Controuler of the Household, the bearer hereof; and this shall be a sufficient warrant unto you so to do. Given under our Signet, at our Court at Salisbury, &c."

The Seal was immediately put into a costly cabinet in Sir John Suckling's presence, and the key of the cabinet was inclosed in a letter to the King, sealed with the episcopal seal of Lincoln, and containing the last words of St. Ambrose and St. Chrysostom, thus translated, " *Non*

[1] Hacket, ii. 26.

ita vixi ut me vivere pudeat; nec mori timeo, quia bonum habemus Dominum; that as I have not lived in my place so altogether unworthily as to be ashamed to continue in the same, so am I not now perturbed in the quitting of the same, because I know I have a good God and a gracious sovereign. *Moriar ego, sed me mortuo, vigeat ecclesia.* Let me retire to my little Zoar, but let your gracious Majesty be pleased to recommend unto my most able and deserving successor an especial care of your church and churchmen. So may God make your Majesty more victorious than David, more wise than Solomon, and every way as great a King as your Majesty's blessed father."[1]

This is the last time that an ecclesiastic has held the Great Seal of England, and notwithstanding the admiration in some quarters of mediæval usages, I presume the experiment is not likely to be soon repeated. No blame can be imputed to Williams while Keeper, for he seems to have been most anxious to perform the duties of the office to the best of his ability. Clarendon represents him as corrupt; but I think without any proof to support the charge.[2] It is quite clear that he was not swayed in his decrees by the solicitations of Buckingham, which was probably one cause of his dismissal. James said that, in sometimes withstanding Buckingham, " he was a stout man that durst do more than himself."

He is blamed for having made a vast many orders privately on petitions, for the sake of the fees, amounting to £3,000 a year; but his friends asserted with much probability, that this complaint arose from the barristers who lost the glut of motions they were accustomed to have in Court.[3]

---

[1] Hacket, ii. 27.

[2] Touching his bribery, the following pleasant anecdote is told: Having retired one summer to Nonsuch House, it chanced, as he was taking the air in the Great Park, that seeing a new-built church at a distance, and learning the name of the chief benefactor, he said, " Has he not a suit depending in Chancery?" and the answer from George Minors, who attended him, being in the affirmative, he added, " and he shall not fare the worse for building of churches." The gentleman being told this saying of the Lord Keeper, sent, next morning, a taste of the fruit of his orchard and the poultry in his yard, to Nonsuch House. " Nay, carry them back, George," said the Keeper, "and tell your friend he shall not fare the better for sending of presents."—*Philips.*

[3] One of these petitions, with the Lord Keeper's answer, is still extant in the Report Office: "*Fitchell* con. *Hickman.* The petition of two orphan children prayed that their uncle and brother might be appointed to put cer-

It is admitted that, at first, he showed his Cambrian origin by his irascibility ; " yet when he had overgone three years in the Court of Chancery, he watched his passions so well that the heat of his old British complexion was much abated, and he carried all things with far more lenity than choler.' He would chide little and bear much. His anger on the bench, if sharp, was short-lived, and the sun never set before he was returned to patience and loving kindness." [2]

Although he was very charitable and munificent, he did not, like some of his predecessors and successors, court popularity by dinner-giving. " He never feasted the King, and very rarely gave any lavish entertainments to others." [3]

If (as it was alleged) a good many of his decrees were reversed by his successor, he was little answerable for them, as he still continued to have the Master of the Rolls or common-law Judges for his assessors,—and these reversals are said to have been chiefly on rehearings, with new evidence.

I have now done with Williams in his judicial capacity, and in my strictures upon him I hope I have not forgotten the good-natured admonition of Bishop Hacket : " I do not blame lawyers if they would have us believe that none is fit for the office of Chancellor but one of their own profession. But let them plead their own learning and able parts, without traducing the gifts of them that are excellently seen in theological cases of conscience, and singularly rare in natural solertiousness."

When Williams was deprived of the Great Seal he was only in his forty-third year—an age at which, if bred to the bar in our times, he might be aspiring to a silk gown. He lived twenty-five years afterwards, constantly involved in turmoil and trouble ; but as he was no longer connected

tain bonds in suit for their benefit. *Answer.* ' I must be certified from the two justices next adjoyning of a sufficient man who I may trust for the use of the children, *least they fall from the frieing pan to the fire.*'—Jo. LINC. L. K."

[1] It is said that the great Welsh case of *Choleric* v. *Choleric*, which was pending so long in the Court of Chancery, began in his time, and caused some mirth when called on by the Registrar.

[2] Hacket.   [3] Ibid. 79.

with the administration of justice, as he was only a second-rate statesman, as he had not a high name in oratory or literature, and as the events of his time which it is my duty to record will be illustrated in the lives of his successors, I shall be brief in my sketch of his subsequent career.

From Foxley, in Wiltshire, where he surrendered the Great Seal, he went at once to his episcopal palace at Buckden, which he found in a very dilapidated condition. He magnificently restored it, and there he lived in splendor, having public days for entertaining all the surrounding clergy and gentry at his table.[1] Forgetting how he himself employed spies, he talked very freely of the government—not always sparing the failings of the King

[1] The same kinsman to whom I before referred has favored me with a copy of the following original letter, still extant, written by the ex-Lord Keeper soon after his return to Buckden:—

"With the remembrance of my love and best affections unto you, being very sensible of that great goodwill you have ever borne me, I thought it not unnecessarie to take this course with you, which I have done with noe one other freynde in the worlde, as to desire you to be noe more troubled with this late accident befallen unto me, than you shall understand I am myselfe.

"There is nothinge happened which I did not foresee, and (sithence the death of my deare master) assuredlye expect ; nor laye it in my power to prevent, otherwise than by the sacrificinge of my poor estate, and that which I esteeme far above the same—my reputation.

"I know you love me too well to wishe that I should be lavishe of either of these, to continue longer (yeat no longer than one man pleased) in this glorious miserye and splendid slaverye, wherein I have lived (if a man maye call such a toilinge a living) for these five years almost.

"By losinge the Seale, I have lost nothinge, nor my servants, by any faulte of myne, there being nothinge either layde or soe much as whispered to my charge.

"If we have not the opportunitye we hadd before to serve the Kinge, we have much more conveniencye to serve God, which I doe embrace as the onlye end of God's love and providence towards me in this sudden alteration.

"For your sonne Owen Wynn (who together with my debte is the object of my worldlye thoughts and cares), I will perform towards him all that he can have expected from me, if I live ; and if I die, I have performed it alreadye.

"You neede not feare any misse of me, being for such æra reserved in all your desires and requests ; having alsoe your eldest son near the Kinge, and of good reputation in the Court, who can give you a good accompt of any thinge you shall recommende him unto you.

"Hopinge therefore that I shall ever holde the same place I did in your love, which was fixed on my person, not my *late Glare*, and which I will deserve by all the freyndlye and lovinge offices which shall lie in my power, I end with my prayer unto God for the continuance of your health, and doe rest your very assured lovinge freynd and cozen,

"Bugden, 1 Decr., 1625. "Jo. LINCOLN.

"To my very much honored worthy Freynd and Cozen,
 Sr John Wynn, Knt and Baronet."

and the favorite. Some of his indiscreet expressions being reported at Court, Buckingham vowed, "that of all he had given him he would leave him nothing." In the hope of discovering something against him that might be made the subject of prosecution in the King's Bench, in the Star Chamber, or in Parliament, a commission of thirteen was appointed to inquire into all his proceedings while he held the Great Seal—but the attempt proved abortive.

At the approach of the coronation, for which he had been ordered to prepare a sermon, he came to London and dutifully tendered his service. As Dean of Westminster, according to the usage of centuries, he was entitled to a particular place at this solemnity. But he had orders to absent himself, and to depute one of the prebendaries in his stead. He sent in a list of all the prebendaries—and to mortify him the more, *Laud*, his special enemy, was selected.

Not receiving a writ of summons to Charles's second parliament, which met soon after, and feeling that this was an infringement of the rights of the peerage, he wrote to him, remonstrating against the insult, and saying, "I beg, for God's sake, that your Majesty would be pleased to mitigate the causeless displeasure of my Lord Duke against me, and I beseech your Majesty, for Jesus Christ his sake, not to believe news or accusations against me while I stand thus enjoined from your royal presence, before you shall have heard my answer to the particulars." The writ was sent to him, and he gave his proxy to Bishop Andrews, forbearing to sit in the House during this short parliament, in the hope of assuaging Buckingham's resentment, to whom he privately sent some wholesome advice for the management of public affairs.

On the summoning of the famous parliament which passed "the Petition of Right," he received his writ, with an injunction not to attend ; but he wrote back to Lord Keeper Coventry, "I must crave some time to resolve, by the best counsels God shall give me, whether I shall obey your Lordship's letter (though mentioning his Majesty's pleasure) before my own right, which, by the law of God and man, I may, in all humility, maintain." When parliament met, he took his seat in person, and was constant in his attendance during the session.

The Lords entering into an inquiry respecting illegal commitments for refusal to pay the forced loan, he very actively assisted, and, as ex-Lord Keeper, spoke with the authority of a law lord. The Judges of the King's Bench, who had refused to liberate these prisoners on a *habeas corpus*, were ordered to attend, but scrupled to answer the questions put to them, and "desired to be advised whether they being sworn, upon penalty of forfeiting body, lands, and goods into the King's hands, to give an account to him, may do this without warrant from his Majesty." The Bishop of Lincoln said, "this motion proceeded from him; and he took it for clear that there is an appeal even from the Chancery, which is a higher Court than the King's Bench; and that Court hath ever given an account of their doings."[1]

He was one of the managers for the Lords of the open conferences between the two Houses on this subject, and gave a very elaborate report of the speeches of the managers for the Commons, particularly those of Sir E. Coke and Mr. Noy,—afterwards the inventor of the writ for ship money,—then a flaming patriot.[2]

When the Petition of Right came up from the Commons, Williams warmly supported it; but, to show his moderation, he proposed to add a clause, "That, as they desired to preserve their own liberties, so they had regard to leave entire that power wherewith his Majesty was intrusted for the protection of his people." The Lords agreed to the amendment; but it was rejected by the Commons, under a suspicion that the Bishop had been "sprinkled with some Court holy water."

He afterwards gained unqualified applause for his assistance in carrying through the measure. The royal assent being for some time refused, he made a very excellent speech, showing that, as it stood it was agreeable to our laws and constitution; and that it was no less honorable for the King, as it made him a King of freemen not of slaves.

At last the words were pronounced, "*Le droit soit fait come il est desiré;*" and the Petition of Right was law.

In the general joy which followed, the King, for a short time, sought to add to his popularity by appearing to take Williams again into favor. A private conference

[1] 2 Parl. Hist. 288.   [2] Ibid. 322.

then took place between them, which was made the foundation of all the Bishop's subsequent persecutions and misfortunes. To a question, "how the King might ingratiate himself with the people?" he answered "That the Puritans were many, and strong sticklers; and if his Majesty would give but private orders to his ministers to connive a little at their party, and show them some indulgence, it might, perhaps, mollify them a little, and make them more pliant, though he did not promise that they would be trusty long to any government." The King said he took the advice in good part and promised to follow it;—and happy would it have been for him if he had so acted,—instead of throwing himself into the arms of Laud, and for nearly twelve years (during which parliaments were intermitted) doing every thing to irritate and insult that party which, growing strong by persecution deprived him of his crown and of his life.

It was thought that when Buckingham had perished by the fanaticism of Felton, Williams might have recovered his ascendancy; but this event only added to the power of Laud, who was successively made Bishop of London, and Archbishop of Canterbury, and presided both in the Court of High Commission, and in the Star Chamber. This wrong-headed man no doubt persuaded himself that he had no object in view but the welfare of the Church and the King, and that he was doing God good service by all the cruel measures he resorted to.

Unfortunately for the Church, and fatally for himself, he forthwith originated a controversy very similar to that which has recently sprung up at Oxford; but, thank God, the very learned and pious Tractarians have neither the power nor the wish to enforce their opinions by violent means. The Archbishop, without being a Roman Catholic, longed to come as near as possible to the doctrines and ceremonies of Rome, and issued a number of new regulations with respect to the position of the communion-table, the mode of administering the sacrament of the Lord's Supper, and other religious rites. These Williams considered not only contrary to the spirit of the Reformation, but in violation of ecclesiastical canons, and the Articles of the Church of England,—and to oppose them, he published a book, entitled "The Holy Table,"—pretty plainly insinuating that they led to Romanism, but at the same time using Scripture language, and such general arguments, that his book could not itself be made the subject of prosecution.[1]

Laud, however, denounced all who differed from him as "Puritans," and eagerly looked out for an opportunity to prosecute Williams as their leader.

There was a suit depending in the episcopal court at Lincoln, against some persons who had refused to comply with a prescribed ecclesiastical formality. The Bishop was unwilling to proceed to extremities against them, and the prosecutors at the trial having called them "Puritans," he said something about "the Puritans being good subjects, and of his knowing that the King did not wish them to be hardly dealt with." Complaint of this language was immediately brought to Laud, and he directed it to be made the subject of an information in the Star Chamber—the *charge* to be, for spreading false news, and disclosing what had passed between the defendant and the King, contrary to the oath of a Privy Councillor,"—and the *evidence*, "that he had published and misrepresented his conversation with the King about indulgence to the Puritans." As a preliminary step his name was struck out from the list of Privy Councillors.

Noy was then Attorney General, and filed the information, but on looking into the case he was so much ashamed of it, that it went to sleep for several years. On his death, —at the instigation of Laud, who had in vain tried to induce Williams to recant the doctrines of "The Holy Table," and to resign the deanery of Westminster,—it was revived. Still there was a difficulty in carrying it through without any evidence,—when Sir John Banks, the new Attorney General, dexterously and unscrupulously filed another information against the Bishop, imputing to him that he had tampered with the King's witnesses in the former suit.

This was equally unfounded, but, after a trial which lasted nine days, the Right Reverend Defendant was found guilty. Archbishop Laud, in pronouncing judgment, hypocritically said, "Sorry I am, my Lords, that such a man as my Lord Bishop of Lincoln for profession, and sorry that he, being so wise, so discreet and under-

[1] Clarendon says of it that it displayed "much good learning, but too little gravity for a Bishop."

standing a man every way, should come to deserve the censure of this Court. When I look upon and consider his excellent parts, both of nature and achieved unto by study and art; when I think upon his wisdom, learning, agility of memory, and the experience that accompanies him with all those endowments, it puts me to stand." The sentence was, that the defendant should pay a fine of £10,000; should be imprisoned in the Tower during the King's pleasure; should be suspended from his ecclesiastical functions *tam a beneficiis quam officiis;* and should be referred over to the High Commission Court, there to be further dealt with as his offense should deserve.

Under this judgment he was immediately arrested and carried to the Tower, where he was kept a close prisoner between three and four years, till he was released by the Long Parliament. Meanwhile he was, in other respects, treated with excessive severity. He petitioned that "his fine might be taken up by £1,000 yearly, as his estate would bear it;" but Kilvert, a pettifogging attorney, and an infamous tool of his persecutors, was sent down to Buckden with an immediate execution for the £10,000,—seized all his furniture, plate, and books,—felled his timber, —slaughtered his deer,—sold for five pounds pictures which had cost him £400,—and continued reveling for several years in the palace without accounting for the moneys he received, or paying any part of the fine.

Laud, not yet satiated, in the spring of 1639, caused another information to be filed against Williams, along with Lambert Osbaldeston, one of the Masters of Westminster School, "for divulging false news and lies to breed a disturbance between the late Lord Treasurer Weston and the Archbishop himself; for giving them nicknames, and for contriving to work the Archbishop's ruin." This charge was founded on certain private letters of the defendants, in which they had reflected on some of the measures of the Lord Treasurer, and had called the Archbishop "the great little man." Being found guilty, the sentence upon the Bishop of Lincoln was, that he should be fined £5,000 to the King, and £3,000 to the Archbishop; imprisoned during the King's pleasure, and acknowledge his fault. He was supposed by his judges to be rather leniently dealt with; for Osbaldeston had a similar sentence, with the addition of *standing in the pillory and having his ears nailed to it.*

When it was thought that the ex-Lord Keeper's spirit was broken by these proceedings, an offer was made to liberate him on his giving up his bishopric and all his preferments in England, and taking a bishopric in Ireland. He answered, "that it were a tempting of God to part with all he had willingly, and leave himself no assurance of a livelihood; that his debts, if he came out of the Tower, would cast him into another prison; that he would never hazard himself into a condition to beg his bread; and as to going into Ireland, that as he was imprisoned here under the King, he plainly saw he should soon be hanged there under the Lord Deputy."[1] So he resolved to exercise his patience, and wait a better day.

His deliverance arrived much sooner than could then have been expected. The parliament which was assembled in the beginning of 1640, upon the Scottish invasion, was abruptly dissolved before Williams could apply to it for redress; but the November following was the memorable era of the meeting of "the Long Parliament." He now hoped for his own liberation, and vengeance on his oppressor. About this time he said to Hacket, his biographer, "I am right sorry for the King, who is like to be forsaken by his subjects. But for the Archbishop, he had best not meddle with me, for all the friends he can make will be too few to save him."

In a few days after the commencement of the session he presented a petition to the House of Lords praying that he might be set at liberty, and that a writ of summons might be sent to him as a Peer. This was opposed by Finch, the Lord Keeper, and by Archbishop Laud; but the Lords agreed on an address to the King in his favor, and sent their own officer, the Gentleman Usher of the Black Rod, to the Tower to deliver him out of custody. He was brought to Westminster forthwith, and, in the midst of many congratulations, took his seat on the Bishop's bench.

He could not refrain, at first, from launching out rather

---

[1] Hacket, part ii. 136. According to Clarendon, "he had much to defend himself against the Archbishop here; but if he was in Ireland there was a man (meaning the Earl of Strafford) who would cut off his head within one month."

violently against those who had persecuted him, but after this ebullition he conducted himself with moderation; showing himself a friend to the monarchy and the church; and, were it not for the Jesuitical advice which he gave to Charles, about assenting to the execution of Strafford, his subsequent conduct must be applauded by all parties in the state. Some Peers, to whom chiefly he owed his liberation, having spoken with personal disrespect of the King, who was still residing at Westminster in the full exercise of the royal functions, he sharply rebuked them, —pointing out how the use of such language was contrary to the duty of good subjects, and was inconsistent with all notion of kingly government. They exclaimed: " We have conjured up a spirit, and would we could lay him again." Clarendon relates, that now preaching before the King in his turn as Dean of Westminster, when mentioning the Presbyterian discipline, he said, "it was a government only fit for tailors and shoemakers and the like—not for noblemen and gentlemen,"—which giving great scandal to his patrons, "he reconciled himself to them by making merry with certain sharp sayings of the Court." But the noble historian had such a spite against Williams, that this representation must be received with some suspicion.[1]

From whatever cause,—the King, pretending to approve of his conduct, sent for him one evening, had a conference with him that lasted till after midnight, and, as a token of a full pardon, ordered the records of all the proceedings against him in the Star Chamber to be cancelled.

To some of his more respectable opponents Williams said, " If they had no worse foes than him, they might fear no harm, and that he saluted them with the charity of a Bishop;" but when Kilvert, who had behaved so abominably at Buckden, came to crave pardon and indemnity, he said passionately, " I assure you pardon for what you have done before; but this is a new fault, that you take me to be of so base a spirit as to defile myself with treading on so mean a creature. Live still by pettifogging, and think that I have forgotten you."[2]

He strongly advised Charles not to assent to the act which deprived him of the power of dissolving this

[1] Hist. Reb. i. 536 542, 548.   [2] Hacket, part ii.

parliament at pleasure, and which must be considered the foundation of the impending revolution. Long before the King's captivity, the House of Commons had become unpopular, so that there was a strong reaction throughout the nation in his favor; and if he could have called a new parliament he would have been safe.

But Williams' conduct with respect to Strafford can not be defended. In the first place, although the trial for the high treason was *causa sanguinis*,—he contended, contrary to the canons and immemorial usage, for the right of the Bishops to be present and to vote upon it, and that they ought to exercise this right.[1]

The Bill of Attainder being passed, although he professed to disapprove of it, he agreed to go with three other prelates to try to induce the King to assent to it, and thus he stated the question:—"Since his Majesty refers his own judgment to his Judges, and they are to answer it, if an innocent person suffers,—why may he not satisfy his conscience in the present matter, since competent Judges in the law have awarded that they find the Earl guilty of treason, by suffering the judgment to stand, though in his own mind he is satisfied that the party convicted was not criminous?" The other three Bishops, trusting to his learning and experience, joined with him in sanctioning this distinction, in laying all the blame on the Judges, and in saying that the King, with a good conscience, might agree to Strafford's death. Clarendon mainly imputes Strafford's death to Williams's conduct on this occasion, saying that "he acted his part with prodigious boldness and impiety." It is stated as matter of palliation by others, that Usher, the celebrated Archbishop of Armagh, was one of this deputation, and that Strafford, although aware of the advice he had given, was attended by him on the scaffold, and received from him the last consolations of religion.

Williams now visited his diocese, and tried to put down unlicensed preaching, which was beginning to spread for-

---

[1] There is a striking instance of the inaccuracy of Lord Clarendon in relating this transaction. He strongly blames Williams for denying the right of the Bishops to be present and to vote—that he might deprive Strafford of their support; whereas Hacket gives at full length a very long speech which Williams delivered, to prove that the Bishops on trials for life and death were to sit and vote like other Peers.—3 St. Tr. 823. 2 Parl. Hist. 732. In capital cases the Bishops always withdraw under protest.

midably. On his return, being violently attacked in parliament for this proceeding, he ably defended himself in a conference between the two Houses, held in the Painted Chamber.

While afraid of the displeasure of the popular party, a new change of fortune awaited him. It was said he experienced almost as many vicissitudes as Marius, *Consul toties exulque; ex exule Consul.* Instead of being sent to Newgate, as he expected, by the influence of the Puritans whom he had protected,—he was made by the King Archbishop of York, and placed, *de facto,* at the head of the Church of England. Laud, the Archbishop of Canterbury, was under impeachment in the Tower, and the clergy of the establishment looked, as their last hope, to him who had been for years persecuted and imprisoned as their enemy.

CHAPTER LX.

CONCLUSION OF THE LIFE OF LORD KEEPER WILLIAMS.

WILLIAMS had scarcely taken his seat in the House of Lords as Metropolitan when he had to defend the right of his order to sit there. A Bill came up from the Commons to exclude the Bishops entirely from parliament, and to disqualify them for all secular employments. When it got into Committee, he delivered a very long and able speech against it, which made such an impression on its supporters, that it was allowed to go to sleep for five months.[1] The King complimented him on this occasion, saying, "My Lord, I commend you that you are no whit daunted with all disasters, but are zealous in defending your order."—"Please it your Majesty," replied the *Arch*-BISHOP, "I am a true Welshman, and they are observed never to run away till their general do first forsake them. No fear of my flinching whilst your Majesty doth countenance our cause."

But after the fatal attempt of the King to seize the five members in the House of Commons, all hope of a peaceable settlement was at an end. The cry against the

[1] 2 Parl. Hist. 794.

Bishops was revived, and it was greatly exasperated by Williams having, as Dean of Westminster, gallantly defended the Abbey against a mob who wished to seize the regalia deposited there, and having put them to flight by an armed force. The Bishops were threatened with personal violence, and were prevented from entering the House of Lords.

Hereupon Williams drew up a protest, addressed to the King, which was signed by himself and eleven other Prelates. After dwelling upon their privileges as a constituent part of the Assembly and one of the estates of the realm, "they humbly protest, before his Majesty and the noble House of Peers, that, saving unto themselves all their rights and interests of sitting and voting in the House at other times, they dare not sit or vote in the House of Peers until his Majesty shall further secure them from all affronts, indignities, and dangers. And whereas their fears are not built upon fantasies and conceits, but upon such grounds and objects as well may terrify men of good resolution and much constancy, they do, in all duty and humility, protest against all laws, orders, votes, resolutions, or determinations, as of themselves null and of none effect, which, in their forced and violent absence, have already passed, or which, during their forced and violent absence, shall hereafter pass, in that most honorable House."

This gave furious offense to the Commons, who immediately complained of it to the Upper House,—and all the twelve Prelates who signed it being arrested, ten of them, with the Archbishop of York at their head, were committed to the Tower; the other two, on account of their age and infirmities being allowed to remain in the custody of the Sergeant at Arms.[1]

It was an affecting circumstance that the two Archbishops, who had so long been foes, were now both in the Tower; and it is recorded, to their honor, that, in a Christian spirit, forgetting all past injuries and animosities, they were cordially reconciled. They did not personally converse together, that they might avoid the suspicion of plots, but they often sent each other messages of love and consolation.

The Commons proceeded with articles of impeachment

[1] 2 Parl. Hist. 893.

for high treason against the twelve Bishops, and, afterwards, by bill of attainder; but to construe into high treason a protest against the validity of the acts of the assembly of which they were members, while they were by violence prevented from being present, was too flagrantly unjust even for those times, and the proceeding was allowed to drop.[1]

The Bill for excluding the Bishops from sitting in parliament now passed the two Houses without further opposition,[2] and the question arose, whether it would receive the royal assent? Many, who thought they well knew Charles, believed that he would sooner have resigned his crown and his life than sanction such "a heavy blow and great discouragement to the Church." What was their horror when, with his free assent, the Act became the law of the land! His reluctance is said to have been overcome by the last request of his beloved Henrietta, as he was attending her embarkation for the Continent at Dover. She had little respect for Protestant Prelates; she had been persuaded that this concession would so far gratify the Commons, that they would forego their other demands; and she was always more influenced by the love of present ease than by a strict adherence to principle, or the apprehension of distant consequences.

Soon after this, Williams and his brethren who had been committed along with him, were liberated; and it had been well for the reputation of the Parliamentary party if Laud, who could no longer be formidable, had been included in the order for their discharge. These holy men, when at large, found themselves still so much under popular odium in the metropolis, that it was necessary for them all to make their escape into the country as soon as possible. While they lay in prison ballads were composed upon them, and they were made the subject of caricatures, for which the English were beginning to show a genius. One print, that had a great sale, represented the Archbishop of York in his lawn sleeves and episcopal robes; a square cap on his head; and (to celebrate his defense of the Abbey, and his assault on the populace) with bandoleers about his neck, a musket on his shoulder, and a rest in his hand. By these means he became as unpopular as Laud had ever been, and instead of resuming

---

[1] 4 St. Tr. 63.   [2] 2 Parl. Hist. 916.

possession of the Deanery, he found it necessary to follow the King to York, where the royal standard was unfurled, and preparations were proceeding for the commencement of hostilities.

He took possession of Cawood Castle, which belonged to his see, but he was soon obliged to fly from it in the dead of the night. Sir John Hotham and his son, who began the civil war, having been proclaimed traitors for refusing to admit the King into Hull, made a sally out of that town with the design of taking Cawood Castle, where the Archbishop was collecting men and provisions for the King's use. News was brought, that young Hotham would arrive there by five o'clock next morning with a large force, and that he had drawn his sword in " a hectoring manner," uttering a vow that he would cut off the head of the Archbishop for having spoken very sharply against his disloyalty. The castle was in a ruinous state, and incapable of making any defense. The Archbishop, therefore, was obliged to effect his escape, a little after midnight, with a small band of horsemen and the few valuables he could carry with him at so short a warning. He meant to seek refuge in his own country, and he set off " without a sumpter-horse, or any provision for his journey, without a change of apparel, and almost without money, for all that he had been able to raise among his tenants in Yorkshire he had sent to the royal treasury."[1]

The following day he met the King beating up for volunteers, and handed over to him the stoutest of his men. Having received a royal pass to carry him into Wales,—on bended knee, with tears streaming from his eyes, and hearty prayers for a successful issue to the coming contest, he kissed his Majesty's hand, and bade him adieu,—believing that it was for the last time. He journeyed on with a very slender retinue, and, notwithstanding the disturbed state of the country, after many alarms, safely reached Aberconway, near fifty years from the time when he had left the place as a stripling.

The energy of his character continued without abatement. He was looked up to with great pride by his countrymen, as one of the few Cambrians who had risen to high distinction in England, and he animated them with zeal in the royal cause. To draw down the blessing

[1] Hacket, part ii. 208, 210.

of Heaven upon his endeavors, he set all North Wales on a more earnest practice of religion, and ordered that frequent prayers should be put up in all churches, with fasting,—and he himself was almost daily in the pulpit exhorting his hearers, in their own language, to defend the mitre and the crown. The emulation of the great families among each other had made them indifferent to the public struggle that was now going on, but he contrived to unite them all in one common resolution to resist any invasion by the parliamentary generals. For nothing that he ever did was he so much praised by his contemporaries, as for the manner in which he put Conway Castle in a state of defense. He found it a ruin, but he repaired its walls, threw up important works to strengthen it, victualed it, and collected a stout garrison for it, which he saw regularly trained.

The King hearing of his exertions, sent him a commission signed by his own hand, in which, after much praise bestowed on the Archbishop, and noticing the importance of Conway Castle, he says, "You having begun at your own charge to put the same into repair, we do heartily desire you to go on in that work, assuring you that whatsoever moneys you shall lay out upon the fortification of the said castle, shall be repaid unto you before the custody thereof shall be put into any other hand than your own, or such as you shall recommend." [1]

The Archbishop, in consequence, appointed two of his nephews to hold the castle for him;—but, as we shall see, this arrangement was unavailing, and he met with an ungrateful return for his military services.

While he still enjoyed the royal favor, he repaired to Oxford in consequence of a summons to attend his Majesty during the sitting of a rival parliament to be attempted there. He had now frequent conferences with Charles, and gave him some prophetic advice about Cromwell, who was yet of mean rank, but whom he had known at Buckden. Says he, "That Oliver Cromwell, I am full sure will turn out the most dangerous enemy your Majesty has. I never could make out his religion, but he was a common spokesmen for sectaries, and maintained their part with stubbornness. He loves none that are more than his equals. Above all that live, I think he is the

[1] Hacket, part ii. 208, 210.

most mindful of an injury. He talks openly that it is fit some should act more vigorously against your forces, and bring your person into the power of the parliament. He says, 'his general, the Earl of Essex, is only half an enemy to your Majesty.' Every beast hath some evil properties; but Oliver Cromwell hath the properties of all evil beasts. My humble motion is, either that you would win him to you by promises of fair treatment, or catch him by some stratagem, and *cut him short.*" All this the King received with a smile of incredulity.[1]

The royal, in opposition to the republican, parliament assembled. Such respect was paid to the last regular statute which the King, Lords, and Commons had all assented to, that Williams, and other Bishops then at Oxford, did not take their places in the mock House of Lords, presided over by Lord Keeper Lane.[2] However, the King paid them the compliment to consult them,—on which occasion Williams made him a long speech, particularly complaining of the irregularities of the royal army. "Your soldiers," said he, "in their march and quarters are very unruly, and lose the people's affections everywhere by the oppressions they sustain." He recommended specific measures and concessions,—" with indemnity to the King's adherents; for we save a ship with the loss of the goods, not of the passengers:—thus concluding,—"But if your Majesty disdain to go so low, and will not put the good of the church and kingdom upon their faith, to which misery I fear our sins have brought us, I am ready to run on in the common hazard with your Majesty and to live and die in your service." Charles professed to receive this counsel in good part, and when Williams took leave, again expressly charged him with the care and government of all North Wales,—especially of Conway Castle. Under a military escort he safely returned thither.

But he was not long allowed to remain in his command. The royalist leaders were not satisfied to see a churchman sharing their power, and Prince Rupert, always rash and headstrong, was induced to grant a commission to Sir John Owen, an officer noted for violence and covetous-

---

[1] Hacket, part ii. 212.

[2] This seems to have given offense to those who ought to have constituted the right reverend bench. Hacket says, testily, "Oxford wanted not Bishops at this time, but they were excluded to sit and vote as Peers in parliament."
—Part ii. 214.

ness, to supersede him. The inhabitants of the surrounding country had deposited all their most valuable effects in Conway Castle, and the Archbishop had made himself personally responsible for them. When required to resign, he indignantly denied the validity of Rupert's commission, and refused admittance to the new Governor. Sir John Owen thereupon surprised the castle by a large military force, and scaling the walls and bursting open the gates, he took possession of it, with all the ammunition, stores, and property which it contained. The Archbishop sent an earnest but respectful complaint to the King at Oxford, but could gain no further satisfaction than that "it should be considered at more leisure." He remonstrated no further, "lest he should say too much," but he felt deeply wounded by this great indignity.

During fifteen months he remained in a state of inactivity, hearing of the field of Naseby and the utter ruin of the royal party. At the end of that period, he engaged in an affair which has brought some obloquy upon his memory. Colonel Milton, a parliamentary officer, who had got possession of Chester, marched with a considerable force, across the Dee, through Flint and Denbighshire, to Conway town, and prevailed with the Archbishop to enter into a treaty to assist him to take the castle, still held by Sir John Owen for the King. The chief condition was, that those who had deposited their wealth in the castle, should have everything restored to them which had escaped the rapacity of the royalists. The Archbishop then assembled his kindred and dependents, marched at their head, and joined Colonel Milton's regular troops in assaulting the castle. The garrison was so reduced that they could make but a short and ineffectual resistance, and the Archbishop was again master of the fortress.

He reconciled this proceeding to his principles of royalty by his old casuistry, "*licet uti alieno peccato.*" His apologist, admitting that "his carriage did not become him to thrust himself in among the assailants," mitigates his misconduct by the quotation from Sallust, "*non minus est turpe sua relinquere quam aliena invadere injustum.*"[1] He was loudly accused of having renounced his allegiance and deliberately gone over to the rebels: but though the

[1] Hacket, part ii. 220.

royal cause was then desperate, I believe his great object was to be revenged of the insult offered to him by Sir John Owen, which had been so long rankling in his bosom.

When he had seen all the property found in the castle restored to the right owners, he retired to the house of his kinswoman, the Lady Mostyn, at Glodded, in the parish of Eglwysrose, in the county of Carnarvon, where he remained till his death. In this retreat he still anxiously listened to the news brought him of public affairs; and if his loyalty had suffered a short eclipse, it now shone out with fresh luster. When told that the King, pressed by the forces under Fairfax, had, by the advice of Monsieur Montreville, secretly fled from Oxford, and repaired to the Scottish army before Newark, he wrung his hands, saying, " What! be advised by a *stranger*, and trust the *Scots!* then all is lost." He was more and more afflicted as he successively heard of his fears being verified by the treacherous act of the Scotch army, in delivering up their confiding countryman to the parliament, —of his being seized by Joyce and the Independents,—of his flight to the Isle of Wight,—of the disastrous issue of his negotiations at Newport—of his being made a close prisoner in London,—and of the preparations for the unprecedented proceeding of bringing him to an open trial. But when the news arrived that Charles had been found guilty and doomed to die,—and that the sentence had actually been carried into execution by stiking off his head on a scaffold erected in front of his own palace at midday, before hundreds of thousands of his subjects,—the aged Archbishop fainted away, and vowed that he never would take comfort more.

He survived rather more than a year, remaining constantly in bed, except that every night, as the hall clock struck twelve, he rose, and having nothing but his shirt and waistcoat upon him, he knelt on his bare knees and prayed earnestly a quarter of an hour before he retired to his rest again—observing the season of midnight, because the Scriptures speak of Christ's coming to judge the quick and the dead at midnight,—and the burden of his prayer being " Come, Lord Jesus, come quickly and put an end to these days of sin and misery." He longed for his own deliverance, saying, " I am ready for the Lord."

At last, when his strength was much reduced, he was

seized with a sharp attack of fever, which carried him off in a few hours. When the pangs of death were upon him, after the Visitation of the Sick had been twice read over to him, and he had received absolution, these words being repeated by the priest in his hearing, *the Lord be merciful to thee, the Lord receive thy soul,*—at that instant he first closed his own eyes with one hand, and then lifting up the other, his lips moved, and, recommending his spirit to his Redeemer, he expired. His death happened on the 25th of March, the day of his birth,—when he completed his sixty-eighth year.

Without any very high mental endowments, his extreme industry and energy, and a combination of fortuitous circumstances, against the occurrence of which the probabilities were incalculable, raised him to great distinction, and mingled his name with transactions of permanent public interest. He will always be memorable in English history as the last of a long line of eminent ecclesiastics, who, with rare intervals, held for many centuries the highest judicial office in the kingdom, and exercised a powerful influence over the destinies of the nation.[1]

All accounts represent him as very fiery in his temper, by which he was betrayed into rash measures, and gave great offense,—some, with Lord Clarendon at their head, ascribing this to systematic arrogance and imperiousness, —while his good-natured secretary explains away his "choler and high stomach" by his Welsh blood, asserting that he was speedily appeased, and that "there did not live that Christian that hated revenge more than he, or that would forgive an injury sooner."

Though grasping wealth with eagerness, he spent it most munificently. While he held the Great Seal he was too much devoted to the duties of his office to be much given to hospitality; but when he retired, one of his detractors says, "he lived at Buckden the most episcopal of any of his predecessors."[2] His house was open to all his neighbors of all degrees, lay and spiritual, and when persons of distinction were traveling that way he sump-

---

[1] Humanly speaking, lucky chances must be considered as having chiefly contributed to his extraordinary elevation, notwithstanding the application to him of the quotation: "Cujus ea vis fuisse ingenii atque animi cernitur ut quocunque loco natus esset, in quodcunque tempus incidisset, fortunam ipse sibi facturus videatur."

[2] Sanderson's King James, part ii. p. 507.

tuously entertained them and their retinues. He was likewise very charitable to the poor, and liberally assisted scholars of merit who were laboring under pecuniary difficulties, till he could permanently provide for them.

Although supposed to favor the Puritans, he incurred great scandal with that sect by encouraging stage plays. He used to have the players down from London to Buckden,—when the hall of the episcopal palace was converted into a theater, where comedies were performed—even on a Sunday. Collier, in his "Annals of the Stage,"[1] asserts that "The Midsummer Night's Dream" was exhibited there on Sunday, the 27th of September, 1631; and others add, that on that very day he had held an episcopal ordination, so that the play was for the amusement of the young priests and deacons.

It is difficult to get at the truth in such an age of faction; and, at any rate, we must not judge of an individual who lived two centuries ago by our own notions of propriety. It was long after the Reformation, before there was any essential change in manners and customs, and Hacket,—himself a Bishop, and a very grave and decent divine,—without making any admission, or entering into any specific denial respecting these charges, asserts "that Archbishop Williams did no more in recreating himself with such diversions at Buckden than he himself had seen that grave prelate, Archbishop Bancroft, do at Lambeth." We must remember that King James's "Book of Sports," commanding all good Christians and churchmen to play at football and other such games every Sunday afternoon, after having been present at Divine worship, was read during the morning service in every church and chapel in the kingdom.

Williams had such a sincere love for the Liturgy of the Church of England, that he caused it to be translated into Spanish and other foreign languages. He regularly kept up religious observances in his family, and at dinner a chapter was read in the English Bible daily by one of the choristers, and at supper another, in Latin, by one of his gentlemen.

Some accused him of licentiousness, and it was loudly whispered that about the time he was made Lord Keeper

[1] Vol. ii. 27.

he had an intrigue with the Countess of Buckingham.¹ Others would have it that he had promised to marry her, —that having got the Great Seal as her dowry, he refused to perform his promise,—and that he was displaced because, " now being come to the height of his preferment, hee did estrange himselfe from the old Countesse."²

Wilson, in his History of King James, seeks to refute all these stories, by asserting that Williams was *eunuchus ab utero*. This is denied by Bishop Hacket, who, however, relates what would equally answer the purpose—that while a little boy in petticoats, he, along with his playmates, jumped from the walls of Conway in a windy day, expecting the wind to inflate their clothes, and make a parachute for them; but that, while the rest safely reached the ground, he fell precipately upon a ragged stone, by which he was so mutilated that he could never have thought of marriage, and a want of chastity could not be imputed to him.³

This statement is, in all probability, correct; but Williams, to avoid the contempt or ridicule which might have fallen upon him if it had been known that he had suffered such mutilation, carefully concealed it during his lifetime, and talked and wrote as if he had been a man of perfect integrity both in body and mind.⁴ However, being unmarried,—to avoid scandal, he kept only men servants in his house. To this circumstance his biographers ascribe its dirtiness and its disorders, which, they say, are best prevented by female superintendence.⁵

He was a remarkably handsome man;—" his person proper, his countenance comely, his complexion fair and lovely,⁶ his gait so stately that most people mistook it for pride."⁷

Till he heard of Charles's execution he was merry and

---

¹ This story even reached Scotland. " It was rumored every quher that hes too grate familiaritie with Buckinghame's mother procured him thesse grate favors and preferments one a suddaine."—*Balfour*, ii. 93.
² Weldon.   ³ Hacket, p. 8.
⁴ *E. g.*—in his letter to Buckingham begging the deanery of Westminster, he says, " being *unmarried*, and *inclining* so to continue "—and his conversation with Prince Charles about the courtesan with whom he was in correspondence, rather indicates a desire that he should be considered *potentially* a libertine.—*Ante*, p. 159.   ⁵ Hacket. Philips.
⁶ This corresponds with his portraits: all of which that I have seen represent him wearing a broad-brimmed hat, such as that in which Bradshaw " bullied."   ⁷ Philips.

facetious in adverse as well as prosperous fortune; but after that event, if he would converse with any one, it was only respecting the enormous crime of Cromwell, Bradshaw, and the other regicides, and inquiring whether the Divine vengeance had not yet overtaken them?

Like his great predecessors, Morton and Wolsey, he had the sons of the principal nobility—of the Marquess of Hertford, and the Earls of Pembroke, Salisbury, and Leicester, and many other young gentlemen—reared in his family before they went to the University. They were taught the classics by his chaplains; they had proper instruction in all manly exercises from the officers of his household; and he himself read them lectures on logic, and catechised them in religion during Lent.

He affected to rival Wolsey in his princely expenditure on public buildings. He repaired and beautified Westminster Abbey at his own expense. He rebuilt Lincoln College, Oxford, merely because it had been founded by one of his predecessors; and he was a splendid benefactor to St. John's College, Cambridge, the place of his education.

While Lord Keeper he embraced an opportunity of repurchasing his family estate, which he left, though considerably burdened with debt, to his nephew and heir, Sir Griffith Williams.

His writings, which are entirely theological, I do not presume to criticise. They had long fallen into oblivion, but I should think they might now be read with advantage in the Tractarian controversy. He was superior in learning and acutenesss to Laud, whose reputation is owing to the illegal, barbarous, unprovoked sentence passed upon him,—as little to be palliated as defended,—and the calm, dignified, and courageous manner in which he met it,—whereby all his faults, and follies, and cruelties were forgotten, and he, who if he had been left alone would have sunk into oblivion, or remembered only for his bigotry and intemperance, is now regarded as a martyr and a saint.[1]

Williams's printed speeches which have come down to us show a vile taste in oratory and composition. **They** are most pedantic, quibbling, and illogical.

---

[1] ———"Nothing in his life
Became him like the leaving it."

He might have played a great part, first in opposing the arbitrary measures of the Court on his dismissal from office, and afterwards in checking the excesses of the parliamentary party when he was released from the Tower at the meeting of the Long Parliament; but he wanted moderation and firmness of purpose; he could not command the support of his own friends, and he was constantly laying himself open to the assaults of his antagonists. There is no sufficient ground for Clarendon's censure, that he was "a man of a very corrupt nature, whose passions transported him into the most unjustifiable actions;" but still less can he be taken for the immaculate character represented by Bishop Hacket,—although it speaks loudly for his good qualities, that he so powerfully attached to him a man of learning and discernment, who had known him most intimately for many years, and who continued warmly to defend him after his disgrace, and after his death.[1]

Williams was buried in a little Welsh church near Penrhyn, where a monument was some years after erected to his memory, for which an epitaph was written by the faithful Hacket,—recording at great length his origin, his accomplishments,[2] and his services,—and thus concluding:—

"Postquam inter tempora luctuosissima
Satur esset omnium quæ videret et audiret,
Nec Regi aut Patriæ per rabiem perduellium amplius servire potuit.
Anno Aetatis 68º expleto Martis 25º qui fuit ei natalis
Summa fide in Christum. inconcussâ erga Regem fidelitate
Animam angina extinctus piissime Deo reddidit.
Nec refert quod tantillum monumentum in occulto angulo positum
Tanti viri memoriam servat,
Cujus virtutes omnium ætatum tempora celebrabunt."

[1] Hacket's "Scrinia Reserata, a memorial offered to the great deservings of John Williams, D.D.," is one of the most curious pieces of biography in our language, and should be studied by all who would thoroughly understand the history of the reigns of James I. and Charles I. Consisting of two folio volumes, generally bound up together—what it contains of Williams is like two grains of wheat in two bushels (not of chaff) of various other sorts of grain—but it is full of most rare quotations, and of quaint illustrations. The author must have been a man of extensive learning and most agreeable conversation: he makes us always highly pleased with himself, if not with his hero. Dr. Johnson says, rather harshly, "This book is written with such depravity of genius, and such mixture of the fop and the pedant, as has not often appeared." Philips's "Life of Williams," written in the beginning of the last century, contains little additional information, and is a work of very inferior merit.

[2] (Inter alia) "Novem Linguarum Thesaurus." He was not like the polyglot Sir William Jones, ignorant of his mother-tongue (Welsh).

CHAPTER LXI.

LIFE OF LORD KEEPER COVENTRY FROM HIS BIRTH TILL THE COMMENCEMENT OF THE PROCEEDINGS RESPECTING SHIP MONEY.

WE now come to the life of a steady lawyer,—regularly bred to the bar,—by "a mixture of good and evil arts" advancing to the highest honors of his profession,—of powerful though not brilliant parts,—of great skill in his own science, but without any ornamental accomplishments,—unscrupulous where any great object was to be gained, yet with tact to stop without too much shocking public opinion,—though unaided by principle, knowing how to preserve a certain reputation for honesty,—uniformly prosperous while living—and fortunate in his death.

The Great Seal having been surrendered up by Lord Keeper Williams, at Foxley, in Wiltshire, remained with the King for a few days till he returned to Whitehall, and on the 1st of November, 1625, was delivered to Sir THOMAS COVENTRY.[1]

His family is traced to an inhabitant of the city of Coventry, who, coming to push his fortune in London in the reign of Henry IV., took the name of his native place. He left a son, John, who being an eminent mercer rose to be Sheriff in 1416, and Lord Mayor of London in 1425. He is much celebrated in the Chronicles for his discreet carriage in the struggle which took place during his Mayoralty between Humphrey, Duke of Gloucester, and Henry Beaufort, Bishop of Winchester,[2] and for having been appointed one of the executors of the famous Richard Whittington, who had risen to be thrice Lord Mayor from having had no property in the world but his cat. He bought an estate at Cussington, in Oxfordshire, long possessed by his posterity. From him was descended Sir Thomas Coventry, a very learned Judge of the Court of Common Pleas in the reign of James I.,[3] who married the

---

[1] Rot. Pat. 1 Car. 1, p. 24, n 7.   [2] Ante, vol. I. p. 317.
[3] Appointed Jan. 25, 1606. See in Dugd. Or. Jur. p. 97, a curious account of the procession on this occasion from Sergeants' Inn to Westminster, when

heiress of a family of the name of Jeffreys, settled at Croome, in Worcestershire.

Thomas, the Lord Keeper, was their eldest son, and was born there in the year 1578. He was an instance, not so rare in former as in more recent times, of the son of a great lawyer, proving a greater lawyer, although he labored under the disadvantage of being heir to considerable wealth, both by his father's and mother's side. But he showed from infancy, uncommon quickness and vigor of application. He remained under the paternal roof with a private tutor till he was fourteen, when he was entered a gentleman commoner at Baliol College, Oxford. He resided there three years, till he took his Bachelor's degree. He was then removed to the Inner Temple of which his father was a bencher, and he now diligently devoted himself to the study of the law. Instead of making acquaintance with William Shakespeare, or any of Burbage's company of players, he attached himself to Sir Edward Coke, then Attorney General. To law students and worshippers of his greatness, this tyrant of the bar was condescending and kind, carrying them with him to public disputations, directing their private reading, and warning them against *prepropera praxis* as well as *prepostera lectio*.

When called to the bar, young Coventry's progress was slow but sure. In 1606 his father died, and it was expected that he would have retired to the family estates; but he was ambitious, and he continued assiduously to follow his profession in the hope of political advancement.

So great did his reputation become in the course of a few years, without the *prestige* of office, that when Sir Edward Coke was to be dismissed from the Chief Justiceship of the King's Bench, Coventry, only thirty-seven years old, was designated by the public voice as his successor. Bacon, however, who had then a powerful ascendency, disliked him for having been protected by Coke, and thus wrote to James:—

"I send a warrant to the Lord Chancellor for making forth a writ for a new Chief Justice, leaving a blank for the name, to be supplied by your Majesty's presence; for I never received your Majesty's express pleasure in it. If

the frightful mistake was committed of making those of highest dignity march first, so that the students of the inns of Chancery came last.

your Majesty resolve of Montagu, as I conceive and wish, it is very material, as these times are, that your Majesty have some care that the Recorder succeeding be a temperate and discreet man, and assured to your Majesty's service. If your Majesty, without too much harshness, can continue the place within your own servants, it is best. If not, the man upon whom the choice is likely to fall (which is Coventry) I hold doubtful for your service; not but that he is a well learned and honest man; but he hath been, as it were, bred by Lord Coke, and seasoned in his ways."[1]

Montagu was appointed Chief Justice; and Coventry contriving to make it understood that, however much he respected the learning of his old master, he could not but lament his recent popular courses, was permitted to succeed as Recorder of London. An adhesion to ancient friendships, and a recollection of benefits received, do not seem in those days to have stood much in the way of promotion.

Having lost his first wife, who was of an ancient Worcestershire family, he now married "the widow of a citizen,—lovely, young, rich, and of good fame." "We may represent his happiness," says his biographer, "in nothing more than this, that London had first given him the handsel of a place both honorable and gainful, together with a wife as loving as himself was uxorious; and of that sort which are not unaptly styled housewives; so that these two drew diversely, but in one way, and to one and the self-same end,—he in the exercise of his profession—she in the exercise of her domestic; for they that knew the discipline of their house aver, that he waved that care as a contiguous distraction to his vocation, and left her only as a helper to manage that charge which best suited to her conversation."[2]

Coventry so rapidly got rid of all suspicion of favoring Sir. E. Coke, that on the 14th of March in the following year he was made Solicitor General; and two days after, going down to Theobald's to be presented to the King, he received the honor of knighthood.

He was counsel for the Crown on the trial of the Somersets for the murder of Sir Thomas Overbury, and in

[1] Bac. Works, vi. 131.
[2] MS. Life of Lord Coventry in the British Museum.

all the state prosecutions which followed for some years; but either from his own inclination, or the jealousy of the King's Sergeant and the Attorney General, he did not act a conspicuous part in any of them. Nevertheless he managed not only to enjoy favor while Lord Bacon was Chancellor, but on the disgrace of that great statesman, in which Yelverton, the Attorney General shared, to intrigue himself into the office of Attorney General.

His great object was quietly to nurse his fortune. He devoted himself to the discharge of his professional duties, and to gaining the good graces of all those who might serve him. He not only cultivated Buckingham assiduously, but supported the new Lord Keeper Williams in the Court of Chancery, and tried to veil his deficiencies in legal acquirements, till it was evident that the Bishop's official career was drawing to a close. The Great Seal being then within his own grasp, it would, perhaps, have been too much to have expected that he should not, by a few winks and shrugs, and stories of the Welshman's towering passions and ludicrous blunders, seek to precipitate his fall.

The only public prosecution I find him conducting while Attorney General, was that against Edward Floyde, for slandering the King and Queen of Bohemia. This case has been grossly misrepresented or misunderstood, and I am glad of an opportunity to explain it. It has been often cited as an instance of the abusive exercise of parliamentary privilege, whereas it was an instance of parliamentary impeachment. Floyde, a Catholic barrister, having said, "I have heard that Prague is taken; and Goodman Palsgrave, and Goodwife Palsgrave, have taken to their heels and run away, and, as I have heard, Goodwife Palsgrave is taken prisoner,"—the Protestant zeal of the country was very much excited, and the House of Commons, whose powers were as yet very undefined, took the case up as a fit subject of impeachment, and contended that they had judicial criminal jurisdiction as much as the Lords. They never pretended that any offense had been given to their body, or any member of it; but they alleged that a public crime had been committed, of which they had cognizance. Floyde was accordingly "impeached before the Commons in Parliament assembled," and the words being proved, a heavy sentence was passed upon him. He appealed to the King, who next morning sent to the Commons to inquire on what precedents they grounded their claim to judge offenses which did not concern their privileges, and by what reasoning it could be shown, that a court which did not receive evidence upon oath, could justly condemn a prisoner who asserted his innocence. This led to a conference between the two Houses, the Lords contending that their judicature was trenched upon—and the leaders of the Commons finding that this new pretension could not be supported, it was agreed that Floyde should be impeached before the Lords,—an entry being made in the Journals to soften the defeat, " that his trial before the Commons should not prejudice the rights of either House."

Coventry now conducted the prosecution at the bar of the House of Lords, not as Attorney General, but as manager for the Commons. He stated the case with moderation, and proved it by certain written depositions which he read. The defendant having been heard, he was found guilty *nemine dissentiente*.

Coventry then came to the clerk's table, and recapiulating his offense, prayed judgment against him, whereupon sentence was pronounced, " That he should be incapable to bear arms as a gentleman,—that he should ever be held infamous, and his testimony not taken in any court or cause,—that he should be set on a horse's back at Westminster Hall, with his face to the horse's tail, and holding the tail in his hands, with papers on his head and breast declaring his offense,—that he should ride to the pillory in Cheapside, there to stand two hours on the pillory, and be branded on the forehead with the letter K.,—that he should on a subsequent day be whipped from the Fleet to Westminster Hall, at the cart's tail, and then stand on the pillory there two hours,—that he should be fined in the sum of £5,000,—and that he should be imprisoned in Newgate during life." So shocked were the Lords themselves with this inhuman punishment, that they made a standing order, " That in future, when upon any person prosecuted before the House, being found guilty, judgment shall not be given till a future day, that time may be taken to consider thereof." Still upon this occasion, the Lords were acting in the exercise of their power of trying commoners for misdemeanors on the accusation of the Commons, and there is no pretense for citing the case to throw odium upon parliamentary privilege.[1]

Buckingham had found it difficult to get rid of Williams as Lord Keeper in the latter end of James's reign, but he held the Crown in his pocket on the accession of "Baby Charles." Sir Henry Hobart, the Chief Justice of the Common Pleas, who was first thought of for the Great Seal, having shown some symptoms of independence, the dictator resolved to give it to the discreet Coventry, on whom he thought he might implicitly rely. He accordingly wrote him an offer "to step into the shoes of my Lord of Lincoln," giving him time to consider of it. Mr. Attorney returned an answer, in which he declares that he had undergone a sharp conflict and perplexity of thoughts in measuring his fitness for such promotion, but concludes by expressing the dutiful resolution, "to lay himself in all humility and submission at the feet of his Sovereign, to dispose of him as should seem best to his own princely wisdom and goodness," which, says he, "if it be that way as your Grace told me his Highness did incline, I shall dutifully obey, and faithfully undergo it, my hope being that God and the King's Majesty will bear with my infirmities, and accept my true heart and willing endeavor."

Before his formal appointment, when his approaching elevation was known, Lord Bacon, now living in retirement in his chambers in Gray's Inn, applied to him to provide for an old dependent who had been cast away like his master, and was now in great straits. Coventry's refusal is unfeeling and discreditable. After adverting to Bacon's polite compliment, on his elevation, and declaring "his unaptness to so great an employment, nothingtheless

---

[1] 2 St. Tr. 1153. The sentence is happily ridiculed by Sheridan, who said of a person who had published a pamphlet against him: "I suppose that Mr. —— thinks I am angry with him; but he is mistaken for I never harbor resentment. If his punishment depended on me, I would show him that the dignity of my mind is superior to all vindictive feelings. Far should I be from wishing to inflict a capital punishment upon him grounded on his attack upon me; but yet, on account of his general character and conduct, and as a warning to others, I would merely order him to be publicly whipped three times; to be placed in the pillory four times; to be confined in prison seven years; and then, as he would enjoy freedom the more after so long a confinement, I would have him transported for the remainder of his life."—
2 John Taylor's Records, 174.

his submission to stand in that station where his Majesty will have him," he says—" as for the request you make for your servant, though I protest I am not yet engaged by promise to any, because I held it too much boldness towards my Master, and discourtesy towards my Lord Keeper, to dispose of places while he had the Seal ; yet in respect I have some servants, and some of my kindred apt for the place you speak of, and have been already so much importuned by noble persons when I lately was with his Majesty at Salisbury, as it will be hard for me to give them all denial ; I am not able to discern how I am able to accommodate your servant, though for your sake, and in respect of the former knowledge myself have had of the merit and worth of the gentleman, I should be most ready and willing to perform your desire, if it were in my power." How different from this heartless civility would have been his reply to a worthless courtier basking in the sunshine of court favor.

The new Lord Keeper was appointed by patent, whereby he was empowered " to hear, examine, and determine such causes, matters, and suits as shall happen to be, as well in the Chancery as in the Star Chamber, like as the Chancellor of England might and was accustomed to do." The Close Roll of this year is lost, and I find no account of the delivery of the Great Seal to him by the King, or of his installation.

He set to work very assiduously in the Court of Chancery, and there were many rehearings before him—as he was considered an accomplished Equity lawyer, and so little confidence could be placed in the skill of his right reverend predecessor. He is said to have behaved with great moderation, always speaking of Williams respectfully, reversing as seldom as possible, and under color of some fresh evidence, or of some new point being taken before him.

"At his first accession to the Seal, he found 200 causes in the paper ready for hearing, all which (with such as fell in the way) he determined within the year, so that the clients of the Court did not languish in expectation of the issue of their causes."[1]

But although he was allowed to be an able Judge, it is plain that the jurisdiction of the Court was still in a very

[1] Life of Lord Coventrie, in the British Museum.

unsettled state. We have a report of one of the earliest cases before him, showing that, while he decided legal rights himself, when difficult questions of equity arose, he sent a case to the common-law Judges.[1]

A commission was issued to Sir Julius Cæsar, Master of the Rolls, and others, to assist him in hearing causes; but unless at the commencement of his judicial career, he had no distraction from parliaments, and he himself did the great bulk of the business of the Court.[2]

In his second term he took his place on the woolsack, and was obliged to watch over a short but stormy session.

One reason of Charles I.'s dislike of Parliaments may have been his repugnance to speaking in public, from the hesitation in his utterance. At the opening of his second parliament, he merely said that he hated long speeches, and was not a very good hand at speaking, and therefore he meant to bring in the old custom which many of his predecessors had used—that my Lord Keeper should explain the royal will.

The Lord Keeper, going through the usual form of conferring with the King, as if taking instructions from him at the moment, then made a long and elaborate oration. The practice of taking a text of Scripture for a theme, which we have so often noticed, had now fallen into desuetude, and, I believe, was never adopted by lay Chancellors. Coventry, having dwelt much upon the use of parliaments, proceeded to an eulogium on the new Sovereign, "who doth strive whether he should be accounted *major* or *melior*, a greater King or a better man," justly complimenting him on " his daily and unwearied access to this House before his access to the Crown, and his gracious readiness in all conferences of importance."[3] Then came a declaration of his Majesty's good intentions during his future reign. " For his Majesty doth consider that

---

[1] See Farmer *v*. Compton, Chancery Reports in reign of Charles I., p. 1.

[2] At this time the judicial and political duties of the Lord Chancellor clashed much, for the Court of Chancery and the House of Lords both met punctually at eight o'clock in the morning. The Commons assembled at the same hour—never sitting later than twelve, and giving the afternoon to committees.

[3] Notwithstanding the errors into which Charles was led when he came to the throne, it is impossible not to admire his amiable and praiseworthy demeanor during his father's lifetime. The Journals of the House of Lords show that he was constant in his attendance there, and he seems to have been ever anxious to quiet all disputes, and to do a good turn to everybody.

the royal throne on which God, out of his mercy to us, hath set him, is the fountain of all justice, and that good laws are the streams and rills by which the benefit and use of this fountain is dispersed to his people. And it is his Majesty's care and study that his people may see, with comfort and joy of heart, that this fountain is not dry."[1]

Coventry was not yet a Peer, and he acted only as Speaker in putting the question, without taking a share in the debates; but he must be considered responsible for the measures of the government as far as law was concerned, and they were very unfortunate. The Commons were incensed by the trick of trying to disqualify Sir Edward Coke and several of the popular leaders, by nominating them Sheriffs of their counties.[2]

The same policy was pursued, with the like effect, in the Upper House. Buckingham, dreading the disclosures which might be made respecting his Spanish negotiations by the Earl of Bristol, a writ of summons was not sent to that nobleman; and on this being complained of as a breach of privilege, the Lord Keeper accompanied the writ with a mandate, that "his Lordship's personal attendance should be forborne." Bristol insisting on his right to take his seat as a Peer, the Attorney General was directed to exhibit articles of impeachment against him for high treason, and he was committed to the Tower. But these violent proceedings only irritated both Houses the more. The Commons impeached Buckingham, and the Lords showed no disinclination to listen to the charges against him. Notwithstanding an urgent letter of the King to the Speaker of the House of Commons to hasten the supply, they there talked only of grievances; and Clement Coke, Sir Edward's eldest son, said, "it was better to die by an enemy than to suffer at home."

By the Lord Keeper's advice both Houses were summoned to attend the King at Whitehall,—when the King gently, and the Lord Keeper bitterly, reproached them for their refractory conduct. The latter was particularly severe upon the Commons for the language they had permitted Clement Coke to hold among them,—dwelt upon

[1] 2 Parl. Hist. 39.
[2] I have often thought that it must have been an amusing spectacle at the Bucks assizes, to see the great Ex-Chief Justice with his white wand attending the Judges, who must have found it very convenient, if they were puzzled by any point of law which arose, to take the opinion upon it of the High Sheriff.

their unfounded charges against the Duke of Buckingham,—and went through all their proceedings since the commencement of the session, which, he said, showed an entire forgetfulness of duty.¹ The King at parting, no doubt prompted by Coventry, plainly intimated to them that, as parliaments were altogether in his power for their calling, sitting, and dissolution, if they were not more submissive he must govern without them.²

A curious constitutional question arose a few days after, which very much perplexed the Lord Keeper, and remains to this day undetermined. The Earl of Bristol, in his defense, relied upon communications which had passed between him and the King, when Prince, at Madrid, and to prove these proposed to call the King himself as a witness. The Lord Keeper gave it as his opinion, that the Sovereign can not be examined in any judicial proceeding under an oath, or without an oath, as he is the fountain of justice, and since no wrong may be imputed to him, the evidence would be without temporal sanction. On the other side they pointed out the hardship of an innocent man being deprived of his defense by the heir to the Crown becoming King, and urged that substantial justice ought to be paramount to all technical rules.

A proposal was made which could not be resisted, that the Judges should be consulted,—and two questions were propounded for their consideration: 1. "Whether, in case of treason or felony, the King's testimony was to be admitted or not?" 2. "Whether words spoken to the Prince, who is after King, makes any alteration in this case?" But when the Judges met on a subsequent day, the Lord Chief Justice declared that his Majesty, by his Attorney General, had informed them that, "not being able to discern the consequence which might happen to the prejudice of his crown from these general questions, his pleasure was that they should forbear to give an answer thereto."³

---

¹ One complaint which he makes shows how searching the inquiries were which the popular leaders were now disposed to institute, and excuses the warrants of Secretaries of State to open letters at the Post Office. "Your committees have presumed to examine the letters of secretaries of state, nay his own (the King's), and sent a general warrant to his signet office, and commanded his officers not only to produce and show the records, but their books and private notes which they made for his Majesty's service. This his Majesty holds as insufferable as it was in former times unusual."   ² 2 Parl. Hist. 60.

³ I humbly apprehend that the Sovereign, if so pleased, might be examined

The Lord Keeper further increased the irritation in the Lords by committing to the Tower the Earl of Arundel, Earl Marshal, for marrying, without the King's consent, his son to a daughter of the Duke of Lennox, allied to the royal family. The Lords voted his imprisonment pending the session an infringment of their privileges, and refused to proceed with any business till he was restored to liberty. This interposition was a heavy blow to the Court, as he held five proxies, which he was resolved to use in favor of Bristol and against Buckingham.

Seeing that all threats and violent measures were unavailing to sway the parliament, the usual resolution of the Stuarts under such circumstances was taken—of an abrupt dissolution. The Lords so far sympathized with the Commons, that, hearing of what was intended, they petitioned the King for a short delay. His answer, the Lord Keeper being at his elbow, was, "No, not of one minute."[1]

Angry recriminations were circulated through the country, under the titles of "The King's Reasons for dissolving Parliament," and "The intended Remonstrance of the Commons." The Earls of Bristol and Arundel, with the popular leaders of the Commons, were imprisoned by order of the King in Council. An attempt was now made to commit in the King's name, without specifying any offense; and if it had succeeded "Lettres de cachet" would have been established in England.

But the exhausted state of the Exchequer on this, as on many other occasions during the seventeenth century, proved the safeguard of our liberties. Buckingham's inglorious expedition to the Isle of Rhé caused a lavish expenditure, which all the irregular modes of raising money resorted to were unable to supply. The Lord

---

as a witness in any case, civil or criminal, but must be sworn, although there would be no temporal sanction to the oath. See 2 Rol. Ab. 686. "King James I. yielded testimony in many things in the Countess of Exeter's case;" whether sworn does not appear.—*Huds. Treatise on Star Chamber*, 2 Coll. *Jur.* 206. The simple certificate of King James I. as to what had passed in his hearing, was received as evidence in the Court of Chancery —*Abigny* v. *Clifford*, Hob. 213. But Willis, C.B., stated that in every other case the King's certificate had been refused.—*Omichund* v. *Barker*, Willis, 550. In the Berkeley Peerage case before the House of Lords in 1811, there was an intention of calling George IV., then Prince Regent, as a witness, and I believe the general opinion was that he might have been examined, but not without being sworn. [1] 2 Parl. Hist. 193.

Keeper was so imprudent as to sanction an attempt directly to impose new duties on merchandise by proclamation; but this being a palpable attempt to violate existing statutes, and not to evade them,—even the Judges declared it to be illegal. At last, in the beginning of 1628, such was the want of money, that no expedient remained but the calling of a fresh parliament. As a slight concession to public opinion, the jails were all cleared of their patriotic inmates; but the obstinacy of the King was not subdued, and he was not prepared to lower his pretensions.

On the first day of the session he said to the two Houses,—"Should you not do your duties in contributing what the state at this time needs, I must, in discharge of my conscience, use those other means which God hath put in my hands to save that which the follies of other men may otherwise hazard to lose;" and the Lord Keeper concluded a long oration with these words; "Therefore, so resolve of your supplies that they may be timely and sufficient, sorting the occasion; your aid is lost if too little or too late, and his Majesty is resolved that his affairs can not permit him to expect it overlong. This way of parliamentary supplies, as his Majesty hath told you, he hath chosen not as the only way, but as the fittest; not because he is destitute of others, but because it is most agreeable to the goodness of his own most gracious disposition, and to the desire and weal of his people. If this be deferred, necessity and the sword of the enemy make way for others. Remember his Majesty's admonition; I say, remember it."[1]

To the intelligence, moderation, and firmness of this parliament we are mainly indebted for the liberty we now enjoy.

A sufficient aid being voted, but not definitively,—the subject of arbitrary imprisonment was taken up by the two Houses, and many conferences were held between them, in which Sir Edward Coke displayed the fire of youth with the wariness of age.[2] Pym, in spite of his

---

[1] Rush. i. 477. 2 Parl. Hist. 221.

[2] Yet he sometimes discoursed as if commenting on a section of Littleton. He says that an Englishman hath and ought to have a fee in his liberty, and not a mere tenancy at will; "for no tenant at will will support or improve anything, because he hath no certain estate: ergo, to make men tenants at

minute subdivisions, gained the admiration of the House
and of the country by his energy, and laid the foundation
of that reputation which shone out with such splendor in
the Long Parliament. Wentworth, still a patriot, showed
what ascendancy he could give to which ever side he
espoused.

A plan was laid to put an end to these discussions by
calling the two Houses before the King, and making a
declaration to them of the King's respect for liberty. Accordingly the Lord Keeper, in his presence, said, "He
holdeth *Magna Charta,* and the other six statutes insisted
upon for the subjects' liberty, to be all in force, and assures you that he will maintain all his subjects in the just
freedom of their persons and safety of their estates, and
that he will govern according to the laws and statutes of
this realm, and that you shall find as much security in
his Majesty's royal word and promise as in the strength
of any law ye can make, so that hereafter ye shall never
have cause to complain."

The answer to this speech was "the Petition of Right,"
Wentworth exclaiming, sarcastically, "Never parliament
trusted more in the goodness of their King, so far as re-
gardeth ourselves; but we are ambitious that his Majesty's
goodness may remain to posterity." A statutable recognition was required of the illegality of raising money in
the shape of loans, or by any other contrivance, without
the authority of parliament; of commitments by the
King, without stating a sufficient cause in the warrant; of
quartering soldiers in private houses; and of trying
soldiers, mariners, and their accomplices, in time of peace,
by martial law.

Coventry assisted in all the shifts and contrivances by
which Charles attempted to evade giving an unqualified
assent to this act, but stood by his side, when he at last,
with his own lips, pronounced the words, "Soit droit fait

will of their liberties, destroys all industry and endeavors whatsoever; and
so much for these six principal reasons:—

"Taken {
 A re ipsa,
 A minore ad majus,
 A remediis,
 From the extent and universality,
 From the indefinitenesss of the time,
 A fine.
} Loss of {
 Honor,
 Profit,
 Security,
 Industry."
}

come il est désiré," amidst the plaudits of all present, followed by unbounded rejoicing throughout the nation.[1]

The good understanding, however, was of short duration, for the King, receiving very bad advice from Coventry and other courtiers, insisted on his authority to levy tonnage and poundage by his prerogative alone; and the Commons resumed with fresh ardor the impeachment of Buckingham. To put an end to these proceedings, the King came to the House of Lords one morning at nine o'clock, without his crown or his robes,—the Peers likewise being unrobed. Mounting the throne, he ordered the Black Rod to summon the Commons, who had met at eight, and were framing a remonstrance to remind him that by the Petition of Right he was precluded from levying duties on merchandise without the previous consent of parliament.

When they had come to the bar he made a speech, trying to explain away the Petition of Right, which, he said, he had been told would not interfere with his lawful prerogative; and he insisted on his inherent and hereditary title to tonnage and poundage. He then gave the royal assent to the subsidy and other bills which had passed, and the Lord Keeper, by his orders, prorogued the parliament.[2]

Coventry's conduct during the session had given so much satisfaction to the Court, that he was now raised to the peerage by the title of Baron Coventry, of Aylesborough, in the county of Worcester.

A few weeks after, his position was considerably altered by the assassination of Buckingham, to whom he owed his elevation;—and, till the apostasy and rise of Wentworth under a new name, which followed after no long interval, he was himself the most influential adviser of the Crown. Unhappily, instead of checking Charles's arbitrary propensities, he zealously encouraged and abetted them.

In the beginning of the following year the same parliament re-assembled; but all confidence in the sincerity of Charles, and the honesty or prudence of the Lord Keeper and his other ministers, was gone, by the disgraceful artifice resorted to of circulating as by authority, copies of

[1] 2 Parl. Hist. 374.   [2] 2 Parl. Hist.

the Petition of Right, with the evasive answer to it which had first been pronounced.

The Lord Keeper was strongly suspected of being the author of this proceeding; and a direct attack was made upon him along with the Barons of the Exchequer, for having decided in their Courts that tonnage and poundage might be lawfully levied without an act of parliament. Charles, when it was too late, tried to conciliate, by declaring that he did not challenge tonnage and poundage as a right, and that he was willing that an act should pass to confer them upon him. The Commons threatened to punish the officers who had levied these duties unlawfully,—when Secretary Cook declared that the King would not separate the obedience of his servants from his own acts, nor suffer them to be punished for executing his commands.

This led to the famous resolutions, "that whosoever shall advise the taking of tonnage and poundage, not being granted by parliament, shall be reputed a capital enemy to this kingdom and government; and that whatever merchant or other person shall pay tonnage and poundage, not being granted by parliament, shall be reputed a betrayer of the liberties of England." [1]

Finch, the Speaker, refusing to put the resolutions, and wishing to leave the House, was forcibly held in the chair till they were carried. Meanwhile, the King was in the House of Lords, impatient to put an end to these proceedings by a dissolution, and (the Lord Keeper standing by his side) he ordered the Usher of the Black Rod to summon the Commons to attend his Majesty at the bar forthwith. This officer went, with the emblem of his office in his hand, and knocked at the door of the House of Commons, but was barred out, and obliged to report on his return that he could not procure admittance. The Captain of the Guard, in a little time, was ordered to break the door open; but going for that purpose, he found that the Commons had adjourned. On the day of the adjournment the King again went to the House of Lords; and the Lord Keeper, without asking the attendance of the Commons, dissolved the Parliament.

This was the last time that Coventry ever appeared in the House of Lords; for an interval followed of near

[1] 2. Parl. Hist. 490.

twelve years without a Parliament, and before another met he was snatched away from the impending troubles.

A settled resolution was now formed to establish despotism in England, and, but for the formidable insurrection which broke out in Scotland, there is scarcely a doubt that the scheme would have succeeded, and that " parliament" would have been read of in our history as an obsolete institution, showing that our ancestors were free I must consider Lord Keeper Coventry the most culpable of the conspirators, although, from the wariness of his nature and the mediocrity of his talents, he has escaped the full measure of indignation which his conduct deserved. Charles himself was an absolutist *par métier* (as Frederick the Great said of himself), and, considering the notions of Divine right which he inherited from his father, and which were assiduously inculcated by the ministers of religion around him, we need not wonder that after the three attempts he had made to hold parliaments, his conscience was satisfied with the conviction that, being useless and mischievous, they might be safely superseded by prerogative. Laud, a narrow-minded priest, looked with such horror upon the Puritans, that he mixed up their love of freedom with their dislike of episcopacy, and might excusably think that he was promoting both the temporal and spiritual interests of the community by assisting in obtaining supreme power for the pious Head of the Church. Strafford, with great genius, had been educated only as a country gentleman, and, passing, with the zeal of a renegade, from the popular to the prerogative side, he perhaps incurred less moral blame than if he had been regularly trained in a familiar acquaintance with the laws and constitution of his country. Noy, the Attorney General, and Littleton, the Solicitor General, who had gone over along with him, thought they were little to blame while they imitated the example and received the warm applauses of the head of their profession,—a Peer of parliament and in possession of the Great Seal. Lord Coventry had not even the poor apology set up for Lord Bacon, that he was acting under the uncontrollable influence of an imperious minister. After the death of Buckingham, Charles thought for himself, and was open to any advice that might be offered to him by any of his councillors. There can not be a doubt, therefore, that Coventry might have interposed, effectively, to deprecate the unconstitutional, illegal, cruel, and oppressive measures which were now resorted to; but, instead of this, in a cool, quiet, and cunning manner he suggested them, he executed them, and he defended them. Thinking that a time of retribution might possible arrive, he studied, as far as he could, to avoid the appearance of taking a prominent part at the council-table or in the Star Chamber; but his were the orders, his were the proclamations, his were the prosecutions, and his were the sentences which marked the next eleven years of arbitrary rule, and which, if he had succeeded in his enterprise, might have made him be celebrated as another Richelieu.

As soon as parliament was dissolved, the popular leaders of the House of Commons were summoned before the Council, and being examined by the Lord Keeper respecting their conduct at the conclusion of the session—particularly in keeping the Speaker in the chair and forcing him to put the question on the resolution against taxing without the authority of parliament,—they were all committed to prison by warrants which did not express the cause of commitment. The legality of such warrants had been denied; and if they could be established, a great step was gained, for thereafter no redress could be obtained by an appeal to the ordinary legal tribunals.

Some apprehension was entertained respecting the firmness of Sir Randolph Crew, the Lord Chief Justice of the King's Bench, a very learned lawyer, who had gone considerable lengths in supporting the measures of the Government, but was supposed not to be entirely free from principle, or the dread of the House of Commons, if there should ever be another parliament. He was therefore unceremoniously dismissed from his office by the Lord Keeper, and Sir Nicholas Hyde, in whom the event showed that entire confidence was rightly placed, was appointed his successor.

The Lord Keeper then directed certain questions to be put to the Judges, with the view of for ever extinguishing freedom of speech in parliament, and subjecting refractory members to the jurisdiction of the King's Judges for their words and conduct as representatives of the people. These venerable sages, who, it is contended, ought constitutionally to have been considered the arbiters of parliamentary privileges, unanimously returned for answer, "that freedom of speech only extends to things debated in parliament *in a parliamentary course*, and that a parliament man, committing an offense against the King or Council in parliament, not in a parliament way, may be punished for it after the parliament ended; for the parliament shall not give privilege to any one *contra morem parliamentarium* exceeding the bounds of his place and and duty,"—whereof the Courts were necessarily to be the sole Judges.[1]

Writs of habeas corpus were sued out in vain, and Sir John Eliot and others were convicted and sentenced for what they had done in the House of Commons. No writ of error could then be brought, as parliament was not allowed to sit; but the judgment was reversed after the death of Lord Coventry, and many years after the defendants had suffered the punishment so unjustly inflicted upon them.[2]

In Chamber's case the Lord Keeper was supposed to show commendable moderation for those times. The defendant, an eminent Turkey merchant, being required to pay exorbitant duties on goods not imposed by parliament, had the temerity to say that "merchants are in no part of the world so screwed as in England, and that in Turkey they had more encouragement." Being prosecuted in the Star Chamber for this seditious speech, he was of course found guilty, and Laud and several others were for fining him £3,000; but the Lord Keeper mildly proposed £1,500, and the fine was at last fixed at £2,000, the defendant likewise being ordered to read an acknowledgement of his great offense, dictated by the Attorney General.[3]

In the next case, which was a prosecution against Dr. Alexander Leighton, a Scotch divine, for slandering prelacy, there was no division of opinion, and the Lord Keeper pronounced sentence, in which all concurred, "that the defendant should be imprisoned in the Fleet

---

[1] It should, however, be recollected, to the credit of the Judges, that the year before, in Felton's case, there being abundant evidence to convict him, and neither the King, the Lord Keeper, nor the Attorney General pressing them for a contrary opinion, "they agreed that he ought not to be tortured by the rack, for no such punishment is known or allowed by our law."—3 St. Tr. 371.   [2] Ibid. 331.   [3] Ibid. 380.

during life,—should be fined £10,000,—and after being degraded from holy orders by the High Commissioners, should be set in the pillory in Westminster,—should there be whipt,—should after being whipt again be set in the pillory,—should have one of his ears cut off,—should have his nose slit,—should be branded in the face with a double S. S. for a Sower of Sedition,—should afterwards be set in the pillory in Cheapside, there whipt, and after being whipt again be set in the pillory, and have his other ear cut off."[1]

A book was now industriously circulated, entitled "A Proposition for his Majesty's Service to bridle the Impertinency of Parliaments," recommending that, after the fashion of France and other Continental states, all the towns in England should be fortified and garrisoned; that all highways should lead through these towns; that no one should be allowed to enter them without a passport, showing whence he came and whither he was going, and that the gates be shut all night, the keys being kept by the Mayor or Governor; that innkeepers be required to deliver in the names of all strangers who come to their houses; that the ruined castles to be found near most cities should be repaired, bulwarks and ramparts for ordnance being added according to the rules of fortification; that an oath should be required, acknowledging that the King is as absolute as any other Christian Prince, and may by proclamation either make or reverse laws without consent of parliament; that the example of Louis XI. should be followed, who found the like opposition from popular assemblies, and effectually suppressed them; that instead of parliamentary subsidies, a tax, to be called "a decimation," should be imposed by the King, importing the tenth of all subjects' estates to be paid as a yearly rent to their Prince; that the monopoly of the sale of salt should be assumed by the King, as in foreign countries; that £5 *per cent.* on the value of all property in litigation be demanded by the Crown, and for recompense thereof to limit all lawyers' fees and gettings (so excessive in England), whereby the subject should save more in fees and

---

[1] Laud's Journal shows that this sentence was rigorously carried into execution. After minutely describing the punishment at Westminster, he says, "on that day sevennight his sores upon his back, ear, nose, and face being not cured, he was whipt again at the pillory in Cheapside, and there had the remainder of his sentence executed upon him by cutting off the other ear, slitting the other side of the nose, and branding the other cheek."

charges than he would give in this new gabella, reckoned to bring in £50,000 a year; that there should likewise be imposed a gabella, as in Tuscany, on all cattle, horses, flesh, fish, and other victuals, bread excepted; and, lastly, that the King should strictly enforce the keeping of fast days, granting a dispensation to those willing to pay for it, which it was calculated would yield £100,000 a year, without any disgust, because it would be every one's choice to give it or no. Thus was the King of England for ever after to be powerful, rich, and independent, and without distraction to exercise a paternal rule over his dutiful and loving subjects!

But the scheme caused much scandal, being considered a plain proof that the King was avowedly aiming at despotic sway, and it excited such dangerous discontents, that the Lord Keeper thought the discreet course would be to disclaim it, and to institute a sham prosecution against some who had read the book, which the Court had at first warmly patronized. Accordingly, an information in the Star Chamber was filed against the Earl of Bedford, the Earl of Clare, Sir Robert Cotton, John Selden, Esquire, Oliver St. John, Esquire, and several other patriots, for publishing a seditious writing, entitled "A Proposition for his Majesty's Service to bridle the Impertinency of Parliaments."

However, when this case was coming to a hearing, the Lord Keeper declared in the Star Chamber that the King, in respect of the great joy upon the birth of his son,[1] had ordered the proceedings to be stopped, and the defendants to be discharged; yet to mark his dislike of such advice, commanded the writing to be burned as seditious and scandalous.[2]

But the scheme was in reality highly agreeable to the Court, and was steadily acted upon. Not only were tonnage and poundage still levied without authority of parliament, but the duty on goods imported was, from time to time, increased by the Council, and extended to new commodities. A new stamp duty was imposed upon cards. To accustom the people to obey the royal mandate, proclamations were issued from time to time respecting subjects connected with trade, the public health, and supposed public convenience, and these were enforced in the Star

[1] Charles II., born May 29, 1630. [2] 3 St. Tr. 387.

Chamber,—with the intention that breaches of them should, by-and-by, be punished by indictment in the Courts of common law, and that, by degrees, a proclamation might in all respects be considered equivalent to an act of parliament.[1]

If persons, to escape from these oppressions, wished to seek refuge in another hemisphere, they were restrained from emigrating by proclamation. Thus was the ship stopped that was to carry to New England Cromwell, Pym, Hampden, and Hazelrig; and a violation of the law which, being compared with others, was considered so slight as not to be much regarded at the time, led to a revolution in the state.[2]

Not more respect was paid to private property than to public rights, as many shops and houses were pulled down, by order in Council, to make way for supposed improvements in the city of London, such compensation being made to the owners as an agent of Government chose to fix.[3]

The Lord Keeper was in a more special manner answerable for the revival of monopolies. In direct violation of the statute law, he passed many patents under the Great Seal for the exclusive manufacture and vending of soap, leather, salt, and other commodities, without any pretense of invention or improvement,—merely in respect of the large sums that were given for the grants. A parliament was talked of to redress these grievances; but, to drive the people to despair, a proclamation came out, countersigned by the Lord Keeper, wherein the King reciting the late abuses in parliament, declared that " he would consider it presumption for any one to prescribe to him any time for calling that assembly,"—so that a petition for a parliament would afterwards have been prosecuted as a seditious libel.

[1] These proclamations prohibited the importation of certain commodities, regulated the mode of carrying on manufactures at home, fixed the prices of marketable goods, forbade the erection of houses in London, and enforced residence in the country. For disobedience of this last proclamation, 167 persons were prosecuted in one year. One Hillyard was fined £5,000 for selling saltpeter contrary to proclamation.—*Rushworth*, ii. 144.

[2] Ibid. 409, 418.

[3] Mr. Hume defends or palliates these illegal acts by observing that, as parliament did not meet, they were necessary, thereby making the unconstitutional disuse of parliaments the excuse for the assumption of legislative power by the Crown.—*Hume's Hist.* c. 52.

The attention of the public was for a short time, diverted from these measures by the trial, before Lord Coventry, as Lord High Steward, and his Peers, of Lord Audley, Earl of Castlehaven, in Ireland, for assisting in committing a rape on his wife, and for other abominable offenses. The custom was still kept up of previously taking the opinion of the Judges on any points likely to arise in a criminal case, even though not of a political nature; and on this occasion, for the guidance of the Lord High Steward, they told him "that a Peer of Parliament could not, if so inclined, waive his privilege, and be tried by Commoners; that a Peer can not challenge a Peer on his trial; that a Peer was not entitled to counsel for matter of fact more than a Commoner; that a wife may be a witness against her husband in case of personal violence; and that in clergyable offenses a Peer can not pray his privilege till he confesses or is found guilty."

The trial took place with great pomp and solemnity, in Westminster Hall. When the prisoner had been placed at the bar, the Lord High Steward, after alluding to the heavy charges against him, said, "His Majesty brings you this day to your trial, doing herein like the mighty King of kings, in the 18th of Genesis, ver. 20, 21, who went down to see whether their sins were so grievous as the cry of them. 'Because the cry of Sodom and Gomorrah is great, and their sins be grievous, I will go down (saith the Lord) and see whether they have done altogether according to the cry of it.' And kings on earth can have no better pattern to follow than the King of heaven; and therefore our Sovereign Lord the King, God's Vicegerent here on earth, hath commanded that you should be tried this day, and to that end hath caused these Peers to be assembled." The trial then proceeded, on three indictments, for three several felonies at the same time. Both written depositions and *vivâ voce* evidence were adduced against him. Being found guilty, sentence was pronounced upon him very impressively by the Lord High Steward, and he was afterwards executed.[1]

The King soon after went into Scotland, ostensibly to be crowned, but, in reality, to enforce the attempt to introduce Laud's episcopacy into that country; an attempt which for ever alienated from him the hearts of his

[1] 3 St. Tr. 402.

countrymen, and which may be considered the remote cause of all his misfortunes. Laud accompanying him, Coventry was left at the head of affairs in England, and no way relaxed the arbitrary system pursued by his master.

Charles returned from Scotland under the delusion that he had completely effected his object, and more thoroughly determined to make himself absolute all over the island. The death of Archbishop Abbot enabled him to raise Laud to the primacy; and Juxon, the new Bishop of London (to the general disgust, and to the deep concern of all the enlightened friends of the Church), was made Lord High Treasurer,—to preside in the seat of Lord Burleigh over the finances and councils of the nation.

Now the innovations to bring the rites of the Church of England as near as possible to those of Rome were pushed with fresh energy, and the Puritans were persecuted with redoubled zeal. Lord Coventry, neither in the Council nor in the Star Chamber, did anything for the law, the constitution, or the public safety. He sometimes pretended to disapprove of the excesses of Laud, but in reality countenanced them. Henry Sherfield, an ancient barrister of Lincoln's Inn, being prosecuted in the Star Chamber for breaking a painted glass window in a church at Salisbury, the Lord Keeper at first gave it as his opinion that the defendant should only be reprimanded, make an acknowledgment before the Bishop, and repair the broken window; but he easily allowed himself to be overruled by Laud, and pronounced the sentence that the defendant should further be fined £500, and be committed to the Fleet prison.[1]

The sentence of the Star Chamber on the learned Prynne for his "HISTRIOMASTIX, or a Scourge for Stage Players," was unanimous—"that he should be disbarred, —that he should be fined £10,000,[2]—that he should suffer perpetual imprisonment, 'like monsters that are not fit to live among men, nor to see light,'—that he should stand in the pillory in Westminster and Cheapside,—that he should have his ears cropped,[3]—that his nose should be

---

[1] 3 St. Tr. 561.
[2] It was avowed that this fine was more than he was able to pay, so that Magna Charta was ostentatiously violated.
[3] It was pleasantly observed, that "he might conceal his loss of ears by

slit,—and that he should be branded on the forehead, and that all who had any copies of his book should deliver them up to be burnt, under pain of the high displeasure of the Court.[1]

Now came the two prosecutions, in the Star Chamber, of Ex-Lord Keeper Williams,[2] which Hume imputes to "the haughty Primate," and denounces as "the most iniquitous measure pursued by the Court during the time that the use of parliaments was suspended." But the sentences of fine, pillory, ear-cropping, and imprisonment for life in distant gaols, pronounced and executed upon Bastwick, the physician, and Burton, the divine, for reflecting upon the Bishops, might well bear a comparison.

In the case of Lilburn, the Lord Keeper took a very active part in supporting the jurisdiction of the Court. An information being exhibited against the defendant for a libel, he was called upon to answer interrogatories that he might criminate himself,—and refusing to answer them, he was brought up before the Lord Keeper, and the other dignitaries forming this awful tribunal, for his contempt. —*Lord Keeper.* "Why will you not answer?"—*Lilburn.* "My honorable Lord, I have answered fully before Mr. Attorney General to all things that belong to me to answer unto."—*Lord Keeper.* "But why do you refuse to take the Star Chamber oath?"—*Lilburn.* "Most noble Lord, I refused on this ground, because that when I was examined, although I had fully answered all things that belonged to me to answer unto, and had declared myself of the thing for which I am imprisoned, yet that would not give content, but other things were put unto me concerning other men, to ensnare me and get further matter against me. And withal I perceived the oath to be an oath of inquiry, and for the lawfulness of which oath I have no warrant."—*Lord Keeper.* "Well, come, submit yourself unto the Court."—*Lilburn.* "Most noble Lords, with all willingness I submit my body unto your Honors' pleasure; but for any other submission, I am conscious to

a periwig, although in his 'Histriomastix' he had inveighed against that ornament."

[1] 3 St. Tr. 562. Hume can not conceal his delight in recording the punishment of Prynne, and openly praises the good intention of the Court in thus trying to inspire better humor into the Puritans, but adds, with much *naïveté*, "whether pillories, fines, and prisons were proper expedients for that purpose, *may admit of some question.*" [2] Ante, pp. 173, 174.

myself that I have done nothing that doth deserve a convention before this illustrious assembly, and therefore for me to submit, is to submit I know not wherefor." He was committed to the Fleet, and, being brought up on a subsequent day, still refused, in spite of all threats, to be sworn. *Lord Keeper.* "Thou art a mad fellow, seeing things are thus, that thou wilt not take thine oath."—*Lilburn.* "My honorable Lord, I have declared unto you the real truth ; but for the oath, it is an oath of inquiry, and of the same nature as the High Commission oath, which oath I know to be unlawful." The Lord Keeper then sentenced him to be fined £500, to be whipt through the streets, to be set in the pillory, and to be remanded to the Fleet till he conformed. When in the pillory he distributed some papers, said to be seditious, because they vindicated his innocence,—and for this new offense an order was made, on the suggestion of the Lord Keeper, to which Laud and all the other Judges assented, "that he should be laid alone—with irons on his hands and legs —in the wards of the Fleet, where the loosest and meanest sort of prisoners are used to be put."[1]

These were sentences of the Star Chamber, Coventry's own Court, and generally pronounced with his own lips. But he must likewise be held responsible for the greater iniquities of the High Commission, which, if he did not prompt, he might easily have restrained, either by his private influence, or judicially by writs of prohibition,— which he refused to issue.

He was further grievously to blame for vexations which he countenanced in extending the bounds of royal forests, and for the extortions practiced under his superintendence in reviving obsolete claims by the Crown to estates that had for generations been quietly enjoyed by the families now in possession of them.

[1] 3 St. Tr. 1315.

CHAPTER LXII.

CONCLUSION OF THE LIFE OF LORD KEEPER COVENTRY.

WE have been relating the grievances of individuals which, though they excited much commiseration, might long have been borne without any general movement; but "SHIP-MONEY" now threw the whole nation into a flame. The Lord Keeper, if not *artifex*, was *particeps criminis*. Noy, who had gained eminence in his profession by practicing "in the sedition line," having *ratted* and been made Attorney General, was eager to show his devotion to the Court,—and, after a long examination of musty records in the Tower, finding that in time of war the King had first pressed ships into his service, had then asked the seaports to equip ships for him, and had occasionally afterwards ordered the adjoining counties to contribute to the expense,—framed his famous scheme, which, if it had succeeded, would have effectually superseded parliaments. He disclosed his invention to the Lord Keeper, and to Strafford, now high in the ascendant, and they both rapturously approved of it:—but foreseeing that its legality would come in question, and entertaining some misgivings respecting Sir Robert Heath, Chief Justice of the Common Pleas, they, as a prudent preliminary, removed him from his office, and substituted for him Sir John Finch, one of the most unprincipled and reckless Judges who ever disgraced the English Bench. The writs under the Great Seal, directed to the Sheriffs of every county in England, fixing, by royal authority, the sum to be raised in each county, and requiring that it should be ratably assessed, were then concocted; but before they were issued their author suddenly died, and the chief burden of prosecuting the measure fell upon the Lord Keeper.

Not flinching from the task, he assembled all the Judges in the Exchequer Chamber previous to the Summer Circuit, and after addressing them on various other topics, came to the legality of ship-money.

"I have but one thing more to give you in charge, and it is a thing of great weight and importance; it concerneth the honor of his Majesty and the kingdom, and the safety of both. Christendom is full of war, and there is nothing but rumors of war. No doubt it hath ever been accounted the greatest wisdom for a nation to arm that they may not be enforced to fight, which is better than not to arm and to be sure to fight. Therefore his Majesty, in those doubtful times, hath not only commanded that all the land forces of the kingdom should be set in order and readiness, but to set to sea a royal fleet at his Majesty's great charge, but with the assistance of the maritime places of this kingdom. The causes, and occasions, and times of war, with the preparation and ordering of them, is proper to the King; and dutiful obedience in such things does best become the subject. And yet his Majesty hath vouchsafed, even by his writ, to declare enough to satisfy all well-minded men, and to express the dearness of his princely heart in aiming at the general good of his kingdom. Upon advice with his Council he hath resolved that he will forthwith send forth new writs for the preparation of a greater fleet next year, and that not only to the maritime towns, but to all the kingdom besides; for since that all the kingdom is interested, both in the honor, safety, and profit, it is just and reasonable that they should all put to their helping hands. Now that which his Majesty requireth from you and doth command is, that in your charges at the assizes, and in all places else, where opportunity is offered, you take an occasion to let the people know how careful and zealous his Majesty is to preserve his honor, and the honor of this kingdom, and the dominion of the sea; and to secure both sea and land with a powerful fleet, that foreign nations may see that England is both ready and able to keep itself and all its rights. And you are to let them know how just it is that his Majesty should require this for the common defense, and with what alacrity and cheerfulness they ought and are bound in duty to contribute to it: that foreign nations may observe the power and readiness of this kingdom, which will make them slow to contend with us, either by sea or land; and that will be the best way to confirm unto us a sure peace."[1]

The writs were issued, and were generally obeyed; but many grumbled,—some openly asserted that the imposition was unlawful, and it became of the utmost import-

[1] 3 St. Tr. 837.

ance to ensure a favorable decision, should the question come before a court of law. The Lord Keeper therefore applied to the Judges,—dealing in the first instance in fraudulent generalities,—and obtained from them an unanimous resolution, that " as were the benefit redounded to the ports and maritime parts, the charge was, according to the precedent of former times, lawfully laid upon them; so by parity of reason, where the good and safety of the kingdom in general is concerned, the charge ought to be borne by the whole realm."

Having laid this foundation, he in the following Term put two specific questions to the Judges: 1. " Whether, in cases of danger to the good and safety of the Kingdom, the King could not impose ship-money for its defense and safeguard, and by law compel payment from those who refused?" 2. " Whether the King were not the sole Judge both of the danger, and when and how it was to be prevented?"

The twelve Judges having assembled in Sergeants' Inn Hall, they were told that their opinion was merely required for the private satisfaction of the royal conscience. Ten agreed to answer both questions, without qualification, in the affirmative. Two, Crooke and Hutton, dissented, but were induced to subscribe the opinion—upon the representation that, when the Judges were thus consulted, the judgment of the majority was that of the whole body.

To the dismay of Crooke and Hutton, and to the utter astonishment of them and of all their brethren,—as soon as the Lord Keeper was armed with this opinion he assembled them all openly in the Star Chamber, and, with a full knowledge of the manner in which it had been obtained and signed,—after another elaborate panegyric on ship-money, and heavy complaint of those who disloyally questioned the King's power to demand it, he thus proceeded: " When his Majesty heard of some refusals, though he had cause to be sensible of it, yet he was far from being transported with passion, but thought good to resort to the advice of you his Judges who are sworn to give him faithful and true counsel in that which pertaineth to the law; and this his Majesty, as well for the direction of his own course as for the satisfaction of his subjects, required you to deliver your opinion herein, to which you returned an answer under your hands." He then ordered the opinion to be read by the clerk, with the names of all the twelve as they were in order subscribed; which being done before a crowded audience, he continued: " My Lords, *this being the uniform resolution of all the Judges of England, with one voice and act under their hands;* I say, this being so resolved, as they do here express upon every man's particular studying the case, and upon a general conference among themselves, it is of very great authority, for the very lives and lands of the King's subjects are to be determined by these reverend Judges; much more a charge of this nature, which, God knows, can not be burdensome to any, but is of singular use and consequence, and for the safety of the whole kingdom. The command from his Majesty is, that I should publish this your opinion in this place, and give order that it should be entered in this Court, in the High Court of Chancery, and in the Courts of King's Bench, Common Pleas, and Exchequer, for this is a thing not fit to be kept in a corner. And his further command is, that you the Judges do declare and publish this general resolution of all the Judges of England through all parts of the kingdom, that all men may take notice thereof, and that those his subjects which have been in an error may inform themselves and be reformed. You have great cause to declare it with joy, and you can hardly do it with honor enough to the King, that in so high a point of his sovereignty he hath been pleased to descend and to communicate with you his Judges;—which showeth that justice and sovereignty in his Majesty do kiss each other."

The reverend sages of the law all remained mute while this trick was played off upon them, those who were eagerly looking for promotion approving of it in their hearts, and the dissentients not being able to deny their handwriting, or publicly to enter into any explanation of their conduct.

One man in England remained unconcerned and undismayed by this supposed unanimous opinion of the twelve Judges, and that was JOHN HAMPDEN! He refused to pay the twenty shillings assessed upon him in respect of his estate in Buckinghamshire, and being sued for the amount, he, in due form, denied his liability. The case, on account of its importance, was adjourned into the

Exchequer Chamber, before all the Judges, and was there argued many days. Lord Chancellor Ellesmere, on a similar occasion, was present in the Exchequer Chamber, and pronounced judgment;[1] but Lord Keeper Coventry does not seem to have publicly interfered with the decision of this case, though he was, no doubt, very active in privately reminding the Judges of the opinion they had given. To the immortal honor of Crooke and Hutton, notwithstanding the manner in which they had been entrapped, and notwithstanding all the attempts now made to work upon their fears and hopes, they delivered a clear and decided opinion upon the merits,—that the tax was unauthorized by the common law, and was forbidden by statute. Three other Judges, Davenport, Brampston, and Denham, without denying the King's right, voted for the defendant on certain points of form. But there being a majority, with Lord Chief Justice Finch at their head, who held that the power to impose this tax belonged to the Crown at common law, and that, even if there were statutes to abolish it, these statutes were not binding on the King,—judgment was given *quod defendens oneretur*, and process of execution issued to levy the twenty shillings.

Coventry and Strafford were short-sighted enough to rejoice in the victory they had won, thinking arbitrary government was firmly established. "Since it is lawful," said they, "for the King to impose a tax towards the equipment of the navy, it must be equally so for the levy of an army; and the same reason which authorizes him to levy an army to resist, will authorize him to carry that army abroad, that he may prevent invasion. Moreover, what is law in England is law also in Scotland and Ireland. This decision of the Judges will, therefore, make the King absolute at home and formidable abroad."[2] But "it is notoriously known that the pressure was borne with more cheerfulness before the judgment for the King than ever it was after; men before pleasing themselves with doing somewhat for the King's service as a testimony of their affection, which they were not bound to do; many really believing the necessity, and therefore thinking the burden reasonable; others observing that the advantage to the King was of importance, when the damage to them was not considerable; and all assuring

[1] Case of Postnati, *ante*, vol. ii. p. 376.   [2] Strafford Papers, ii. 61.

themselves that, when they should be weary or unwilling to continue the payment, they might resort to the law for relief, and find it. But when they heard this demanded in a court of law as a right, and found it, by sworn Judges of the law, adjudged so, upon such grounds and reasons as every stander-by was able to swear was not law, and so had lost the pleasure and delight of being kind and dutiful to the King; and instead of giving were required to pay, and by a logic that left no man any thing which he might call his own, they no more looked upon it as the case of one man, but the case of the kingdom, nor as an imposition laid on them by the King, but by the Judges, which they thought themselves bound in conscience to the public justice not to submit to. When they saw in a court of law reasons of state urged as elements of law; Judges as sharp-sighted as Secretaries of State, and in the mysteries of state; judgment of law grounded upon matter of fact of which there was neither inquiry nor proof; and no reason given for the twenty shillings in question but what included the estates of all the standers-by,—they had no reason to hope that doctrine, or the promoters of it, would be contained within any bounds; and it is no wonder that they, who had so little reason to be pleased with their own condition, were no less solicitous for, or apprehensive of, the inconveniences that might attend any alteration." [1]

Notwithstanding the general discontent, there is too much reason to believe that the scheme to establish absolute government on the ruins of free institutions would have succeeded in England, as it did about this time in France, had it not been for the troubles which now broke out in Scotand. Charles's violent attempt to introduce episcopacy into that country, though he had so far succeeded as to have the Archbishop of St. Andrew's for his Chancellor, and several other Prelates invested in the high offices of state,—produced the most sudden, peaceful, and complete revolution recorded in history. In the course of a few weeks, without a drop of blood being spilt, the King was virtually dethroned, and a new government was established, under the title of "The Tables," with the almost unanimous consent of the nobles, the gentry, and commonalty,—having a well disciplined army at its com-

[1] Clarendon.

mand, and recognized by all the civil functionaries in the kingdom. "The solemn League and Covenant" immediately followed.

The first effect produced in England by this movement was a ludicrous trial, at which the Lord Keeper presided with apparent gravity. When the news arrived at Whitehall, Archy, the King's Fool, who, by his office, had the privilege of jesting, even on his Master, happened unluckily to try his wit upon Laud, and called out to him, "*Who's fool now, my Lord?*" For this offense the Primate insisted that he should be prosecuted, on the maxim, "*non licet ludere cum sacris;*" and after a solemn hearing before the Council, Archy was sentenced "to have his fool's coat pulled over his head, and to be dismissed the King's service."[1]

But more serious consequences were at hand. The King, notwithstanding the moderate counsels which were given to him by the Lord Keeper, and even by Laud himself, was resolved to make no concessions to the Scottish rebels, and to suppress the insurrection by military force. He directed summonses under the Great Seal to issue to all the nobility to meet him at York with trains suitable to their rank and possessions, and he marched to the north at the head of a feudal army, like another Edward I., to conquer Scotland.

But in England the national prejudice against the Scotch was overpowered by sympathy in their cause. The King's forces dwindled away as they approached the border, and were not in a condition to engage their opponents, under the veteran Leslie. At Berwick, Charles found it indispensably necessary to negotiate, and after agreeing to abolish episcopacy (under a secret protest that he would restore it on the first favorable opportunity), he was obliged, for want of money, to disband his troops, and he ingloriously returned to London.

Fresh writs, to raise ship-money to the amount of £200,000, were issued, and all sorts of expedients were resorted to for the purpose of filling the Exchequer,—but in vain. The Covenanters, becoming more insolent, talked of invading England, so that Presbytery, the only true form of church government, might be established all over the island,—and there were no means of raising an

[1] Rush. ii. 470.

army to resist them. A new tax might be imposed by proclamation, but in the present temper of the people, there was no chance of its being paid.

Under these circumstances, Coventry, and the whole Council, including even Archbishop Laud, and Juxon, the Lord Treasurer, recommended that a parliament should be called—a calamity, they privately said, from which England had now been happily exempt for eleven years, and with which they had well hoped that the country would never more be visited. The King for some time resisted, looking for assistance from Strafford and the Irish; but finding his ministers steady in their unanimous advice, he put to them this pertinent question: " If the new parliament should prove as untoward as some has lately been, will you then assist me in such extraordinary ways as in that extremity may be thought fit?" They all replied in the affirmative; and the Lord Keeper was ordered to prepare a proclamation, and writs of summons for a parliament, to meet in the month of April following, —the interval being allowed for the meeting of a parliament in Ireland, which, it was hoped, the Lord Deputy could manage at his pleasure, and would set a good example for England.

Although Coventry had concurred in the advice to call a parliament as an inevitable evil, he looked forward to it with the deepest apprehension. The fate of Lord Bacon twenty years before was ever present to his imagination; and although he might have consciousness of being free from personal corruption, notwithstanding the charges against him on that score,—he knew well that a considerable share of the misgovernment while he held the Great Seal was imputed to him by the public, and that he was particularly obnoxious for the illegal patents of monopoly which he had sealed,—for the arbitrary proclamations which he had countersigned,—for the cruel sentences of the Star Chamber pronounced by him,—and for the active part he had taken in procuring the corrupt judgment in favor of ship-money.

There can be little doubt that, had he survived, the storm which burst upon his successor would have overwhelmed him, and that if he had escaped the scaffold, he would have been driven into exile.

But, while in possession of the high office and of the

great fortune which he had amassed,—without any judicial exposure of his misdeeds, or temporal retribution for them, he was snatched away from impending misfortunes. On the 13th of January, 1640, he suddenly died at his residence, Durham House, in the Strand, in the 60th year of his age. Upon his death-bed he sent this last request to the King,—"that his Majesty would take all distastes from the parliament summoned against next April with patience, and suffer it to sit without an unkind dissolution."[1]

The only contemporary writer who bestows upon him any thing like unqualified praise, is Lloyd, the author of "The State Worthies,"—who even lauds his love of constitutional government—saying, "of all those counsels which did disserve his Majesty he was an earnest dissuader, and did much to disaffect those sticklers who labored to make the prerogative rather tall than great, as knowing such men loved the King better than Charles Stuart; so that, although he was a courtier, and had had for his master a passion most intense, yet had he always a passion reserved for the public welfare, an argument of a free, noble, and right-principled mind." But Whitelock says, "he was of no transcendent parts of fame;" and Sir Anthony Weldon, that "if his actions had been scanned by a parliament, he had been found as foul a man as ever lived." L'Estrange is more impartial: "His train and suit of followers was disposed agreeably to show both envy and contempt; not like that of Viscount St. Alban's, or the Bishop of Lincoln whom he succeeded, ambitious and vain; his port was state, theirs ostentation. They were indeed the more knowing men, but their learning was extravagant to their office; of what concerned his place he knew enough, and, which is the main, acted according to his knowledge." Fuller observes, with happy ambiguity, "It is hard to say whether his honorable life or seasonable death was the greater favor which God bestowed upon him." His most valuable eulogium is from Clarendon: "He was a man of wonderful gravity and wisdom, and understood not only the whole science and mystery of the law at least equally with any man who had ever sat in that place, but had a clear conception of

---

[1] Echard, p. 476.

the whole policy of the government both of church and state, which, by the unskillfulness of some well-meaning men, jostled each other too much. He knew the temper, disposition, and genius of the kingdom most exactly; saw their spirits grow every day more steady, inquisitive, and impatient, and therefore naturally abhorred all innovations, which he foresaw would produce effects yet many; who stood at a distance, thought he was not active and stout enough in opposing those innovations. For though by his place he presided in all public councils, and was most sharpsighted in the consequence of things, yet he was seldom known to speak in matters of state, which he well knew were for the most part concluded before they were brought to the public agitation; never in foreign affairs, which the vigor of his judgment could well have comprehended; nor indeed freely in anything, but what immediately and plainly concerned the justice of the kingdom; and in that, as much as he could, he procured references to the Judges. Though in his nature he had not only a firm gravity, but a severity and even some morosity, yet it was so sharply tempered, and his courtesy and affability towards all men so transcendent and so much without affectation, that it marvelously recommended him to all men of all degrees, and he was looked upon as an excellent courtier without receding from the native simplicity of his own manners. He had, in the plain way of speaking and delivery, without much ornament of elocution, a strange power of making himself believed, (the only justifiable design of elocution[1]), so that though he used very frankly to deny, and would never suffer any man to depart from him with an opinion that he was inclined to gratify when in truth he was not, holding that dissimulation to be the worst of lying, yet the manner of it was so gentle and obliging, and his condescension such to inform the persons whom he could not satify, that few departed from him with ill will and ill wishes. But then this happy temper and these good faculties rather preserved him from having many enemies and supplied him with some well-wishers, than furnished him with any fast and unshaken friends, who are always procured in Courts by more ardor and more vehement professions and appli-

---

[1] This is like the well-known observation, that "speech is given to man to enable him to conceal his thoughts."

cations than he would suffer himself to be entangled with. So that he was a man rather exceedingly liked than passionately loved; insomuch that it never appeared that he had any one friend in the Court of quality enough to prevent or divert any disadvantage he might be exposed to. And therefore it is no wonder, nor to be imputed to him, that he retired within himself as much as he could, and stood upon his defense without making desperate sallies against growing mischiefs, which he knew well he had no power to hinder, and which might probably begin in his own ruin. To conclude, his security consisted very much in his having but little credit with the King; and he died in a season most opportune, in which a wise man would have prayed to have finished his course, and which, in truth, crowned his other signal prosperity in the world." But under this blaze of eager commendation, it is easy to discover the features of a character wary, selfish, unprincipled, reckless, plausible, of refined hypocrisy, desirous of preserving the decencies of life, but sincerely anxious about nothing beyond his own ease and advantage, —which by his sagacity and adaptation to the times he cultivated so successfully, that he continued comfortably till death in an office the tenure of which was so precarious that no man died in it for many years before or after him.

As a politician he must ever be held mainly responsible for the troubles arising from the collision between prerogative and law which he brought about. He was checked for a time by Montagu, who had been Chief Justice of the King's Bench, and was afterwards Lord Treasurer and President of the Council; but during nearly the greatest portion of the sixteen years he held the Great Seal, he was the only adviser of the government on legal and constitutional questions: and if he did not originate he is nearly equally culpable for not having strenuously opposed the many fatal measures brought forward during the interval of parliaments, and for having abetted the scheme of subverting the ancient liberties of his country. Lord Clarendon represents that Coventry gave good advice in the Cabinet; and "perplexed the designs and councils of the Court with inconvenient objections in law." But I look to his language in public, and to his acts,—which we authentically know, and which would only acquire a deeper hue of atrocity if they were in opposition to his strong conviction and earnest remonstrances.

He was named in a commission which he drew, and to which he affixed the Great Seal, "to concert the means of levying money by impositions or otherwise—form and circumstance to be dispensed with, rather than the substance to be lost or hazarded." In the Star Chamber, "although the Archbishop of Canterbury was higher in rank, and all the Councillors and Judges who were summoned to attend, had an equal voice, yet the Lord Keeper was specially appointed by his patent to hear, examine, and determine all causes, matters, and suits in that Court;" and he was in reality the President. He is answerable, therefore, for those sentences of frightful and unprecedented cruelty which brought proverbial odium upon that tribunal, and within a year after his death led to its abolition, amidst the universal execrations of the people.

I ought not, however, to omit a story thus told to his credit by Sir Anthony Weldon, which, however improbable it may be, I have no means of contradicting: "Buckingham is grown now so exorbitant, he aspires to get higher titles both in honor and place as Prince of Tipperary and Lord High Constable of England, who herein wrought after Leicester's ambitious example; but he is crossed, too, with Coventry, now Lord Keeper; and, no doubt, on those just grounds his predecessor (Hatton) did.' But Buckingham's ambition could not be so bounded; for, upon the opposing it by Coventry, he peremptorily thus accosted him, saying: 'Who made you, Coventry, Lord Keeper?' He replied: 'the King.' Buckingham sur-replied: 'It's false, 'twas I did make you; and you shall know that I who made you can and will unmake you!' Coventry thus answered him: 'Did I conceive I held my place by your favor, I would presently unmake myself, by rendering the Seal to his Majesty.' Thus Buckingham, in a scorn and fury flung from him, saying: 'You shall not keep it long:' and surely, had not Felton prevented him, he had made good his word."

As an Equity Judge, he seems to have given entire satisfaction. He certainly must have been familiarly acquainted with the law of England, and with the doctrines and practice of the Court of Chancery. Yet it is surpris-

[1] Ante, vol. ii. p. 305.

ing how little progress equity, as a science, made under him. No decision of his, of much value, is recorded; and no great principle or rule of the system can be traced to him. Several writers unaccountably state that few of his decrees were reversed, "because he made the parties come to a compromise, and had an allegation on the face of his decrees that they were pronounced by consent."[1] He took care that none of his decrees should be brought before a Court of Appeal by preventing parliament from ever assembling.

He deserves great credit for "Ordinancies made by the Lord Keeper Coventery (with the advice and assistance of Sir Julius Cæsar, Master of the Rolls) for the redress of sundry errours, defaults, and abuses in the High Courte of Chauncerye." I give No. 1 as a specimen, which shows the evil of prolixity then prevailing, and which will prevail in spite of all efforts to repress it,—while the remuneration of lawyers is regulated by the length of the written proceedings. "1. That bills, answers, replications, and rejoinders be not stuffed with repetitions of deeds or writings, *in hæc verba*, but the effect and substance of so much of them only as is pertinent and material be set down, and that in brief and effectual terms. That long and needless traverses of points not traversable or material, causeless recitals, tautologies, and multiplication of words, and all other impertinences, occasioning needless perplexity, be avoided, and the ancient brevity and succinctness in bills and other pleadings restored. And upon any default herein, the party and counsel under whose hand it passeth shall pay the charge of the copy, and be further punished as the case shall merit."

---

[1] Lloyd. Fuller. From the following passage in "Madagascar," a poem by Sir William Davenant, written about this time, it appears that the reconciliation system was very much acted upon by Judges; and this accounts for the security with which they could then retain the *épices* with which they were presented on both sides:—

"These when I saw, my hopes could not abstain
To think it likely I might twirl a chain
On a judicial bench; learn to demur,
And sleep out trials in a gown of fur;
Then reconcile the rich for gold-fring'd [lin'd] gloves,
The poor for God's sake, or for sugar-loaves."

I myself, when Attorney General, received *tea* from the East India Company, and *sugar-loaves* from the corporation of Kingston-on-Hull; but I was a party to reforms which took away all these *sweets* from the office

To these Orders, the authorship of Coventry is confined. With such a predecessor as Bacon, and such a contemporary as Hyde, he seems to have felt an utter contempt for literature and literary men, and to have lived almost entirely with lawyers. I find no further account of his domestic habits, and no personal anecdotes respecting him. One attempt which he made at a jest has come down to us. When Prynne, Bastwick and Burton were prosecuted in the Star Chamber for libeling the Bishops, they objected that the Bishops ought not to sit as their Judges; whereupon smartly answered my Lord Keeper, "By that plea you can never be tried, for you have libeled all the magistrates in the land."[1]

He died the richest man that had yet held the Great Seal. Weldon says, "Coventry, so generally reputed an honest man, got such an estate by bribery and injustice, that he is said to have left a family worth a million,—which may commend his wisdom but not his honesty." But the anonymous biographer I have before quoted, although he allows that Coventry's enormous wealth was a ground of considerable "*murmuration*" against his integrity in his own time, more good-naturedly, and perhaps more reasonably, says, "The vague objection vulgarly inferred that the amassing of his wealth could not well be done in justice, might be answered to the full in this, that his patrimony considered, and the gainfulness of the places he passed through, together with the great fortunes of his own and his sons' intermarriages, all concurring and falling into a frugal family,—might soon wipe away all imputations of the most malignant, and persuade even detraction itself to rest in peace, and, as we may charitably believe, in glory, as his posterity surviving remains in his house and fortunes."[2]

He was buried in the church of Crome d'Abitot, where a suitable monument, recording his age, family, and offices, was erected to his memory.

He was twice married: first, to Sarah, daughter of Edward Sebright, Esq., of Besford, in the county of Worcester, by whom he had a daughter, and a son who succeeded to his title and estates; and, secondly, to Elizabeth, daughter of John Aldersey, Esq., of Spenstow, in the county of Chester, by whom he had several sons

[1] Lloyd.   [2] Sloane MS. Brit. Mus.

and daughters. His grandson, Thomas, the fifth Baron, his last male descendant, was advanced in the peerage by King William to be Earl of Coventry and Viscount Deerhurst, with a special limitation on failure of his own issue to that of Walter, the third son of the Judge, and brother of the Lord Keeper. This remainder came into operation in the year 1719, by the death of the fourth Earl without issue, and under it the honors of the family are now enjoyed.[1]

CHAPTER LXIII.

LIFE OF LORD KEEPER FINCH FROM HIS BIRTH TILL THE MEETING OF THE LONG PARLIAMENT.

WE now come to one of the worst characters in English history. It is rather fortunate for his memory that he has not had his full share of notoriety with posterity. He was universally execrated in his own times, and ought now to be placed in the same category with Jeffreys and Scroggs. He raised himself to eminence in bad times by assisting to upset law and liberty, and when on the bench he prostituted, in the most shameless manner, his judicial duties for his private ends. It is some consolation to think that, if he did not meet the fate he deserved, he did not escape unpunished.

Although, previous to the death of Lord Keeper Coventry, it had been resolved to submit to the necessity of once more calling a parliament, the King and his advisers were by no means fully aware of the state of the public mind, or of the difficulties which surrounded them. Instead of making concessions, and trying to gain over opponents, they were resolved still to stretch the prerogative, and if they could not obtain a supply of money by dictating to the House of Commons, to throw aside all profession of respect for the constitution, and to govern by open force. The most violent and unscrupulous supporter of arbitrary power that could be found in the profession of the law was therefore to be chosen as Lord Keeper, and there was no hesitation in fixing on Sir John

[1] Grandeur of the Law, p. 49.

Finch, Lord Chief Justice of the Court of Common Pleas, although he was, in reality, "a man exceedingly obnoxious to the people upon the business of ship-money, and not of reputation and authority enough to advance the King's service."[1]

He disgraced a family of considerable antiquity, which, in the seventeenth century, rose to great distinction by producing several very eminent lawyers. They were said to be descended from Sir Henry Fitzherbert, Chamberlain to King Henry I., and in the time of Edward I. to have assumed their present surname from the acquisition of the manor of *Finch's*, in Kent. Their possessions were enlarged by the marriage of Sir Thomas Finch with the heiress of Sir Thomas Moyle, Chancellor of the Court of Augmentations in the reign of Henry VIII. The eldest son of this marriage was Sir Moyle Finch, the ancestor of the Earls of Winchelsea and Nottingham. The second son, Sir Henry Finch, from whom sprang the subject of this memoir, was twice representative in parliament for the city of Canterbury, in the reign of Elizabeth, and the first great lawyer of the family. He was autumn reader of Gray's Inn in 1603, took the coif in 1614, and was made King's Sergeant in 1616. He wrote the treatise called "Finch's Law," which, till the production of Blackstone's Commentaries, was the chief elementary text-book for law students. From his preface, he seems to have had himself a very high opinion of his own performance, and to have thought it of infinitely greater importance than the NOVUM ORGANUM: "Inter innumeros tam augustæ disciplinæ alumnos, surrexit adhuc nemo, qui in eo elaboravit ut rerum præstantiam methodi præstantia consequatur. Aut ego vehementer fallor, aut superavi rei vix credendæ difficultatem maximam; syrtesque et scopulos, Scyllam et Charybdin præternavigavi."

John, his son, whom we have now to take in hand, was born on the 17th of September, 1584, and was of a very different character, being, from his early years, noted for idleness, though he showed a talent for turning the industry of other boys to his own advantage.

He was entered of Gray's Inn, and there professed to study the law, but instead of reading his father's black-letter treatise, or attending "moots and readings," he

[1] Clarendon.

spent his time in dicing and roistering. When called to the bar, he had little acquired learning of any sort,—no clients, and many debts. He saw that he had no chance to get forward in the regular routine of his profession, and that he was in considerable danger of being sent to prison by his creditors; but his parts were lively, his manners were agreeable, he had powerful friends at Court, and he determined to make his fortune by politics. He avoided the degree of the coif, as he knew he could make no figure in the Court of Common Pleas, among the drowsy, long-winded Sergeants, but he contrived to be employed occasionally in libel cases, in the Star Chamber. What he looked forward to with most eagerness was the meeting of a parliament; a chance which an aspiring lawyer, in those days, might for years expect in vain. " Having led a free life in a restrained fortune, and having set up upon the stock of a good wit and natural parts, without the superstructure of much knowledge in the profession by which he was to grow, he was willing to use those weapons in which he had most skill." [1]

He was disappointed in not being returned to Charles's first parliament, but he took his seat as a burgess in that which met in February, 1626. He was one of the lawyers then accused of " taking retainers on both sides," and " of waiting to see which way the cat jumped." The popular party had been gaining strength every new parliament since the middle of the reign of Elizabeth, and now had a complete ascendancy in the House of Commons, but they had no preferment to bestow, and John Finch would have been much better pleased with the appointment of Attorney to the Court of Wards than with the reputation of a flaming patriot. An expectation prevailed, which was not disappointed, that some of the most formidable leaders, who gave least open offense to the Court, would be offered employment.

Under the pretense of great moderation, the new member contrived to get himself appointed Chairman of the Committee, to whom was referred the very important question, " whether Sir Edward Coke, late Chief Justice of the King's Bench, having been appointed, against his will, Sheriff of Buckinghamshire before the general election, was disqualified to sit in the House of Commons for

[1] Clarendon.

another county?" The Committee very much deferred to Finch as a gentleman of the long robe, who, among *lay gents*, could talk very glibly of law, and appointed him to draw up the report, " wherein many cases were cited, *pro et contra*, as to the nature of a High Sheriff for one county being elected knight of the shire for another; on all which cases, he said, the Committee would give no opinion, but desired that a search might be made amongst the records for more precedents of the like nature."[1] A dissolution took place before the point was decided. In the meantime, Coke was not allowed to sit, and the Court was relieved from his invectives, which proved so formidable in the next parliament, when the " Petition of Right" was passed; but Finch, to show his impartiality, the day before the dissolution, moved a resolution, which was carried, "that Sir Edward Coke, standing *de facto* returned a member of that House, should have privilege against a suit in Chancery commenced against him by the Lady Clare."

It must have required considerable ingenuity to mystify so clear a point as that though a Sheriff could not return himself as member for his own county, the Crown could not, at pleasure, disqualify him for being returned for another county, or for a borough, over which he had no official control; but Finch had the good luck, from his conduct of this case, to establish the reputation of a constitutional lawyer, and to be courted, if not confided in, by both parties.

In consequence of this, at the meeting of Charles's third parliament, in March, 1628, he was actually elected Speaker of the House of Commons. He had now *his foot in the stirrup*, and he resolved to push forward, appalled by no obstacle, Though elected by the voice of the popular party, he instantaneously deserted them, and made himself the mere tool of the Court. His conduct as Speaker might have been anticipated from the slavish and fulsome language he held as soon as his formal disqualifying of himself had been overruled, and his appointment had been confirmed by the King:—

" It is now no longer good time nor good manners to dispute with my Lord the King; but with all joy and alacrity of heart, humbly and thankfully to meet so great

[1] 2 Parl. Hist. 46.

hath enjoyed, the very religion we profess hath taught us whose image you are."

He was constantly closeted with the King and Buckingham, telling them all that passed in the House, and plotting with them how the schemes of the popular leaders might best be defeated. After one of these conferences he brought down a very indiscreet message from the King, intimating that the session would be speedily closed, and commanding the Commons "not to enter into or proceed with any new business which might spend time, or might lay any scandal or aspersion upon the state, government, or ministers thereof." This, as might have been foreseen, set the whole House in a flame.

Sir Robert Philips thus began the debate: " I perceive that towards God and towards man there is little hope. I consider mine own infirmities, and if ever my passions were wrought upon, it is now. This message stirs me up: especially, when I remember with what moderation we have proceeded."

Sir John Eliot followed, and was alluding to certain supposed aspersions on the ministers of state, when the Speaker started up from the chair, and, apprehending that Sir John intended to fall upon the Duke of Buckingham, said, with tears which he knew how to bring into eyes, " There is a command laid upon me to interrupt any that should go about to lay an aspersion on the ministers of state."

A scene of great confusion ensued, which was put an end to by the contrivance of resolving themselves into a grand committee of the whole House "on the state of the nation," and so getting Finch out of the chair. An order was at the same time made, " that the doors be locked, and that no one depart the House upon pain of being sent to the Tower." Finch, against whom this resolution was passed, before quitting the chair, earnestly begged that he might be allowed to be absent for half an hour on urgent private business, and the permission was magnanimously accorded to him.

A hot discussion now ensued, and a resolution was moved, "that the Duke of Buckingham was the cause of all the evils under which the state labored." A member observed, that for the Speaker to desire to leave the House in such a manner was never heard of before, and he feared would be ominous. Finch, in truth, had posted off privately to the King, and now returned with this message, "that his Majesty commands, for the present, they adjourn the House till to-morrow morning, and that all committees cease in the mean time." An immediate adjournment took place in consequence.

The following morning he brought a soothing message from the King, which they, with the moderation and good sense which distinguished them, agreed to accept as satisfaction for the insult offered to them; but they firmly defeated his purpose, which was to divert them from proceeding with the "Petition of Right."

An evasive answer had been given by the King, which, under words of seeming consent, would have been construed into *Le Roy s'averisa ;* but they held a conference with the Lords, and both Houses being now equally suspicious of their Speakers, they put down in writing what the Lord Keeper should say on the subject to the King on the throne in the House of Lords, and they agreed "that he should stand in his place as a peer, and there deliver this request to his Majesty, and aftewards go to his place of state."

At last, Finch was obliged to come to the bar at the head of the Commons, and after the "Petition of Right" had been read at full length; he had the mortification to hear the words pronounced, *Soit fait come il est désiré.*

In spite of this, Charles insisted on levying tonnage and poundage without authority of parliament, although they were willing to pass a bill to authorize the levy, whereupon notice was given in the House, on the 25th of June, of a motion to be made next morning for a remonstrance to the King against this proceeding. Early next morning, Finch went to Court to take his orders, but there much perplexity existed, and they at last resolved on an instant prorogation. He had been detained so long by this consultation, that he had kept the House above an hour waiting for him, and he did not make his appearance till past nine o'clock. He had scarcely been seated in the chair when,—while the member who had given the notice was beginning to read the proposed remonstrance,—three knocks were heard at the door, and the Black Rod entering, commanded them forthwith to attend his Majesty in the House of Lords. Finch hurried thither, and the

King sitting on the throne, without his robes (so precipitate was the proceeding) ordered the prorogation.

During the second short and stormy session of this parliament, Finch continued to act as the puppet of the Court. The Commons, being very indignant at the manner in which the King tried to retract his assent to the "Petition of Right," were preparing a remonstrance—when the Speaker delivered a message from his Majesty ordering them to adjourn for a week, but they resolved that "it was not the office of the Speaker to deliver any such message unto them, for the adjournment of the House did properly belong to themselves."

Sir John Eliot then moved "the remonstrance;" but Finch refused to put the question from the chair, saying, that "he was commanded otherwise by the King." Selden asked him if he refused to act as Speaker. He replied "he had an express command from the King, so soon as he had delivered his message, to rise." Thereupon he rose and was leaving the chair, when Hollis, Valentine, and others, in spite of the efforts of certain Privy Councillors to free him, forced him back into the chair saying, "he should sit there till it pleased them to rise." Finch, with abundance of tears, answered, "I will not say I will not, but I dare not. Command me not to my ruin,—in regard I have been your faithful servant, and would sacrifice my life for the good of my country; but I dare not sin against the express command of my Sovereign."

Selden urged, that he, being the servant of the House could not refuse their command under any color, and that his obstinacy would be a precedent to posterity if it should go unpunished; but "he still refused, with extremity of weeping and supplicatory orations."[1]

This *fracas* terminated in the barring out of the Black Rod, the abrupt dissolution of Charles's third parliament, and his resolution thereafter to govern by his absolute prerogative.[2]

For some years there was a lack of law promotion, and Finch did not receive the reward of his subserviency. He was not much of a favorite with Lord Keeper Coventry, who felt some jealousy of his courtly arts. He laid himself out for practice at the bar, but there was no confidence

[1] 2 Parl. Hist. 491. 3 St. Tr. 235.   [2] Ante, p. 205.

in his learning or integrity, and he could only hope for advancement from royal patronage.

Prynne had incurred the high displeasure of the government by his *Histriomastix*, inveighing bitterly against theatrical amusements, in which the Queen herself took a part. After he had been condemned in the Star Chamber for this publication as for a seditious libel, Finch thought it would be a good hit to show that the legal profession thoroughly disapproved of its principles,—by getting up a masque, to be acted by the four Inns of Court before their Majesties. Two benchers were chosen by each Inn of Court to conduct the pageant. Finch represented Gray's Inn, and appears to have acted as " Master of the revels." There were sixteen grand masquers, " four gentlemen of each Inn of Court, most suitable for their persons, dancing, and garb." The members of the several Inns of Court were to intermingle, and each party of four was to be drawn in a chariot with six horses,—but great difficulty arose in settling the precedence of the chariots which respectively represented the dignity of each Inn of Court, —till that thorny point was decided by lot. The next controversy was, by what rule the four were to be placed in each chariot,—which was resolved by the happy thought of having them made, like the Roman triumphal chariots, " of an oval form, so that there should be no precedence in them."

The procession to Whitehall exceeded the glories of the installation of a Lord Chancellor. First marched the Marshal and his men; after him came one hundred gentlemen of the Inns of Court mounted on horse back, " in very rich clothes, scarce anything but gold and silver lace to be seen of them, with a page and two lacqueys to each. Then came the " anti-masques," intended for humor and jocularity,—the first, anti-masque being of cripples and beggars on horseback, on the poorest jades that could be gotten, and ingeniously habited so as to ridicule the great officers of the law,[1] and another to satirize such projectors as sought patents for useless schemes, as " the fish-call, or a looking-glass for fishes in the sea, very useful to fishermen to call all kinds of fish to their nets,"—" the new invented wind-mate, very profitable when common winds

[1] Finch himself had the chief hand in this, and from his bad success in the profession hitherto, probably took great delight in it.

fail, for a more speedy passage of calmed ships and vessels on seas and rivers,"—"a movable hydraulic, which, being placed by a bedside, causeth sweet sleep to those who, either by hot fevers or otherwise can not take rest."[1]

Then, to the admiration of all beholders, came the Grand Masquers in their oval chariots, "their habits, doublets, trunk-hose, and caps of most rich cloth of tissue, and wrought as thick with silver spangles as they could be placed, large white silk stockings up to their trunk-hose, and rich sprigs in their caps; themselves proper and beautiful young gentlemen." Starting from Ely House, in Holborn, they marched down Chancery Lane, through the Strand to the Palace, where they paraded round the tilt yard, that the King and Queen "might have a double view of them." They alighted at Whitehall gate, when the Masque began and "was incomparably performed." Then followed a ball, in which Queen Henrietta danced with some of the Masquers, and (*gaudeo referens*) "did judge them as good dancers as ever she saw." The whole concluded with a banquet, after which all departed. "And thus," says with quaint solemnity the historian of this masque, imitating the well-known passage from "The Tempest," "this earthly pomp and glory, if not vanity, was soon past and gone as if it had never been."[2]

Finch and three others were deputed to the office of returning thanks, in the name of the four Inns of Court, to the King and Queen, "for their gracious acceptance of the tender of their services in the late masque;" and as it had given peculiar delight to Henrietta, who, since the death of Buckingham, had acquired great influence, it perhaps contributed to his elevation almost as much as his services in the chair of the House of Commons, for he was immediately appointed Attorney General to the Queen; and notwithstanding his ignorance of law and want of experience he was shortly after appointed a Puisne Judge of the Court of Common Pleas.

What he wanted in law and professional experience, he

---

[1] This was the contribution of Mr. Attorney General Noy. It appears from Rymer's Fœdera, vol. xix., that there were actually patents granted for these inventions, and while I was Attorney General, several as absurd were applied for. The "*wind-mate*" may have been an anticipation of the *steam-engine*.

[2] Whitelock's Memorials, p. 21. The cost to the four Inns of Court was calculated to be above £20,000.

supplied in zeal for the prerogative, and in severity to Puritans and to all persons obnoxious to the government who came before him.[1] In little more than a year the grand question of ship-money arose. Heath, the Chief Justice, being considered a Judge not fit to be trusted, was removed, and Finch, well known to be ready to go all lengths, was appointed to preside in his place.

He did not disappoint expectation. By laboring his own puisnes and some of the other Judges, he was mainly instrumental in obtaining the extra-judicial opinion that the King might lawfully impose ship-money in case of necessity, and that he was the sole judge of the necessity for imposing it.

When Hampden's case came to be decided in the Exchequer Chamber, Lord Chief Justice Finch exceeded all the other Judges in the slavish doctrines which he laid down.

"A parliament (said he, among many other things quite as strong) is an honorable court; and I confess it an excellent means of charging the subject and defending the kingdom; but yet it is not the only means. Certainly there was a King before a parliament, for how else could there be an assembly of King, Lords, and Commons? And then what sovereignty was there in the kingdom but his? His power, then, was limited by the positive law; then it can not be denied but originally the King had the sovereignty of the whole kingdom, both by sea and land, with a power of charging the whole kingdom. Then the law that hath given that power hath given means to the King to put it in execution. It is a very true rule that the law commands nothing to be done, but it permits the ways and means how it may be done, else the law should be imperfect, lame, and unjust. Therefore, the law that hath given the interest and sovereignty of defending and governing the kingdom to the King, doth also give the King power to charge his subjects for the necessary defense and good thereof. And as the King is bound to defend, so the subjects are bound to obey, and to come out of their own country if occasion be, and to provide horse and

---

[1] Clarendon thus characterizes Noy and Finch at this time, "the one knowing nothing of, nor caring for the Court; the other knowing or caring for nothing else."

arms in foreign war; and such are compellable now to find guns, powder, and shot, instead of bows and arrows. Then if sea and land be but one entire kingdom, and the King lord of both, the subject is bound as well to the defense of the sea as of the land; and then all are bound to provide ships, men, ammunition, victuals, and necessaries for that defense. As to the observations of my brother Crooke, that we are compellable by our persons and arms, but not with any sum of money, I answer that *bona corporis* are above *bona fortunæ*. If this power to command the persons of his subjects is in the King, then, I say, more reason that their estates should be in his power in this case of defense." He then goes on to examine the statutes and authorities cited on the other side, making very light of them. *Magna* CHARTA he dismisses with the observation, that to the enactment "nullum tallagium imponatur nisi per commune concilium," there is the implied exception, *unless for the public good*. To the statute 25 Ed. I, c. 5, and all subsequent statutes on the subject, he gives the answer, that " acts of parliament may take away flowers and ornaments of the Crown, but not the Crown itself. No act of parliament can bar a King of his regality, or his trust and power to defend his subjects; therefore, acts of parliament to take away his royal power in the defense of his kingdom are void. They are void if they profess to take away the power of the King to command the persons, goods, and money of his subjects: no acts of parliament make any difference." " The Petition of Right" he treats with great contempt,—on the ground that, from having been Speaker when it passed, he knew there was no intention thereby to alter the old law. With text writers, of course, he is very unceremonious. Fortescue, he says, is entitled to no weight, because the treatise " De Laudibus" was written during the wars of York and Lancaster, when the author was in exile, and wished to please the people, and to return to his own country. After getting rid of all the authorities in a similar manner, he arrives at the conclusion, "that the King has a clear right, in case of danger, to impose a tax for the defense of the realm;—that the expectancy of danger is sufficient ground for the King to charge his subjects;—that the King is the sole judge of the danger;— that the King's averment of danger is not traversable,—

and therefore, that the defendant was bound to pay the sum assessed upon him."¹

Lord Clarendon says—" Undoubtedly, my Lord Finch's speech in the Exchequer Chamber made ship-money much more abhorred and formidable than all the commitments by the Council-table, and all the distresses taken by the Sheriffs of England: the major part of men (besides the common unconcernedness in other men's sufferings) looking upon those proceedings with a kind of applause to themselves to see other men punished for not doing as they had done;—which delight was quickly determined when they found their own interest, by the unnecessary logic of that argument, no less concluded than Mr. Hampden's."

But this logic endeared him to the Court, and insured him further preferment as soon as any opportunity should occur. In the meanwhile he strengthened his claim by his conduct in the Star Chamber, where, having been made a Privy Councillor, he now acted as Judge. We may take as an example, his proof that he would not be swayed by private considerations to spare an old acquaintance, when he proposed an aggravation to the punishment of Prynne, whom he had known well at the bar. The Court having agreed that for a new libel which he had published along with Bastwick and Burton, "he should stand in the pillory, lose his ears, pay a fine of £5,000, and be perpetually imprisoned in a distant fortress." the Chief Justice moved, by way of amendment, "that he should likewise be stigmatized in the cheeks with the two letters S. and L: for a Seditious Libeler,"— to which all the Lords agreed.²

He likewise distinguished himself in pressing for severe punishment on Bishop Williams, when that Prelate was the second time brought before the Star Chamber on pretenses more frivolous than the first, although he had then rather taken the part of the defendant, not aware that he was so odious to the Government. Being now reproached for his inconsistency, he replied with candor: "I was soundly chidden by his Majesty for my former vote; and I will not destroy myself for any man's sake."³

At last, on the death of Lord Keeper Coventry, Finch's ambition was fully gratified. That event having happened

¹ 3 St. Tr. 1216, ² Ibid. 725. ³ Hacket's Life of Williams.

on the 13th of January, 1640, on the 17th of the same month the Great Seal was delivered to him as Lord Keeper, and on the 23rd, the first day of Hilary term, he was installed with great pomp in the Court of Chancery, and was raised to the peerage by the title of Baron Finch of Fordwich.[1]

This appointment caused great dismay at the time, as a proof of the spirit which still actuated the King's councils, even after the difficulties in which he had been involved by his arbitrary government, and after he had found it absolutely necessary again to summon a parliament. Modern historians, even those who are impartial, pass over the promotion of Finch at this juncture without a censure, and with Hume he is a decided favorite.

He held the Great Seal little more than three terms, and during this short space of time the proceedings in the Courts of justice were much interrupted by political disputes, so that we do not know much of him as an Equity Judge; but we have an account of one of his early cases, showing that his legal and equitable principles corresponded, and that he acted in an enlarged sense on the doctrine that "equity follows the law." A bill was filed to carry into effect an order of the Lords of the Council, upon a matter over which they had no jurisdiction. The defendant demurred for want of equity, and the demurrer coming on to be argued, Finch decreed for the plaintiff, saying, "that while he was Keeper no man should be so saucy as to dispute these orders, and that the wisdom of the Board should be always ground enough for him to make a decree in Chancery."[2]

When Easter term came round, he was called away to preside in the House of Lords. Parliaments having now been intermitted above eleven years, the very forms of proceeding were almost forgotten, and none of the officers knew the duties they had to perform. The Lord Keeper was answerable for all, and much time was occupied in inquiries and preparations. The public looked forward with eager expectation to a redress of grievances, but the

---

[1] Crown Office Minutes' Book, fol. 1. He had the extraordinary honor, when he was sworn, of having the book held for him by the Bishop of London, Lord Treasurer, and so had his successor, Littleton. On all other occasions of this sort the book is stated to have been held by the Master of the Rolls. [2] 1 Clarend. 131.

Court had resolved that the attention of both Houses should be confined to the granting of supplies.

There was a grand procession the first day of the Session, and the people, delighted once more to witness such a spectacle, were so good-humored and grateful, that the less penetrating expected a happy result. The King being seated on his throne, and the Commons attending at the bar of the House of Lords, he merely said, "that never King had a more great and weighty cause to call his people together, but that he would not trouble them with the particulars, which they would hear from the Lord Keeper."

Finch began by celebrating the goodness of the King in calling a parliament, notwithstanding the memory of former discouragements, but strongly deprecated their interference with affairs of government. "His Majesty's kingly resolutions are seated in the ark of his sacred breast, and it were a presumption of too high a nature for any Uzziah, uncalled, to touch it." He then warned them by the example of Phaeton, not to aim at that of which they were incapable. "Let us beware how, with the son of Clymene, we aim not at the guiding of the chariot, as if that were the only testimony of fatherly affection, but let us ever remember that though the King sometimes lays by the beams and rays of Majesty, he never lays by Majesty itself." After taking a view of the foreign relations of the country, which he justly represented as highly satisfactory, he says, "But what availeth this, *si foris hostem non inveniat, si modo domi inveniat ?*" He launches out into a bitter invective against the Scots, who had made a most ungrateful return for all the King's affection and bounty. "For when his Majesty had most reason to expect a grateful return of loyalty and obedience from that nation, some men of Belial, some Zelia hath blown the trumpet there, and by their insolences and rebellious actions draw many after them, to the utter desertion of his Majesty's government. Following the wicked counsels of some Achitophels, they have seized on the trophies of honor, and invested themselves with regal power and authority." He draws a striking contrast between Scotland and Ireland, where all was loyalty and obedience, and the parliament had lately voted large subsidies to assist his Majesty in restoring tranquillity in this island. He desires the English parliament to follow so good an example, and "for a while laying aside all other debates, to pass such and so many subsidies as should be thought fit and convenient for so great an occasion." To avoid all questions about tonnage and poundage, he said his Majesty had caused a bill to be prepared to authorize the collection of the tax from the commencement of his reign. This was the only concession alluded to; but he assured them, that "after the grant of such a supply as the urgency of the King's affairs instantly required, which he would accept as the pledge of their loving, happy, and dutiful affection to him, his person and government, they should afterwards have an abundant opportunity for considering of such petitions as they should conceive for the good of the commonwealth."[1]

But the Commons instead of yielding to this request on the faith of this promise, immediately fell upon grievances,—ship-money,—the levying of duties on merchandise without the authority of parliament,—the cruelties of the Star Chamber and High Commission Court,—and breach of the privilege of the House in prosecuting and punishing members for words spoken in the House. Above all, they took up with earnestness the conduct of the Lord Keeper Finch, when Speaker of the House of Commons, on the last day of the last parliament. Sir Harry Vane gave a circumstantial account, from notes taken at the time, of the whole transaction, and of the Speaker's expressions, "that he dared not put the question, that he was commanded not to put the question, and that they should not force him to his ruin." A motion was thereupon made and carried, that a select committee be appointed to prepare a representation to his Majesty of the violation of the liberties of this House that happened the last day of the last parliament, humbly beseeching his Majesty "that the like violation may not hereafter be brought in practice to his prejudice or theirs." And a resolution was carried, "that it is the opinion of this House, that the Speaker's refusing to put the question after a verbal command from his Majesty, signified to this House by the Speaker, to adjourn, and no adjournment made by this House, is a breach of the privileges of this House."

[1] 2 Parl. Hist. 529.

The Lord Keeper thought that all these mutinous dispositions might be quelled by a proper display of vigor. Accordingly, on the 20th of April, both Houses were summoned to attend in the banqueting house at Whitehall, and there, in the King's presence, he read a lecture upon the necessity of giving supply precedence over grievances; but the Commons were obstinate, and on returning to their Chamber after a long debate, resolved to prefer grievances to supply. Charles then, without the Lord Keeper's advice or privity, took one of those rash steps which led to such fatal consequences in the dispute now commencing. He came suddenly into the House of Lords, and seating himself in his chair of state, without his robes, he addressed the Peers, and solicited their good offices in prevailing on the Commons to grant an immediate supply. When he withdrew, the Lords, flattered by his appeal to them, immediately agreed, on the motion of the Lord Keeper, "that the supply should have precedency, and be resolved upon before any other matter whatsoever, and that there should be a conference desired with the Commons in order to dispose them thereto."

The Commons having agreed to the conference, it was managed on the part of the Lords by the Lord Keeper, who strongly urged the Commons to postpone the consideration of their supposed grievances, reminding them that " they had the word of a King, and not only so but *of a gentleman*," [1] for all they required respecting religion, property and privilege. "Lastly, he told the Commons that the Lords had voted and declared as their opinion, that his Majesty's supply should have precedency and be resolved on before any other matter whatsoever; therefore he desired the House of Commons to go on with that first, as that which in the opinion of the House of Lords is held most necessary." [2]

As might easily have been foreseen, the Commons were highly incensed by these proceedings, and came to a resolution " that their Lordships voting, propounding, and declaring, concerning matter of supply before it was moved from this House, was a breach of privilege, and that a remonstrance should be sent to the Lords to this

[1] One of the earliest instances of "gentleman" being used in this sense.
[2] 2 Parl. Hist. 553.

effect; and the Lords voted a counter-resolution, that their merely expressing an opinion on the order in which the subject of supply should be considered, was no breach of the privileges of the Commons."

Under the advice of Pym and Waller the Commons still insisted on proceeding with grievances. The King sent them two other messages to hasten the supply, and finding them inflexible,—by the rash and ruinous advice of the Lord Keeper, he suddenly made his appearance on the throne, and having praised the Lords and severely censured the Commons, abruptly dissolved the parliament from which such national benefits had been expected. This measure is deeply deplored by Clarendon, who truly says that there never was a parliament in which Charles had so many true friends, and there can be no doubt that if he had evinced any sincere disposition to correct the errors of his government, an adequate supply would readily have been granted to him, the Scottish insurrection would have been suppressed, and he would soon have been relieved from all his difficulties. Again, had Strafford been at hand, the business would have been conducted with more dexterity, and there would have been a fair chance of success to arbitrary rule. But that able minister being in Ireland, a country then as distant from us for practical purposes as America now is, Charles was left with such councillors as Finch and Laud, more inconsiderate and violent than himself, and all tended to a popular revolution. Bellasis and Sir John Hotham, who had opposed the Court in the Lower House, were immediately summoned before the Council, and refusing to answer the questions the Lord Keeper put to them respecting their conduct in parliament, were committed to prison. Crew, the chairman of the committe of religion, shared the same fate, because he would not deliver up the petitions and complaints which had been intrusted to him.

The Lord Keeper gave a fresh instance of his ignorance and folly by publishing an opinion in which he induced some of the Judges to join him, that the Convocation, after the dissolution of the parliament, was still entitled to sit and grant supplies from the clergy,—and by a novel commission under the Great Seal, he authorized them to frame an ecclesiastical code adapted to the exigency of the times. The more timid members of the Convocation were still much alarmed, but a majority agreed to seventeen new canons, and although they in various particulars affected the rights of the laity and were clearly illegal, they all received the royal assent, one of them being "that every clergyman, four times in the year, should instruct his parishioners in the Divine right of Kings, and the damnable sin of resistance."[1] These ecclesiastical enactments added greatly to the general excitement. The vessel was already full, and this last drop made the waters of bitterness to overflow."[2]

Nothing so strikingly proves how universally the feeling of resentment against the government prevailed in the nation, as that it infected the camp, and unnerved the English soldier,—insomuch, that now occurred the only instance in our history of an English army flying from the field of battle. "The King saw plainly that both divers officers of his army, and even the private soldiers generally (which was a most remarkable inclination), would not fight against the Scots."[3]

After the rout at Newburn, and the flight to Durham, Charles and his councillors were in a state of the utmost perplexity. Without funds, his troops must be immediately disbanded, and Leslie, with his Covenanters, might march triumphant to join the discontented in London.[4] The late unfortunate dissolution of the parliament was already deeply deplored, but to meet a new House of Commons seemed a measure not only humiliating but hopeless. The Peers had been willing to grant a supply, and the King had parted amicably with them. Finch suggested that they might be summoned without the Commons, and treated as a national assembly,—pretending that there were various precedents for a great Council of the Peers so acting in cases of imminent national danger. The advice was relished, and he issued writs of summons under the Great Seal to all the Peers, requiring them to

---

[1] Rush. i. 1205. Wilk. Con. iv. 553.   [2] Clarendon.   [3] Whitelock.
[4] Another difficulty was then experienced (which we now meet by the annual Mutiny Act), that the Petition of Right having abolished martial law, there were no means of punishing military offenses. Even Finch was obliged to acknowledge this, and he privately passed pardons under the Great Seal to officers who had found it necessary to execute a mutineer. Lord Conway said upon the occasion, that if any lawyer were so imprudent as to discover the secret to his soldiers, it would be necessary instantly to refute him, and to hang him by sentence of a court-martial.—Rush. iii. 1199.

meet at York on the 25th of September to consult with the King *de arduis regni.*

Before the day arrived, petitions poured in from all quarters for the calling of a parliament, as the only remedy to save the nation from anarchy and ruin; and many Peers joining in these, Charles foresaw that this would be the first recommendation of the Great Council. He yielded to the torrent, which he despaired of being able to stem. But though it was announced that a parliament should be summoned, the Peers were allowed to assemble, and "the Grand Council" was constituted. In his address to them, the King, according to the information he had received from the Lord Keeper, stated "that upon sudden invasions, where the dangers were near and instant, it had been the custom of his predecessors to assemble the Great Council of the Peers; and, by their advice and assistance, to give a timely remedy to such evils which could not admit a delay so long as must, of necessity, be allowed for the assembling of parliament." But Lord Clarendon says, " this assembly of the Peers was a new invention, not before heard of; or so old, that it had not been practiced in England for some hundreds of years;" and, in truth, since the time of Henry III., when the Commons became a constituent part of the legislature, there had been no instance of the Peers being summoned without them to deliberate on public affairs. As nothing was done at this Council, historians have been much puzzled to explain the motive for calling it; but there can be little doubt that when the writs for it issued, the intention was that it should take upon itself all the functions of parliament, and that it was, by a *coup-d'état,* to supersede the House of Commons, which had been found so troublesome. The attempt created serious alarm among the middling and lower orders of the people, and was regarded as another proof of a deep-laid scheme to crush public liberty.

Although Charles announced to the Great Council that he had already given orders to his Lord Keeper to issue writs for a parliament, the general conviction was, that this was the result of his altered purpose, and that the nation was to have been taxed by an ordinance of the House of Lords. To save appearances they held several meetings, —advised the negotiation with the Scots, which ended in the treaty of Ripon,—and sent a deputation to London, to assist in borrowing money for the support of the army. They then all quietly dispersed.

CHAPTER LXIV.

CONCLUSION OF THE LIFE OF LORD KEEPER FINCH.

ON the 3rd of November began the most memorable parliament recorded in our annals. Instead of the usual grand procession, the King, attended by the Lord Keeper and a few of the great officers of state, came privately by water from Whitehall, and landed at the parliament stairs, near where Westminster Bridge now stands. The King, after a few general observations, in a very conciliatory and touching tone, said he had commanded his Lord Keeper to give a particular account of what had happened since the last dissolution.

Finch's address was very artful; his great object being to divert indignation from himself to the Scots. Having eulogized the bravery, and genius, and greatness of the natives of England, he boldly denied that they had ever been conquered either by Saxons, Danes, or Normans. "It were an easy task," he said, "to make it appear that they never changed the old established laws of England, nor ever brought in any new, so that you have the frame and constitution of a commonwealth, made glorious by antiquity; and, with states as with persons and families, certainly an uninterrupted pedigree doth give luster." He then pointed out the extreme presumption of the Scots, in passing with an army the rivers Tweed and Tyne, seizing upon Newcastle, and levying contributions on Northumberland and Durham "to the prejudice of monarchy, and rendering less glorious this kingdom." Next came the indispensable necessity of instantly providing funds for supporting an army, by which the invasion might be opposed, the King's authority vindicated, and the honor of the country maintained. Aware of the ill construction that had been put upon the Council of the Peers at York, he pretended to say that it was after a custom which had been frequently used:[1] "This was not done to prevent, but to prepare for a parliament. It was not to clash or interfere with this assembly, by acting or ordering any thing which belongeth to this high and supreme jurisdiction, but only to give their assistance for the present to render things more fit for this great assembly. They could never attempt, nor had the least thought to make, by any act or order, any thing tending to charge the subject."[2]

Nevertheless, there was a greater disposition to sympathize with the Scots than to raise an army for their destruction, as they declared their only object was to lay their grievances before their Sovereign. The elaborate denial of all bad intentions in calling the Council of the Peers at York strengthened the previous suspicions on this subject, and the Commons only waited till their Speaker was chosen that they might proceed against the authors of their grievances,—of whom the Lord Keeper himself was considered one of the most guilty.

In a few days he had a specimen of the temper of the Commons, and a forewarning of his own fate,—in the impeachment, suddenly voted with closed doors, against the Earl of Strafford ;—and, as the organ of the Peers, he was obliged to issue the order for the commitment of his colleague, and to direct that he should at once be carried off by the Sergeant-at-arms, without then being permitted to say a word in his own defense.[3]

It is said that Finch gave out now privately that he was willing to go over to the popular party, and to do every thing he could to assist them, and that he had actually made some impression on the most violent leaders, who hoped to have turned him into a useful tool ; but that Lord Falkland, Hyde, and the more moderate reformers, put an end to the negotiation, thinking that he might, in his new-born zeal for liberty, suggest measures which would be dangerous to the monarchy.

The Lords seem to have originated no proceeding before Finch's fall, except an inquiry into the manner in which the studies and the repositories of Lord Warwick

---

[1] Although Camden and Selden flourished about this time, it is certain that the general mass of men of education were by no means so well acquainted with the history and antiquities of the country as at the present day—or the Lord Keeper durst not have ventured on such an assertion.

[2] 2 Parl. Hist. 630.   [3] Ibid. 734.

and Lord Brook had been searched at the conclusion of the last parliament within time of privilege; and upon this occasion he took the liberal side, although the acts complained of must have been done with his privity. Sir William Beecher, the clerk of the Council, being brought to the bar, the Lord Keeper demanded of him " by what warrant he had searched and carried away the papers of the aforesaid Peers?" The witness having demurred to answer, on the ground "that he was the King's sworn servant, and that he must acquaint the King with the matter before he answered," the Lord Keeper ordered him to show his warrant, and blamed him for naming the King in the business; and, he again refusing to give a direct answer till the King was made acquainted with it, the Lord Keeper told him that " the Lords did take him to be the chief actor of the fact, and were resolved to proceed against him as the principal." Sir William was finally committed to the Fleet, but in two days after, on acknowledging his error, he was released. At this time there certainly was a large majority of the Lords against the Court, and, though attached to the monarchy, eager for a correction of the abuses which had prevailed both in the church and the state. But as, according to the adjustment of the respective functions of the two Houses in Floyde's case, *they* were to sit as Judges, the Commons being the Accusers,—they properly remained quiet till charges should regularly be brought before them.

In the meanwhile the Commons having liberated Prynne, Bastwick, and Burton, and procured the commitment of Strafford and Laud to the Tower, proceeded against Lord Keeper Finch as the person next most obnoxious to them. The chief grounds of complaint against him were his conduct as Speaker, in refusing to put the question; his oppressive perversion of the Forest Laws; his endeavors to incense the King against parliaments; and, above all, his conduct with respect to ship-money, in obtaining the extra-judicial opinion of the Judges against Hampden, and in declaring on his circuit that the right to ship-money was so inherent in the Crown, that no act of parliament could take it away.

Bagshaw, the member for Southwark, referring to the Lord Keeper's recent honeyed words, said, "If these troublers of our Israel do go unpunished, it will never be

Strafford and Laud, and might not have an opportunity of following the example of Secretary Windebank, who, on a charge being originated against him, had fled to the Continent. His friends, on the contrary, were sanguine in the expectation that he might make a favorable impression on the House, so that, with the secret countenance he expected from some of the leaders, the impeachment might be negatived—and, at any rate, they were resolved that he should have " a run for it."

Next morning, the House having met at eight, as soon as prayers were over, a chair was set for the Lord Keeper to make use of if he pleased, and a stool to lay the purse upon, a little within the bar, on the left hand as you enter. He presented himself in his robes, carrying the purse in his own hand; and having bowed to the Speaker, he laid it on the chair. He would not sit down himself, nor put on his hat, though he was moved to do it by the Speaker, but spoke all the while bare-headed and standing, the Sergeant-at-Arms attending the House continuing by him with the mace on his shoulder.

Lord Finch appears to have gained more applause on this occasion than he had ever before done. Whitelock, who says, "it was a sad sight to see a person of his greatness, parts, and favor, to appear in such a posture before such an assembly to plead for his life and fortune,"—declares that " the apology was elegant and ingenious, and delivered with an excellent grace and gesture, and that many were exceedingly taken with his eloquence and carriage,"—and Rigby, the Member for Wigan, who spoke first after he had withdrawn, thus began : " Mr. Speaker, though my judgment prompts me to sit still and be silent, yet the duty I owe to my King, my country, and my conscience moves me to stand up and exhort you to be firm and inflexible. Had not this siren so sweet a tongue, surely he could never have effected so much mischief to this kingdom. You know, Sir, *optimorum putrefactio pessima*, the best things putrefied become the worst, and as it is in the natural so in the body politic."[1]

Yet such as it has come down to us, it by no means merits these encomiums, and it must either be very imperfectly reported, or he must have had the full measure of favor at all times shown in the House of Commons to

[1] 2 Parl. Hist. 692.

any one vindicating himself with tolerable address from a personal accusation. He begins well by trying to insinuate himself into the good graces of his audience:— "Mr. Speaker, I do first present my most humble thanks to this honorable assembly for this favor vouchsafed me, in granting me admittance to their presence, and do humbly beseech them to believe it is no desire to preserve myself or my fortune, but to deserve your good opinions, that hath drawn me hither. I do profess in the presence of Him who knoweth all hearts, that I had rather go from door to door, and crave *Da obolum Belisario*, with the favorable censure of this assembly than live and enjoy all honor and fortune under your displeasure." He then goes on to justify his religion, "which was well known to be pure Protestantism by all the members of the Society of Gray's Inn, where he lived thirty years." He declares that the two places of Puisne Judge and Chief Justice of the Common Pleas were conferred upon him when he was far from the thoughts of the one and from the ambition of the other. He asserts that while he was Speaker he served the House with candor, never doing ill office to any. He excuses his refusal to put the question from the chair by the King's express command, and desires each of his hearers to consider how he would have comported himself between the displeasure of a gracious master and the ill opinion of this honorable assembly. He then goes to *ship-money*, on which he makes a still lamer excuse, asserting that it was a mere accidental coincidence that he was made Lord Chief Justice four days before the writs issued: that the Lord Keeper Coventry had made an improper use of the extrajudicial opinion upon the legality of the tax which the King had required to be kept secret; that he never used the least promise of preferment or reward to any of them; that his judgment in Mr. Hampden's case might be erroneous, but was conscientious; and that he had always maintained that ship-money could only be lawfully levied when the kingdom was in danger,—suppressing his doctrine that the King was the sole judge of the danger. He last of all justified himself from the charge of violating the *Charta de Foresta* by enlarging the boundaries of the royal forests, and concluded by submitting all that he had done to the goodness and justice of the House.

At the meeting of the Lords next morning, it was known that the Lord Keeper had absconded; and Littleton, Chief Justice of the Common Pleas, under a commission from the King, was placed on the woolsack as Speaker. Lord Falkland immediately appeared at the bar to prefer the impeachment. Having read the articles, he said:

"Nil refert tales versus qua voce legantur.

"The charge was such as required no assistance from the bringer; when voted, having been attended with all possible evidence, and all possible aggravation, that addition only excepted which my Lord Finch alone could make, and had made, by his confession, signified in his flight."

The Lords sent back a message to the Commons, that they had taken into consideration the charges against John, Lord Finch, late Keeper of the Great Seal; but having received intimation that he was not to be found, they had ordered him into safe custody as soon as he could be discovered.

It was generally suspected that his escape had been connived at by the popular leaders; but there seems to have been a large majority in the House of Commons who wished to bring him to the block.

The noble and learned fugitive arrived safely in Holland; and on the 3rd of January, 1641, wrote the following letter to Lord Pembroke, to be laid before the two Houses:

"My most well-beloved Lord, the interest your Lordship hath ever had in the best of my fortunes and affections, gives me the privilege of troubling your Lordship with these few lines, from one who hath now nothing left to serve you withal but his prayers. These your Lordship shall never want, with an heart as full of true affection to your Lordship as ever any was. My Lord, it was not the loss of my place, and with that of my fortunes, nor being exiled from my dear country and friends, though many of them were cause of sorrow, that afflicts; but that which I most suffer under is, that displeasure of the House of Commons conceived against me. I know how true a heart I have ever borne towards them, and your Lordship can witness, in part, what ways I have gone in; but silence and patience best become me. With these I must leave myself and my actions to the favorable construction of my noble friends; in which number your Lordship hath a prime place. I am now at the Hague, where I arrived on Thursday, the last day of last month, where I purpose to live in a fashion agreeable to the poorness of my fortunes. As for any views in this world, I have utterly cast off the thoughts of them; and my aim shall be so to learn *to number my days, that I may apply my heart unto wisdom,* —that wisdom, that shall wipe all tears from mine eyes and heart, and lead me by the hand to true happiness, which can never be taken from me. I pray the God of Heaven to bless this parliament with both a happy progress and conclusion; and if my ruin can induce but the least to it, I shall not repine. I truly pray for your Lordship and your noble family, that God would give an increase of all worldly blessings, and in the fullness of days to receive you to his glory. If I were capable of serving any body, I would tell your Lordship, that no man should be readier to make known his devotion and true gratitude to your Lordship, than your Lordship's most humble and affectionate poor kinsman and servant, " FINCH."

He remained in exile about eight years, in great penury and misery. Even the royalists who, from time to time, escaped beyond seas to avoid the tyranny of the parliament, generally shunned him, although they could not avoid sometimes coming in contact with him at hotels and boarding houses.[1] At last, by making an abject submission to Cromwell, and agreeing to pay a sum of money as a delinquent, he was allowed to return; and he lived in retirement till the Restoration.

He was then most indecently put into the commission for the trial of the Regicides,—which calls forth this indignant complaint from Ludlow: "Finch, who had been accused of high treason twenty years before, by a full parliament, and who, by flying from their justice, saved his life, was appointed to judge some of those who should have been his his judges."[2]

He is only reported to have spoken once during the trials. This was upon the observation of General Harrison, "Whereas, it has been said, we did assume and

[1] "Arrived at the Hague, I find my Lord Finch, not long before fled out of England from the fury of the Parliament." "I lodged at Brown's. There was in pension with us my Lord Finch."—*Evelyn's Private Correspondence.*
[2] Mem. 365.

usurp an authority; I say this was done rather in the fear of the Lord."

Lord Finch.—"Though my Lords here have been pleased to give you a great latitude, this must not be suffered that you should run into these damnable excursions, to make God the author of this damnable treason committed by you."[1]

He died soon after, universally despised by cavaliers as well as republicans,—by high churchmen as much as by puritans. Leaving no issue, this branch of the family of Finch became extinct; and with it the barony of Finch of Fordwich.

We must rejoice that he escaped the scaffold, of which he was in such danger; but we can not regret the subsequent misfortunes which befel him. Nothing can be conceived more subversive of public virtue, than the continued prosperity of an unprincipled judge and reckless politician, who has notoriously advanced himself by his profligacy, and set at naught all regard to consistency and decency.

CHAPTER LXV.

LIFE OF LORD KEEPER LITTLETON FROM HIS BIRTH TILL THE COMMENCEMENT OF THE CIVIL WAR.

THE Great Seal remained for some time with the King after the night of the 21st of December, when he so unexpectedly received it from Lord Finch, about to fly for his life.

In such an extraordinary emergency there was much difficulty in the appointment of a successor. Banks, the Attorney General, had been actively engaged in all the unconstitutional and cruel government prosecutions which had taken place during the suspension of parliament; and Herbert, the Solicitor General, though recently appointed, had rendered himself almost equally obnoxious to the popular party, by the blind zeal he had displayed in support of the arbitrary principles on which the government had been conducted. The promotion of either

[1] 5 St. Tr. 1025.

of them would therefore have been considered a direct insult to the House of Commons, and an acknowledgment by the King that all his professions of amendment were insincere. There was a disposition to offer office to some of the lawyers on the other side,[1] but none of them could be prudently trusted to preside in the House of Lords, particularly when it was considered that the impeachments against Strafford and Laud would soon be coming on to be heard. Strafford, now in the Tower, still kept up a private intercourse with his royal Master,—and it is said to have been by his recommendation that, on the 29th of January, 1641, the Great Seal was delivered to Sir EDWARD LITTLETON, Chief Justice of the Common Pleas, as Lord Keeper.

Although the appointment did not turn out felicitously, either for him who suggested it or for the public,—apparently a better choice could not have been made, as Littleton was a very profound lawyer, and a man of excellent private character. Although he had changed sides in politics,—considering the times, he was to be praised for his moderation,—for he had not violently persecuted his ancient opinions or his ancient friends. With more moral courage and energy he might have gained for himself a high reputation, and prevented the coming collision ; but, entertaining the best intentions, he sadly disappointed the expectations of his friends, and he pursued a vacillating course, which ended in his own disgrace, and aggravated the calamities of his country.

Edward Littleton, the subject of this memoir, was of an ancient family of the robe, being lineally descended in the male line from the great Littleton, author of "The Tenures," and judge of the Common Pleas in the reign of Edward IV. This legal patriarch left three sons, the eldest of whom is the ancestor of Lord Lyttleton, and the second of Lord Hatherton. From the third was descended the Lord Keeper, who was born at Mounslow, in Shropshire, in the year 1589, being the eldest son of Sir Edward Littleton, of Hewley, in the same county, likewise of the profession of the law, having been one of the Justices of the Marches, and a Judge of North Wales. Young Edward Littleton was educated at a provincial

[1] Oliver St. John, long in "the sedition line," was soon after made Solicitor General.

grammar school till he was sent to Oxford, and entered a gentleman commoner at Christ Church. Here he applied very diligently to study, and in 1609 he took the degree of Bachelor of Arts, having gained great applause for his proficiency in logic and in classical learning. He continued a very diligent student during the remainder of his life.

Being removed to the Inner Temple, he devoted himself to the Year Books and antiquarian lore. He was a bosom friend of Selden, and for some years they carried on their studies in common, often going together to the Tower of London, there to regale themselves with a smell of ancient parchment.[1] He continued at the same time to keep up an acquaintance with more elegant pursuits. He was a famous swordsman, and he showed in his youth a taste for the military art, which afterwards broke out in maturer years, and placed him at the head of a regiment, —with the Great Seal in one hand, and a pike in the other. But he was determined to rise by his profession, and when he was called to the bar he was reckoned the best grounded common lawyer which his Society had sent forth for many years. He soon rose into very extensive practice.

In 1626 he was returned a member of the House of Commons, and eagerly joined the patriotic party then struggling against the ascendancy of the Duke of Buckingham, and he took an active part in supporting the impeachment carried on against that powerful favorite.[2]

He again sat in Charles's third parliament, called in 1628, and fought zealously for the cause of liberty under the auspices of Sir E. Coke. He was much noticed by the venerable patriot, and through his influence was chosen chairman of the Committee which examined into grievances since the preceding dissolution, and prepared the "Petition of Right." He moved four resolutions, which were unanimously agreed to by the House: 1st, "That no freeman ought to be committed or detained in prison, or otherwise restrained by command of the King or the Privy Council, unless some cause of the commitment, detainer, or restraint be expressed, for which by law he ought to be committed, detained or restrained."—2ndly, "That the writ of Habeas Corpus can not be denied, but

---

[1]   "Oh, Tewkesbury, the smell
    Of ancient parchment pleased thee well."—*Pleader's Guide.*
[2] 2 Parl. Hist. 53.

ought to be granted to every man that is committed or detained in prison, or otherwise restrained by the command of the King, the Privy Council, or any other, he praying for the same."—3rdly, "That if a freeman be committed or detained in prison, or otherwise restrained by command of the King, Privy Council, or any other, no cause of such commitment or detainer being expressed, and the same be returned upon a Habeas Corpus granted for the said party, that then he ought to be delivered or bailed."—4thly, "That the ancient and undoubted right of every freeman is, that he hath a full and absolute property in his goods and estate, and that no tax, tallage, loan, benevolence, or other like charge, ought to be commanded or levied by the King or his ministers, without common assent of parliament."

Afterwards, at a conference with the Lords, who were called upon to concur in these resolutions, he made a very learned and admirable speech, showing that they were founded on acts of parliament and precedents. Sir E. Coke followed, loudly praising his young friend, and saying, "Your Lordships have heard seven acts of parliament in point, and thirty-one precedents, summarily collected, and with great understanding delivered. I am transported with joy, because of the hope of good success in this weighty business."

In a subsequent stage of the proceeding, Heath, the Attorney General, having attempted to prove that commitments by the King himself were not subject to the ordinary rules of law, and stood up for *lettres de cachet*, Littleton made a furious attack upon him, and successfully demolished his authorities and arguments, showing that "it is equal whether the King do it himself or by the agency of others."[1] He had a no less triumphant conflict with Secretary Cooke, who, although he had signed most of the illegal warrants by which members had been sent to gaol for their conduct in the House, now found it convenient strongly to recommend moderation. "We have moderation preached to us," said Littleton, "and we follow it. But what is the conduct of those who preach it? Let the parties have their doom who have violated the liberties of parliament."[2] When the "Petition of Right" passed the Commons, he had the honor to be

[1] 2 Parl. Hist. 256, 262, 295. 3 St. Tr. 85.   [2] 2 Parl. Hist. 441.

appointed, along with Sir E. Coke and Sir Dudley Digges, to carry it up to the Lords.

The flaming patriot, however, could not resist the tempting offers made to him when the system was begun of buying off opposition, and he went over to the Court along with Noy, Saville, and Wentworth. But it must be acknowledged that he did not like them show the zeal of a political convert from the errors of opposition, and he continued to enjoy the good-will and to cultivate the society of his early friends. His first preferment was a Welsh Judgeship, (in after times so perilous to patriotism), and soon after, by the support of the government, he was elected Recorder of London.

When Lord Keeper he must have looked back with much regret to this period of his life. He still continued to practice at the bar, and without political office was easily at the top of his profession. Noy, the Attorney General, a most learned man, confined himself to his official duties, and was day and night among the musty records from which he was inventing, and preparing to justify his writ of ship-money. The Solicitor was one Shilton, silly and ignorant—put in by a caprice of the Duke of Buckingham, and universally despised. Brampston, the King's Sergeant was lengthy and laborious, but seldom went beyond the drowsy atmosphere of the Common Pleas. Littleton, who had "taken great pains in the hardest and most knotty part of the law as well as that which was more customary, and was not only very ready and expert in the books, but exceedingly versed in records, so that he was looked upon as the best antiquary of the profession, and upon the mere strength of his own abilities had early raised himself into the first rank of the practices in the Common Law Courts, now grew into the highest practice in all the other Courts,"[1] and he was eagerly retained in every cause of consequence depending not only in the King's Bench and Exchequer, but in Chancery, in the Star Chamber, and at the Council Table. Though subject to a few sarcasms for the countenance he now gave to the unconstitutional measures of the government, and the altered tone of his conversation on political subjects—as parliament never met, he did not incur any public obloquy, and in private society he was

[1] Clarendon.

much sought after, not only by flatterers, whom he contemned, but by the numerous class of agreeable persons who are always desirous of cultivating the acquaintance of a man rising into great professional eminence.

On the lamented death of Noy at the moment when his writs of ship-money were ready to be launched, Banks, a brazen-faced lawyer, was put in his place, but he was more remarkable for boldness than for skill or weight to defend the measures now in contemplation. "When the King found he should have much to do in Westminster Hall, he removed an old, useless, illiterate person who had been put into that office by favor, and made Littleton Solicitor General, much to his honor, but not to his profit, the obligation of attendance upon that office depriving him of much benefit he used to acquire by his practice."[1] A more unpleasant consequence must have been to him, who was always defective in nerve and energy, that he was now obliged to appear as counsel for the Crown in all public prosecutions, however obnoxious they might be. But in looking through the state trials of this period, it is wonderful to see how he contrived to throw the odious parts upon the King's Sergeant and the Attorney General, and how he betook himself to comfortable obscurity. In the prosecution against Bastwick, Burton, and Prynne, although he could not be silent, he confined himself when he followed Sir John Banks and Sergeant Whitfield, to vindicating the memory of Noy, who was said in "The Divine Tragedy," one of the publications included in the information, to have been struck, as a judgment from Heaven, with a mortal disease when scoffingly looking at Prynne having his ears cut off in the pillory under a former sentence.[2]

At last came *Rex* v. *Hampden*, and Littleton was obliged to take the laboring oar. Ship-money was to be proved to be legal by precedents, processes, records, and

[1] Clarendon.
[2] A ludicrous circumstance happened on this occasion, which shows that, even in the Star Chamber, in cases of libel, the truth of the charge might be inquired into. Littleton undertook to prove by three or four gentlemen of good credit and rank, that Mr. Noy labored long before under the infirmity of which he died. "The Solicitor then called out for room for the gentlemen to come in, but none such appeared."—3 St. Tr. 719. So late as Queen Anne's time, Lord Holt, in Tuchin's case, called upon the defendant to prove the truth of his charges, and the judge-made doctrine that "the greater the truth the greater the libel," now statutably repealed, was of later origin.

writings of different æras, from the Heptarchy downwards—which were to upset all the acts of parliament which had been passed to forbid taxation without authority of parliament, and were to show that acts of parliament upon such a subject were *ultra vires* and void. Noy being gone, it was felt that no one could so well use his materials as Mr. Solicitor. He was heard before all the Judges in the Exchequer Chamber, for the Crown, three entire days, after Oliver St. John had spoken two days for the defendant. His argument is certainly very learned and ingenious, and much more modest, or rather less outrageously offensive, than that of Chief Justice Finch and several of the Judges, who openly avowed the principles of pure despotism, insisting that the prerogative of the Crown was essentially absolute, and could not be controlled by legislative enactments. He candidly allowed that, in England, subjects have a property in their goods; but he contended that the law of property must give place to the law of nature for the common defense, and that the levying of a debt or duty upon property, so far from destroying, doth confirm it. " *Quicquid necessitas cogit defendit;* the law of the time must regulate the law of the place. A chirurgeon may cut off one member to save the rest. If a storm arise at sea, to cast out goods is lawful, and they whose goods are saved shall contribute to the loss. A man may pull down the house of another when the next house to it is on fire. *Jam tua res agitur paries cum proximus ardet.* If two men are fighting, a passer-by may part them, and put them into several chambers, because it is for the good of the commonwealth. If a madman be abroad, he may be taken, whipped, and imprisoned, lest he do violence to himself or others. The King may compel all to defend the realm, and he may vary the mode of contributing to the public defense. Judges are not to fight, but they are to be knighted;[1] nay, a Sergeant sworn in the Common Pleas is compellable; Rolfe, a stout Sergeant, pleaded that he was of the degree of a coif, and not bound to be a knight, but he was forced to it. Imminent perils to a state dispensed with ordinary proceedings in law; *inter*

---

[1] One judge in my time successfully resisted this supposed obligation, by refusing to go to court or to appear in the King's presence after his appointment. He said that he was determined to die " *John Heath, Esquire.*"

arma silent leges. Nay, if there are but rumors of war, laws are silent." He then undertakes to prove his general doctrines by going through English History from the foundation of the kingdom to the Norman Conquest—thence to *Magna Charta*—to the statute *De Tallagio non concedendo*—to the first granting of tonnage and poundage—and, finally, to the Petition of Right, "which did no ways concern the dispute." He relied mainly on *Danegelt*, arguing, that " if usurpers could lay this tax on the people, much more may our natural born King do the like—which shows it to be an undoubted inalienable right in the Crown of England. Oh, say they, but this *may be* done by a parliament. By a *may be* a man may answer any argument. Oh, but they tell us that Fortescue, Chief Justice of the King's Bench, to show the law of England to be better than the law of France, saith, that nothing can be taken from an Englishman but by parliament, he himself consenting thereto. That, my Lords, is *in the ordinary way.* Doth he say that no man without parliament may contribute to defend himself? *Ne verbum quidem !*"—But this taste of the reasoning of the law officers of the Crown in those days must suffice.

Although he acquired considerable reputation on this occasion, he became more and more dissatisfied with his position and with the aspect of public affairs. He lamented the inhuman punishments to which his colleagues instigated the Star Chamber, and, amidst the growing discontents of the nation, he saw distinctly that the day of retribution was at hand.

Finch being made Lord Keeper on the death of Coventry, a vacancy occurred in the office of Chief Justice of the Common Pleas, to which Banks had the best right, this being called " the Attorney General's cushion ;" but Mr. Attorney being of a stouter heart, and not unwilling to enjoy a little longer the sweets of his lucrative place, waived his claim, and Littleton, to his inexpressible delight, from being tossed on a tempestuous ocean, found himself at once in the delicious harbor for which he had long prayed, and which he had hardly hoped ever to reach. " He was made Chief Justice of the Common Pleas, then the best office of the law, and that which he was wont to say in his highest ambition in his own private wishes, he had most desired; and it was indeed the sphere in which he moved most gracefully and with most advantage, being a master of all that learning and knowledge which that place required, and an excellent Judge, of great gravity, and above all suspicion of corruption."[1]

He was soon after made a Privy Councillor, against the wishes of Lord Keeper Finch, who was desirous of preventing other lawyers from entering into any rivalship with himself. The succeeding twelve months must have been a very agreeable portion of his existence, from his considering not only what he actually enjoyed, but that from which he had escaped, and to which he saw others exposed. While he was securely reaping the public applause in a high office, the duties of which he felt that he thoroughly understood and could satisfactorily perform, he must have thought to himself what he must have suffered buffeting in the House of Commons,—vainly attempting to palliate the enormities of the government, which he had secretly lamented and condemned. When the fatal step was taken of abruptly dissolving the parliament, if still a law officer of the Crown, he would have been required to give an opinion that the Convocation might sit on, vote supplies, and make canons binding on the laity,—he would have been called upon to sanction modes of filling the Exchequer if possible more illegal than ship-money,—and he would have seen the dire necessity of being soon exposed to another parliament in which the misgovernment of twelve years was inevitably to be examined and punished.

When the Long Parliament met, he little thought that his further elevation and his troubles were approaching; and he still hoped that he might long repose on his "cushion" in the Common Pleas. In the morning after Finch's flight, he suddenly found himself on the woolsack, as Speaker of the House of Lords. Still he trusted that this appointment was only temporary, till the Great Seal should be delivered to another Lord Keeper.

But he discovered in a little time that the King, by the secret advice of Strafford and Laud, wished that he should become Lord Keeper. Sincerely declining the elevation, he was gently reminded of his obligations to the King, and strongly assured, that he might not only be instrumental in saving his old friends and patrons about to be

[1] Clarendon.

tried for high treason in the House of Lords, but that he might be the means of bringing about a happy settlement of all the existing differences, and of saving the state. Conscious of his own mental infirmities, and foreseeing the perplexities in which they might involve himself and others, he long resisted; but Hilary term approaching, there being an absolute necessity that the vacancy should be filled up for the ordinary administration of justice, and the King's importunity continuing, he yielded, and took the step which he for ever repented;—for he had not another day of peace of mind, and he experienced nothing but doubt, anxiety, mortification, and self-reproach, till his eyes were closed in death.

He received the Great Seal, as Lord Keeper, at Whitehall, on the 19th of January, 1641; and two days after, on the first day of Hilary term, he took his place in the Court of Chancery in the presence of the Lord Treasurer, the Earl Marshal, the Marquis of Hamilton, the Earl of Pembroke, and many others of the nobility.[1] On the 18th of February following, he was raised to the Peerage by the title of Lord Littleton, of Mounslow,—this promotion likewise being said to have been suggested by Lord Strafford, who thought he might be more useful if permitted to take part in the proceedings of the House as a Peer than if he could only put the question as Speaker,—a plan destined to end in disappointment and discomfiture.

The first business which came before the House of Lords after the new Lord Keeper's elevation, was the "Triennial Bill," by which, if there was any intermission of parliaments for three years, the Peers were to meet and issue writs, in the King's name, for the holding of a parliament; and in case of default by the Peers, the returning officers were to elect representatives to the House of Commons; and in case of their default, the constituents were to meet and choose representatives of their own authority, so that this law might not be evaded—as that had been which required "that parliaments should be held yearly, and oftener, *if need be.*" The passing of this act caused ringing of bells and bonfires all over England; and the Lord Keeper, by the direction of both Houses, returned thanks to his Majesty for giving his assent to it;

[1] Crown Off. Min. Book, fol. 5.

saying, that it would be of singular security for the present, of infinite honor to his Majesty's royal crown and dignity, and of great comfort to posterity.' He then took an oath before the Lords spiritual and temporal, that while he held the Great Seal, he would duly issue writs for the summoning of parliaments as the act directs.[2]

We now come to a passage in his life which justly subjects him to the charge of the basest pusillanimity. Treachery even was imputed to him; but I think his conduct is to be explained by a lamentable deficiency of moral courage, not of principle. He had been recently raised to the Peerage in the belief that he might be of essential service by presiding as a member of the House of Lords, at the important trial about to take place, on which the life of Strafford, and the fate of the monarchy, were supposed to depend. According to Clarendon,— when he had been made Lord Keeper, he was a little mortified in not at once having a Peerage, and he himself expressly pointed out to the King the important services he should be able to render to the royal cause if that dignity were conferred upon him.

On the day when Strafford was to be arraigned, the King unexpectedly came to the House of Lords, and seating himself on the throne without his robes, merely said that he wished to hear the nature of the charges. The ceremony having been once gone through, he withdrew, and several Peers testified high resentment at this intrusion, insisting that it was an attempt to intimidate, and that all that had taken place while the King was present was to be considered *coram non judice*, and void.

Now it was expected that "Baron Littleton of Mounslow" would have stood up for the King, and he certainly might have urged that both on principle and precedent, Charles in this instance had done nothing irregular, for the King is always supposed to be present in parliament, and in former times was actually on the throne, not only at the opening and conclusion of the session, but almost constantly while any business was going on. Although it belonged to the Peers to regulate the conduct of this impeachment, and to decide by a majority of the votes upon the guilt or innocence of the accused, the King, without interfering with the proceeding, was

[1] 2 Parl. Hist. 718.   [2] Crown Off. Min. Book, fol. 5.

entitled to be present at it, and might at any moment have put a stop to it by a dissolution. But the Lord Keeper was so frightened by this sudden storm, that he had not a word to say even by way of apology for the King, and a motion being carried without opposition, that the Earl of Strafford be again called to the bar, that the articles of impeachment might be read to him and his plea taken *de novo ;*—without leaving the woolsack he a second time went through the ceremony of the arraignment.[1]

Some thought that the Lord Keeper would make amends when the trial actually came on; but the day before that fixed for its commencement, he sent a message to the House of Lords, intimating that he was taken so ill that it was impossible for him to attend, and besides that he had some doubts whether the objection of the Commons was not well founded, that no Peers created since the impeachment was voted ought to sit on the trial, as the impeachment was in the name of all the Commons of England, and therefore such Peers being prosecutors were disqualified as Judges.[2]

This was justly considered a material advantage gained for the impeachment. The Earl of Arundel, the Earl Marshal, an enemy of Strafford, was elected by the House to sit Speaker in the absence of the Lord Keeper.

The truth was, that when Littleton heard of the preparations in Westminster Hall for this great solemnity,—the court for the Peers, the closet for the King and royal family, the galleries for the House of Commons, the seats for the Scottish Commissioners and the deputation from the Irish parliament, and, above all, the crowds that were to assemble, and the cries for vengeance that had already been uttered in the streets,—his heart entirely failed him, and a real illness afterwards came on, which confined him for some weeks to his bed.

Before he would acknowledge that he had recovered, Strafford, by an unparalleled display of constancy and talent,—without professional assistance,—and three na-

---

[1] 2 Parl. Hist. 742.

[2] In point of law there is no foundation for this objection. The creation of peers to influence a pending impeachment would be highly unconstitutional, and would subject those who advised such a step to severe punishment; but peers, when created, have all the rights and privileges of the peerage, and no exception can be taken to the competency of any peer.

tions marshaled against him,—had defeated the proceeding by impeachment; a bill of attainder had been brought in to put him to death without the forms of justice; the Judges, yielding to popular, as they formerly did to royal intimidation, had iniquitously pronounced that the charges against him amounted in point of law to high treason; amidst the apprehension of new plots against the nation, the bill had rapidly passed both Houses; the King's scruples had been overcome by the solicitations of the Queen and the sophistry of the Bishops; and the noble victim, after exclaiming, "Put not your trust in princes," had met his fate with such courage and composure as to enlist all sympathy in his favor, and to make his name respected by posterity, although, having been once the champion of public rights, he had long systematically labored to subvert the liberties of his country.

After Strafford's execution, Littleton resumed his place on the woolsack; but he offered no resistance to any of the bills which came up from the Commons. He was well justified in agreeing to those for abolishing the High Commission Court and the Star Chamber. He proposed an amendment to that for preventing a dissolution without the consent of the two Houses,—that it should be in force only for three years,—by the end of which time it might be expected that the reformation of the state would be completed;—but this being objected to by the Commons, he withdrew it, and Charles was virtually dethroned.

At last there was some respite from these troubles, the two Houses having adjourned while the King went on a visit to Scotland, and Littleton was allowed to enjoy repose at his villa at Cranford.

Meanwhile the Irish rebellion broke out; the alarm of a counter-revolution by a Roman Catholic force was universally spread, and parliament again meeting, measures were proposed by the popular leaders inconsistent with monarchical government. None of these had the Lord Keeper the spirit to resist. His excuse was, that he cultivated the good-will of the republican party so that he might be able more effectually to serve the King. He might have stopped the bill for turning the Bishops out of the House of Lords, by insisting on the objection that a bill to the same effect had been rejected during the same session ; but yielding to the clamor of the mob, he voted for it, and joined in advising the King to assent to it.

He then suddenly took another turn, which was still more fatal to the royal cause. The Queen, the ladies of the Court, and Lord Digby, resolved that they would put down the movement by a display of vigor, and that the prosecutors of Strafford should share his fate. A charge of high treason was to be suddenly brought against Lord Kimbolton, Pym, Denzill Hollis, Sir Arthur Hazelrig, Hampden, and Strode, upon which they were to be committed to prison, and it was thought that the disaffected, thus deprived of their leaders, would instantly become powerless. The charge was to be made—not by indictment before a grand jury, or by the impeachment of the Commons,—but by the Attorney General *ex officio* in the House of Lords.

When this scheme was disclosed to the Lord Keeper, he must have seen the madness of it. As a lawyer, he must have known that the House of Lords had no jurisdiction to try commoners for a capital offense ; and that the Attorney General had no power to originate such a prosecution.[1] As a man of sense and observation, he must have been aware that the House of Commons and the public would not allow such a prosecution to proceed ; and that the attempt would only add to the popular excitement, and prevent all chance of reaction. But finding that the King was strongly bent upon it, he had not the courage to oppose it ; and he communicated a royal message to the Lords, "that the Attorney General, by the King's special command, was to lay before them a charge, for high treason, against one member of that House and five members of the other House of parliament." Herbert, the Attorney General, who had ceased to be a member of the House of Commons, and had taken his seat in the House of Lords, under his writ of summons as an assistant, then rose from the Judges' woolsack where he had been placed, and standing at the clerk's table, said "that the King had commanded him to tell their Lordships that great and treasonable designs and practices against him and the state had come to his Majesty's knowledge ; for which the King had given him command

---

[1] Appeals of treason in Parliament had been abolished by 1 Hen. IV. c. 14. See Bl. Com. 314.

to accuse six persons of high treason, and other high misdemeanors, by delivering the articles in writing, which he had in his hand, which he received from his Majesty, and was commanded to desire their Lordships to hear read."

The articles being read, they were found to charge the accused with subverting the fundamental laws of the kingdom,—with attempting to alienate the affections of the people from the King,—with sowing disaffection in the army,—with inviting the Scots to invade England,—with endeavoring to overturn the rights and being of parliaments,—with exciting tumults,—and with conspiring to levy war against the King. Mr. Attorney then moved, that their Lordships would take care for securing the persons of the accused. Lord Kimbolton was in the House sitting by Lord Digby, with whom he had a great private intimacy; and who, although he had recommended the measure, pretended to him that it struck him with surprise and horror. According to the concerted plan, and according to the course pursued with Strafford and Laud, the Lord Keeper ought to have moved the immediate commitment of Lord Kimbolton; but his courage failed him, and the House adjourned.

There is no direct evidence that Littleton was privy to the fatal course now pursued by the King, in going to the House of Commons personally to demand and arrest the five members, when they were not delivered up to his messenger; but it is hardly possible to impute to Charles such culpable misconduct, such folly, as well as such criminality, as that he should proceed in a matter of such infinite importance, depending upon the legal extent of his prerogative, without consulting his chief law adviser and the Keeper of his conscience, with whom he was in constant intercourse. We know that a private council had been held upon the subject, from the intelligence conveyed to those most interested by the French ambassador,[1] and by "that busy stateswoman, the Countess of Carlisle, who had now changed her gallant from Strafford to Pym."[2] If Littleton was present when it was debated and approved of, we may be sure from his character that however much he might disapprove, he would not venture to oppose it. To his timid acquiescence in

---

[1] "J'avois prévenu mes amis, et ils s'étoient mis en sureté."—Mazure, iii. 429.
[2] Warwick, 204.

whatever was proposed on either side, however imprudent or unconstitutional, may in no small degree be attributed the fatal collision which followed. All historians agree, that the prosecution of Lord Kimbolton and the five members, which he might easily have prevented, was the proximate cause of the civil war; for the popular leaders now saw that no faith was to be placed in any of the professions of the Court; and that without an appeal to the sword, their own lives must certainly be sacrificed.

When it was too late, the Lord Keeper brought down a message from the King, "that in all his proceedings against the Lord Kimbolton and the five members, he had never the least intention of violating the least privilege of parliament; and that he was willing to have the matter cleared up in any way that parliament should advise." But this concession was imputed to a temporary apprehension from the burst of indignation which the previous outrage had universally called forth.

Preparations were now made on both sides for hostilities; and the country party brought in their bill for regulating the militia, which they thought indispensable for their own safety, although they could not expect that the King would agree to it, as it appointed a military chief in every county, and in substance transferred the command of the army from the Crown to the Parliament.

CHAPTER LXVI.

CONCLUSION OF THE LIFE OF LORD KEEPER LITTLETON.

THE King now withdrew from London, and after passing some time at Newmarket, was proceeding towards York, communicating from time to time with the Lord Keeper, in whom he still placed some lingering confidence. Being determined to dismiss the Earl of Essex and the Earl of Holland from the offices of Chamberlain and Groom of the Stole, he sent an order to Littleton that he should require the staff and key from the one and the other. The Keeper trembled at the task, and not being able to summon up courage to undertake it, went privately to Lord Falkland and desired him to assist him in presenting his excuse to the King. Making many professions of loyalty, he expressed a hope that his Majesty would not command him in an affair so unsuitable to the office he held; that no Keeper had ever been employed in such a service; and that if he should execute the order it would be voted a breach of privilege, and the House would commit him to prison, by which not only would he himself be ruined, but the King would receive the greatest affront; whereas the thing itself might be done by a more proper officer without inconvenience. "How weak soever the reasons were," says Lord Clarendon, "the passion was strong," and his representation being transmitted to the King, he was excused, and the harsh duty was imposed upon Lord Falkland himself.

But the conduct of the Lord Keeper was now so unsatisfactory that the King resolved to get rid of him. Since the failure of the prosecution of the five members, Littleton had abandoned all effort to put on a show of vigor in the House of Lords, and had silently suffered the most objectionable votes to be carried without opposition. He was even suspected of perfidy, for he not only declined performing the duty which the King had enjoined in reference to the Earls of Essex and Holland, but he had private conferences with the leaders of the parliamentary party, who frequently resorted to him, and whom he appeared very much to court. At last, having supported the Militia Bill to which the King refused the royal assent, —when it again came up from the Commons in the form of an ordinance by the two Houses, omitting the King's name,—he put the question upon it from the woolsack, and himself actually voted for it, "to the infinite offense and scandal of all those who adhered to the King."[1] This was in reality the abolition of monarchy and the establishment of a republic.

Hyde, who had a kindness for him, and suspected that his nerves might be more in fault than his principles, went early next morning to call upon him at Exeter House, and finding him in his study, began to express great astonishment and regret at his recent conduct, and plainly told him how he had lost the esteem of all good men, and that the King could not but be exceedingly dissatisfied with him. Some attendants being heard in an outer room,

[1] Clarendon. 2 Parl. Hist. 1091, 1110, 1114.

Littleton desired them to withdraw. Then locking the door of that room and of the study, he made Hyde take a seat, and sitting down near him, thus unburdened his mind :—

"The best proof I can give of my value for this proof of your friendship is by concealing nothing from you. You see before you the most wretched of mankind. I have not had an hour of peace or comfort since I left the Common Pleas, where I knew both the business and the persons I had to deal with. I am supposed to be preferred to a higher dignity, but I am now obliged to converse with another set of men who are strangers to me, and with affairs which I understand not. I have had no friend with whom I could confer on any doubt which might occur to me. The state of public affairs has been deplorable and heart-breaking. The King is ill-counseled and is betrayed by those about him. The proceedings of the parliament which I may have appeared to countenance, I more bitterly condemn; and I am filled with the most gloomy forebodings, for they would never do this if they were not resolved to do more. I know the King too well, and I observe the carriage of particular men too much, and I have watched the whole current of public transactions these last five or six months, not to foresee, that it can not be long before there will be a war between the King and the two Houses. I often think with myself of what importance it will then be, which party shall have the Great Seal, the *Clavis Regni*, the token of supreme authority. In my heart I am and ever have been for the King, both out of affection to his person and respect for his high and sacred office. When the trial comes, no man shall be more ready to perish either with or for his Majesty than myself. It is the prospect of this necessity that has made me carry myself towards that party with so much compliance, that I may be gracious with them,— at least that they may have no distrust of me. I know that they have had a consultation within a few days whether, as I may be sent for by the King or another put in my stead, it would not be best to appoint the Seal to be kept in some secure place, so that they might be in no danger of losing it, and that the Keeper should receive it from time to time for the execution of his office. The knowledge I had of this consultation, and the fear I had of the execution of it, has been the reason why, in the debate on the militia, I gave my vote in such a manner as must make a very ill impression with the King and many others who do not inwardly know me. If I had not now submitted to those I mislike, this very night the Seal had been taken from me. But my compliance will only prejudice myself, not the King. I have now got so fast into their confidence, that I shall be able to preserve the Seal in my own hands till the King require it of me, and then I shall be ready to attend his Majesty with it, wherever he may be, or whatsoever fortune may betide him."

Hyde, convinced of his present sincerity, although not altogether satisfied with the explanation of his past wavering, asked him "whether he would give him leave, when there should be a fit occasion, to assure the King that he would perform this service when required of him?" Littleton solemnly passed his word for the performance of it as soon as his Majesty pleased; and so they parted.

When the news of the Lord Keeper's vote on the Militia Bill reached York, the whole Court was thrown into amazement and dismay. The King, exceedingly displeased and provoked, sent a peremptory order to Lord Falkland instantly to demand the Great Seal from the traitor, and desired him to consult with Hyde as to who would be the fittest person to be appointed to succeed, suggesting the names of *Banks*, now Chief Justice of the Common Pleas, and *Selden*, the celebrated antiquary. The positive order to require the Seal from the present Lord Keeper would have been obeyed, had not Falkland and Hyde been so much puzzled about recommending a successor; but they thought the Lord Chief Justice Banks might be as timorous as the other in a time of so much disorder, although he had been bold enough in the absence of danger, and they concluded that he was not equal to the charge. "They did not doubt Mr. Selden's affection to the King any more than his learning and capacity, but they were convinced that he would absolutely refuse the place if it were offered to him, as he was in years, and of a weak constitution, and had long enjoyed his ease, which he loved, and was rich, and would not have made a journey to York, or lain out of his own bed, for any preferment."[1] Neither Herbert nor St. John, the Attorney and Solicitor General, of extreme opinions on opposite sides, could be thought of for a moment. Hyde then disclosed to Falkland, the conference he had had with Littleton, the Lord Keeper's loyal professions, and the solemn pledge he had given; and proposed that they should, along with their opinions of the other persons, submit advice to his Majesty to suspend his resolution concerning the Lord Keeper, and rather to write kindly to him to bring the Seal to York, instead of sternly sending for it and casting him off. Hyde finished by offering to stake his own credit with the King that Littleton would be true.

Lord Falkland had no esteem of the Keeper, nor believed that he would go to the King if he were sent for, but would find some trick to excuse himself, and was for immediately getting the Great Seal out of his hands. Hyde, as a professional lawyer, pointed out how absolutely necessary it was, at such a juncture, that the King should first resolve into what hands to put the Seal before he reclaimed it, for that it could not be put out of action for one hour, but that the whole justice of the kingdom would be disordered, which would raise a greater and juster clamor than there had yet been; and again urged that care should be taken that no man should be able to say he had refused the office, an occurrence which would be most prejudicial to the royal cause. He observed, "that the great object was to have the Seal where the King himself resolved to be, and that if the Lord Littleton would perform his promise, it were desirable that he and the Seal were both there; if, on the contrary, he were not an honest man, and cared not for offending the King, he would refuse to deliver it up, and inform the disaffected Lords of his refusal, who would justify him for his disobedience, and they rewarding and cherishing him, he must ever after serve their turn, and thus his Majesty's own Great Seal should be every day used against him, the mischief whereof would be greater than could well be imagined."[2]

Falkland yielded, and they resolved to give an account of the whole to the King and expect his order. Charles naturally had great misgivings of the fidelity and firmness

[1] Clarendon.   [2] Ibid.

of Littleton, notwithstanding Hyde's confidence, but approved of the course recommended, and wrote back that on Saturday, in the following week, as soon as the House of Lords had adjourned, a messenger from him should arrive at Exeter House and order the Keeper with the Seal to repair to him forthwith at York. This resolution was communicated by Hyde and Falkland to Littleton, who expressed much joy at it, and promised that all should be arranged to the King's contentment.

On the Saturday he privately intimated that he was going to his villa at Cranford for his health, and induced the Lords to adjourn the House to as late an hour as ten o'clock on the Monday morning, that he might sleep two nights in the country. He had not long got back to his house in the Strand, when about two o'clock in the afternoon, Mr. Elliot, a groom of the bed-chamber to the Prince, entered his study, where in breathless expectation he was waiting the royal messenger, and delivered to him an autograph letter from the King, requiring him, with many expressions of kindness and esteem, to make haste to him; and if his indisposition, for he was often troubled with gravel, would not suffer him to use such speed upon the journey as the occasion required, that he should deliver the Seal to the person who gave him the letter, who being a strong young man, would make such haste as was necessary, and that he might himself perform his journey by degrees suitable to his infirmities.

Littleton was surprised and mortified to find that the purpose of his journey had been communicated to the messenger, who bluntly demanded the Seal from him, and he at first declared that he would not deliver it into any hands but the King's; but he considered that it would be hazardous to carry the Seal himself in such a journey,—that if, by pursuit of him which he could not but suspect, he should be seized upon, the King would be very unhappily disappointed of the Seal, and that this misfortune would be imputed to imprudence in him, perhaps to unfaithfulness. So he delivered the Seal to the person trusted by the King to receive it, without telling him anything of his own purpose. Elliot was instantly mounted, and having provided a relay of horses, with wonderful expedition presented it to the delighted King at York, who, for a moment, supposed he had recovered all his authority; and, to enhance his merit, Elliot told a vaporing story which he had invented, "how the Lord Keeper had refused to deliver the Seal, and how he got it by force by having locked the door upon him, and threatened to kill him if he would not give it to him, which upon such his manhood, he did for pure fear consent unto."[1]

As soon as the messenger was gone, Littleton pretended to be much indisposed, and gave orders that no one should be admitted to speak with him. He then called in Lee, his purse-bearer, on whose fidelity he could entirely rely, and putting his life in the power of this dependent, told him he was resolved to go next morning to the King, who had sent for him; that he knew the malice of the parliament would use all means to apprehend him; that he knew not how he should be able to bear the fatigue of the journey; that his horses should be ordered to be ready against the next morning: that his own groom only should attend him, and that his purpose should be imparted to no one else living. The faithful purse-bearer, who was a keen royalist, was greatly delighted with his confidence, and insisted on being of the party.

At day-break next morning, the Lord Keeper and his purse-bearer stepped into his carriage, as if they had been going to Cranford; but when they had got into the part of the country where Piccadilly now stands, they discovered by the side of a hedge the groom and two led horses. They immediately mounted, and taking by-paths till they were at a considerable distance from the metropolis, at noon felt themselves tolerably secure. The Lord Keeper's health stood the severe exercise beyond his expectation, and before the end of the third day he kissed the King's hand at York.[2]

---

[1] Life of Clarendon, i. 120. I am informed by Lord Hatherton that "there is a tradition in the family that Elliot forced it from him with a pistol, and that the Lord Keeper, foreseeing the bad consequences such an outrage might produce to the credit of the King and Elliot, prudently followed Elliot to York, in order to prevent it, by giving it the appearance of being his own voluntary act." But the account of the transaction which I have adopted, not only stands on positive testimony, but is supported by probability. If Littleton had broken his promise, and tried to retain the Seal against the King's mandate, he would have proceeded to York—only to be hanged in the Castle Yard.

[2] This was considered an extraordinary journey, being performed, I presume, on the same horses; but by relays of horses there was sometimes in

Sunday passed over in London without any alarm, those who inquired about the Lord Keeper believing, as they were told, that he was at his country-house, at Cranford; but when he did not appear at the hour to which the Lords had adjourned on Monday, the truth of his flight was discovered, and the confusion in both Houses was very great. The few friends of the King rejoiced; but the popular leaders, who imagined they knew all Littleton's thoughts, and had secured him to their interests, hung down their heads, and were distracted with shame. When they had a little recovered their spirits, although they concluded that he was out of their reach, yet to show their indignation, and perhaps in the hope that his infirmities might detain him on the journey, they issued a warrant for apprehending him, and bringing him and the Great Seal back to Westminster, as if they had been making hue and cry after a felon with stolen goods.[1] The two Houses made a further decree, that if he did not return in fourteen days he should lose his office, and that all patents afterwards sealed with the Great Seal which he had carried off should be void. We shall see in the sequel, however, that they repaired the loss by manufacturing a Great Seal of their own, under which they issued edicts in the King's name in defiance of his authority.[2]

Littleton's conduct at York was extremely mysterious, and seems to show that he is liable to the charge of duplicity as well as timidity. He was again declared Lord Keeper, though for some time the King would not trust the Seal out of his own presence, and when it was

those days a dispatch which, till railways came up, must have seemed marvelous. Between Charles at York and Hyde in London, papers were transmitted by royalist gentlemen, who voluntarily offered their services, and who sometimes performed the journey and brought back the answer in the short space of thirty-four hours. See the account of the transmission of the news of Elizabeth's death to James, *ante*, vol. ii., p. 368.

[1] 2 Parl. Hist. 1270. The warrant was addressed " To the gentleman usher, or his deputy; and all sheriffs, mayors, and other his Majesty's officers, shall be aiding and assisting to the gentleman usher or his deputies."

[2] In this narration of Littleton's flight to York, I have closely followed the authority of Clarendon, who ought to be accurate, as he was personally privy to the whole transaction; but according to the Journals of the Lords—on the 20th of May, "the Lord Keeper not being well, and so unable to sit as Speaker, the House gave him leave to be absent, and appointed the Lord Privy Seal to sit as Speaker;" and on Saturday the 21st, the House " ordered that the Lord Keeper have leave to be absent two or three days for his health."—Lords' Journals, v. 76, 77. It is possible that he may have attended and made his excuse, and obtained leave of absence in person.

to be used, produced it to Littleton, and received it back from him as soon as the sealing was over. Credit was given by many about the Court to Elliot's story, till Hyde arrived at York, and stood up for the Lord Keeper's fidelity. The King then expressed a wish to take the Great Seal from him; but Hyde told him "that he would discourage many good men who desired to serve him very faithfully if he were too severe for such faults as the infirmities of their nature and defects in their education exposed them to, and that if the Keeper, from those impressions, had committed some faults which might provoke his Majesty's displeasure, he had redeemed those errors by a signal service, which might well wipe out the memory of the other." The King allowed that he had made expiation, but complained of his present conduct, and that he still raised difficulties about putting the Great Seal to proclamations against the parliament. Hyde replied, that "the poor gentleman could not but think himself disobliged to the highest extremity in the presumption of Mr. Elliot, and that his extravagant and insolent discourses should find credit without his Majesty's reprehension and vindication, who knew the falsehood of them; that his Majesty should remember he had newly escaped out of that region where the thunder and lightning is made, and that he could hardly yet recover the fright he had been often in, and seen so many others in; and that his Majesty need not mistrust him,—he had passed the Rubicon, and had no hope but in his Majesty." Charles promised to show him countenance and protection in future.

The exclusive custody of the Great Seal was then offered to him, but he, expressing great joy at this mark of confidence, begged that it might remain with his Majesty, to be given to him when necessary, lest, by any violence or stratagem, it might be taken from him, and carried back to the parliament.[1]

One would have thought that he would now have been disposed to set the parliament at defiance; but as soon as he heard of the steps taken against him at Westminster, he sent to the House of Lords "the humble petition of Edward Littleton, Lord Keeper of the Great Seal," showing that he was very willing to submit to their Lordship's

[1] Life of Clarendon, i. 125.

order, but that this was impossible (as appeared by the annexed affidavit), without danger of his life ; and that, having been ordered by the King to come to York, he was further ordered, on his allegiance, to remain there. The affidavit purported to be sworn by his servant, who accompanied him in his journey, and stated what was palpably false, that he was so ill on Monday, the 23rd of May (when he was proceeding so swiftly to the north), that it was conceived he would then have died ; and that he had since been disabled from traveling by his diseases and infirmities.[1]

Nay, further, when he got among the cavaliers, there being no " Times," " Morning Chronicle," or " Hansard " to refer to, he pretended that he had never favored the parliamentary party, and he had the hardihood to assert that he had not voted in support of the Militia Bill.

These statements being reported to the Lords at Westminster, they ordered a committee of three to search the Journals for the truth of this matter, who immediately reported " That the Lord Keeper was present when the petition to the King concerning the militia was agreed on ; that he was present, argued, and voted for the following resolution : *That in case of extreme danger and of his Majesty's refusal, the ordinance of both Houses doth oblige the people, and by the fundamental laws of this kingdom ought to be obeyed ;* and, lastly, that he himself, under the MILITIA ORDINANCE, named deputy-lieutenants, and consented to the several forms of deputations of the militia."[2]

In the history of the Great Seal I ought here to mention that the two Houses, in their celebrated " Petition and Advice " of 2nd June, 1642, proposed that the Lord Chancellor or Lord Keeper, with some other officers, should always be chosen with the approbation of both Houses ; but the King received the proposal with mockery and scorn.

Although Littleton was continued in his office by the King till the time of his death, and although he ever after adhered to the royal cause, he does not seem to have been much trusted, and his name seldom occurs in subsequent transactions. He was not admitted with Hyde and Falkland into the secret consultations of the royalists,

[1] 2 Parl. Hist. 1319. [2] Ibid. 1367.

and his only official duty was to put the Great Seal to proclamations and patents. As Lord Keeper he was allowed, according to his precedence, to put his name first to the declaration issued by forty-eight Peers, just before the commencement of hostilities, "that to their certain knowledge the king had no intention of making war upon the parliament." He fixed his residence at Oxford, now considered the seat of government, but was sometimes called upon to attend the King in his campaigns. Without a bar, solicitors, or suitors, he pretended to sit in Chancery, and he went through the form of passing a commission under the Great Seal, appointing certain other persons to hear and determine causes in his absence.[1] His most solemn judicial act at Oxford was calling Sir Richard Lane to the degree of Sergeant at Law, and swearing him in Chief Baron of the Exchequer.

After the battles of Edge Hill and Newbury there was, in the beginning of 1644, the form of a parliament at Oxford, and a much greater number of Peers attended here than at Westminster, although the Bishops were not allowed to sit, in consequence of the act for excluding them from parliament, to which the King had given his assent. The Hall of one of the Colleges was fitted up in the fashion of the House of Lords, and Littleton presided on the supposed woolsack. But though Charles so far complied with the forms of parliament as to make the two Houses a short speech at the opening of the Session, he did not say, according to the precedents, that the Lord Keeper would further explain to them the causes of their being assembled. Littleton still being allowed his rank, subscribed next after the Princes of the blood the letter to the Earl of Essex, proposing an accommodation; and the two Houses, without venturing to propose a tax, having resolved to raise £100,000 for the public service by loan, he, jointly with the Speaker of the House of Commons, addressed to all who were supposed able to contribute to it, official letters of solicitation bearing a very considerable resemblance to privy seals for the raising of a " Benevolence."[2]

[1] Jan. 3, 1643.
[2] By the kindness of my friend, Lord Hatherton, I am enabled to lay before the reader a copy of one of these letters, which must be considered a very interesting historical document :—

He had fled so suddenly from London, that he had been obliged to leave all his books and manuscripts behind

"CHARLES R.

"Trusty and well-beloved, We greet you well. Whereas all our subjects of the kingdome of England and dominion of Wales are both by their allegiance and the Act of Pacification bound to resist and suppresse all such of Our subjects of Scotland as have in a hostile manner already entred, or shall hereafter enter into this kingdome. And by law, your personall service, attended in a warlike manner for the resistance of this invasion, may be required by Us, which we desire to spare, chusing rather to invite your assistance for the maintenance of Our army in a free and voluntary expression of your affections to our service and the safety of this kingdome. And whereas the members of both Houses of Parliament, assembled at Oxford, have taken into their consideration the means of supporting our army, for the defense of Us and Our people against this invasion, and for the preservation of the religion, laws, and liberties of this kingdome, and therefore have agreed upon the speedy raising of the summe of one hundred thousand pounds by loane from particular persons, towards the which themselves have advanced a very considerable proportion, and by their examples hope that Our well-affected subjects, throughout the kingdome, will in a short time make up the remainder, whereby We shall not only be enabled to pay and recruit Our army, but likewise be enabled to put Our armies in such a condition as Our subjects shall not suffer by free quarters, or the unrulinesse of Our soldiers, which is now in present agitation, and will (we no way doubt, by the advice of the members of both Houses assembled) be speedily effected. We doe towards so good a worke, by the approbation and advice of the said members of both Houses here assembled, desire you forthwith to lend us the summe of one hundred pounds, or the value thereof in plate, toucht plate at five shillings, untoucht plate at foure shillings foure pence per ounce; and to pay or deliver the same within seven daies after the receipt hereof, to the hands of the high sheriffe of that our county, or to such whom he shall appoint to receive the same (upon his acquittances for the receipt thereof), who is forthwith to returne and pay the same at Corpus Christi College in Oxford, to the hands of the Earle of Bath, the Lord Seymour, Mr. John Ashburnham, and Mr. John Pettyplace, or any of them, who are appointed treasurers for the receiving and issuing thereof by the said members (by whose order only the said money is to be disposed), and to give receipts for the same, the which We promise to repay as soone as God shall enable us ; this summe being to be advanced with speed, We are necessitated to apply ourselves to such persons as your selfe, of whose ability and affection We have confidence, giving you this assurance, that in such further charges, that the necessity of Our just defense shall enforce us to require of Our good subjects, your forwardness and disbursements shall be considered to your best advantage. And so presuming you will not faile to express your affection herein, We bid you farewell. Given at Our Court at Oxford, the 14th day of February, in the nineteenth year of our raigne, 1643,

"By the advice of the members of both Houses assembled at Oxford. "ED. LITTLETON, C."

The above letter is among Lord Hatherton's family papers. The direction on it is torn and illegible ; but no doubt it was addressed to the owner of his estate, at that time, Sir Edward Littleton, Bart., of Pillaton Hall. In a corner of the letter are a few lines, signed "Tho. Leveson Arm. Vic. Com. Staff," which are almost illegible. They begin, "I am commanded to send you this letter ;" the remainder seems to refer to the time and manner of remitting the money.

him. The parliament did not generously send them after him for his consolation, but made an order that "in respect to the learning of Mr. Whitelock, and his other merits in regard to the public, all the books and manuscripts of the Lord Littleton, late Keeper of the Great Seal, which should be discovered, should be bestowed on Mr. Whitelock, and that the Speaker grant his warrant to search for them, seize them, and put them into his possession."[1]

Being practically without civil occupation, the Lord Keeper thought that he might agreeably fill up his leisure, and that he might raise his reputation, by looking like the times and becoming a soldier. We have mentioned that he was a famous swordsman in his youth. Though so notorious for moral cowardice, he was by no means deficient in natural bravery, and on whichever side he happened to fight, he would have shown an English heart. He now proposed to raise a volunteer corps, which he himself was to command,—to consist of lawyers and gentlemen of the Inns of Court and Chancery, officers of the different Courts of Justice, and all who were willing to draw a weapon for Church and King under the auspices of the Lord Keeper. The offer was accepted, and a commission was granted to him, of which the doquet remains among the instruments passed under the Great Seal of King Charles I. at Oxford.

"A commission granted to Edward, Lord Littleton, Lo. Keep. of the Great Seale, to raise a regiment of foot souldiers, consisting of gent. of the Inns of Court and Chauncy, and of all ministers and officers belonging to the Court of Chauncy, and their servants, and of gent. and others who will voluntarily put themselves under his command to serve his Matie for the security of the Universitie and Cittie of Oxford. T^e apud Oxon. xxi^o die Maij. A^o R. R. Caroli, xx^o."[2]

"per ipsm Regem."[3]

---

[1] Life of Whitelock, 55.   [2] May 21, 1645.

[3] According to a statement by the Editor of his "Reports," the Lord Keeper's military zeal was felt by all members of the profession of the law then at Oxford, the Judges included. "He was colonel of a foot regiment, in which were listed all the Judges, lawyers, and officers belonging to the several courts of justice."—*Pref.* ed. 1683. This reminds me of the gallant corps in which I myself served in my youth, "the B. I. C. A.," or "Bloomsbury and Inns of Court Association," consisting of barristers, attorneys, law

The Lord Keeper devoted himself to this new pursuit with great zeal and energy, acting the part of Adjutant as well as Commander, and as he was a remarkably tall, handsome, atheletic man in a green old age, he made an excellent officer. All connected with the law flocked to his standard, and their number was greatly increased by recruits from the different colleges who mixed military exercises with their logical contentions in the schools. As a mark of respect for his military prowess, the University now conferred upon him the degree of Doctor of the Civil Law.¹ Whether these learned volunteers could ever have been made capable of facing the psalm-singing soldiers of Cromwell—commanded by "Colonel Fight-the good-fight-of-Faith" and "Captain Smite them-them-hip-and-thigh,"—is left in doubt, for the "Lord Keeper Commandant," while drilling his corps one morning in Bagley Wood, was overtaken by a thunder storm, and caught a violent cold. This being neglected turned into a fever which carried him off on the 27th of August, 1645, to the regret of the royalist party, notwithstanding his backslidings and the serious suspicions which had formerly been entertained of his fidelity.

He was buried with military honors in the cathedral of Christ Church, not only his own regiment, but the whole garrison attending. All the nobility of Oxford and the heads of houses joined in the procession. The solemnity was closed with a funeral eulogium upon him, by the "incomparable Dr. Hammond," then Orator of the University.

After the Restoration, a monument was erected over

students, and clerks, raised to repel the invasion threatened by Napoleon; but none of the reverend sages of the law served in this or the rival legal corps named the "Temple Light Infantry," or "The Devil's Own," commanded by Erskine, still at the bar. Lord Chancellor Eldon *doubted* the expediency of mixing in the ranks, and did not aspire to be an officer; Law, the Attorney General, was in the awkward squad, having always looked to his feet when the word of command was given " Left leg forward," and having replied to the reprimand of the drill-sergeant, "By what process can I know that I put my left leg forward except by looking?" Lord Keeper Littleton has, therefore, the glory of being recorded as the last successor of Turketel, Thomas-à-Becket, and the Earl of Salisbury, who ever carried arms while head of the law.

¹ I do not find any account of the ceremony, but I presume the public orator, after enumerating his high civic distinctions, added, "et militavit non sine gloriâ," the compliment paid on a similar occasion to Sir WILLIAM GRANT, Master of the Rolls, who had served as a volunteer in Canada.

his grave—recording his origin, the high offices he had held, and the virtues his family wished to have attributed to him—above all—

"FORTITUDE AND UNSUSPECTED FAITH TO HIS SOVEREIGN."

In quiet times he would have passed through the world with honor and applause. Had he died Chief Justice of the Common Pleas, he would have left behind him, if not a splendid, a respectable reputation. But his elevation placed him in situations for which he was wholly unfit ; and if he is saved from being classed with the treacherous, the perfidious, and the infamous, it is only by supposing him to be the most irresolute, nerveless, and pusillanimous of mankind. So completely did his faculties abandon him after he received the Great Seal, that he driveled as a Judge,—not only in political cases before the Privy Council,—but also in the common run of business between party and party. His deficiency in the Court of Chancery has been accounted for by a suggestion that he was previously acquainted only with the practice of the common-law Courts; but this is wholly unfounded ; for, during the whole time that he was Solicitor General, he was in the first business at the equity bar, though neither he, nor any other counsel, then confined themselves to that branch of practice.

Lloyd, with the undistinguishing panegyrics he bestows on all, says of Littleton, that " his learning was various and useful; his skill in the maxims of our government, the fundamental laws of the monarchy, with its statutes and customs, singular; his experience long and observing; his integrity unblemished and unbiassed ; his eloquence powerful and majestic, and all befitting a statesman and a Lord Keeper." But Clarendon, though inclined to screen him, having some regard to candor and truth, is obliged to say—" Being a man of grave and comely presence, his other parts were overvalued. From the time he had the Great Seal he seemed to be out of his element, and in some perplexity and irresolution in the Chancery itself, though he had great experience in the practices and proceedings of that Court; and made not that dispatch that was expected at the Council table; and in the parliament he did not preserve any dignity, and appeared so totally dispirited that few men showed any respect to him, but they who most opposed the King, who indeed did exceedingly apply themselves to him, and were with equal kindness received by him."

In 1683 there was published a folio volume of his Reports of Cases decided in the Court of Common Pleas and Exchequer in the beginning of the reign of Charles I. They are in Norman French, and they are not very valuable; but he had not intended them for publication, and they were found among the papers of his brother, Sir Timothy Littleton, a Baron of the Exchequer.[1] The Lord Keeper never aspired to the honors of authorship.

He was twice married, but his only issue was a daughter, and his title became extinct. It was revived, however, in the elder branch of his family,—Sir Thomas Littleton, descended from William, the eldest son of the founder, having been created Lord Lyttleton in the reign of George II. In the south window of the Inner Temple Hall there is a fine shield of the Lord Keeper's arms, with fifteen quarterings, distinguished by a crescent within a mullet, which shows him to have been of the third house.[2]

CHAPTER LXVII.

LIFE OF LORD KEEPER LANE.

I HAVE now to introduce to the reader a man, who, although he was never installed in the "marble chair" in Westminster Hall, nor ever presided on the woolsack, was the legitimate successor of the illustrious Lord Chancellors and Lord Keepers whose names are known to fame. I regret that my researches respecting him have not been more successful, for all that I have discovered of him is to his honor. He was a very high royalist, but sincere, firm, and consistent.

---

[1] The title is curious as showing the strange Gipsy jargon then used by English lawyers: "LES REPORTS des tres Honorable EDW. SEIGNEUR LITTLETON, BARON DE MOUNSLOW, CUSTOS de le Grand Seale d'Angliteur, et de ses Majesty pluis HONORABLE PRIVY COUNCEL, en les Courts del COMMON BANCK et EXCHEQUER en le 2, 3, 4, 5, 6, 7 ans del reign de Roy CHARLES le I."

[2] I am indebted to Lord Hatherton, representative of the second house of the Littletons, for several interesting particulars of the Lord Keeper, which I have above related.

His father was Richard Lane, of Courtenhall, in the county of Northampton, who, though of little wealth, was entitled to arms.[1] Young Lane seems to have raised himself from obscurity by talent, industry, and perseverance. Having never sat in parliament, nor been engaged in any great state prosecution, he had not much celebrity till the troubles were breaking out; but he was known to discerning men as an admirable lawyer, as well as a steady friend of the prerogative, and in the hope that he might be useful to the Crown in the proceedings which were now anticipated, he was made Attorney General to the Prince of Wales.

Soon after this promotion the Long Parliament met, and Strafford was impeached for high treason. However much Charles wished to protect him, he could not be defended by Banks or Herbert, the Attorney and Solicitor General to the Crown,—and Mr. Lane was retained as his leading counsel, along with Gardiner, Recorder of London, a man of great eminence in his profession, and Loe and Lightfoot, two promising juniors.

An order being made by the House of Lords for assigning them and giving them access to their client, the Commons most unreasonably complained that such a step should be taken without their consent, and inveighed with much bitterness against those lawyers who durst be of counsel with a person accused by them of high treason. Nay, one member went so far as to move that they should be sent for and proceeded against for contempt: but it was suggested that they not only were obliged to it by the honor and duty of their profession, but that they would have been punishable for refusing to submit to the Lords' order. It appeared too revolting to make this matter a breach of privilege, and the debate dropped. Such attempts at intimidation have ever been scorned by the bar of England, and Lane and his brethren were now only more eager and determined to do their duty at every hazard.

When Strafford was brought up to be arraigned, Lane made a heavy complaint of the length of the articles of impeachment, which contained the actions of the Earl's service for thirteen years past, both in England and Ire-

---

[1] Herald's Hist. of Northamptons, A.D. 1618, c. 14.

land, and he prayed further time to prepare the answer. This, after considerable difficulty, he obtained.

During the seventeen days which the trial lasted on matter of fact, Lane and the other counsel were not allowed in the slightest degree to interfere, and the noble prisoner, unassisted carried on against the most distinguished lawyers and statesmen of the country party, and against public prejudice and passion, that heroic struggle which seemed to render the result doubtful, and which shed such a luster on his closing scene.

> "Now private pity strove with public hate,
> Reason with rage, and eloquence with fate;
> So did he move the passions, some were known
> To wish, for the defense, the crime their own."

He then prayed that he might be heard by his counsel upon the question, whether any of the charges amounted to treason in point of law? and in spite of a stout resistance by the managers of the Commons, who felt that the case was going against them, leave was given.

The 17th of April, 1641, was the most memorable day in the life of Lane. The Commons resentfully refused to attend as a body, but almost all the members of the House were present from curiosity. The Scottish and Irish Commissioners filled the galleries; the King and his family were known to be in the royal closet, the Prince occasionally showing himself and nodding to his Attorney General; the uninclosed part of Westminster Hall was filled by an an immense mass of anxious spectators from the city and from the provinces, once strongly incensed against Strafford, but now beginning to doubt his guilt, and strongly inclined to admire and pity him. How insignificant in comparison was the trial of Warren Hastings, of which we have heard such boastful accounts from our fathers.

Lane surpassed all expectation. Knowing that a majority of the Peers were now favorable to his client, and being unchecked by any opponents,—although he professed to carry himself with all content and satisfaction to the House of Commons, and to abstain from touching on the merits of the cause,—he said that it was impossible to argue the question of law without stating the facts (as he understood them) out of which that question arose. Accordingly he took a short, rapid, and dexterous view of the evidence adduced. Having then shown very distinctly and incontrovertibly that none of the charges amounted to treason under the statute of Edward III., which provides against "compassing the King's death, levying war against him, violating his companion, and counterfeiting his Great Seal," but is entirely silent with respect to "subverting the fundamental laws of the kingdom," he came to the main point which had been urged by the Commons, "whether the salvo in that statute as to parliament declaring a new case of treason could apply to a parliamentary impeachment?" and he argued to demonstration that this power could only be exercised by parliament in its "legislative capacity,"—that the House of Lords was then acting judicially according to promulgated law,—and that the Earl must be acquitted, unless he could be proved to have done an act which had been legislatively declared treason before it was committed. He finally contended that, assuming the subversion of the fundamental laws of the kingdom to be high treason, one or more acts of injustice, whether maliciously or ignorantly done, could in no sense be called the subversion of the fundamental laws; for otherwise, possibly "as many judges, so many traitors," and all distinction and degrees of offenses being confounded, every man who transgresses a statute may lose his life and his estate, and bring ruin upon his posterity. He then went over all the cases supposed to be in point, from that of John de la Pole downwards, showing that, in the worst of times, no man had been convicted of treason except upon a specific charge of having violated one of the express provisions of the Statute of Treasons—a statute made to guard the subject from constructive and undefined offenses against the government—a statute which had been the glory of Englishmen—for which respect had been professed by our most arbitrary sovereigns—but which was now to be swept away by those who avowed themselves the champions of freedom, and the reformers of all abuses.

He sat down amidst great applause; and, after a short address from the Recorder on the same side,—it being as late as between two and three o'clock in the afternoon, the House adjourned.[1]

An acquittal was now considered certain; but in the

[1] 3 St. Tr. 1472. 2 Parl. Hist. 732.

night the parliamentary leaders entirely changed their plan of proceeding. Instead of praying the judgment of the Lords upon the articles of impeachment, they said they intended not to offer any reply to the argument of law made by Mr. Lane, it being below their dignity to contend with a private lawyer; and, next morning, they put up Sir Arthur Hazelrig, "an absurd, bold man," a pupil of Pym, and employed by the party on any desperate occasion, to prefer a bill in the House of Commons " for the attainder of the Earl of Strafford of high treason."

This bill was opposed by Seldon and the more moderate lawyers on the liberal side, and could hardly have been pushed through but for the newly-discovered evidence brought forward by Sir Harry Vane respecting Strafford's declaration in council, "that the King having tried the affection of his people, was absolved from all rule of government; and that the army of Ireland might reduce this kingdom to obedience." The effect was heightened by the disgraceful opinion obtained from the trembling Judges, that this charge amounted to high treason.

When the bill came up to the Lords, Lane having no longer an opportunity of being heard, Oliver St. John, who had accepted and retained the title of "King's Solicitor General," but was the most furious of the prosecutors of Strafford, boldly attempted to answer Lane's argument: and, feeling that he had failed, he unblushingly said, "that in that way of bill, private satisfaction to each man's conscience was sufficient; and why should they take such trouble about law in such a case? It was true we give law to hares and deer, because they are beasts of chase; but it was never accounted either cruelty or foul play to knock foxes and wolves on the head, where they may be found, because they are beasts of prey."[1]

After Strafford's conviction, Lane remained in London quietly pursuing his profession, and privately advising the Royalists, till the King, by proclamation under the Great Seal, having ordered all the law Courts to be adjourned to Oxford, and the parliament, by an ordinance, having required them to continue sitting at Westminster, the cavalier lawyers thought they could no longer publicly practice in the metropolis without acknowledging the usurped

[1] 3 St. Tr. 1477.

authority of the Roundheads. While some of them took to conveyancing and chamber business, Lane resolved to go to Oxford, where, although there was not likely to be much *pabulum* for barristers, he should at least testify his respect for the King's proclamation, and his devotion to the royal cause. He had a strict private intimacy with Whitelock, afterwards Keeper of the Great Seal, although they were on opposite sides in politics; and to him he intrusted his books and the furniture in his chambers in the Inner Temple, which, in the disturbed state of the country, he could not carry along with him. On his arrival at Oxford, his loyalty was rewarded with the honor of knighthood.

He found Lord Keeper Littleton, with the Great Seal, sitting in the Philosophy Schools; and two or three Judges having joined, they went through the form of holding the Courts to which they respectively belonged. But there was no one to represent the Exchequer, and the office of Chief Baron being vacant, it was offered to Lane, who was considered at the head of the Oxford bar. He could not expect his salary to be very regularly paid, but he did not sacrifice a very lucrative practice, and he accepted the offer.

To be regularly installed as a Judge, he was first to be raised to the dignity of the coif; and, accordingly, in the roll of the proceedings under the Great Seal at Oxford, we have the following entry:—

"1643-4, January 25. M^d. that Sir Richard Lane, Kt., the Prince's Highness' Attorney, made his appearance the first day of Hilary term at the Chancery bar in the Philosophy Schools at Oxford, and was there sworn a Sergeant-at-law, his writ being returnable Octobis Hillarij before the Right Hon[ble] Edward Lord Littleton, Lord Keeper of the Great Seal of England, in open court, Sir J. Colepeper Master of the Rolls, Dr. Littleton and Sir Thomas Mainwaring, Masters of the Chancery, being present, and the oaths of supremacy and allegiance, and the oath of a Sergeant-at-law, were read to him by the Clerk of the Crown."

The following day he was sworn in as Chief Baron in a corner of the Schools called the "Court of Exchequer," and likewise received the honor of knighthood, the Lord Keeper complimenting him on his loyalty and learning, which had procured him such special marks of the King's favor—and the new Chief Baron expressing a hope that notwithstanding the recent successes of the rebels in England, from the assistance of our loyal brethren in Scotland and Ireland,[1] they would speedily be put down, and his Majesty would be acknowledged as God's Vicegerent throughout all his dominions.

At this time there was a large batch of promotions at Oxford—Hyde being sworn in Chancellor of the Exchequer, Cottington, Lord Treasurer, Brerewood, a Justice of the King's Bench, Colepeper, Master of the Rolls and a Peer, Gardiner, Solicitor General, to say nothing of several Masters extraordinary in the High Court of Chancery[2]—and I dare say, on the first day of the following Term (although I do not find the fact recorded, and therefore do not venture to assert it) there was a grand *levée* at the Lord Keeper's rooms in Christ Church, and a procession from thence to the Philosophy Schools, where the Courts were opened in due form, the Counsel were asked if they had anything to move, and the Judges rose early—having at least this consolation, that they could not be reproached with the accumulation of arrears.

But Lane was soon after employed in real and very serious business. After the battle of Marston Moor, the surrender of Newcastle, and the third battle of Newbury, the Royalists were so much disheartened that a negotiation for peace was proposed to the parliament, and Charles, instead of styling them as hitherto "the Lords and Commons of Parliament assembled at Westminster," was induced to address them as "the Lords and Commons assembled in the Parliament of England at Westminster." The proposal could not be refused without incurring popular odium, and Uxbridge, then within the parliamentary lines, was named as the place of conference.

The King sent a list of his commissioners—"Sir Richard Lane, Knight, Chief Baron of the Exchequer, Hyde, Chancellor of the Exchequer, Gardiner, Solicitor General;" and the others with the dignities lately conferred upon them. The parliament took offense, having declared on Littleton's flight to York with the Great Seal, that all patents afterwards passing under it should be void, and

---

[1] Alluding to Montrose and Glamorgan.
[2] Doquets of patents at Oxon. Temp. Car. 1.

they were particularly hurt that any one should be denominated "Solicitor General" except their beloved St. John, who under that title had been directing all their movements, and whom they intended to employ as their commissioner in this very treaty. They insisted therefore that Lane and the rest of the King's commissioners should be mentioned in the pass and in the full powers conferring authority upon them to negotiate for the King, simply by their names, without any office or dignity as belonging to them. This concession was made, and the royal ambassadors arrived at Uxbridge with a commission under the Great Seal which was rejected, and another under the King's sign-manual, which was recognized as sufficient. The great bone of contention was still the militia, and Lane proved very clearly that by the ancient constitution of England the power of the sword belonged exclusively to the Sovereign, and that there could be no military force lawfully in the kingdom except under his warrant. The parliamentary commissioners did not much combat this law, but peremptorily insisted that the command both of the army and the navy should be in the two Houses,—a precaution indispensably necessary for the safety of those who had been standing out for the liberties of the nation. Twenty days were ineffectually consumed in such discussions—when the conference broke up. The pass was to expire next day, and as Lane and his colleagues might require two days to perform their journey to Oxford, they having spent two days in coming thence to Uxbridge, they were told by the parliamentary commissioners that they might safely make use of another day, of which no advantage should be taken; but they were unwilling to run any hazard, and they were in their coaches so early in the morning that they reached Oxford that night and kissed the hand of the King,—who received them very graciously, and thanked them for the pains they had taken in his cause. His Majesty was particularly pleased with the zeal and ability manifested by the Chief Baron in supporting his constitutional right to the power of the sword, and marked him for further promotion.

Lane remained at Oxford with the sinecure office of Head of the Court of Exchequer during the disastrous campaign of 1645. The gleam of hope from Montrose's victories in Scotland was extinguished by the news of the fatal field at Naseby, the surrender of Bristol by Prince Rupert, and the defeat of the royalists at Chester and Sherburn. In the midst of these disasters Lord Keeper Littleton had been suddenly carried off, while making an effort to provide for the safety of Oxford, now threatened on every side.

The Great Seal was little thought of till the King made good his retreat from Newark, and took up his winter quarters in this city. He still displayed unshaken firmness; the growing difference between the Presbyterians and Independents held out a prospect of his being able to obtain favorable terms from either of these powerful parties, and he looked forward to important assistance from Scotland and Ireland, by which he might be in a situation again to make head against the parliament. Whether for negotiation or action, it was important that he should keep up the appearance of a regular government;—and that he might make use of the Great Seal for proclamations and grants, he resolved to appoint a new Lord Keeper.

If he had had a wider choice, he could not have selected a better man than the Lord Chief Baron, and when he proposed this appointment it was approved by the whole Council. Accordingly, on the 23rd of October, "Sir RICHARD LANE, Knight, was sworn at the Philosophy Schools, in Oxford, into the office of Lord Keeper of the Great Seal of England, taking the oaths of supremacy and allegiance, the oath of office, together with the oath according to the statute lately made for issuing forth of writs of summons of parliament, the Lord Treasurer and divers others being then present."[1] It has been said, that "the new Lord Keeper had neither a court, suitors, nor salary;"[2] but this is not altogether correct, for on the 17th of November following, "a grant was made by patent to the Right Honorable Sir Richard Lane, Knight, Lord Keeper of the Great Seal of England, of 23s. *per diem* for his diet, and of £26 13s. 4d. *per annum* for a winter livery, and £13 6s. 4d. for a summer livery, and £300 *per annum* pension out of the Hanaper, and of all such part of finable writs to be answered by the Cursitors as former Lord Keepers have had, and of all other fees

---
[1] Doquets of patents at Oxford, Temp. Car. I.   [2] Parke's Chanc. 117.

and allowances belonging to the office of Lord Keeper; the said allowances to begin upon and from the 30th day of August last, and so forward, so long as he shall continue in the office."[1] However, as all these allowances were to come from fees on patents and writs, it is to be feared that the Lord Keeper's "diet, liveries, and pension" were poorly provided for, and that having already contributed to the supply of the King's wants the small remnant of his private fortune, he now found it difficult to conceal the poverty and misery with which he had to struggle. Only three patents are recorded as having passed the Great Seal after his appointment, one to make Sir Thomas Gardiner Attorney General, another to make Sir Jeffrey Palmer Solicitor General, and the third for authorizing the Master of the Rolls, and others, to hear causes in Chancery in the absence of the Lord Keeper.

In the following spring, Charles found that the offers made to him were only "devices to amuse the royal bird till the fowlers had inclosed him in their toils." He resolved, therefore, rather than be taken prisoner by Fairfax and Cromwell, who were marching to lay siege to Oxford, to fly to the Scotch army encamped before Newark, and to throw himself upon the generosity of his countrymen. With a view to his flight, and that some order might be preserved for the safety of his friends when he was gone, he appointed a Council "for the better management of the garrison and defense of the city," and placed the Lord Keeper at the head of it.

Great was the consternation in Oxford on the morning of the 27th of April, when the King was not to be found, and it was known that he had escaped at midnight, disguised as a servant, following his supposed master, Ashburnham, on the road to Henley.

Lane, however, behaved with courage and constancy,— resolved that if the place could not be successfully defended, it should not capitulate except on honorable terms. Cromwell, on hearing of the King's escape, employed himself in schemes, by bribing the Scots, to get possession of his person, and Fairfax did not arrive before Oxford till the beginning of June. During the war, this city had been rendered one of the strongest fortresses of

---

[1] "T° apud Oxon. xvii°. Novemb. A°. R.R°. Caroli, xxi°." Doquets, &c.

the kingdom. On three sides, the waters of the Isis and the Cherwell spreading over the adjoining country, kept the enemy at a considerable distance, and on the north it was covered by a succession of works erected by skillful engineers. The garrison now amounted to near 5,000 men, the last remnant of the royal army, and a plentiful supply of stores and provisions had been collected in contemplation of another campaign. A stout resistance might have been made; but without the possibility of relief, it must have been hopeless, and all deliberation on the subject was put an end to by an order from the King addressed to the Governors of Oxford, Lichfield, Worcester, and Wallingford, the only places in the kingdom that still held out for him, whereby "the more to evidence the reality of his intentions of settling a happy and firm peace, he required them *upon honorable terms* to quit those places, and to disband all the forces under their command."

The terms for the surrender of Oxford were negotiated by Lane. He wished much to have inserted an article, stipulating that he should have leave to carry away with him the Great Seal, the badge of his office, together with the Seals of the other Courts of justice, and the swords of state, which had been brought to Oxford; but to this Fairfax most peremptorily objected, under the express orders of the parliament, by whom they were considered the emblems of sovereignty. Rather than stand the horrors of an assault, Lane signed the capitulation, by which the Seals, along with the swords of state, were all delivered up.[1]

On the 3rd of July, the parliament with loud exultation received a letter from Fairfax, signifying that he had sent by the Judge Advocate of the army the several seals and swords of state, surrendered at Oxford, under the fourth

[1] "Articles of Agreement concluded and agreed on by his Excellency Sir Thomas Fairfax, Knt., general of the forces raised by the parliament, on the one party, and the Right Honorable Sir Richard Lane, Knt., Lord Keeper of the Great Seal of England, &c., for and concerning the rendering of the garrison of Oxford."

Art. IV. "That the seals called the Great Seal, Privy Seal, the signets, and the seals of the King's Bench, Exchequer, Court of Wards, Duchy, Admiralty, and Prerogative as also the swords of state, shall at such time and in the presence of two such persons as the General Sir Thomas Fairfax shall appoint, be locked up in a chest, and left in the public library."—*Whit. Mem.* 210.

article of the treaty, to be disposed of as the two Houses should direct, and an order was immediately made, "that the King's Great Seal, sent by the general from Oxon, be defaced and broken." In the mean time, those seals were all delivered to Speaker Lenthal, to remain in his custody till the House should call for them.

The ceremony of breaking the King's Great Seal took place with much parade on the 11th of August, the day fixed for the installation of the parliamentary Lord Keeper. Lenthal appearing at the head of the Commons, produced it at the bar of the Lords. A smith being then sent for, it was by him openly defaced and broken, amidst much cheering,—and the fragments were equally divided between the Speakers of the two Houses.

I should have been delighted to relate that Charles's last Lord Keeper lived in an honorable retirement during the rule of those whom he considered rebels and usurpers, and survived to see the restoration of the monarchy under the son of his sainted master; but I regret to say that I can find no authentic trace of him after the capitulation of Oxford. From the language of Lord Clarendon, it might be inferred that he did not long survive that misfortune,[1] while others represent that he followed Prince Charles to the Continent, and died in exile.[2]

Considering Sir Richard Lane's spotless integrity, and uniform adherence to his principles,—notwithstanding his comparative obscurity and his poverty, he is more to be honored than many of his predecessors and successors who have left behind them a brilliant reputation, with ample possessions and high dignities to their posterity.

Although the life of Charles was prolonged near two years and a half from the time when Lane surrendered

[1] Hist. Reb. part iii. 778.
[2] By the kindness of my friends at the Heralds' Office, I am now enabled to clear up this difficulty. There is extant a commission to the Lady Margaret, his widow, dated 22 April, 1651, to administer to his effects, stating that he had died in France.

Lady Margaret survived until 1669, when she was buried in Kingsthorpe Church, where there is this inscription:—

"Here lieth the body of the Lady Margaret Lane, late wife to the Right Honorable Sir Richard Lane, Lord Keeper of the Great Seal of England to K. Charles the First and K. Charles the Second; who *dyed* in his *banyshment* for his loyalty to the Crown. She departed the 22 day of April, 1669."—See Brydge's Hist of Northampton, i. 412

the Great Seal to the parliament, yet he never appointed another Chancellor or Lord Keeper, and his reign may be considered as having then closed. We must, therefore, now take a short retrospect of the changes which the law underwent while he was upon the throne.

In consequence of the abrupt dissolution and long intermission of parliaments, only fifty-one public acts were added to the statute-book in this reign, and by none of these was the letter of the law materially altered. But an unspeakable improvement was introduced in the practical administration of justice by the suppression of the Star Chamber. Not only was the pretension of legislating by proclamation gone with the power of enforcing it, but trial by jury was secured to all who were charged with common-law offenses, and there was much less danger of cruelty in the infliction of discretionary punishment when the sentence was not to be pronounced by the ministers of the Crown, who had instituted the prosecution, and who tried to outbid each other for royal favor by the severity they displayed.

The King, on the petition of the two Houses agreed to make out the Judges' patents *quamdiu se bene gesserint*, instead of *durante bene placito;* but this concession, not being secured by statute, was disregarded by his sons, and the independence of the Judges was not properly provided for till the reign of King William III.[1] There is no ground, however, for the vulgar error, that the Judges were all removable at the will of the Sovereign till the reign of King George III., who, in reality, acquired his popularity on this subject merely by taking away the power of his successors on their first coming to the throne.

The Triennial Act[2] was a noble law, and framed for the real benefit of the Crown as well as of the public, notwithstanding the stringent clauses authorizing elections, on a certain contingency, without the King's writ. Had it not been inconsiderately repealed by Lord Clarendon, the Stuart dynasty might long have ruled over England.

Considering the insane conduct of the Bishops during the first two Stuart reigns, so severely condemned by Lord Clarendon and all true friends of the monarchy, it is not wonderful that the act should have passed for depriv-

[1] 13 W. 3, c. 2. [2] 16 Car. 1, c. 7.

ing them of their seats in the House of Lords:[1] but I can not consider this a permanent improvement in the constitution; for hereditary honors and wealth are so enervating, that the Upper House could scarcely maintain its position without the infusion of fresh blood from the church as well as the law; and by reason of the talents and character of the right reverend bench, its proceedings are more effective and more respected. I therefore rejoice that this act was condemned at the Restoration, and I trust that there never will be occasion for repealing the act by which it was repealed.

The Courts of common law were filled with able Judges in this reign, but their decisions are badly reported by Crooke, and others still more loose and indiscriminating; and till Saunders arose there was no legitimate successor of Plowden and Coke.

Equity as a system made little progress. Coventry was contented to dispose of each case that came before him according to his notions of what was right, without laying down any broad general principles; and Finch, Littleton, and Lane were too much occupied with political broils to think of judicial improvement.[2]

CHAPTER LXVIII.

LORD KEEPERS OF THE PARLIAMENTARY GREAT SEAL DURING THE COMMONWEALTH, TILL THE FIRST APPOINTMENT OF LORD COMMISSIONER WHITELOCK.

WHEN Lord Keeper Littleton fled to York in May, 1642, the parliamentary leaders were thrown into perplexity. Knowing the importance of the Great Seal, they had cultivated him very assiduously, and, from his vote upon the militia ordinance, they believed he had so completely committed himself against the Court that he must remain entirely under their control. After that occurrence, the precaution they had contemplated of ordering the Great Seal to be kept in some secure place, appeared unnecessary. They were thus

[1] 16 Car. 1, c. 27.
[2] See Tothill; Nelson's Chancery; Reports in Chancery, vol. i.; Godbolt's Reports; Popham's Reports.

quite unprepared for the misfortune of this machine of government being transferred from them to the King.

While he now had the advantage of duly issuing whatever grants, commissions, or proclamations he might think proper, they foresaw that the administration of justice would be materially impeded in the metropolis,—that they could not even have new elections to fill up vacancies in the House of Commons,—and that they could not do any act of state to which the Great Seal was necessary. Having assumed the exercise of supreme power, their policy was to carry on the government in the King's name, according to the forms of the constitution.

Encouraged by Littleton's submissive petition to the House of Lords, they thought it possible that he might be playing a double part; and, by way of experiment, they sent some "proclamation writs" to Nottingham, where he then was with the King,—about the time when the royal standard was first raised there,—and he was required to seal them according to the duty of his office.

Littleton, still dreading an open rupture with the parliament,—as an equivocating excuse wrote the following letter to the Clerk of the Crown in Chancery:—"Sir, I could not seal the proclamation writs you sent unto me from the Lords, for that I never could have the Seal sithence the receipt of them until this hour."

After several conferences between the two Houses, who wished to throw all the odium upon the King, it was resolved to set forth "a declaration showing to the people the grievous obstruction of justice by the taking and detaining the Great Seal out of the custody of the Lord Keeper." Committees were likewise appointed to consider "how these and the like inconveniences may be remedied and prevented for the future;" and that of the Commons was particularly to report upon a method "how the House may be replenished of their members notwithstanding writs for a new election instead of those cast out of the House cannot be sealed as is usual."[1]

The declaration accordingly came out, heavily complaining of the infraction of the clause in Magna Charta —"Nulli negabimus, nulli deferemus justitiam vel rectum;" but a long time elapsed before any measure to

[1] Lords' Journ. v. 343. Com. Journ. ii. 771.

meet the evil could be agreed upon. It was vain to expect that proceedings which had immemorially been under the Great Seal could take place without its authority, and many lawyers were startled by the express enactment in the statute 25 Edw. III., that "to counterfeit the King's Great Seal shall be High Treason"—an enactment which might have been very inconveniently put in force against all those who voted for a new Great Seal, should the royal party prevail. They therefore contented themselves for the present with passing an ordinance to make void all patents and grants under the King's Great Seal since the time it ceased to attend the parliament, and forbidding obedience to any proclamation for removing the Courts of Justice from Westminster.[1]

The inconvenience, however, was more and more severely felt, particularly by the professors of the law. Says Whitelock, "The courts of justice were not yet open, and *there was no practice for lawyers*."[2] About this time, there came out a pamphlet, which caused a considerable sensation, entitled "St. Hilary's Tears shed upon all Professors of the Law, from the Judge to the Pettifogger, for want of a stirring Term, written by one of his Secretaries that had nothing else to do."[3]

At last, in May, 1643, Oliver St. John, as yet styled "Solicitor General," and Sergeant Wilde, the two boldest lawyers on the popular side, resolved upon a strenuous effort to have a new Great Seal, and they induced the Commons, without a division, to agree to the following resolutions:—1. "That the Great Seal of England ought, by the laws of the land, to attend the parliament." 2. "That the Great Seal of England doth not attend the parliament as it ought to do." 3. "That by reason thereof, the commonwealth hath suffered many mischiefs, tending to the destruction of the King, parliament, and kingdom." 4. "That it is the duty of both houses to provide a speedy remedy for these mischiefs." Then came the 5th and

---

[1] Jan. 21, 1643. [2] Whit. Mem. 71.
[3] Thus it began: "A term so like a vacation; the prime Court, the Chancery (wherein the clerks had wont to dash their clients out of countenance with long dashes); the examiners to take the depositions in hyperboles, and roundabout *Robinhood* circumstances with *saids* and *aforesaids*, to enlarge the number of sheets;"—alluding to the abuse which it has never yet been found possible to correct, of allowing costs according to the number of written words, by so much a folio.

startling resolution, "THAT A GREAT SEAL OF ENGLAND SHALL BE FORTHWITH MADE TO ATTEND THE PARLIAMENT, FOR THE DISPATCH OF THE AFFAIRS OF THE PARLIAMENT AND THE KINGDOM."

But a strong opposition sprung up to this proceeding,—the more cautious members suggesting that it would be a direct renunciation of all allegiance to the Crown,—that the two Houses still acknowledged Charles for their sovereign, and were in treaty with him for a peaceable settlement of all differences, notwithstanding his misgovernment by advice of evil counselors,—and that the making of a new Great Seal would be a direct infraction of the law, for which they might hereafter be made criminally responsible. On the other hand, the more determined urged that it was unworthy to start technical difficulties as to the mode of exercising the authority of the parliament in the manner most effectual and most beneficial to the public,—that a new Great Seal, which would so much facilitate the transaction of public business, would not be a greater departure from law than issuing orders in the King's name against his person,—and that it was much too late to talk prudishly of a regard to law, after they had fought the King at Edgehill, and he had declared by proclamation, not only that all who had appeared against him in arms, but all who had contributed money, or stores, or provisions for the use of those whom he designated *Rebels*, were guilty of high treason. After a long debate, the last resolution was carried only by a majority of 12,—the yeas being 86, and the noes 74.[1]

The Lords, whose deliberations were chiefly guided by the Earl of Manchester (formerly Lord Kimbolton), now presiding on the woolsack as Speaker, the Earl of Northumberland, and the Earl of Essex when he could be spared from the army,—were by no means as yet prepared to go the full length of these resolutions. On the 1st, they voted "that the Great Seal ought to be applied to the commands of the parliament according to the laws of the land, but that it ought not, according to the laws of the land, to attend the commands of the parliament."

---

[1] With the tellers, making a house of 164, I believe there was seldom afterwards a more numerous attendance, even before Pride's Purge, or the violent exclusion of members—a considerable number having joined the King, many of the parliamentary party being with the army, and there being long no means of filling up vacancies.

The 5th resolution, for making forthwith a new Great Seal, they met with a direct negative.

Several conferences upon the subject were held between the two Houses to no purpose. At the last of these, the Commons submitted the following reasons for the measures they recommended, divided into two general heads:—

" I. *Mischiefs occasioned by conveying away the Great Seal from the Parliament.*

" 1. It was secretly and unlawfully carried away by the Lord Keeper, contrary to the duty of his place; who ought himself to have attended the parliament, and not to have departed without leave; nor should have been suffered to carry away the Great Seal if his intentions had been discovered.

" 2. It hath been taken away from him and put into the hands of other dangerous and ill-affected persons; so as the Lord Keeper, being sent unto by parliament for the sealing of some writs, returned answer, that he could not seal the same because he had not the Seal in his keeping.

" 3. Those who have had the managing thereof have employed it to the hurt and destruction of the kingdom sundry ways: by making new Sheriffs in an unusual and unlawful manner, to be as so many generals or commanders of forces raised against the parliament; by issuing out unlawful commissions of array, with other unlawful commissions for the same purpose; by sending forth proclamations against both Houses of parliament, and several members thereof; proclaiming them traitors against the privileges of parliament and laws of the land; by sealing commissions of oyer and terminer to proceed against them and other of his Majesty's good subjects, adhering to the parliament, as traitors; by sending commissions into Ireland to treat a peace with the rebels there, contrary to an act of parliament made this session; besides, divers other dangerous and illegal acts have been passed under the Great Seal since it was secretly conveyed away from parliament, whereby great calamities and mischiefs have ensued to the kingdom's prejudice.

" II. *Mischiefs proceeding through want of the Great Seal.*

" 1. The terms have been adjourned; the courts of justice obstructed.

"2. No original writs can be sued forth without going to Oxford; which none who holds with the parliament can do without peril of his life or liberty.

"3. Proclamations in parliament can not issue out for bringing in delinquents impeached of high treason, or other crimes, under pain of forfeiting their estates according to the ancient course.

"4. No writs of error can be brought in parliament to reverse erroneous judgments; nor writs of election sued out for choosing new members upon death or removal of any; whereby the number of the members is much lessened, and the House in time likely to be dissolved if speedy supply be not had, contrary to the very act for continuance of this parliament.

"5. Every other court of justice hath a peculiar seal; and the parliament, the supreme court of England, hath no other but the Great Seal of England; which being kept away from it, hath now no seal at all; and therefore a new seal ought to be made.

"This Seal is *clavis regni*, and therefore ought to be resident with the parliament (which is the representative of the whole kingdom) while it continues sitting, the King as well as the kingdom being always legally present in it during its session."

The Lords having sent a message "that their Lordships do adhere to their former resolutions concerning the making of a new Great Seal," the Commons, the following day resolved, "That a Great Seal of England shall be presently made, and that a committee be appointed for this purpose, and that Sir Robert Harley take care of the speedy and effectual execution of this order."[1] They meant this by way of a hint, that they might exclusively assume sovereign authority, and they hoped that when the Seal was made the Lords would acquiesce in the use of it.

There seems to have been a difficulty in finding an artist who would undertake the work without the direct order of the House, and about a week afterwards it was resolved, "that Mr. Marten (the regicide) do to-morrow bring hither the man who will undertake to grave the Great Seal to receive his directions."[2] Simonds, the eminent medalist, was accordingly introduced, and was

[1] Lords' Jour. vi. 117, 119. Com. Jour. iii. 154, 155. [2] Com. Jour. iii. 162.

fortified with the following warrant, signed by the Speaker:—" Ordered that Mr. Simonds be required and enjoined forthwith to make a new Great Seal of England, and that he shall have £100 for his pains, £40 in hand, and three-score pounds as soon as he shall finished his work."[1]

On the 28th of September a Seal engraved on silver, copied from an impression of the King's Great Seal, and in all respects resembling it, was brought into the House, when an order was made " that it should be sealed up and delivered into the custody of Mr. Speaker, not to be made use of until the House take further order."[2]

The leaders of the Commons were now very much perplexed as to their next move, for they were by no means yet prepared to throw off the authority of the Lords, that House retaining considerable influence with the public, and the Earl of Essex and other Peers being indispensably necessary for carrying on the war. They resolved to make another effort to obtain the concurrence of the other House. In the meanwhile the battle of Newbury had been fought; the exasperation of the contending parties had considerably increased; and Essex had been recently gratified by the dismissal of his rival, Sir William Waller, who, from temporary successes, had been quaintly called " *William the Conqueror,*" and had excited the jealousy of the " Lord General." It was likewise hoped that some impression had been made by Prynne's famous treatise, written for this occasion, which the House had ordered to be printed,[3] entitled,

"THE OPENING OF THE GREAT SEALE OF ENGLAND,
"CONTAINING
" Certain brief, historicall, and legall observations touching the originall antiquity, use, necessity of Great Seale of the Kings and kingdom of England, in respect of charters, patents, writs, commissions, and other processe,
" Together with the King's kingdom's parliament's severall interests in and power over the same, and over the Lord Chancellor and the Lords and Keepers of it, both in regard of its new making, custody, administration for the better execution of publike justice, the republique, necessary safety and utility;

---

[1] Com. Jour. iii. 174. This same artist made the other Great Seals for the Commonwealth, and, after the battle of Dunbar, was sent to Scotland, to take the effigies of Oliver for a medal, to celebrate the victory. Such was his reputation, that he continued to be employed by the government after the Restoration.—Carlyle's Cromwell, vol. ii. 291–293, 2nd ed.
[2] Com. Jour. iii. 257.   [3] Sept. 15, 1643.

"Occasioned by the over-rash censures of such who inveigh against the parliament for ordering a new Great Seale to be engraven to supp'y the willful absence, defects, abuses of the old, unduely withdrawne and detained from them.

"By WILLIAM PRYNNE, utter Barrister of Lincoln's Inne.

"Esther, viii. 8. 'Write ye also for the Jews, as it liketh you, in the King's name, AND SEAL IT WITH THE KING'S RING: for the writing which is written in the King's name, AND SEALED WITH THE KING'S RING, may no man reverse.'"

In this treatise, the author of HISTRIOMASTIX having lost his ears, but not his learning or his dullness, nor his perverse ingenuity,—by a misapplication of Scripture and legal authorities, had attempted to prove that the Great Seal of England was meant to express the will of the King and the other estates of the realm, and that upon the default or deficiency of any one branch of the legislature, it might be lawfully used by the remainder.[1]

A committee was appointed "to consider what is fit to be done concerning the Great Seal, and the use of it, and of the former votes of both Houses concerning it, and to report their opinions to this House; and this business is especially recommended to Mr. Sergeant Wilde, and all the lawyers of the House."

Mr. Sergeant Wilde reported from the committee that another conference on the subject should be demanded from the Lords,—which was agreed to, and he was appointed to manage it. He forcibly recapitulated the former reasons, introducing a little of Prynne's argumentation—dwelt upon a proclamation lately put forth by the King for seizing the estates of all parliament men, and any who adhered to the parliament—and pointed out the absolute necessity for the use of a new Great Seal to preserve the government of this kingdom, and to provide for the administration of justice.[2]

The Lords yielded; and "taking into serious consideration the necessity of preserving the government of the kingdom and his Majesty's authority in parliament, and the being thereof, and the due administration of justice, and perceiving, by the mischiefs already experienced, how

---

[1] It was pretty much on this reasoning that Mr. Pitt's Regency Bill proceeded in 1789, which was adopted by the Tory party—the heir-apparent, in whom was the hereditary right, being supposed to be adverse to them. A Great Seal was fabricated for the occasion, after the example of the Long Parliament, as the commission to go through the form of giving the Royal consent was purely the act of the two Houses.

[2] Lords' Jour. vi. 252, 253.

absolutely indispensable it is to have the Great Seal attending the parliament,—after a mature debate this question was put,—Whether a Great Seal of England shall be forthwith made to attend the parliament for dispatch of the affairs of the parliament and of the kingdom?—and it passed affirmatively."[1]

A message to this effect coming down to the Commons, they resolved, on the motion of Sergeant Wilde, that "an ordinance should forthwith be framed for more effectually invalidating all proceedings under the Great Seal at Oxford, and for vesting the Seal of the parliament in Commissioners, with the powers of Lord Chancellor or Lord Keeper, to be exercised under the directions of both Houses."[2]

An ordinance to this effect speedily passed through the House of Commons; but it seems to have met with some obstruction in the Lords, and not fewer than six messages were sent up from the Commons praying their Lordships to concur with them in putting the new Great Seal in execution, and to expedite their answer concerning the Great Seal,—the messengers from the Commons always being informed that "their Lordships would send an answer by messengers of their own." At last Sergeant Wilde came to the bar of the Lords, and, with his characteristic energy, read them a lecture on their long delays, telling their Lordships, "that the ordinance concerning the Great Seal was of such absolute necessity that the Commonwealth suffered great prejudice for want thereof." The difficulties, whatever they might have been, were now overcome; and, after some conferences to fix the names of the Commissioners, the ordinance received the assent of both Houses, and, according to the doctrine then prevailing, became law. Six Commissioners were appointed —two members of the House of Peers, and four members of the House of Commons, "which said persons, or any three or more of them, whereof one member or more of the Lords' House, also one member or more of the House of Commons, should be present, were authorized to have the keeping, ordering, and disposing of the new Great Seal, as also all such and the like power as any Lord Chancellor, or Lord Keeper, or Commissioners of the Great Seal ever had, used, or ought to have."[3]

[1] Lords' Jour. vi. 254.   [2] Com. Jour. iii. 278.
[3] Lords' Jour. vi. 300, 301.   "It must surely excite a smile that men who

After some preliminaries had been settled as to the form of the oath to be taken by the Commissioners, and the place where the Seal was to be kept by them,[1]—on the 30th of November the Speaker of the Commons, attended by the whole House, appeared at the bar of the Lords, and said,—" My Lords, Whereas the Great Seal of England was, by order of the House of Commons, appointed to be in my custody, without being made use of until it should be settled and disposed of by authority of ordinance of both Houses of parliament, I am now commanded by the House of Commons to deliver the same to the Speaker of your Lordships' House, so that the Commissioners may be sworn, and the Great Seal delivered to them in full parliament." The Speaker of the Lords went down from his place to the bar, and received it from the hands of the Speaker of the Commons and brought it to the woolsack. Thereupon the Earl of Kent and the Earl of Bolingbroke, the two Peers Commissioners, were sworn at the table, the Speaker of the Lords administering the oath of office to them. Next the four Commissioners, members of the House of Commons, viz. Oliver St. John, Solicitor to his Majesty; Mr. Sergeant Wilde, Samuel Brown, Esq., and Edward Prideaux, Esq., took the oath, the Clerk of the Parliament reading it to them. Then the Speaker of the Lords carried the Great Seal to the bar, and delivered it to the Six Commissioners in full parliament, and the Commons and their Speaker returned to their own House.[2]

On a subsequent day the Lords Commissioners all took the oath required by the Triennial Act, and the oaths of allegiance and supremacy[3] before both Houses,—at the same time that Lenthal was sworn in Master of the Rolls,

had raised armies and fought battles against the King, should be perplexed how to get over so technical a difficulty. But the Great Seal in the eyes of English lawyers has a sort of mysterious efficacy, and passes for the depositary of royal authority in a higher degree than the person of the King."—*Hall. Const. Hist.* ii. 222.

[1] That this Seal might not be carried off to the King, or applied to any improper purpose, it was to be kept in the office of the clerk of the House of Peers, sealed up with three of the Commissioners' seals, in an iron chest, under three different locks, each Commissioner having one key.—*Lords' Jour.* vi. 300, 32.

[2] This graphic description of the ceremony is nearly in the very words of the Lords' Journals vi. 318.

[3] These oaths continued to be taken by all persons in employment under the parliament till the end of the civil war.

having been appointed to that office by ordinance, while Colepeper enjoyed the same title at Oxford under the King's patent.[1]

As soon as the news of these proceedings reached Oxford, a proclamation was issued by the King, under his Great Seal, denouncing the counterfeiting of the Great Seal by the parliament as "High Treason,"—forbidding the use of it,—declaring null and void all done under it,—and threatening to prosecute, as traitors or accessories, all who should use it or pay respect to it. But this was treated at Westminster as *brutum fulmen*, and was not thought even worthy of an answer.[2]

By several supplemental ordinances and resolutions of the two Houses, offices were provided for the "Lords Commissioners" and "His Honor,"—and, after an interruption of nearly two years, the Court of Chancery was re-opened at Westminster, and the business proceeded with full vigor. On the first day the Commissioners sat, they sealed above five hundred writs. In judicial matters they were left to their own discretion; but in putting the Seal to grants and appointments to offices they acted ministerially, under the orders of the two Houses.

The House of Commons immediately ordered an account of all sums paid into the Court of Chancery for the last twenty years, and that if any should prove to be the moneys of malignants or delinquents, or to be dead stock, it should be applied to the public service.[3] This is the origin of the "Suitor's Fund."

In answer to a proclamation under the King's Great Seal, adjourning the Courts to Oxford, the first state document to which the Lords Commissioners put their Great Seal was a counter-proclamation, by which all judges, officers, suitors, and other faithful subjects of his Majesty, were enjoined under a heavy penalty, to attend the Courts at Westminster.[4]

Sergeant Wilde appears to have been by far the most active of the Six Commissioners, and next to him at a

---

[1] In the absence of royal authority, great importance seems to have been attached to the allegation that these acts were done "*en plein parliament,*" an expression frequently occurring in the early rolls respecting the granting of honors and offices.

[2] Nov. 29, 1643. Docquets of Great Seal at Oxford, Temp. Car. I.

[3] Com. Jour. iii. 346. The return made would be very curious, but I have not been able to meet with it. [4] Jan. 6, 1644. Com. Jour. iii. 359.

long interval, came Oliver St. John, who was an able lawyer, but devoted much of his time to politics. One of the noble Lords Commissioners always sat along with the Commoners, but did not interfere unless on occasions of ceremony.

A commission was soon after issued, authorizing the Master of the Rolls, and certain of the Judges, to assist in the hearing of causes in the Court of Chancery.

Things continued on this footing at Westminster till the month of August, 1646, when the King's Great Seal, having been taken at Oxford, was broken in pieces with much solemnity in the presence of both Houses, and there ceased to be rival Great Seals in England.[1] At the same time the Earl of Salisbury, who had been appointed in the place of the Earl of Bolingbroke, deceased, was sworn as a Lord Commissioner. The Earl of Kent, having taken his place as a Peer, came down to the bar and received the parliamentary Great Seal from the other Commissioners. He presented it to the Clerk of the Parliament, by whom it was carried to the Speaker of the House of Lords, and laid on the woolsack. The Earl of Salisbury, then at the table, took the oath of supremacy, *the oath of allegiance*, the oath of office, and the oath under the Triennial Act. Finally, the Speaker of the House of Lords carried the Seal to the bar, where the Commons, with their Speaker, then stood, and delivered it to the Earl of Salisbury to be kept by him with the rest of the Commissioners.[2]

Violent disputes now arose respecting the Commissionership of the Great Seal and other offices. Oliver Cromwell, who at first was probably influenced only by a fanatical zeal for religion and liberty, had for some time been goaded on by personal ambition, and distinctly aimed at supreme power. With this view he was pursuing his "Self-denying Ordinances,"—from which he meant that he himself should be excepted, whilst they should deprive of all power the Earl of Essex, the Earl of Manchester, and the leaders in both Houses, whose ascendency he dreaded. Accordingly, on the self-denying principle, he caused an ordinance to be brought in by which it was declared that the Great Seal should not, in future, be held by any member of either House, and three new

[1] Ante, p. 303.   [2] Lords' Jour. 458.

Commissioners, not in parliament, were named to supersede the six now in office. In the Commons, a vote was obtained, by a majority of 75 to 65, " that no member of either House should be a Commissioner of the Great Seal," and three Commissioners were agreed upon, who were not in parliament,—Sir Rowland Wandesford, Sir Thomas Biddingfield, and Bradshaw, afterwards President of the High Court of Justice. At the same time it was provided that the presentations to livings and the appointment of Justices of the Peace should be in the two Houses; and an order was made, " that the Commissioners for the custody of the Great Seal do not relieve any person in Chancery in any case where the party may be relieved by the common law." [1]

But the self-denying principle was not at all approved of by the Lords, as it operated most unequally, by at once disqualifying the whole body of the Peerage for holding any public employment. They therefore rejected the ordinance for transferring the Seal to the three new Commissioners.

The Commons then passed another ordinance, as a compromise for the present, " That the Speakers of both Houses should have power to seal all original writs and processes, and likewise commissions and pardons, which have usually passed and ought to pass, under the Great Seal, as fully as any Lord Keeper or Commissioner for the Great Seal for the time being ought and might have done;" and sent it up to the Lords with a message, "That in regard of the great obstruction of the proceedings in Chancery because the Commissioners of the Great Seal are not settled, and in regard of the great prejudice the subject suffers for want of sealing of writs, there being now 8,000 writs ready to be sealed, the Commons had framed an ordinance for preventing of these inconveniences, wherein they desire their Lordships' concurrence."

The Lords agreed to the ordinance with some immaterial amendment; and it was followed by another, for appointing the Master of the Rolls and certain Judges to hear causes in Chancery in the absence of the Lords Commissioners.

An order was thereupon made that the late Commissioners should deliver the key of the chest in which the

[1] Com. Jour. iv. 701.

Great Seal was kept to the Speaker of the House of Commons; and Lenthal, accordingly, received it from Sergeant Wilde. The sum of £1,000 was voted to each of them for their trouble, and it was ordered that such of them as were of the Long Robe should thenceforth have the privilege of practicing within the bar.

On the 31st of October the two Speakers were sworn in, both Houses being present. The Earl of Manchester, standing in his place on the woolsack, took the following oaths:—1. The oath of supremacy. 2. The oath of allegiance. 3. The oath of office, which he read himself; —and 4. The oath under the Triennial Act, administered to him by the clerk of the Crown. Then Lenthal had the same oaths administered to him,—the two first at the bar, the third read to him by the Speaker of the Lords' House. This being done, the Earl of Manchester went down to the bar, and the Great Seal being brought from the woolsack and taken out of the purse and opened, the Speaker of the Lords' House took it into his hand, and said,— "According to the ordinance of both Houses of parliament authorizing me to be a Commissioner of the Great Seal, I do receive it and deliver it unto you (the Speaker of the House of Commons) as the other Commissioner."[1]

On the 2nd of November, the new Lords Commissioners began the business of the Seal, and a Judge and a Master in Chancery by turns assisted them; but their sittings were very irregular, and there were heavy complaints of delays and ill-considered decrees. Their authority was set at defiance by Jenkins, a common-law Judge, who had stoutly adhered to the King, and had tried and executed several persons for taking arms against him. This spirited Welshman being brought up in custody for disobedience to the process of the Court of Chancery, was required to put in an answer to a bill filed against him, imputing to him gross fraud and breach of trust; but he told them "that he neither ought nor would submit to the power of that Court, for that it was no Court, and their Seal was counterfeit."

An ordinance being introduced to attaint him for this contumacy and his other misdeeds, he was brought to the bar to make his defense; but he refused to kneel, denied their authority, and told them that they wronged

[1] Lords' Jour. viii. 552.

the King, and that there could be no law without a King. The House fined him £1,000 for his contempt. Soon after he was specifically called upon to plead to the charges of "having given judgment of death against men for assisting the parliament, having been himself in arms against the parliament, having persuaded others to do the like, and having denied the power of the parliament;" but he still said they had no power to try him, and he would give them no other answer. The attainder passed the Commons, but was allowed to drop in the Lords; and afterwards, in the year 1651, when the government was better established, on a slight submission Jenkins received a pardon under the Great Seal of the Commonwealth.[1]

It was meant that the present arrangement respecting the Great Seal should only be temporary, and a joint committee of the two Houses, consisting of fifteen Peers and thirty Commoners, repeatedly met in the Painted Chamber, with the view of devising some plan that might be more satisfactory to the public. The Commons, now more and more under the influence of Cromwell, were for extending the self-denying ordinance to the Great Seal; but the Lords, feeling their influence declining, would not part with this remnant of their power, and came to a resolution "that among the Commissioners of the Great Seal there should be one or more members of their House."

These disputes rendered it necessary that the time should be prolonged for which the two Speakers were to be the Lords Commissioners, and this was repeatedly done by ordinance,—generally from twenty days to twenty days.[2] But the King was now a prisoner: military despotism was established under the semblance of liberty,— and the discerning saw that the struggle of the Peers to maintain their independence being unavailing, everything must bend to the mandate of Cromwell.

[1] Whit. Mem. 291, 292, 301, 347, 389, 464, 511.
[2] Lords' Jour. viii. 560 *et seq.*

CHAPTER LXIX.

LORDS COMMISSIONERS OF THE GREAT SEAL FROM THE FIRST APPOINTMENT OF WHITELOCK TILL THE ADOPTION OF A NEW GREAT SEAL BEARING THE INSIGNIA OF THE REPUBLIC.

AMIDST the stirring political events which for some time occupied the public,—the negotiations with the King at Holmby,—his being violently carried off by Joyce,—his flight from Hampton Court,—his imprisonment in Carisbrook Castle,—and the attempts of the army to overpower the parliament,—the custody of the Great Seal, and the administration of justice in the Court of Chancery, excited little attention.

But in an interval of comparative quiet which occurred in the spring of 1648, loud complaints were heard of the absurdity of having for the two supreme Equity Judges a lay Peer, because he happened to be Speaker of the House of Lords and the Speaker of the House of Commons, who, though he had been bred to the law, was now completely absorbed in his parliamentary duties.

In the hope of satisfying the people and reconciling the clashing pretensions of the two Houses, an ordinance was introduced into the Commons, and immediately passed, for the appointment of three new Lords Commissioners, —the Earl of Kent, Bulstrode Whitelock, Esq., and Sir Thomas Widdrington, Sergeant-at-law. When the ordinance came up to the Lords, they insisted that there should be an equal number of their body appointed Commissioners, and added the name of Lord Grey de Werke, —with a proviso that no act should be done by the Commoners, unless with the concurrence of one Peer and one Commoner. To these amendments the Commons reluctantly assented, and the ordinance was law.

Three of the new Lords Commissioners of the Great Seal were mere ciphers, and there would be no amusement or instruction in trying to trace their origin or their career; but WHITELOCK is one of the most interesting as well as amiable characters of the age in which he lived,— and as afterwards, on the deposition of His Highness, the Lord Protector Richard, he was for a time sole Lord

Keeper of the Great Seal under the Commonwealth, I am required to write his Life as if he had presided in the Court of Chancery and on the woolsack by the authority of an hereditary sovereign.

This distinguished republican lawyer was of an ancient family, and very proud of his seventeen descents recorded at the Heralds' College. He was the only son of Sir James Whitelock, a Judge of the Court of King's Bench, and Elizabeth, daughter of Edward Bulstrode, Esq., of Hedgely Bulstrode, in the county of Buckingham, and sister of Bulstrode, the famous law reporter. He was strongly connected with the law, Sir George Croke, a Judge successively of the Common Pleas and King's Bench, and the publisher of law cases in three reigns,[1] being his mother's uncle. In the house of this venerable magistrate in Fleet Street, young Bulstrode Whitelock first saw the light, on the 6th of August, 1605.

After passing with credit through Merchant Taylors' school, he was entered in Michaelmas term, 1620, a gentleman commoner of St. John's College, Oxford. Laud was then the master of the College, and from him he received many kindnesses, which he never afterwards forgot. Having quitted the University (for what cause does not appear) without a degree, he was placed in chambers in the Middle Temple, and commenced the arduous course of study necessary to fit him for the bar. His father was his instructor, and, together with the sound maxims of the common law, early imbued his mind with the principles of constitutional freedom, then little regarded among lawyers. The old Judge, when himself a practicing barrister, had been subjected to a Star Chamber prosecution for a professional opinion he had given to a client upon the legality of a "benevolence" exacted by James I.; and when on the bench, he had differed from all his brethren in pronouncing against the power of the King and Council to commit to prison, without specifying in the warrant the cause of the commitment.[2] Yet he conducted himself

---

"But some amidst the legal throng
Who think to them thy streams belong,
Are forced to cite opinions wise,
Cro. Car.—Cro. Jac.—and Cro. Eliz."
—*Plead. Guide.*

[1] Judge Croke's Reports are thus cited by the names of the princes in whose reigns the cases were described.   [2] Darnel's case, 3 St. Tr. 1

with such propriety, that Charles I. was forced to characterize him as "a stout, wise, and learned man, and one who knew what belonged to uphold magistrates and magistracy in their dignity." While a student, young Whitelock was fond of joining amusement with instruction by acting as marshal to the Judges of assize. He himself tells us that, "according to the leave he had from his father, and by his means from the several Judges, he rode all the circuits of England to acquaint himself with his native country, and the memorable things therein."

In 1628 he was called to the bar, and went the Oxford circuit of which he afterwards became the decided leader.[1] He likewise rose into respectable practice in London. He sat, when very young, in the parliament which passed the "Petition of Right," and without taking any prominent part in the debates, he steadily voted for that great measure. During the long intermission of parliaments which followed, he did not mix in politics, and he seems to have associated a good deal with the courtiers. Being now Treasurer of the Middle Temple, he formed an acquaintance with Mr. Attorney General Noy, to whom he tells us, he thus came to be introduced. "A student of the Inn having died in chambers, the Society disbursed money for his funeral, which his father refused to pay. A bill was thereupon preferred against that gentleman in the Court of Requests, in the name of the Treasurer, ingeniously and handsomely setting forth the customs of the Inns of Court, with the whole matter, and praying that he might be compelled to pay the money so disbursed, with damages. Upon my carrying the bill to Mr. Attorney General Noy for his signature, with that of the other Benchers, he was pleased to advise with me about a patent the King commanded him to draw, upon which he gave me a fee for it out of his little purse, saying, 'Here, take these single pence,' which amounted to eleven groats, 'and I give you more than an attorney's fee, because you will be a better man than an Attorney General. This you will find to be true.' After much other drollery, wherein he delighted and excelled, we parted,

---

[1] As a proof of this he mentions that at the last assizes for the county of Oxford which he attended, thirty-five causes were tried, and he had forty-four retainers—his ascendancy being as great in the other seven counties on the circuit.

abundance of company attending to speak to him all this time."

Whitelock was manager for the Middle Temple of the famous masque given to the Queen, by the Inns of Court, in confutation of "Histriomastix" against interludes, and he has left us a most circumstantial and entertaining account of it. To him was committed "the whole care and charge of the music," which he assures us "excelled any music that ever before that time had been heard in England."[1] His head was quite turned by the Queen's compliment, "that she never saw any masque more noble or better performed than this was, which she took as a particular respect to herself, as well as to the King her husband, and desired that her thanks might be returned to the gentlemen of the Inns of Court for it."[2]

He now passed his vacations in Oxfordshire, affecting while there merely to be a country squire; yet from his knowledge of the law, he was called upon to preside as Chairman of the Justices of Peace. Speaking of one instance which occurred in 1635, he gives us a statement containing a lively representation of the opinions and manners of the times. "At the Quarter Sessions at Oxford, I was put into the chair in Court, though I was in colored clothes, a sword by my side, and a falling band, which was unusual for lawyers in those days, and in this garb I gave the Charge to the Grand Jury. I took occasion to enlarge on the point of jurisdiction in the temporal Courts in matters ecclesiastical, and the antiquity thereof which I did the rather because the spiritual men began in those days to swell higher than ordinary, and to take it as an injury to the church that anything savoring of the spirituality should be within the cognizance of ignorant laymen. The gentlemen and freeholders seemed well pleased with my charge, and the management of the business of the Sessions; and said they perceived one might speak as good sense in a falling band as in a ruff."[3]

He now began gradually to associate himself with those who were opposing the arbitrary measures of the Court. He was active in resisting the encroachments of the Crown upon the rights of the landholders in Whichwood Forest, and he encouraged his kinsman, Hampden, in the great case of ship-money. Yet he was always moderate, and he did

[1] Mem. p. 19.   [2] Ibid. p. 22.   [3] Ibid. p. 23.

not wish even to take advantage of the discontents of the Scots on account of episcopacy. "I persuaded my friends," said he, "not to foment these growing public differences, nor to be any means for encouraging a *foreign nation, proud, and against our natural Prince.*" He still continued intimate with Hyde, Falkland, and the more reasonable reformers.

When the Long Parliament was summoned he stood for Great Marlow, and was beaten by unfair means; but upon a petition it was pronounced by the House of Commons to be a void election,—and on a new writ being issued, he was returned. He made his maiden speech in the debate which arose upon the motion that Selden, and the other members of the House who were illegally imprisoned in 1629, should receive indemnification out of the estates of the Judges who had been parties to the judgment of the Court of King's Bench,—his own father being alleged to be one of them;—and he at once defended his father's memory and his own patrimony, by showing that his father had expressed a clear opinion for admitting the defendants to bail, and had himself undergone persecution in behalf of the liberty of the subject.

So favorable an impression did he make by the earnestness and modesty of his demeanor on this occasion, that he was elected chairman of the committee appointed to draw up the impeachment against Lord Strafford, and employed by the House to manage the seven last articles of the impeachment. He objected to have anything to do with one of them, which charged the Earl with a design of bringing over the army of Ireland for the purpose of reducing England to subjection, as not being supported by sufficient evidence, "thinking it not honorable for the House of Commons to proceed upon an article whereof they could not make a clear proof." On his motion this article would have been struck out, had it not been warmly supported by Sir Walter Earle. Whereupon it was retained, and assigned to this gentleman to manage; but he made such a wretched hand of it, that the Queen, inquiring his name, said, "that water-dog did bark, but not bite, but the rest did bite close." Strafford himself bore testimony to the candor and fairness, as well as talent, with which Whitelock discharged his part in the prosecution. "Glynne and Maynard," he said, "used him like advocates; but Palmer and Whitelock like gentlemen, and yet left out nothing that was material to be urged against him." Whitelock bears ample testimony to the admirable defense of the noble culprit. "Certainly," says he, in closing his touching narrative of Strafford's trial and execution, "never any man acted such a part on such a theater, with more wisdom, constancy, and eloquence, with greater reason, judgment, and temper, and with better grace in all his words and gestures, than this great and excellent person did, and he moved the hearts of all his auditors, some few excepted, to remorse and pity."[1]

At this time it depended a good deal upon accident to which party Whitelock should be permanently attached, for some, with whom he now co-operated became the chief advisers of the King in carrying on the war against the parliament, while the residue assisted in bringing the King to the scaffold, and in abolishing monarchy in England. He himself still supported pacific measures; and in the debate on the bill for arming the militia, he joined with those who urged that the King should be again petitioned to place the sword in such hands as he and the parliament should jointly nominate, and " who would be more careful to keep it sheathed than to draw it." When the ordinance of the two Houses upon this subject passed without the concurrence of the King, whereby in reality his authority was renounced, though all in public employment continued to swear allegiance to him,—Whitelock had serious thoughts of joining the royalists, or of retreating into private life; but he was persuaded by the leaders of the popular party that they had no purpose of war with the King, and that they were only arming to defend themselves and the liberties of the nation. Accordingly he agreed to continue to keep his station in the House of Commons at Westminster, and he accepted a commission as a deputy lieutenant in the military array about to be organized in Bucks and Oxfordshire, where his property and family connections chiefly lay. Still he implored the parliament to make the experiment of further overtures of peace, and to name a committee to review the former propositions which the King had rejected. In his Memoirs he draws a lively picture of the silent but rapid strides

[1] Mem. 44.

which lead to civil war. " We scarce know how, but from paper combats, by declarations, remonstrances, protestations, votes, messages, answers, and replies, we are now come to the question of raising forces, and naming the general and officers of an army. But what may be the progress hereof the poet tells you:—

> "'Jusque datum sceleri canimus, populumque potentem
> In suâ victrici conversum viscera dextrâ.'"[1]

The die, however, was now cast ; and, instead of being, like Hyde, Chancellor of the Exchequer to Charles I., and Lord Chancellor to Charles II., Whitelock was destined to draw an ordinance for establishing a pure republic in England, and to hold the Great Seal under a Lord Protector.

When he heard of the King erecting the royal standard at Nottingham, instead of going to fight under it, he accepted the command of a company of horse in Hampden's regiment, composed of his tenants and neighbors in Oxfordshire; and, marching against the royalist commander, Sir John Biron, he took military possession of Oxford, "being welcomed by the townsmen," he tells us, "more than by the scholars." In consequence, a regiment of horse of Prince Rupert's brigade quartered themselves in his house, Fawley Court, near Henley, and, "indulging in excess and rapine of every kind, destroyed his books, deeds, and manuscripts, cut open his bedding, carried away his coach and four horses and all his saddle-horses, killed his hounds, of which he had a very fine pack, and destroyed all his deer and winged game." He was so much horrified by the ravages of civil war, that his martial ardor very quickly subsided; and, leaving the field of arms to those who had a greater taste for it, he returned to his post in the parliament, and ever after, as a noncombatant, steadily supported the popular side.

We next find him on a very different scene—as a lay member of the famous Assembly of Divines at Westminster.[2] Here, in conjunction with Selden, he in vain combated the position that "presbytery being *jure divino*, no human legislature had a right, in any degree, to interfere with or control the Presbyterian church,"—and he was branded with the opprobrious appellation of "Erastian."

[1] Mem. 61.   [2] Ibid. 99.

He was more successful when the resolution of the Assembly in favor of the "Covenant" came to be debated in the House of Commons, although, on one occasion, he could only prevent its being carried by making a very long and wearisome speech against time, till a sufficient number of "*Independent*" members could be got together, who, for the nonce, coalescing with a small body of *Episcopalians*, threw it out.

In January, 1643, he was named, along with Holles and other popular leaders, a Commissioner to carry propositions of peace to the King at Oxford. This appears to have been a very disagreeable service, although they had a safe conduct. At the inn where they were stationed during the negotiation, a great bustle being heard in the hall, it was found that some of the officers of the royal army had fallen foul of the Commissioners' servants, calling them, and their masters, and the parliament who had dispatched them, "rogues, rebels, and traitors." The Commissioners having ascertained the cause of the disturbance, behaved with becoming spirit. "Holles went presently to one of the King's officers, a tall, big, black man, and taking him by the collar shook him, and told him it was basely and unworthily done of them to abuse their servants in their own quarters, contrary to the King's safe conduct, and took away his sword from him."—"I did the same," adds Whitelock, "to another great mastiff fellow, an officer also of the King's army, and took his sword from him."[1] Nevertheless, they fell under a lively suspicion of having, during this mission, intrigued with the King, and betrayed the parliament. Having paid a visit of courtesy to the Earl of Lindsey, who lay at the royal quarters languishing from the mortal wounds he had received in the battle of Edge Hill, the King, attended by Prince Rupert, came as if casually, into the chamber, and, after many professions of esteem for their persons and characters, requested their advice as to the answer he should give to the propositions of the parliament, and desired them to confer together and set down something in writing that might be fit for him to say, with a view to bring about a happy settlement of all differences. They, acting with perfect good faith to their party, retired into another room, and having agreed on

[1] Mem. 67.

such a declaration as they thought might best tend to a pacific issue of the negotiation, Whitelock wrote it out in a feigned hand and left it on a table, where Charles soon found it. This had been perceived by the Lord Saville, one of the King's attendants, who shortly afterwards revolted to the parliament. He, joining the Presbyterian party, who were eager to get rid of Holles and Whitelock, accused them to the House of being well affected to the King, and of having secretly corresponded with him during their residence at Oxford. The charge was referred to a select committee, who, after a long inquiry, reported in favor of the accused, being mainly influenced by the bad character of the accuser. "Thus ended this knotty and malicious prosecution in the honorable discharge of those two great men. Mr. Whitelock absented himself from the House when they came to give judgment. It was observed that most if not all of the gentlemen of the best interest and quality in the House were for acquitting of them, and that it had never been known in any affair before that held so many days that the young gentlemen and others who were wont, whatever business was in agitation, to go out to dinner or to some refreshments and diversions, should attend so constantly at the time that business was in debate, and not stir from it."[1]

Whitelock, although he never deserted his political associates, seems to have talked of them very freely, even to their opponents. Clarendon asserts positively, that both during the negotiations at Oxford, and at the treaty of Uxbridge in the following year, where also Whitelock was one of the parliamentary Commissioners, and was in daily intercourse with the King's Commissioners, whom he had formerly familiarly known, "he used with them his old openness, and professed his detestation of all the proceedings of the parliamentarians, yet could not leave them."

In the struggle that soon arose between the early

---

[1] Life of Whitelock, p. 51. This passage shows us that even when the House met at eight in the morning, and in the fervor of the Long Parliament, *dinner* caused a serious interruption to the proceedings of the legislature. The hour of twelve approaching, "the young gentlemen and others" disappeared, and the House was deserted. Whether the system of *pairing* had then begun, I do not find, but in all probability a *Presbyterian* and an *Independent*, differing on everything else, often came to an understanding that they should go out together to dine at the ordinary.

leaders of the popular party and him who was now striving to supersede them, and to get all power into his own hands. Whitelock long strenuously opposed the plan, which he detested, for the establishing of a military government. He spoke and voted against "the self-denying ordinance" as a device, not only to put down the Presbyterian sect, whom he still disliked, but to strip all civil functionaries of office and of influence. Nevertheless, ever a mild and time-serving politican, he would not quarrel with Cromwell; and when consulted by the Lord General Essex and his friends, whether the leader of the Independents might not be proceeded against as an "Incendiary," he advised them to wait for better proofs before they ventured to attack a person of such quick and subtle parts, and who had secured such an interest in the House of Commons.

When Cromwell's ascendency had been established, Whitelock completely succumbed, being desirous of doing as much good as he could for his country and for himself under the dominion which he had mildly attempted to prevent. Cromwell now treated him with consideration and kindness, and defeated a plan of his enemies to get rid of him by sending him "Lord Justice into Ireland," saying "*he was against his going away*," and desiring his company, began to use his advice in the administration of civil affairs.

Whitelock, while he did his duty in parliament, attended zealously to his profession. The civil war being over, the practice of the law was very flourishing, and he not only was the favorite leader of the Oxford Circuit, but had the first business in Westminster Hall.

In September, 1647, the offer was made to him of being elected Recorder of the City of London; but he declined the appointment, as he thought it might interfere with the great object of his ambition, which was to preside in the Court of Chancery.

We have seen how, in March, 1648, he was, by an ordinance of the two Houses, named Lord Commissioner of the Great Seal, along with the Earl of Kent, Lord Grey de Werke, and Sir Thomas Widdrington. The following is his own modest account of this transaction:—

"These Commissioners were said to be agreed upon by the private junto of Cromwell's party beforehand to be trusted with this great charge; and in the debate of the business, several others of both Houses were propounded: but, after a great debate, these three only were pitched upon.

"The Earl of Kent being a very honest, just man of good rational parts and abilities, and of an ancient, great family, who would be a countenance to this business, was held a fit person for the Lords' House.

"Sir Thomas Widdrington, being a gentleman of known integrity, and of great abilities in his profession, and brother-in-law to the General, whose sister he had married, was very fit to be one of the House of Commons to be intrusted with so weighty an employment.

"I was less considerable than the other in all respects, yet was well known and understood in the House by my long attendance there, and by them judged not incapable of this employment. Besides, the General had an affection for me, and he had a good interest in the House, and Cromwell and his party were willing to engage me as far as they could with them.

"I can truly say I never heard of this business beforehand, nor was in the least privy to it or acquainted with it; but God was pleased so to order it, not my ambition that sought or contrived it, for I may be believed on much experience, that such employments are not desirable by a prudent and quiet spirit; they seldom afford quiet, never safety. I was at this time on the circuit in great practice, wherein none of my profession had a greater share than myself, and at Gloucester received this unexpected news. The counsel, the officers, and the attorneys, with great respect and much civility, wished me joy of that honorable employment. I sent to my friends of the House to know if my present attendance was expected by the House; but that without a special summons I did not intend to return to London till after the circuit should be ended, where I was engaged in many men's businesses."[1]

Sergeant Widdrington was at this time likewise upon his circuit, and it was ordained "that, till the beginning of the next term, the Lords Kent and Grey should be empowered to seal all commissions and writs." The two noble Commissioners were accordingly both sworn in

[1] Mem. 293.

forthwith in the presence of both Houses. Although the King was now in solitary confinement in Carisbrook Castle, allowed to see no one but "the decrepit old man who kindled his fire," and "the vote of non-addresses" had passed, by which the House of Commons had resolved that they would have no further communication with him, and that if any other persons did so, without leave, they should be subject to the penalties of high treason,—the Earl of Kent and Lord Grey began with swallowing the old oaths of "allegiance and supremacy," and having further taken the oath of office, and the oath under the Triennial Act, the Earl of Manchester, Speaker of the House of Lords, surrendered the Great Seal into their hands.[1]

On the first day of Easter Term, Whitelock and Widdrington having returned from the circuit, were sworn in with the same solemnity, and the four Lords Commissioners went in procession from the House of Lords to the Court of Chancery, in Westminster Hall, having the Great Seal carried before them.[2] A salary of £1,000 a year was voted to each of them, to be paid out of the revenue of the customs, in full of all pensions, fees, wages, and allowances from the Crown.[3]

A few days after they had been installed, the Lords Commissioners went into the Court of Exchequer, and having taken their seats on the bench, with the Barons on each hand of them, a great many lawyers and others standing round, they swore in Mr. Sergeant Wilde to be Chief Baron. Lord Commissioner Whitelock appears always to have taken the lead, and he now thus began his address to the new Judge:—

" Mr. Sergeant Wilde,

" The Lords and Commons in parliament, taking notice of the great inconveniency in the course of justice for

---

[1] Lords' Journ. x. 116, 117.   [2] Whitel. 300.
[3] Com. Jour. v. 528. Whitelock says he was a loser by his elevation, as his professional income had amounted to £2,000 a year.
[4] At this time there was great promotion in the law, by order of the two Houses, on the recommendation of the Lords Commissioners; Sergeant Rolle being made Lord Chief Justice of the King's Bench; Jermyn and Browne, puisne Judges of that Court; Solicitor General St. John, Chief Justice of the Common Pleas; Beddingfield and Cresswell, puisne Judges of that Court; Sergeant Wilde, Chief Baron of the Exchequer; and Gates a puisne Baron.

want of the ancient and usual number of Judges in each of the high Courts of Westminster, whereby is occasioned delay, and both suitors and others are the less satisfied, and desirous and careful that justice may be administered *more majorum*, equal rights done to all men according to the custom of England; they have resolved to fill up the benches with persons of approved fidelity and affection to the public, and of piety, learning, and integrity; and having found by long experience among themselves, that you, Mr. Sergeant Wilde, are a person thus qualified, and very well deserving from the Commonwealth, they have thought fit to place you in one of the highest seats of judicature, and have ordained you to be Lord Chief Baron of this Court. The freedom of this choice, without seeking or other means of promotion, this public consent for your preferment, can not but bring much satisfaction to your own conscience, and encouragement to your endeavors, against all burdens and difficulties which attend so great and weighty an employment." He then proceeds at enormous length to dilate upon the antiquity of the Court of Exchequer, and the dignity and duty of the Chief Baron. On this last topic he says, "The life of a Judge is *militia quædam*, if not *martyrium quoddam*, in both which courage is requisite against the assaults of friends, of family, of servants, and the many importunities and temptations which he shall meet withal: and a martyr he must be in bearing provocations, censures, scandals, and reproaches, which will be cast upon every Judge; one party being always displeased, and not sparing, especially in these times, to censure the judgment, be it never so upright. He must want no courage to resist even the highest and greatest powers." He concludes with a warning which one might have hoped would have been unnecessary for the republican Judge. "Hate covetousness, which embraceth bribery. Bribery doth blind the eyes of the wise and pervert judgment. How odious this was to the people of Rome, appears by the oration of Piso, in the senate, mentioned in Tacitus; and in our nation, by the great examples of Justice upon corrupt Judges, as in Edward I.'s time when the Lord Chief Baron, among others was ransomed at 30,000 marks, which in our account at this day is £10,000." He softens all, however, by the quotation—

> "Qui monet ut facias quod jam facis, ille monendo
> Laudat et hortatu comprobat acta suo."

The same term there was a still more elaborate display of his learning and eloquence on a "call of Sergeants," in which Lord Commissioner Whitelock was himself included. The new Sergeants having presented themselves at the bar, he thus addressed them:[1]—"It hath pleased the parliament in commanding these writs to issue forth, to manifest their constant resolution to maintain the old settled form of government and laws of the kingdom,[2] and to manifest their respect for the profession of the law, and to bestow a particular mark of favor upon you as eminent members of it." He then proposes to discourse on the antiquity and dignity of "the order of the Coif," stating many reasons for undertaking the task,—more especially "his own affection to the degree, he being himself the son of a Sergeant, and having the honor to be one of their number in this call, and acknowledging that both in his descent and fortune he was a great debtor to the law." He is particularly indignant when he comes to wipe off an aspersion cast upon the Sergeants by a libelous author, that formerly they publicly plied for business, each having a stand which was against one of the pillars in St. Paul's Cathedral,—"that they kept their pillars at Paul's where their clients might find them,—as if they did little better than *emendicare panem*." He explains this by the custom, upon a call, of every one of them being brought to a pillar in Paul's, and there left for a time for private devotion: "Our English poet Chaucer (whom I think not improper to cite, being one of the greatest clerks and wits of his time) had a better opinion of the state of a Sergeant, as he expresseth in his prologue of 'The Sergeant':—

---

[1] The Commissioners of the Great Seal having sat in the Court of Chancery, hearing motions till past two o'clock, the new Sergeants presented themselves in their parti-colored robes with gentlemen of the Inns of Court. Then came the Judges of the King's Bench, and the Commissioners and Judges went into the Court of Common Pleas, where they took their places on the Bench. When the new Sergeants had counted, their *Colts* delivered rings—first to the Earl of Kent, then to Lord Grey, next to Lord Commissioner Whitelock, then to the Chief Justice, and the other Judges according to their rank.—*Whit. Mem.* 356.

[2] N.B. They were now deliberating about the King's trial—to be followed by the suppression of the House of Lords and abolition of monarchy.

> 'A Sergeant at law, wary and wise,
> That oft had been at the Pervise,
> There was also, full of rich excellence,
> Discreet he was, and of great reverence.'

"And in his description of the Franklin he saith to him:

> 'At Sessions there was he Lord and Sire,
> Full oft had been Knight of the Shire,
> A Sheriff had been, and a Contour;[1]
> Was nowhere such a worthy Vavasour.'[2]

Brook saith that *Serviens ad legem est nosme de dignite comme chevalier;* and it is *character indelibilis*, no accession of honor, or office, or remotion from them takes away this dignity, but he remains as Sergeant still. Their robes and officers, their bounty in giving rings, their feasts, which Fortescue saith were *coronationis instar*, and continued anciently seven days, and Kings and Queens were often present at, and all ceremonies and solemnities in their creation do sufficiently express the state due unto them."[3] He concludes by giving some wholesome advice, the necessity for which does not exalt our ideas of the liberality and honor of the bar in those days: "For your duty to particular clients you may consider that some are rich; yet with such there must be no endeavor to lengthen causes to continue fees. Some are poor; yet their busi-

---

[1] Sergeant.   [2] An ancient title of nobility.

[3] Without any disrespect to the coif, I must be allowed to say that the result of an investigation I had once occasion to make on this subject, was, that anciently the Sergeants, after going into Court at eight, and dining at twelve, did regularly repair in the afternoon to Paul's to meet their clients who resided within the walls of the city of London. This is corroborated by the assignment of a pillar to each on their call, and by the quotation from Chaucer—for the "Pervise" was a sort of *Exchange* at Paul's, where all ranks met to do business. But there was nothing discreditable in this custom. In those times, and long afterwards, barristers of every degree were consulted without the intervention of attorneys. An attorney was only employed in the actual processes of the Court. Even in Anne's reign the counselor used to see his clients, before breakfast and at night, at the coffee-houses around the Temple. (See *The Spectator*.) An eminent counsel in the reign of George IV. talked of reviving this practice, when the attorneys conspired against him. I suppose that in those days the Sergeant or barrister made up his own brief, and himself took what fee he could bargain for, or was customary, from the client. The attorney has now become an adviser, and keeps the key of the barrister's chambers.—So the apothecary has invaded upon the physician.—The young barrister had then also the stewardship of manors; settlement-drawing, even when on circuit—(See *The Clandestine Marriage*, and Hogarth's *Marriage à-la-Mode*)—all now usurped by attorneys. But it is said that some provincial counsel still "keep the market" in the towns near which they reside.

ness must not be neglected if their cause be honest. Some are peaceable; stir them not to strife. Some are contentious; advise them to reconcilement with their adversary. Amongst your clients, and all others, endeavor to gain and preserve that estimation and respect which is just to your degree, and to an honest and discreet person. Among your neighbors in the country, never foment, but pacify contentions. The French proverb is—

    'Bonne terre, mauvais chemin ;
    Bon avocat, mauvais voisin.'

I hope this will never be turned by any here into English."

It seems marvelous to us, although we live in quiet and dull times, that sensible men could then have felt an interest in such mummeries. The treaty of Newport, the last attempt at reconciliation with Charles, had just been broken off, and the crisis of the struggle between the parliament and the army was close at hand. After a debate in the Commons, which lasted three whole days and one night, a resolution was passed against Cromwell's party, "that the offers of the Sovereign furnished a sufficient ground for the future settlement of the kingdom."[1]—The remedy prescribed for such disorders was *Pride's purge*.

The Lords Commissioners had appointed the following day for holding their "second seal after term." When they arrived at the House of Lords' door, a little before eight, they found two troopers there, who denied them entrance, till saying "they were going about Chancery business," they were allowed to pass. They found the Court of Requests, the stairs of the House of Commons, and the passage leading thence down to Westminster Hall, full of soldiers. While they were meditating retreat, Lord Grey de Groby, who was acting in concert with Colonel Pride, came up to them, and advised them to sit, assuring them that they were in no danger, and that the preparations they saw were only against *malignant* members of the House of Commons. They accordingly proceeded to the Court of Chancery, and began to call over the bar for motions. In a little time Lord Commissioner Widdrington was fetched away by a message from Cromwell, who expressed a desire to see him; and a member of the House of Commons came into Court, and mentioned how all who had voted in the preceding night

[1] 3 Parl. Hist. 1239.

were refused permission to take their seats, and many of them had been made prisoners. The Lords Commissioners thereupon rose, thinking that the counsel and suitors could not attend with freedom, and not being without apprehensions for their own personal safety. The Earl of Kent and Lord Grey de Werke asked Lord Commissioner Whitelock to go with them to the House of Peers, where they were sure to be protected. On their way thither they met Colonel Pride and Lord Grey de Groby, watching for obnoxious members, many of whom they had secured; but the Lords Commissioners were allowed to pass unmolested. They were advised by the assembled Peers to return to the Court of Chancery,—but Whitelock would not act without the sanction of the House of Commons. He proceeded thither, and stated the doubt which he and his brother Commissioners entertained as to whether, in the existing confusion, they should sit or adjourn. The party now dominant, afraid of the imputation upon the army, that they interrupted the course of justice, advised the Commissioners by all means to sit, and proceed with business. Whitelock then went to the Court of Wards, where he was joined by the two Peers and Widdrington, and they sat till six in the evening,—when the soldiers were gone, and all was tranquil. Meanwhile Pride excluded ninety-six members and imprisoned forty-seven—reducing the assembly, once so numerous and respectable, to a small number of individuals, who, in the quaint language of the times, were afterwards dignified with the appellation of the "Rump."

As soon as the Court rose, Whitelock and Widdrington went to the house of Lenthal, the Speaker and Master of the Rolls, in Chancery Lane, where they met General Cromwell, and had a long conversation with him respecting the present posture of affairs,—he trying to persuade them that he still hoped for a settlement with the King. Two days afterwards he made them draw up a paper for general circulation, to palliate the violence offered to the House of Commons, and holding out a prospect of the restitution of the secluded members.

But on the 23rd of December a debate arose in the Commons on the proposal for bringing "delinquents" to justice, in which the design of taking off the King was distinctly avowed. Several members made no scruple to mention his Majesty by name, as "the greatest delinquent," and as such to be brought to justice. They said he had been guilty of treason against the nation, and it remained for the representatives of the nation to bring him to punishment; he had shed the blood of man, and God made it a duty to shed his blood in return. They urged that the life of the King was incompatible with their safety; if he were restored, they would become the objects of royal vengeance; if he were detained in prison, the public tranquility would be disturbed by a succession of plots in his favor; and though in private assassination there was something base and cowardly, from which all Englishmen revolted,—to bring him to a public trial would be to proclaim their confidence in the goodness of their cause, would give to the world a splendid proof of the sovereignty of the people and of the responsibility of Kings, and would shed glory on the English name to the latest generation.

Whitelock, and several other members still allowed to sit, disapproved of this course, and contended that the person of the King was sacred; that history afforded no precedent of a sovereign compelled to plead before a judicature composed of his own subjects; that measures of vengeance could only serve to widen the bleeding wounds of the country; and that a deed which would be regarded with horror by the nation would only hasten a reaction in favor of those arbitrary principles which they had hitherto successfully combated.

Cromwell pretended to be neuter. "Sir," said he, "if any man whatsoever have carried on this design of deposing the King and of disinheriting his posterity, or if any man have still such a design, he must be the greatest traitor and rebel in the world; but since Providence has cast this upon us, I can not but submit to Providence, though I am not yet prepared to give you any advice." His wish was well known to be strongly in favor of the measure, and the fear of seclusion and of personal violence lowered the tone and lessened the number of its opponents. They did not venture to divide the House, lest their names should be handed about like those of the "Straffordians," and a committee of thirty-eight members was appointed to receive informations and examinations, and to prepare charges against the King and all other delinquents whom it might be thought fit to bring to condign punishment.¹

On the 26th of December, the Lords Commissioners Whitelock and Widdrington received a summons to attend this Committee. It would have been a great advantage to Cromwell if he could have prevailed on either of them to preside in the High Court of Justice he was planning, from their reputation as lawyers, and the authority they had gained by having sometime filled the highest office in the law; and he had hopes of overcoming their scruples, the one being his kinsman and the other his fast friend. But he was disappointed. They happened to be consulting together on a case which had been argued before them when the summons was served upon them. Whitelock immediately announced his resolution " not to meddle with the King's trial, it being quite contrary to his judgment, as he had freely declared himself in the House." Widdrington said he was of the same opinion, but that he knew not where to go out of the way, that the Committee might not know where to send for him. Whitelock replied, " My coach is ready : I had made up my mind to go out of town this very morning, on purpose to avoid this unhappy business. I pray you go along with me: I shall be glad of your company, and we may remain quiet at my country-house till it is over."

They instantly drove off, and remained concealed till the trial was actually begun. They certainly would have acted a more manly part if they had boldly attempted to prevent that which they so much condemned; and if Bradshaw sincerely approved of the prosecution, he incurred less moral guilt, by accepting the office which they declined.

After their flight, all opposition to the proceeding ceased in the Commons. A preliminary resolution was unanimously voted, "that by the fundamental laws of this kingdom, it is treason in the King of England to levy war against the parliament and kingdom of England;" and an ordinance was unanimously passed constituting a Court of Justice, to consist of the four Lords Commissioners of the Great Seal, the two Chief Justices, the Chief Baron, the Lord Fairfax, Lieutenant General Cromwell, Sergeant Bradshaw, and various other noblemen,

¹ 3 Parl. Hist. 1253.

members of the House of Commons, and military officers, for the trial of CHARLES STUART for the various treasonable offenses recited in the preamble,—which roundly asserts that he is guilty of them, and that he is deserving of condign punishment.

When the resolution and ordinance came to be discussed in the Upper House, there were only thirteen Peers present, the rest being kept away by apprehension, although no actual violence had been used to exclude them. The Earl of Manchester remembered that, when Lord Kimbolton, he had been himself very irregularly prosecuted for high treason by the King's personal order, and knew that it was certainly then intended to proceed to extremities against him and the five members of the House of Commons; yet he began the debate, and generously moved to negative the resolution, and to reject the ordinance. He showed that, by the fundamental laws of England, the parliament consists of King, Lords, and Commons; that the King only hath power to call and dissolve them, and to confirm all their acts; that, without him, there can be no parliament: and therefore that it was absurd to say, "the King can be a traitor against the parliament."

The Earl of Northumberland, who had taken the popular side throughout the contest, now said, "the greatest part, even twenty to one, of the people of England were not yet satisfied whether the King made war against the Houses first, or the Houses first against him; and, besides, if the King did levy war first, there was no law extant to make it treason for him to do so." The Earl of Denbigh complained that the Commons had had the presumption to put in his name as one of the King's Judges, and swore that he would sooner be torn to pieces than have any share in so infamous a transaction. The motion being put to agree with the resolution and ordinance, it was negatived *nemine dissentiente;* and the Lords, rashly presuming that nothing could be done in the way of legislation without their assent, and resolving to avoid any importunity upon the subject, adjourned for a week.—But before that week expired, the shadow of their power had vanished.

The Commons having gone though the form of appointing a committee to examine the Lords' Journals, for the purpose of finding what they had done upon the resolution and ordinance sent up to them respecting the trial of Charles Stuart, and having had a long debate with closed doors, came to the following resolutions: "That the people are, under God, the original of all just power; that the Commons of England in parliament assembled, being chosen by and representing the people, have the supreme power in the nation; and that whatsoever is enacted or declared for law by the Commons in parliament assembled hath the force of law, and all the people of this nation are concluded thereby, although the consent of King or House of Peers be not had thereunto." They then passed an ordinance for the trial of the King in the same terms as the former, only omitting all notice of the Lords.

At the same time it was resolved to have a new Great Seal instead of that hitherto used, which bore the King's name and insignia. A committee appointed to consider the subject reported, that the new Great Seal ought to have on one side the map of England, Ireland, Jersey, and Guernsey, with the arms of England and Ireland, and the inscription, "The Great Seal of England, 1648;"— and that on the other side there should be a representation of the House of Commons sitting,—with the Speaker in the chair,—and the inscription, "In the first year of freedom, by God's blessing restored, 1648." This Seal was immediately ordered, and a sum of £60 was voted towards the expense of making it.[1]

Lords Commissioners Whitelock and Widdrington remained in concealment till they heard that the High Court of Justice had met, had elected Sergeant Bradshaw for President, and had made all the preliminary arrangements for the trial. On the 20th of January, the day when the trial actually began in Westminster Hall, they did not appear when their names were called; but the King having refused to plead, or to recognize the authority of his Judges, the Court rose at an early hour, and the House of Commons sitting as usual, they took their seats in that assembly. In reality, they were acting a trimming, cowardly, and base part, and without incurring the danger of being accessory to the King's death, wished to preserve the favor of the ruling party. Whitelock says,

[1] 2 Parl. Hist. 1255-1258. Com. Jour. vi. 115

"Some looked very shy upon us, but others bid us welcome, and seemed to be glad to see us there."[1]

As Hilary Term ought regularly to have begun on the 23rd of January, and Westminster Hall was entirely occupied with the High Court of Justice, the Lords Commissioners were required to issue an order under the Great Seal for postponing the term, according to a power which had belonged to the prerogative of the Crown; but the Earl of Kent and Lord Grey de Werke positively objected to this, saying that under the "ordinance of the *Lords* and Commons for regulating the Great Seal," which still remained in full force, no act could be done without the concurrence of one noble Commissioner; and the twelve Judges being consulted, declared that without an order under the Great Seal they must go to Westminster Hall, and begin the business of their several Courts at the accustomed time. Whitelock went to the House of Commons and explained this difficulty—when an ordinance was immediately passed commanding him and Lord Commissioner Widdrington, without the concurrence of either of the other Commissioners, to use the Great Seal for all purposes—and the required order was issued, although Kent and Grey were present when it was sealed, and protested against it. The King's trial proceeded without interruption; and on the 27th of January the awful sentence was pronounced, that CHARLES STUART should be beheaded as "a tyrant, traitor, murderer, and public and implacable enemy to the Commonwealth of England."

Lords Commissioners Whitelock and Widdrington were absent from the meeting of the House of Commons held on the 30th of January after the bloody scene had been acted in front of the banqueting house at Whitehall, and they seem to have thought that they were *functi officio*, as there had been no ordinance for the use of the new Great Seal which the House of Commons had ordered. Indeed, Widdrington, who was by much the more scrupulous of the two, had been horror-struck by the King's execution, and for some time adhered to a resolution he expressed not to acknowledge a regicide government.

Lord Grey de Werke retired into the country in despair; but the Earl of Kent, who had firmer nerves, made a dying effort for his office and his order. On the 1st of

[1] Memorials.

February, to which day the House of Lords had adjourned, he and four other Peers met, and having called the Earl of Denbigh to the woolsack, as Speaker, they proceeded to business without taking any notice of the proceedings of the Commons, by which their authority had been disowned. They were willing to have passed a prospective ordinance, " that if hereafter a King of England should try to subvert the fundamental laws of the kingdom, and make war against the Parliament, he should be guilty of high treason, and liable to be brought to trial before a High Court of Justice." On the motion of the Earl of Kent, a message was sent down to the Commons " that the Lords had thought fit to name a committee of nine of their House, in this conjuncture of time, to join with a proportionable number of the Commons to meet the next morning in the Lord Keeper's lodgings, if it might stand with their conveniency, and so from time and place to adjourn as they shall see fitting, to consider of the settlement of the government of England and Ireland. But when the messengers came down to the Commons, the doors of the House were barred against them; and the following day, having renewed their application to be admitted, they met with a similar reception.

A member of the House of Commons who thought that the authority of the Lords might still be useful in carrying on the government, moved "that this House shall take the advice of the House of Peers in the exercise of the legislative power;" but, after a long debate, it was carried in the negative by forty-four against twenty-nine; and then it was resolved, without a division, "that the House of Peers in parliament is useless and dangerous, and ought to be abolished, and that an act be brought in for that purpose." As a malicious pleasantry an amendment was moved and carried, "that Lord Commissioner Whitelock do forthwith prepare and bring in the same."

Whitelock, now dragged from his retirement,—in deep distress came to the House and begged to be excused,— urging that he was not present when the vote passed, and that he had in no way connived in it; but, being told that it was his duty to obey the orders of the supreme power of the state, and finding that all recalcitrants were excluded from office, and even from sitting in the House[1] he yielded, and next morning laid on the table this famous Ordinance,—which, in a few minutes, was read a first and second time, committed, read a third time, passed, and pronounced to be law.

Much more was done on this memorable day. A resolution was moved, that " it hath been found by experience, and this House doth declare, that the office of a King in this nation is unnecessary, burdensome, and dangerous to the liberty, safety, and interest of the people, and ought to be abolished." Lord Commissioner Whitelock having recently acquitted himself so well, was ordered to withdraw and prepare an Ordinance to carry this resolution into effect. He no longer pretended any coyness; and the Ordinance, as he speedily produced it, was immediately hurried through—like that for abolishing the Lords.[2]

An order was then made " that Sir Thomas Widdrington and Mr. Whitelock, the Commissioners of the Great Seal, be required to surrender the Great Seal now in use, bearing the name and insignia of the late King; and that an ordinance be brought in to authorize the use of the new Great Seal made by order of the House, and to appoint them the keepers thereof."

Accordingly, at the sitting of the House next morning, the old Great Seal was produced; and, after it had been broken by a smith, the Speaker being in the chair, the fragments, and the purse with the royal arms embroidered upon it, were given to the Commissioners " for their fees."

The ordinance respecting the new Great Seal was then read a first time;—when Widdrington, courteously but resolutely refused to accept the appointment offered to him. His excuse was accepted, and in consideration of his services, an order was made that he should have a quarter's wages more than was due him, and that he should thereafter be privileged to practice within the bar.

Whitelock then made a long, canting, hypocritical, speech, in which he took care to disclaim all doubt as to the supreme authority of the House. " Unavoidable necessity," said he, " hath put you on these courses, which otherwise, perhaps, you would not have taken. I

[1] An order had been made that no member who had voted for treating with the King should be admitted.   [2] Scobell's Acts, A.D. 1649, c. 16, 17, 27.

am sure, Mr. Speaker, that my acting and sitting here is according to the known laws of England. My protection at this time cometh only from you, and my obedience is due only to you. There is no other visible authority in being in this land but yourselves." But, although he allowed that the highest place of ordinary judicature, to which their favor and good opinion had been pleased to name him, was an object of honorable ambition, and that he should be desirous to do right and justice,—to relieve the oppressed, and to serve God and his country,—he dwelt much on his own insufficiency for so great and weighty a charge. In pointing out its arduous duties, he made observations which, coming from a man regularly bred to the bar, an accomplished lawyer and an experienced Judge, show that "Equity" down to this time had not acquired any systematic form, and was not yet based upon principle. "The Judges of the common law have certain rules to guide them; a Keeper of the Seal has nothing but his own conscience to direct him and that is oftentimes deceitful. The proceedings in Chancery are *secundum arbitrium boni viri* and this *arbitrium* differs as much in different men as doth their complexion or the length of their foot." He therefore implored them to make another and better choice. "But he confessed that, if he declined absolutely, it would be a kind of disavowing of their authority as unwarrantable and illegal,—which was far from him,—and he submitted himself to their pleasure and judgment. This was taken, as it was intended, for acquiescence."[1]

The next person named was John Lisle, who now went by the title of "Major Lisle." He was the son of a respectable gentleman in the Isle of Wight, and was bred to the bar, but was noted for his idleness and profligacy, and never had any practice or knowledge of the law. Being returned a member of the Long Parliament, he was distinguished by his violence against the King. When the war broke out he left his profession and took to arms; but not showing military genius like Ireton and Jones, he

---

[1] Mem. 378. In his Journal he says, "The most considerable particulars which influenced me in this determination were, that I was already very deeply engaged with this party; that the business to be undertaken by me was the execution of law and justice, without which men could not live one by another, a thing of absolute necessity to be done."

never rose above the rank of Major. He is generally represented as having been one of the King's Judges, but he was only assessor, or legal adviser to the High Court of Justice.[1] He was bold, bustling, confident, and unscrupulous. After a short and no eager excuse by him on the score of his incompetence, and his "ready owning the authority of the House to act without King or Lords," his appointment as Commissioner of the Great Seal was carried by acclamation.

A drowsy Sergeant of the name of Keble, known only for some bad Law Reports, was added to the number, and joyfully accepted his appointment.

The ordinance was forthwith passed, constituting these three persons Keepers of the Great Seal *quamdiu se bene gesserint*.[2] The former salary of £1,000 a year was voted to them. A sharp discussion arose whether they should be called "*Lords*" Commissioners, the word "*Lord*" having become distasteful to some; but the opinion of the great majority was, that to drop it would be derogatory to the authority of the parliament.[3]

An order was generously made at the same time, that the arrears due to the Earl of Kent and Lord Grey de Werke, for their salary as Lords Commissioners of the Great Seal, should be immediately paid to them.

[1] For this he was excepted from the general pardon at the Restoration; and though he made his escape, he was assassinated by the royalists at Lausanne.—*Whit.*

[2] I copy the ordinance as a specimen of the manner of legislating which then prevailed: "Be it enacted by the present parliament and the authority of the same that the Great Seal of England shall be committed to the keeping of Bulstrode Whitelock, Sergeant-at-law, Richard Keble, Sergeant-at-law, and John Lisle, Esq., who are hereby appointed Lords Commissioners for that purpose, *quamdiu se bene gesserint*, which said persons are hereby constituted and appointed to be Lords Commissioners for the custody of the Great Seal of England during the time aforesaid, and they or any two of them shall have, and are hereby authorized to have the custody, keeping, ordering, and disposing thereof, as also all such and the like powers and authorities as any Lord Chancellor, Lord Keeper, or Commissioners of the Great Seal of England for the time being, have lawfully had and used, or ought to have had or used."

[3] The preservation of titles is one of the many circumstances which distinguish this revolution and that of France in 1789; but the English Commons had been little aggrieved by aristocracy, and had little objection to it—whereas the injuries and insults heaped upon the *roturiers* by the French *noblesse* created an utter abhorrence and abomination of that order, which still continue, and account for the devoted attachment of the French nation to the law of equal partibility, considered by them the only safeguard against the return of such evils.

The following day the three new Lords Commissioners were sworn in before the House of Commons by the Speaker in these words:—"Whereas, by an act of this present parliament, and by authority thereof, you are made Lords Commissioners of the Great Seal of England, you shall swear that well and truly, according to your skill and knowledge, you will perform your duty in the execution of the said office, according to law, equity, and justice." There was no longer any oath of allegiance or supremacy, and the Triennial Act was considered obsolete. So the Lords Commissioners being ordered to provide a purse for the new Great Seal, with suitable emblems and ornaments, they were dismissed, and proceeded to the Court of Chancery,—where Lord Commissioner Whitelock made a short oration, and intimated that, "on the morrow they should begin to dispatch the business of the suitors, as it was the determination of the parliament, in whom God had placed the supreme power, that right should be done to all, and that justice, like the copious river of Egypt, should overflow and bless the country."[1]

The day following was the day to which the term had been postponed, and there was great confusion in Westminster Hall. Six only of the Judges would agree to serve under the parliament, and they considered their authority gone by the King's death. Early in the morning an ordinance was run through the House of Commons to abrogate the oaths of allegiance and supremacy;—the Lords Commissioners of the Great Seal passed new patents to the Judges;—Lord Commissioner Whitelock made a long speech, explaining and justifying all that had been done;—and then the Judges took their seats in their respective Courts, and the business proceeded as if nothing remarkable had happened.

Cromwell was so well pleased, that he and Ireton, his son-in-law, went home with the Lord Commissioner to

[1] Whitelock, conscious of his equivocal conduct at this time, says, "I resolved to hazard, or lay down all, how beneficial soever or advantageous to me, rather than to do any thing contrary to my judgment and conscience. I paid a visit to the Lord Chief Justice Rolles, a wise and learned man; he seemed much to scruple the casting off of the Lords, and was troubled at it. Yet he greatly encouraged me to attend the House of Commons, notwithstanding the present force upon them, which could not dispense with their attendance and performance of their duty who had no force upon them."—*Whit.* 367, 368.

supper, "where," says Whitelock, "they were very cheerful, and seemed extremely well pleased. We discoursed together till twelve at night, and they told me wonderful observations of God's providence in the affairs of the war, and in the business of the army's coming to London and seizing the members of the House, in all which were miraculous passages. As they went home from my house their coach was stopped, and they examined by the guards, to whom they told their names; but the captain of the guards would not believe them, and threatened to carry these two great officers to the court of guard. Ireton grew a little angry, but Cromwell was cheerful with the soldiers, gave them twenty shillings, and commended them and their captain for doing their duty."[1]

CHAPTER LXX.

LORDS KEEPERS FROM THE ADOPTION OF THE REPUBLICAN GREAT SEAL TILL CROMWELL BECAME "PROTECTOR."

THERE were nominally three Lords Commissioners of the Great Seal, but Whitelock was chiefly looked to; and it is allowed that, though sometimes much harrassed by his colleagues, he presided in the Court of Chancery with impartiality and ability. He was powerfully assisted by Lenthal, who continued Master of the Rolls as well as Speaker, and though occupied at Westminster in the morning, held sittings in the evening at his official house in Chancery Lane.

That the example which the parliament had set might not be imitated, an ordinance was passed to make it high treason to counterfeit the new Great Seal.[2]

The Lords Commissioners were ordered "to take care that all indictments, outlawries, and other acts against any person for adhering to the parliament remaining upon record be searched out, taken off the file, cancelled, and burnt, as things scandalous and void."[3]

While Cromwell was engaged in his Scotch and Irish

---

[1] Whit. Mem. 384.   [2] Scobell's Acts, A.D. 1649, c. 44.   [3] Whit. 449.

campaigns, the march of government was smooth and regular in London, and the holders of the Great Seal were engaged in few transactions which require our notice.

On the 5th of April, 1649, they were ordered to assist at the solemnity of the Lord Mayor-elect being presented to the House of Commons for approbation, when Lord Commissioner Whitelock, taking the purse containing the Great Seal by one corner, and Lord Commissioner Lisle by the other, they carried it up, making obeisances to the Speaker, and laid it on the table, both being in their black velvet gowns; but they were not allowed, as in times of royalty, to express approbation of the choice of the citizens, this task being now performed by the Speaker, as organ of the supreme authority in the state.

Whitelock, in his "Memorials," presents to us a very amusing account of a grand banquet given soon after at Guildhall by the City to the Parliament. The Lord Mayor, when at Temple Bar he met the members of the Commons' House coming in procession, delivered the sword of State, carried before him, into the hands of the Speaker, who graciously restored it to him, after the fashion of the Kings of England. The highest place at the table was assigned to the Speaker, and the next to the Lord General. The Earl of Pembroke then called upon Whitelock, as first Commissioner, to be seated; and on his wishing the old courtier to sit above him, said, in a loud voice to be heard over the whole hall, "What; do you think that I will sit down before you? I have given place heretofore to Bishop Williams, to my Lord Coventry, and to my Lord Littleton: you have the same place that they had, and as much honor belongs to the place under a Commonwealth as under a King, and you are a gentleman as well born and bred as any of them: therefore I will not sit down before you." Whitelock yielded, and had the Earl of Pembroke next him,—the President of the Council and the other Commissioners of the Great Seal sitting lower down.[1] There seems to have been full as much importance attached to such trifles in these republican times as at the Court of Charles I.

A house and grounds at Chelsea, belonging to the Duke of Buckingham, now in exile, were assigned to the Lords

[1] Whit. Mem. Life of Whit. 99. 3 Parl. Hist. 1315.

Commissioners as a private residence. Their general seal days after term they held in the hall of the Middle Temple, of which Lord Commissioner Whitelock continued a bencher.

Six of the common law Judges having refused to act under the parliament—others of learning and character were appointed in their stead, and Lord Commissioner Whitelock, in swearing them in, congratulated them on being the first Commonwealth Judges, and delivered to them a lecture of enormous length, on the duties of their office, which he deduced from the Druids, who were the Judges of the Britons, and the ancient Germans, "'Graff' among whom signified both a Judge and a noble, showing the nobility of Judges."

Among Whitelock's faults and follies, it should be recorded to his honor, that he was most zealous and useful in preserving the medals, books, and monuments of learning which, having belonged to the King personally, had become the property of the state, and which certain Vandals were now eager to sell or to destroy.

I must likewise gratefully mention a noble struggle which he made in the autumn of this year in defense of the profession of the law. One of Cromwell's officers, an ignorant, fanatical fellow, had made a motion "that all lawyers should be excluded from parliament, or at any rate, while they sit in parliament they should discontinue their practice,"—introducing his motion with a violent invective against the conduct of the lawyers both in and out of the House, and being particularly severe upon their loquacity in small causes, and their silence when the lives of their clients were at stake. Whitelock showed that the multiplicity of suits in England did not arise from the evil arts of lawyers, but from the greatness of our trade,—the amount of our wealth,—the number of our contracts,—the power given to every man to dispose of his property as he pleases by will,—and the equal freedom among us, by which all are entitled to vindicate their rights by an appeal to a Court of Justice. He showed that the silence of counselors on capital cases was the fault of the law, which kept them silent; and he "ingenuously confessed that he could not answer that objection, that a man, for a trespass to the value of sixpence, may have a counselor to plead for him; but that, where life and posterity were concerned, he was debarred of that privilege. What was said in vindication or excuse of that custom,—that the Judges were counsel for the prisoner,—had no weight in it; for were they not to take the same care of all causes that should be tried before them? A reform of that defect he allowed would be just."[1] He then showed the valuable services of lawyers in parliament, instancing Sir Edward Coke, with whom he himself had the honor to co-operate in the beginning of the late reign, and who carried "the Petition of Right," and the exertions of St. John, Wilde, and others in the recent struggles. He likewise pointed out the oppressive laws passed at the *Parliamentum Indoctum*, from which lawyers were excluded. "As to the sarcasms on the lawyers for not fighting, he deemed that the gown did neither abate a man's courage or his wisdom, nor render him less capable of using a sword when the laws were silent. Witness the great services performed by Lieutenant General Jones, and Commissary Ireton, and many other lawyers, who, putting off their gowns when the parliament required it, had served stoutly and successfully as soldiers, and had undergone almost as many and as great hardships and dangers as the honorable gentleman who so much undervalued them.[2] With respect to the proposal for compelling lawyers to suspend their practice while they sat in parliament, he only insisted that, in the act for that purpose, it be provided *that merchants should forbear their trading, physicians from visiting their patients, and country gentlemen from selling their corn or wool while they were members of that House*."[3] He was loudly applauded, and the motion was withdrawn.[4]

[1] But it was nearly 200 years before that reform came, and, I am ashamed to say, it was to the last opposed by almost all the Judges.
[2] Whitelock himself served with great distinction.
[3] Life of Whitelock, 109-120.
[4] Although on the rare occasions when it was my duty to speak while a member of the House of Commons, I had the good fortune to experience a favorable hearing, I must observe that there has subsisted in this assembly down to our own times, an envious antipathy to lawyers, with a determined resolution to believe that no one can be eminent there who has succeeded at the bar. The prejudice on the subject is well illustrated by a case within my own knowledge. A barrister of the Oxford circuit taking a large estate under the will of a distant relation, left the bar, changed his name under a royal license, was returned for a Welsh county, and made his maiden speech in top-boots and leather breeches, holding a hunting-whip in his hand. He was most rapturously applauded, till he unluckily alluded to some cause in

Whitelock was a most zealous man and enlightened law reformer. The long vacation of 1649 he devoted, with the assistance of Lenthal, the Master of the Rolls, Keble, his brother Commissioner, and two or three public-spirited barristers, to a review of the practice of the Court of Chancery; and in the following term came out a most valuable set of "Orders" for correcting the abuses which had multiplied there during the late troubles, and for simplifying and expediting the conduct of suits in Equity.[1] These were the basis of the subsequent orders of Lord Clarendon, which are still of authority.

In the following year, on Whitelock's suggestion, a committee was appointed, over which he presided, to consider generally the improvements which might be introduced in the body of the law and the administration of justice.

In 1652, Whitelock prevailed on the parliament to appoint Commissioners, not members of the House, "to take into consideration what inconveniences there are in the law, and how the mischiefs that grow from the delays, the chargeableness, and the irregularities in the proceedings in the law may be prevented, and the speediest way to reform the same." At the head of this commission was placed that most learned and virtuous lawyer, Sir MATTHEW HALE.

They proceeded with great vigor, meeting several times every week in the Chamber in which the Peers had formerly sat, ordering returns from the Judges and the officers in the different Courts, with their fees and duties, examining the most experienced practitioners as to defects and remedies in legal process, and entering scientifically into the whole field of English jurisprudence. They made several valuable reports, but their labors were suddenly interrupted by the violent dissolution of the Long Parliament.

There had for some time been a coolness between Whitelock and Cromwell, in consequence of a private conversation respecting the future plan of government to be adopted. The elated General, after the victories of Dun-

---

which he had been engaged while at the bar—and when it was discovered that he was a lawyer in disguise, he was coughed down in three minutes. In the other House of parliament there is no such prejudice against the law.

[1] See Appendix to Beames's Collection of Chancery Orders.

bar and Worcester, and the subjugation of Ireland, sounded the Lord Commissioner as to the expediency of actually putting the Crown upon his own head; when he was told frankly that the nation would greatly prefer the *Stuarts* to the *Cromwells*, and he was advised to send for Prince Charles and to make him King, on such terms as he might prescribe, whereby he might promote the good of the nation, and for ever secure the greatness of his own family.[1]

Although Cromwell's carriage to Whitelock was thenceforth much altered, he summoned him to attend the meeting of officers of the army and leaders of the independent party, held at his lodgings in Whitehall, the night before he ordered the "bauble" to be removed from the table of the House of Commons. It was here proposed that the Parliament, which had sat above twelve years, should be peremptorily required to pass an act to put an end to its existence,—ostensibly, that the nation might express its will by new representatives,—but, in reality, that the military men might get possession of the civil offices which they considered the just reward of the perils they had undergone. Whitelock, assisted by Sir Thomas Widdrington, his late colleague, strenuously combated this project,—pointing out the glory and prosperity enjoyed under the existing system, and the danger of the attempt to set up a new government, which must lead to tyranny or anarchy,—and strongly asserting that to plot against that authority which they had sworn to respect, was neither consonant to prudence nor justifiable in conscience. The officers of the army, however, inveighed bitterly against the parliament, and declared violently for a change. Cromwell reproved them for these expressions of opinion,—from which those who knew him best conjectured that he had prompted their project, and that he was resolved at all risks to support it. The conference lasted till late at night, when my Lord Commissioner Whitelock went home weary and much troubled in his mind to see the ingratitude and indiscretion of these men. The meeting was resumed before daylight, next morning, and Cromwell himself proposed that the

---

[1] Mem. 548. Cromwell had previously tried to soften him with a present of "a horse and two Scotch prisoners." "The horse," says Whitelock, "I kept for carrying me; the two Scots, unlucky gentlemen of that country, I handsomely sent home again without any ransom."—*Mem.* 484.

present parliament should forthwith be dissolved by its own act, and that a joint council, of officers of the army and those who had served in the House of Commons, should be appointed to rule the affairs of the republic till a new parliament could be assembled. Whitelock again earnestly protested against the formation of such a body, although it was proposed that he should belong to it, and he declared his resolution to stand by the parliament which had conferred such benefits on the country. They separated without coming to any agreement.

Historians profess themselves wholly at a loss to account for the open, imperious and frantic manner in which Cromwell, a few hours after, expelled the members from the House,—which they consider inconsistent with his general character,—not attending to the fact that to gain his object he had previously exhausted all the arts of intrigue, deceit and hypocrisy.

The proposed Council was formed merely as the organ of Cromwell's pleasure, and he published a royal proclamation called "a Declaration by the Council," explaining the reasons of dissolving the late parliament, and requiring all persons to proceed as formerly in the execution of their offices. "The Lord Commissioner Whitelock and his colleagues were in a great quandary what to do till this declaration came out, and did not then proceed in the business of Great Seal; but in a little time, considering that they had their authority from the parliament, they went on as usual."[1] The truth is, that the Lord Commissioner, having given good advice, was generally of a most pliant and conforming temper when his advice had been overruled, and though free from the fumes of fanaticism, was "a waiter upon Providence." He accepted a place in the "Council of State," and though there was no cordiality between him and the President, he abstained from any active opposition to the usurped government. It would be difficult to say where, in law or theory, the sovereign power was supposed to rest between the dissolution of the Long Parliament and the "PROTECTORATE," —but, *de facto*, under the title of "Lord General," Cromwell exercised unlimited sway.

He now resorted to the most absurd and fantastical attempt to constitute a legislative assembly recorded in the

[1] Life of Whitelock, 162. Whit. Mem. 555.

annals of any nation, by calling "Barebones' Parliament." Having succeeded in his late enterprise by means of the violent fanatics, they naturally expected to enjoy power, and his conduct can only be explained by supposing that he was resolved to give them a taste of it, and to demonstrate to them and the world that the government could not be permanently conducted on their absurd principles.

By his own fiat he named one hundred and fifty-six representatives for Great Britain and Ireland,[1] whose qualification was supposed to be that they were "faithful, fearing God, and hating covetousness." One hundred and twenty of these actually attended at the appointed time, and after being inflamed by "a grave, Christian, and seasonable speech" from Cromwell,—in what capacity no one could tell, except that it was believed by his admirers that, on this occasion, "the spirit of God spoke in him and by him,"—and after they had spent several days in "seeking the Lord," praying in turn without the assistance of any chaplain, and affirming that they had never before enjoyed so much of the presence and spirit of Christ,—they at last worked themselves up to the belief that they were divinely inspired, and that the reign of the saints on earth had begun.

In this notable assembly were some persons of the rank of gentlemen; but the far greater part were low mechanics, fifth monarchy men, Anabaptists, Antinomians, Independents—the very dregs of the fanatics.

Having given but an indifferent specimen of their regard to liberty, by prosecuting Lilburne for questioning their authority, and when he had been acquitted by a jury, confining him in the Tower, with an injunction that no obedience should be paid to any writ of habeas corpus in his behalf,—they set about reforming the law. Petitions having been presented complaining of undue delays, vexations, and expenses in the conduct of Equity suits, they disdained to apply palliatives and correctives to such an evil, and resolved "that the High Court of Chancery of England shall be forthwith taken away, and that a bill be brought in for that purpose, and that it be referred to a committee to consider how the causes now depending in Chancery may be determined."

However, more difficulty was experienced in this root-

[1] 139 for England, 6 for Wales, 6 for Ireland, 5 for Scotland.

and-branch reform than had been anticipated. Not only was there a great clamor among the lawyers, "the sons of Zeruiah," as they were called, but all men of sense who attended to the subject were aware that there were many most important rights for which the Courts of law afforded no remedy, and that the proposed measure would be the triumph of fraud and injustice. These considerations were so palpable, that, by degrees, some members of parliament were made to understand them, and to express doubts whether, in this instance, they were not under a delusion of Satan. To give further time for illumination, a resolution was passed to suspend all proceedings in Chancery for one month, the Lords Commissioners for the Great Seal, notwithstanding, being empowered to issue forth, under the Great Seal, "original writs, writs of covenant, and writs of entry," for the purpose of originating actions at law; but a bill for this purpose being introduced, it was finally rejected by the casting vote of the Speaker, the numbers on the division being yeas 39, noes 39.[1]

The abolitionists, however, nothing daunted by this defeat, two days after carried a vote "that the bill for taking away the High Court of Chancery and constituting Commissioners to hear and determine the causes now depending therein, formerly ordered by the House, should be forthwith proceeded with," and it thereupon was read a first and second time, and ordered to be committed. This bill was thrown out on the report; but there was a reference to a select committee to consider what was fit to be done. The committee being nominated by an abolitionist, and composed almost entirely of his party, reported "that another bill should be brought in for taking away the Court of Chancery, and appointing Commissioners to hear and determine as well causes now depending, as also future matters of Equity, and putting in order matters of law which were within the jurisdiction of that Court." Such a bill was accordingly introduced, read a first and second time, and referred to a select committee, who recommended that the famous General Harrison should be added to their number.

But there the bill slept till the members of Barebones' Parliament, themselves convinced of their own insuf-

[1] For the Proceedings of Barebones' Parliament, see 3 Parl. Hist. 1381-1414.

ficiency, voluntarily resigned their authority into the hands of him from whom they had received it, without having passed one single act since they met.[1]

In the meanwhile Whitelock had set out on an embassy to Christina, Queen of Sweden. Cromwell was desirous of having him out of the way during the execution of the scheme now nearly matured; and the Lord Commissioner himself, despairing of being able to ward off the dangers which threatened his Court, was not displeased to submit to this honorable exile, although he had some months before peremptorily refused the offer that he should go to Ireland at the head of a Commission to settle the affairs of that island.

CHAPTER LXXI.

LORDS KEEPERS DURING THE PROTECTORATE OF OLIVER CROMWELL.

WHITELOCK remained absent from England till the 6th of July, in the following year, and on his return found Cromwell regularly installed in the office of Lord Protector, and about to meet a parliament called on the soundest principles of representative government. Scarcely had the Lord Commissioner landed at Gottenburgh on his way to Upsal, when Cromwell, with ill-affected reluctance, agreed to take upon him the office of Chief Magistrate of the State, with the power, though without the name, of King,—pretending that it was forced upon him by the army, and that the public tranquillity required that he should accept it. Lords

[1] A tract on the abuses of the Court of Chancery, published soon after, describes with much drollery the consternation of the legal profession while the bill was depending for abolishing the Court of Chancery: "how sad and sorrowful were the lawyers and clerks for the loss of their great Diana, with their great joy and making of bonfires and drinking of sack, when they were delivered from their fears by the dissolution of the parliament." The imaginative and graphic, but quaint and fantastical Carlyle, in the middle of the nineteenth century, defends the respectability of Barebones' Parliament, and the wisdom of all its proceedings—particularly praising the Bill for the abolition of the Court of Chancery.—Letters and Speeches of Cromwell, vol. ii. 351-434.

Commissioners Lisle and Keble attended the procession to Westminster Hall when this pageant was enacted—jointly carrying the Great Seal before him as he passed through two lines of military, accompanied by the Judges and the Lord Mayor of London; and they administered to him an oath that he would be faithful to the commonwealth, and rule according to the Instrument of Government and other laws of this land.[1] In recompense they were allowed, without molestation, to discharge their judicial duties and to receive their salaries. On the 4th of April, 1654, on the death of Lord Commissioner Keble, Sir Thomas Widdrington, whose scruples were now quieted, was appointed in his place; and on account of the illness of Lisle, on the 30th of May, by warrant under the hand of the Lord Protector, he was appointed to act as sole Commissioner.[2]

Whitelock, now styled Sir Bulstrode, having been created by Christina Knight of the Order of Amarantha, —that he might resume his place as first Lord Commissioner, made no difficulty in recognizing the Protector; and at a grand audience vouchsafed to him at Whitehall, gave "his Highness an elaborate account of his reception at the Swedish Court by the Queen and the Chancellor Oxenstern, and how he had escaped shipwreck by embarking in one of "his Highness's frigates" in the Baltic.[3]

On the 14th of July, Whitelock, Lisle, and Widdrington were sworn in before the Council; and the Lord Protector, after the royal fashion, delivered the Great Seal to them as Lords Commissioners.[4]

Cromwell's second parliament met on the 3rd of September,—a day he considered so auspicious to him. The session was opened with royal splendor, the Protector proceeding to Westminster in a grand state carriage, attended by his life guards. He was followed by the Commissioners of the Great Seal, Whitelock carrying the purse, and by the other officers of state and of the household, all in coaches, bearing swords and other emblems of

---

[1] Whit. 571, 577.
[2] Rot. Claus. 1564, p. 22. When Cromwell was installed Protector, he reappointed the Commissioners of the Great Seal, with the advice of his Council.
[3] See Whitelock's "Journal of his Swedish Embassy"—an amusing book, containing, besides his adventures abroad, some interesting notices of Barebones' Parliament.
[4] Rot. Cl. No. 62, in Petty Bag Office.

sovereignty.' In his speech he boasted much of the appointment of Commissioners to consider how the laws could be made plain, short, and easy,—of putting into the seat of justice men of the most known integrity and ability,—and that the Chancery had been reformed to the just satisfaction of all good men.¹

The Lord Commissioner Whitelock was returned by three constituencies,—the county of Buckingham, the city of Oxford, and the borough of Bedford. He chose to sit for Buckinghamshire, but does not appear to have taken any prominent part in the debates. Other members more adventurous questioned the title of the Lord Protector, and considered whether the government should be in the hands of one individual,—so that, in the month of January, he thought fit, after the manner of the Stuarts, abruptly to dissolve the parliament before it had passed a single act. A bill had been brought in to regulate—not to abolish—the Court of Chancery; but it had not proceeded further than the committee,² and we are not informed of its contents.

Cromwell now for a while assumed legislative power to himself with the advice of his Council, and, under the name of "Ordinances," issued proclamations which he enforced as law. Among these was "an ordinance for the better limiting the jurisdiction of the High Court of Chancery," which had been framed without the slightest communication with the Lords Commissioners, and displayed such ignorance that it might have been the production of General Harrison. The Lords Commissioners were summoned before the Council, where the ordinance was delivered to them, and "they were gravely admonished to be careful not to oppose his Highness's intentions for the common good." Lisle, who was an exceedingly illiterate person as well as very subservient, promised obedience; but Whitelock and Widdrington saw that many parts of the "ordinance" were quite impracticable, and that they should expose themselves to derision if they attempted to put it in execution. Lenthal, the Master of the Rolls, likewise joined them in a remonstrance against it. They represented that it would deprive many persons of their freehold without offense or legal trial, contrary to the Great Charter and various acts of parliament, and they

¹ Carlyle's Cromwell, iii. 22. ² Mem. 600. ³ Com. Jour. vii. 414.

presented a memorial on the proposed rules, showing that in many instances they could not be obeyed, and in others the most mischievous consequences would follow from obeying them. Two of the rules, with the objections to them, may serve by way of specimen of this Chancery Reform:—*Rule.* "Every cause shall be heard and determined the same day it is set down, and for this purpose the Lords Commissioners shall sit if necessary in the afternoon as well as the forenoon, except upon Saturdays." *Objection:*—"This is impossible, for Equity causes depend upon so many circumstances in cases of fraud, that ofttimes three or four days are not sufficient for the orderly hearing of one single cause, and the Commissioners can not sit at the times appropriated to the sittings at the Rolls, as counsel and solicitors can not do their duty in two places at the same time."[1]

Rule.—"No injunction shall be granted to stay the mortgagee from his suit at law, and no injunction shall be granted but upon motion in open court after hearing the merits." *Objection:*—"The mortgagor would often be unjustly turned out of possession, and there is more reason for allowing the interference of a Court of Equity on mortgages than on bonds and other securities, where it is and must be allowed. By the negation to the granting of injunctions in cases of waste, timber might be felled, houses pulled down, meadows and ancient pasture plowed up, to the irreparable loss of the plaintiffs and the Commonwealth."[2]

The Lords Commissioners went on for a whole term after the making of the "ordinance," refusing to observe it. Whitelock said, "that he had taken an oath to execute the place of Commissioner of the Great Seal legally and justly, and for him to execute that 'ordinance' as a law, when he knew that those who made it had no legal power to make law, could not be justified in conscience, and would be a betraying of the rights of the people of England."

The day after term they were summoned before the

---

[1] It was not then foreseen that there would be five courts of Equity sitting together in Westminster Hall.

[2] I find one regulation, however, more reasonable—"that the Masters in Chancery shall sit in public;" to which the only objection was, "that it was so worded as to take away the power of excepting to their Report."

Lord Protector and the Council, and ordered to bring the Great Seal with them,—which they knew was the signal of their dismissal.

His Highness told them " that every one was to satisfy his own conscience in a matter to be performed by himself, and that he had not a worse opinion of any man for refusing to do that which he was dubious of; but that the affairs of the Commonwealth did require obedience to authority, and that the Great Seal must be put into the hands of others who might be satisfied that it was their duty to perform that command.

Whitelock and Widdrington both tried to justify themselves; but the Protector required them to lay down the Seal, and to withdraw. Having, after the example of the Kings, kept the Seal some days in his own possession and personally directed the sealing of various instruments, without any Lord Chancellor, or Lord Keeper, or Lords Commissioners, he delivered it to a new Lord Commissioner,—Colonel FIENNES, a soldier,—and to the noted Major LISLE, " a man for all essays, who had no other knowledge of the business he undertook beyond the little he had learned by accompanying the late Commissioners." " In presence of his Highness and his Council, they took the oaths appointed by his Highness and his Council to be taken."[1]

" Thus," says Whitelock, my fortunes and interest decreased; and now my pretended dear friends and frequent visitors withdrew themselves from me, and began neither to own nor to know me: such is the course of dirty worldlings."[2]

He returned to the bar, and at once got into full practice; but Oliver soon made him and Widdrington Commissioners of the Treasury, with a salary of £1,000 a year.[3]

Nathaniel Fiennes, the new Lord Keeper,—placed the first in the commission, I presume, on account of his superior military rank,—was the second son of Viscount Say and Sele. Having left the University, he passed a short time in the Inns of Court, but merely to finish his general

---

[1] Cl. R. 1625, p. 8, n. 26.
[2] Mem. 627. This is but an indifferent specimen of republican manners, and affords a great contrast with our own times when loss of office does not imply loss of friends.—See Carlyle's Cromwell, iii. 126.
[3] The following year Whitelock officiated at Oliver's installation, " having a drawn sword in his hand."—*Mem.* 661.

education without any view to the profession of the law. He sat for Banbury in the parliament which met in the beginning of 1640, and again in the Long Parliament, and was much in the confidence of Pym and the popular leaders. When hostilities began he had a commission given him, first to be a captain, and afterwards a colonel of horse, under the Earl of Essex, General of the parliamentary forces. Inspiring confidence by his military ardor, he was made Governor of Bristol; but, to the great disappointment and indignation of his whole party, he surrendered that city to Prince Rupert, after a very feeble defense.—He was brought to trial before a court-martial for cowardice, and condemned to death;[1] but by the intercession of his father, he was pardoned, and he afterwards published a justification of his conduct, which very much reinstated him in public opinion. Although not afterwards trusted with any command in the army, he obtained considerable influence in the House of Commons, and was a very active committee-man. He was, for a long time, a violent Presbyterian, and supporter of the Solemn League and Covenant. In consequence, he was expelled from the House by Pride's purge. But he then made a sudden wheel,—struck in with the Independents,—favored the ascendency of the army, and became a tool of Cromwell. Hence his present promotion to the Bench; and the highest civil office in the state was committed jointly to a Colonel and a Major.

I do not find any particular account of the manner in which Lords Commissioners Fiennes and Lisle discharged their judicial duties, although there were loud complaints of their general incompetency. However, their appointment was sanctioned by Oliver's third parliament,[2] and they remained in office till his death.

[1] 4 St. Tr. 186.
[2] On the 10th of October, 1655, there came the following message from his Highness, addressed, "To Our right trusty and right well beloved Sir Thomas Widdrington, Knight, Speaker of the Parliament:

"OLIVER, P.

"Right trusty and well beloved, We greet you well. It being expressed in the 34th article of the Government that the Chancellor, Keeper, or Commissioners of the Great Seal shall be chosen by the approbation of parliament, and in the intervals of parliament, by the approbation of the major part of the Council, to be after approved by the parliament, and We having before the meeting of the parliament appointed, with the approbation of the Council, Our right trusty and right well beloved Nathaniel Fiennes and John

It may be presumed that they continued the practice of calling in the assistance of the Judges; and we must remember that the common-law bench never was better filled, the Protector not only having said that he wished to govern by "red gowns rather than red coats," but having actually appointed Hale, and the most distinguished and honorable lawyers in the profession to preside in the Upper Bench, the Common Bench, and the Exchequer. The Equity business in Chancery must have had valuable assistance from Lenthal, who, released from his duties as Speaker of the House of Commons, continued Master of the Rolls, and was noted for his assiduity and ability as a Judge.

The two Lords Commissioners of the Great Seal were, at all events, very active politicians, and unscrupulously exerted themselves in fulfilling all the wishes of their master. When pressed for money, and trusting to the popularity he thought he had acquired by his successes against Holland and Spain, and the submissive manner in which his alliance was courted by France, he ventured to call another parliament,—Colonel Fiennes and Major Lisle regulated the preliminary proceedings of the Council of State, by which, to secure a majority in spite of the unfavorable result of the elections, nearly one hundred of the members returned were pronounced disqualified and incapable of sitting, under the pretext of "immorality" or "delinquency." On the day of meeting, when the members had returned to their own House from the Painted Chamber, after the Protector had harangued them, none were allowed to enter without a certificate of being "approved by his Highness's Council;" and loud complaints being made of the exclusions, Lord Commissioner Lisle put them in mind, that their first work was to choose a Speaker, and proposed Sir Thomas Widdrington, Ex-Commissioner of the Great Seal (now devoted to Cromwell), as a person of great integrity and experience in

Lisle, Commissioners of the Great Seal of England, I have thought it necessary to transmit to you their names, to the end that the resolution of parliament may be known concerning their approbation, which I desire may be with such speed as the other public occasions of the Commonwealth will permit, and so I bid you heartily farewell." The required approbation was given forthwith. Sergeant Glynne was approved of the same day as Chief Justice of the Upper Bench, from which it has been erroneously supposed that he was made a Commissioner of the Great Seal.—See *Hardy's Chancellors*, 74.

relation to parliamentary business, and every way qualified for that service. Widdrington being placed in the chair, a motion was made, that the excluded members be permitted to take their places, as it was for the House to decide upon the qualifications of its members; but here Lord Commissioner Fiennes pointed out that by the " Instrument," which now regulated the constitution of the government, the Lords of the Council were to see that no papists or delinquents should be returned to serve in parliament, and asserted, that this trust being vested in them, they had discharged it according to the best of their judgment. It could not be denied that such was the provision of the "Instrument;" but that the Council should decide on secret information, and without the knowledge of the constituents or representatives, was alleged to be contrary to the first principles of justice. By dint of numbers, a motion was carried "that the House should pass to the business of the nation."

Under such management, an act was easily carried for excluding Charles Stuart and his family from the Crown, and the House was prepared for the motion, that the title of King should be offered to Cromwell. This motion was to have been made by Ex-Commissioner Whitelock; but he quailed when the day for it arrived, and the task devolved on Alderman Pack, one of the representatives for the city of London.[1] The resolution being carried without difficulty, the two Lords Commissioners of the Great Seal, with Whitelock, Lenthal, Lord Broghill, and others were appointed to communicate it to his Highness, and to solicit his concurrence. The conferences lasted several days, during which Lords Commissioners Fiennes and Lisle repeatedly addressed his Highness, and, in trying to remove his affected scruples, certainly display more legal acuteness and constitutional learning than could possibly have been expected from their military breeding.[2]

[1] Some time before, by way of a *feeler*, Jephson, during a debate in the House of Commons, had thrown out this suggestion in a random manner, and it was not ill received. When Cromwell afterwards asked him in private what could induce him to do so, "As long," said Jephson, "as I have the honor to sit in parliament, I must follow the dictates of my own conscience, whatever offense I may happen to give to your Highness." "Get thee gone," said Cromwell, giving him a friendly slap on the shoulder, "get thee gone for a mad fellow as thou art."

[2] The most eloquent speaker on this occasion was Lord Broghill, afterwards famous as Earl of Orrery, and he was ably supported by Whitelock

There was no difficulty in convincing the person to whom their arguments were addressed, as the scheme was his own, and he ardently wished to accomplish it. The negotiation was prolonged in the hope of softening the opposition to it among the officers of the army, who aspired to the office of Protector in their turn,—among the determined republicans, who had sworn never again to submit to hereditary rule,—and among the members of the Protector's own family, several of whom were zealous royalists, and were constantly urging him to restore the ancient family. After long hesitation, his apprehensions of insurrection or assassination prevailed, and we do not find the name of Oliver I. in the list of the Kings of England.

But his answer being merely that "he would not undertake the government *with that title of King*," the parliament remodeled the constitution by "the Petition and Advice," in such a way as might lead to hereditary limited monarchy, under "Protectors;" and if Richard had possessed any portion of his father's energy, there might have been a change of dynasty, and, with the advantage of the incorporating union which had been forcibly accomplished with Scotland and Ireland, the nation might sooner have reached the freedom, prosperity, and happiness which it has enjoyed under the mild sway of the House of Brunswick. The Protector was now empowered to name his successor, and "to call parliaments consisting of two Houses," which he construed into a right to create Peers. As soon as his grand inauguration was over,[1] he prorogued parliament, without dissolving it, —that he might have time to model his new House of Lords, which was to be brought into action at the commencement of the following session.

After long deliberation, the Lords Commissioners of the Great Seal were directed to issue writs of summons to the new Lords in the terms of the writ of summons to

and Lenthal. See the speeches at length in the *Life of Whitelock*, pp. 275-295, and an admirable summary of them in Hume, vol. vii. 271.

[1] At this ceremony Lord Commissioner Whitelock acted a conspicuous part, assisting the Speaker to clothe the Protector in his purple robe, to gird the sword about his Highness, and to deliver into his hand the scepter of massy gold—and when the trumpets sounded and the heralds proclaimed him, joining in the shouts of *God save the Lord Protector! ! !—Whit.* 662. Carlyle's Cromwell, iii. 273-316.

Peers under the monarchy; and the Judges gave it as their opinion that those who sat under these writs would gain a peerage in fee descendible to their posterity.[1] At the top of the list of those summoned were the names of the Protector's two sons—the Lord Richard and the Lord Henry Cromwell (as Princes of the Blood), and, next, Lord Fiennes and Lord Lisle, the Lords Commissioners of the Great Seal. Afterwards follow the names of Lord Whitelock, of Lord Morpeth, ancestor of the present Earl of Carlisle, and of Lord Monk (the Restorer). Four or five of the old nobility were summoned, but they refused to attend; and Sir Arthur Hazelrig, and two or three other members of the House of Commons who were included, wisely preferred to continue to sit there.[2]

On the day appointed for the re-assembling of parliament the session was opened by the Lord Protector with all the forms and all the pomp of the ancient sovereigns. The new Lords met in the old chamber which was ornamented with the tapestry of the Armada. A chair of state was there placed for his Highness, resembling the throne. There were no Bishops, for they had been excluded by Charles; but in their place the Judges, in scarlet and ermine, were seated on the right of the throne. The Lord Protector, in splendid attire, and wearing a hat with a gold band, attended by his great officers, and surrounded by his Life Guards, having come from Whitehall in a carriage more splendid than Stuart ever sat in, and seated himself under the "cloth of state,"—the Gentleman Usher of the Black Rod was sent to command the immediate attendance of the Commons, in the name of his Highness. They soon appeared at the bar, headed by Widdrington, their Speaker; and the two Lords Commissioners of the Great Seal, with the other great officers

---

[1] The original warrant was "for the Commissioners of the Seal, with the advice of the Judges, to prepare and frame a writ for summoning the members of the other House of parliament to meet at such time and place as shall be appointed by his Highness; and the Commissioners are to seal such writs and to issue them out to such persons as his Highness, under his sign-manual, shall direct and appoint."—*Whit.* 662.

[2] For an analysis of this House of Peers, see *Carlyle's Cromwell*, iii. 390. Cromwell likewise created knights and baronets, by what authority I know not, for it is not given by the "Instrument of Government," or the "Petition and Advice." Not being a knight himself, he could not deal according to the ancient usages of chivalry, but he must have had the opinion of his law officers on the subject, for both his Attorney and Solicitor General became baronets.—*Whit Mem.* 674.

standing by his side, his Highness, to the great scandal of true republicans, thus began:—

"My Lords, and Gentlemen of the House of Commons."
—After a speech much shorter than his usual tiresome, embarrassed harangues, he said that Lord Commissioner Fiennes would explain more fully the reasons for now calling parliament together; and the Lord Commissioner accordingly delivered a long address to the two Houses, by way of enlargement on that of his Highness; comparing the present state of England to the rising of Cosmos out of chaos, as recorded in Genesis; and observing that "*two firmaments* are made two separate houses of parliament."[1]

But this first attempt at a restoration of the ancient constitution, with modern amendments, proved wholly abortive. Cromwell was much weakened in the Commons by transferring so many active supporters to the other House; and there being an article in "the Petition and Advice" that each House should judge of the qualification of its members, the excluded representatives were all admitted to take their seats, so that there was immediately a decided majority against the Government.

The Peers, however, with Lord Fiennes on the woolsack, having taken the oaths, proceeded to business, and on the second day after their meeting came unanimously to a resolution, "that an humble address be presented to the Lord Protector, praying that his Highness would be pleased to appoint a day of public humiliation throughout the three nations." Two Judges, Wyndham and Hill, were sent down to the Commons to communicate this resolution, and to ask them to concur in the address. The messengers were admitted, and allowed to deliver their message; but when they had withdrawn, a motion being made that they be again called in and informed that this House concurs in the address to his Highness, an amendment was moved, by an opposition member, that "this House will send an answer by messengers of their own;" and, after a sharp debate, the amendment was carried by a majority of 75 to 51. His Highness, greatly enraged at this rebuff, sent for the Commons to Whitehall (without the Lords), and read them a severe

[1] Carlyle's Cromwell, iii. 399. This was an approach to the ancient fashion on such occasions, of taking a text from Scripture as a thesis.

lecture on their contumacy; but this only led to a complaint of breach of privilege, and a debate on the appellation and powers of the other House,—with the expression of some doubts as to the validity of the " Petition and Advice," on the ground that it had not been voted by a free parliament.

"Their new Lordships, desirous to try the pulse of the Commons once more."[1] sent a message to them in writing, by two of the Judges, on a subject expected to rouse all their sympathy, "that the Lords desired the Commons to join with them in an address to the Lord Protector, that his Highness would be pleased to issue a proclamation, by the advice of both Houses, commanding all Papists and others who had been in arms against the Commonwealth, to depart out of London and Westminster, and twenty miles thereof, by a certain day." But as soon as the message was delivered, the Commons resolved, without a division, "that they would send an answer by messengers of their own."

The next morning news was brought to Cromwell, at Whitehall, that they were resuming the debate on "the appellation and powers of the other House;" when, not staying for his state carriage, he threw himself into a hackney-coach standing by, drawn by two shabby horses, and attended only by six of his guards, whom he beckoned to follow him, he proceeded to the House of Lords, and sending the Gentleman Usher of the Black Rod for the Commons, made them an angry speech, which he concluded with these words:—"I think it high time that an end be put to your sitting, and I do dissolve this parliament, and let God judge between you and me."[2]

A bill had been introduced into the House of Commons this session " for better regulating and limiting the jurisdiction of the Court of Chancery, but, along with various others, it was lost by the hasty dissolution."[3]

The Protector was now obliged, on the discovery of a royalist plot, to resort to a very arbitrary measure, by establishing a High Court of Justice, which was to decide on life and death without a jury, and without the control of any known law. The Lords Commissioners of the

---

[1] 3 Parl. Hist. 1524.   [2] 3 Parl. Hist. 1525.   Carlyle's Cromwell, iii. 432.
[3] Com. Jour. vii. 527, 528.

Great Seal were placed at the head of it, and Lord Lisle acted as President.

I will give a short specimen of the judicial mildness of this protectorial functionary on the trial of Colonel Slingsby, which may soften our resentment against the tyranny of the Stuart Judges:—*Lord Lisle.* " Thou here standest charged for high treason; this Court requires that thou give a positive answer whether guilty or not guilty."—*Slingsby.* "I desire to have counsel assigned me."—*Lord Lisle.* "There is matter of fact laid to your charge which amounts to treason, and there is no counsel allowed in matter of fact."—*Slingsby.* "There is also matter of law, and I desire to be tried by a jury which is according to the law of the land."—*Lord Lisle.* "We are all here your jury as well as your judges; we are the number of two or three juries."—*Slingsby.* "If it be by the law of the land that the trial shall be by a jury, I desire I may have that privilege."—*Lord Lisle.* "Acts of parliament make justice and law: they are both. They think fit to change the custom of trials that have been in former times."—*Slingsby.* "I desire that the act of parliament may be read."—*Lord Lisle.* "You are before your jury and judges. Parliament have great care of the rights of the people, and have appointed this Court; and his Highness hath appointed you to be tried by us. All must submit to my Lord Protector. We sit here by authority of his Highness by a commission under the Great Seal, and by authority of parliament, and you must submit to our authority." The prisoner was convicted for having acted under a commission from Charles II., and in passing sentence of death, Lord Lisle thus addressed him: " It grieves my very soul to think that, after so many signal providences wherein God seems to declare himself, as it were, by signs and wonders, that your heart should be still hardened, I may say, more hardened than the very hearts of the Egyptians; for they, at length, did not only see, but confessed, that the Lord fought against them; but you, oh, that you would confess and give glory to God! You can not choose but see that the Lord fights against you, that the stars in their courses fight against you; and yet you will not see, you will not confess, until destruction overtakes you."[1]

[1] 5 St. Tr. 871.

The frightful common-law sentence for high treason was pronounced, all which his Highness was pleased to remit —*except decapitation.*

Whitelock refused to serve on this high Court; yet he continued in favor with the Protector, who himself had a regard for law and justice, as far as was consistent with the enjoyment of his own authority.[1] A patent was even signed by him for raising Whitelock to the dignity of a Viscount. This honor was declined by the Lord Comisioner; but under his former writ of summons to the House of Lords, it was considered that his blood was ennobled; he was treated as a Baron, and he was designated Lord Whitelock till the Restoration.[2]

When the next anniversary of the great victories of Dunbar and of Worcester came round Oliver expired, and it is generally supposed that the day was still auspicious to him; but such had continued to be the success as well as vigor of his administration, so much was he dreaded by foreign states, and so much was he respected at home, not only for raising the national credit to a pitch unknown since the days of the Plantagenets, but for the desire which he had shown to govern according to law, and to improve our institutions, that if his life had been prolonged, there seems reason to think he might have overcome all the difficulties which surrounded him, and that, notwithstanding the imbecility of Richard, his scepter might have been long borne by his posterity.[3]

---

[1] "The government of Cromwell was, to be sure, somewhat rigid, but for a new power, no savage tyranny. The country was nearly as well in his days as in those of Charles II., and in some points much better. The laws in general had their course, and were admirably administered."—Burke, *Remarks on Policy of the Allies.*

[2] I only find one other creation by Oliver above the degree of a Baron, "Viscount Howard of Morpeth, July 20, 1657, afterwards created by Charles II., Baron Dacre, Viscount Howard of Morpeth, and Earl of Carlisle, April 30, 1661."   [3] See Carlyle's Cromwell, iii. 448-460.

CHAPTER LXXII.

LORDS COMMISSIONERS OF THE GREAT SEAL FROM THE DEATH OF CROMWELL TILL THE RESTORATION.

ON the doubtful assertion that Oliver, according to the power conferred upon him by the Petition and Advice, had duly named his eldest son as his successor, Richard was immediately proclaimed Lord Protector in London and throughout the kingdom,—with all the solemnities practiced on the accession of a new Sovereign. Nay, addresses to him came pouring in from all classes in a manner greatly to lower the value of such supposed tokens of affection,—pledging "lives and fortunes" in his support,—and declaring, "that though the sun had set no night followed," and that, "though Providence by one sad stroke had taken away the breath from their nostrils, it had given them in return the noblest branch of that renowned stock—a prince distinguished by the lovely composition of his person, and still more by the eminent qualities of his mind."

The new Protector at first graciously confirmed the Great Seal to the military Lords Commissioners, Lord Fiennes and Lord Lisle; but hearing loud complaints of their incompetency, he soon after, while sitting in Council, desired them to surrender it, and re-delivered it to them jointly with Lord Whitelock, in whose judicial integrity and ability he and the public entertained the highest confidence.[1]

Writs of summons for a new parliament having been issued by the Lords Commissioners under the Great Seal, the session was opened by Richard according to royal forms, except that, having addressed both houses himself

[1] "Dec. 30. I went about the business of the Great Seal, whereof I was now again made a Commissioner. Richard had a particular respect for me and upon the 22nd of this month, by advice of some near to him, without any seeking for it by me, I was sent for to Whitehall, where I met the two Lords Commissioners of the Seal, Fiennes and Lisle, and they together being called to the Council Chamber, the Great Seal was delivered to his Highness sitting in Council, and his Highness presently delivered it to Fiennes, Lisle, and me, as Keepers of the Great Seal of England."—*Whit.* 676. He adds that his appointment was generally attributed to Fiennes, who had found Lisle incompetent.

in a very sensible speech, he did not call upon any Keeper of the Great Seal further to explain the reasons for assembling them.

The three Commissioners, being all ennobled, took the oaths with the other Peers, Lord Whitelock presiding on the woolsack. But they could never get any further recognition of their "order" from the Commons, than "that this House will transact with *the persons now sitting in the other House as a House of Parliament* for the present, without prejudice to the privilege of such Peers as have been faithful to the parliament, of being duly summoned to be members of that House." The parliament was soon found wholly unmanageable, and a majority of Richard's council advised him to dissolve it, and to trust rather to the combination of military officers now struggling for supreme rule. This step was strongly opposed by Lord Whitelock, who foretold that it would eventually lead to the destruction of the Protectorate; but he was overruled, and a commission was made out for dissolving the parliament, Lord Fiennes being named the head Commissioner. The commission being announced to the Lords, and the Commissioners having taken their seats under the steps of the throne, the Black Rod was ordered to summon the Commons to the bar; but they declared they would receive no communication from the Lords except by members of that House, and adjourned for three days. Lord Fiennes, however, in the absence of the Commons, ordered the commission to be read, and in the name of his Highness, the Lord Protector, dissolved the parliament. A proclamation under the Great Seal communicated the information to the nation the same afternoon.[1]

By this dissolution Richard had signed his own deposition. Although he continued to reside at Whitehall, he was deserted by all the world, and the government was in complete abeyance till the council of officers thought fit to restore the Long Parliament, thinking they would have a better chance of power by possessing such an instrument under their control. A majority of the surviving members were Presbyterians and Royalists, but they were still prevented by violence from entering the House, and the "Rump," consisting chiefly of those who had voted

---

[1] 3 Parl. Hist. 1544.

for the King's death, did not exceed the number of seventy.

The new House of Lords had vanished like a morning mist, and Whitelock was allowed to take his place in the Commons as a member for Buckinghamshire, for which he had been returned in 1640; but he was much too moderate and too much of a trimmer to be in favor with the ruling faction, and their first step was to deprive him and his colleagues of the custody of the Great Seal. Two days after the Rump re-assembled they agreed to a resolution "that a new Great Seal be with all speed prepared and brought into this House, according to the form of the last Great Seal made by authority of this parliament, and that the last Great Seal be brought into this House to be broken before the parliament."

A new Great Seal being made, an act was passed for appointing Lenthal the sole Keeper of it for eight days, and for ordering the old Great Seal to be broken.[1]

The old Seal being brought into the House by Lord Whitelock, was accordingly broken by a smith into several pieces, which were given to the Ex-Commissioners for their fees, and the new Seal was put into the hands of Lenthal as "Lord Keeper for the Commonwealth." There being great difficulty in the selection of those who were permanently to hold it, another act was passed to continue him some time longer in the office.

In the meanwhile the parliament resolved "that the Court of Chancery be thoroughly reformed and regulated,

---

[1] "An act for the Great Seal of England: Be it enacted by this present parliament and the authority of the same, that the Seal on the side whereof is engraven the maps of England, Ireland, and the Isles of Jersey, Guernsey, and Man, with the arms of England and Ireland, and this inscription, viz., 'The Great Seal of England, 1651,' and on the other side the sculpture of the parliament sitting, with this inscription, viz., ' In the third year of freedom, by God's blessing restored, 1651,' shall from henceforth be the Great Seal of England, and none other, and shall be and is hereby authorized and established to be of the like force, power, and validity, to all intents and purposes, as any Great Seal of England hath heretofore been or ought to be, and that W^m. Lenthal, Speaker of the parliament, be and he is hereby nominated, constituted, and appointed Keeper of the Great Seal of Commonwealth of England, to have, hold, exercise, and enjoy the said office to the said W^m. Lenthal, from this 14th day of May, 1659, for the space of eight days from hence next ensuing, and no longer, and that in as full, ample and beneficial manner to all intents and purposes as any Lord Chancellor of England, Lord Keeper, or Lords Commissioners of the Great Seal may, might, should, or ought to have had, exercised, or enjoyed the same."—*Scobell's Acts*

and that the whole profits, fees, and perquisites arising from the office of Keeper of the Great Seal, should be sequestered and go to the use of the Commonwealth."[1]

The nomination of the new Commissioners of the Great Seal was referred to "the Council of State," and they recommended Bradshaw, who had presided at the King's trial, with Terryll and Fountain, two lawyers known only for their violent republican principles. There was an objection made to the appointment of such men, but it was carried by a majority of 43 to 15. The Commissioners were introduced into the House, and marching up to the table, with three reverences to the speaker, received the Great Seal from him after he had administered to them the following oath: "You shall swear that you shall be true and faithful to this Commonwealth, as it is declared by parliament, without a single person, Kingship, or House of Peers, and that you shall well and truly execute the office of Commissioners of the Great Seal of England, according to the best of your skill, knowledge, and power."[2]

They were ordered to pass a Commission to authorize the Master of the Rolls, with certain Judges and Masters in Chancery, to hear causes after taking the prescribed oath of allegiance to the Commonwealth, and abjuration of Kingship and House of Peers.[3] These three Commissioners remained in possession of the Great Seal for five months, while the "Rump" was permitted to sit, and was ostensibly the supreme power in the State; but I do not find any account of their judicial proceedings.[4] In the distracted condition to which the nation was reduced the administration of justice must have been nearly suspended, and the executive government was carried on jointly by the parliament and the council of officers.

The dissensions between these bodies ended in General Lambert, with a body of 3,000 guards, intercepting the Speaker in Palace Yard as he was proceeding to take the chair, and forcibly preventing him or any of the members

---

[1] Com. Jour. vii. 670. Whitelock, 680.
[2] The oath was administered to them "holding up their hands," from which I conjecture that the ceremony of *kissing the book* was then abolished.
[3] Com. Jour. vii. 728.
[4] During all this time Bradshaw had been ill of a quartan ague, of which he died on the 31st of October, "a stout man and learned in his profession: no friend to monarchy."—*Whit.* 686

from entering the House of Commons. Thus the Rump was again ignominously expelled, and the officers assembled at Wallingford House were for a time the supreme power in the State. That their rule might appear to be in some degree tempered by the presence of a civilian, they issued the following missive to Whitelock, judging from his pliable character that he would not much obstruct their schemes:—

"To our honored Friend, Bulstrode, Lord Whitelock.
"Sir,
"Upon consideration of the present posture of affairs of this Commonwealth, the General Council of Officers of the Army have thought fit to appoint a Committee of Safety for the preservation of the peace and management of the present goverment thereof; as also for their preparing of a form of a future government for these nations upon the foundation of a Commonwealth, or free state: and yourself being one of the persons nominated for that purpose, we do, by their direction, hereby give you notice thereof, and desire you to repair to-morrow morning, at ten o'clock, to the Horse-chamber at Whitehall, in order to the service aforesaid."

Whitelock's character will be best appreciated by allowing him now to speak in his own person: "I was in some perplexity what to do upon this letter, and had much discourse with my friends about it. Desborough and some other great officers of the army, actors in this business, came to me, and made it their earnest request to me to undertake the trust, and told me that some had a design to overthrow magistracy, ministry, and the law, and that, to be a balance to them, I and some others had been chosen to oppose this design, and to support and preserve the laws, magistracy, and ministry in these nations: that if I should deny to undertake the charge, it would much trouble the General Council of Officers, and be of great prejudice to the intended settlement; and therefore they most earnestly desired me to accept of this employment. I had resolved in my mind the present state of affairs; that there was no visible authority or power for government at this time but that of the army; that if some legal authority were not agreed upon and settled, the army would probably take it into their hands, and govern by the sword, or set up some form prejudicial to the rights and privileges of the people, and for the particular advantage and interest of the soldiery, and that to prevent these evils, and to keep things in a better order and form, I might be instrumental in this employment. Upon these and the like grounds, I was persuaded to undertake it, and did meet with them at the place appointed, where I was received by them with all respect and civility."[1]

The first act of the new government was to restore the Great Seal to the keeping of the gentleman who had first sent in his adhesion, and the following order was made:—

"At the Committee of Safety, at Whitehall.

"The Committee of Safety, taking into consideration the necessity of disposing of the Great Seal so as the same may be made use of for the public service, and the administration of justice,

"Ordered that the custody of the Great Seal of England be committed to the Lord Whitelock, as Commissioner and Keeper of the said Great Seal until further order. And the same was accordingly delivered to his hands by the Lord President, and ordered that an entry of the delivery of the Great Seal to the said Lord Whitelock as Commissioner and Keeper of the said Great Seal be made in the Close Roll in Chancery.[2]

"WM. ROBINSON,
"Clerk of the Committee of Safety."

It does seem most extraordinary that a lawyer of Whitelock's reputation and abilities could be induced to take his seat among these military chiefs, so notorious for their fanaticism, their violence, and their utter ignorance of the principles on which mankind are to be governed. The present revolution was received with more general disapprobation than any preceding change which had surprised and perplexed the nation since the death of the last King. There was no regret for the "Rump;" but all thinking men were alarmed to find themselves under the capricious and arbitrary rule of military adventurers, without a leader to correct their extravagance or to soften their violence.

For two months did Lord Keeper Whitelock continue with that title in possession of the Great Seal. Apart-

[1] Mem. 685, 686.
[2] The entry was made accordingly.—Rot. Cl. 1659 p. 2, n. 39.

ments were assigned to him in Whitehall, where, he says, "he sealed commissions and heard motions and causes, the counsel and clients coming thither very willingly to attend upon their business."[1]

But the public distractions increasing as Monk approached, it soon became necessary to postpone all judicial business to a quieter time.[2]

The Council or Committee of Safety, with Whitelock's concurrence, agreed on seven articles as the basis of the future government:—1. That there be no Kingship.—2. No single person as Chief Magistrate.—3. That an army be continued.—4. No imposition upon conscience.—5. No House of Peers.—6. The Legislative and Executive powers to be in distinct hands.—7. Parliaments to be elected by the people.

The Lord Keeper actually issued a proclamation for a new parliament, a measure which gave general satisfaction; but the officers immediately became alarmed lest they should be superseded by a national assembly freely elected. They said that though very desirous for a parliament they must be sure of being able to preserve an ascendency over it, and they insisted that the Lord Keeper, in the writs to be issued under the Great Seal, should introduce some very novel and fantastical restrictions on the qualifications both of electors and those to be elected. He represented "that these restrictions were expressly contrary to law and to the oath he had taken as Lord Keeper of the Great Seal, and that he could not, without the breach of his duty, seal writs for a parliament after that manner." Some of the officers saying "that if he would not, they would seal the writs themselves in their

[1] Mem. 688.
[2] "Wednesday, Nov. 16, 1659.
"At the Committee of Safety at Whitehall.
"This Committee holding it convenient and necessary for divers weighty reasons to adjourn the remaining part of this present Term from and after Saturday, the 19th of this instant Nov'.—It is therefore ordered, that the remaining part of the aforesaid present Term upon and from the day aforesaid be adjourned until the first day of the next Term ; and to prevent the discontinuance of any process, suits, or causes now depending, or any inconvenience to the people thereby, it is also ordered, that writs of adjournment of the said Term shall be issued and passed the Great Seal of England in the usual form for this purpose ; and the Lord Keeper Whitelock, Keeper of the Great Seal, is authorized to issue forth writs accordingly."

Whitelock says, "I caused these writs to be framed, sealed, and issued forth in time."—688.

own fashion," the Lord Keeper replied "that he was ready to deliver up the Seal to them, and that it was there ready if they pleased to take it from him."

A doughty Colonel, greatly nettled at this speech, exclaimed,—" It is not well that at such a time as this so great a charge as the Great Seal should be intrusted to a lawyer. More seemingly were it that an office of such power and profit should be given to those who have encountered the wars and adventured their lives for the service of the Commonwealth than to such as skulk from dangers and covet fees."—*Lord Keeper.* "The gentleman who so much disparages lawyers would do well to call in mind the services performed by Ireton, Jones, Reynolds, and others of the profession during the war. As for myself, I have been exposed to such perils in the service of the state, particularly in my embassy to Sweden, as would have appalled this much-speaking Colonel. I desire, therefore, that such reproachful language may be forborne." Hereupon General Fleetwood and others justified the Lord Keeper and his profession, and the Colonel was put to silence.

Through the agency of Whitelock, the Restoration had very nearly at this time been brought about in a manner very different from that which actually happened, and a very different turn might have been given to the subsequent history of the constitution and of the country. Perceiving that men openly contrasted the anarchy and confusion now existing with the tranquillity formerly enjoyed under the monarchy, and were not backward in the expression of their wishes for the restoration of the ancient line of their princes,—despairing of being able to devise any measures effectually to stem the prevailing current of public opinion,—strongly suspecting the intentions of Monk, who was now mysteriously advancing with his army from Scotland,—and eager to anticipate him,— the Lord Keeper formed the project of being the first to declare for Charles, and of carrying over the Great Seal to him at Breda. But this bauble by itself would be of little value; and he disclosed his plan to several others, who advised him to try to obtain the concurrence of Fleetwood, the Major General of the army, who was of a more moderate and flexible disposition than Lambert, the Commander-in-Chief. Finding the Major General alone, he said "he was come to discourse with him freely about their present condition, and what was fit to be done in such an exigency as they were brought to; that it was more than evident that it was Monk's design to bring in the King, and that without any terms for those of the parliamentary party; whereby all their lives and fortunes would be at his and their enemies' mercy, they being sufficiently enraged against them, and in great need of repairing their broken fortunes; that all the incensed Lords and secluded members were active in the design, so that the restoration of the King was unavoidable. And, seeing it must be, it was more prudence for Fleetwood and his friends to be the instruments of it than to leave it to Monk; that thereby he might make terms with the King for the preservation of himself and his friends, and, in some measure, of that course wherein they had been engaged; but that, if it were left to Monk, they and all they had achieved would be exposed to utter ruin."[1]

Fleetwood was much struck by this reasoning, and agreed to join in any feasible plan that could be proposed for opening a communication with the King. Whitelock proposed that he should muster his troops, take possession of the Tower, induce the Lord Mayor and citizens of London to join with him in calling a free parliament, and send a messenger forthwith to Breda to make terms with the King,—offering himself to go upon that employment, or to accompany him to the Tower. After a little more discourse, Fleetwood became quite delighted with the enterprise; but, dispensing with the Lord Keeper's aid in the military part of it, desired him to get ready forthwith for the journey to Breda, saying, "that he himself would sit down to prepare his instructions, so that he might be on the road that evening, or at least early next morning."

But just as the conference was about to finish, it was announced that Vane, Desborough, and Berry desired to see the General, and he requested Whitelock to withdraw, and stay a little for him,—which he did with heaviness of heart, knowing the irresolution of his friend. In a quarter of an hour Fleetwood came out, and with much emotion said, "I can not do it! I can not do it!" and being asked the reason for this sudden change, he answered, "These

[1] Mem. 690. Life of Whit. 358.

gentlemen have put me in mind, and it is very true, that I am engaged to do no such thing without the consent of Lord Lambert." Whitelock urged that Lambert was then absent from London, and that the affair admitted no delay; but Fleetwood, repeating that "he could not do it without him," he retired, making this observation, "You will ruin yourself and your friends."[1]

There can be no doubt that Whitelock, as the accredited agent of Fleetwood, would have been most cordially received by Charles, who was still very doubtful as to the intentions of Monk; and perhaps an arrangement might have been made, providing guarantees for religion and liberty, which would have rescued the nation from the misgovernment of the two succeeding reigns, and saved the Stuart dynasty.

Several of Whitelock's private friends strongly urged him for his own sake, to fly with the Great Seal to Breda; but dreading lest representing no party in the state, he should meet with a repulse, he declined the advice, although he afterwards found that Ingoldsby, who had signed the warrant for the execution of Charles I. by a tender of his service about this time, experienced indemnity and favor.

As a last desperate effort to continue the republican government, Lord Whitelock put the Great Seal to writs of summons for the election of a new parliament, but the Lord Mayor and Sheriffs of Middlesex refused to act upon them; no respect was paid to them in any quarter, and, to the astonishment and amusement of mankind, the "Rump" was once more restored. A mob, consisting chiefly of royalists, aided by some soldiers, assembled in Lincoln's Inn Fields, and proceeding to the Rolls, in Chancery Lane, saluted Lenthal as the Speaker of the Long Parliament, not yet legally dissolved, and required that he should go and take his seat in the House of Commons to assist in recalling the King. Fleetwood, after some days spent in weeping, said, "the Lord had spit in his face," fell on his knees before the Speaker, and surrendered his commission. The members, with Lenthal at their head, resumed the possession of the House and of the government.

This was a very alarming state of affairs for the Lord

[1] Mem. 691.

Keeper, who, if he had not actively assisted in their last expulsion, had immediately assented to it, had accepted a seat in "the Committee of Safety," and acted as their chief legal adviser. He was told of many threatening expressions uttered against him, and that one *Scot*, a person of considerable influence, with whom he had had a private quarrel at an election, had publicly declared, "that the Lord Keeper ought to be hanged, with the Great Seal about his neck."[1]

He was afraid, therefore, to take his place in the House, as he would have been inclined to do,—his principle being to conform to every political change as quickly as possible. Having been summoned to attend, he went privately to the Speaker, and stated his apprehensions that if he were to appear in his place he might be called in question for his recent conduct, and committed to prison. Lenthal in a friendly manner advised him to attend, saying, that it wou'd be taken as an owning of their authority if he sat with them. He accordingly summoned up resolution to enter the House, but he was very ill received; many of his most familiar acquaintances looked cool and reserved, and one or two particular friends, who still stuck by him, gave him a hint not to be present on the day that was appointed to consider of the absent members.

The just result of all his political manœuvring was, that he found himself universally despised, and that he was equally afraid for his personal safety which ever side should triumph. Under these melancholy circumstances his heart entirely failed him, and he resolved at once and for ever to withdraw from public life. He therefore locked the Great Seal in a box, and ordered his wife to carry it to the Speaker, and to deliver him the key of it. He then went privately into the country, and remained in strict concealment at the house of a friend. An order was made that he should attend in his place, but he was not further molested.[2]

After the Restoration, he at last found himself safe, when the bill of indemnity had passed. From his precaution in declining to act in the High Court of Justice, he

---

[1] Scot was himself afterwards hanged as a regicide.

[2] Sir Harry Vane, who obeyed a similar order, was expelled the House, and exiled to his castle of Raby, for having taken part with the Council of State on the second expulsion of the Rump.

was not included in the exception leveled at the King's Judges.

He never again appeared on the political stage,—and here we must take leave of him. It is said that after the Restoration he came to Court and asked pardon of the King for "all that he had transacted against him,"—perhaps not without hopes of once more recovering the Great Seal; but Charles bade him "Go live quietly in the country, and take care of his wife and one-and-thirty children."[1]

He retired to Chilton Park, in the county of Wilts. Here he lived quietly, devoting himself to study and country amusements till 1675, when he died in his seventieth year. His remains were interred at Fawley, near Marlow, in Buckinghamshire, where he had constructed a burying place for his family.

In his own time he was reckoned the competitor of Lord Clarendon for fame as well as for power, and as he was at the head of the law of England for twelve years, and mixed up with some of the most striking events during the most important period in our annals, his merits and defects must continue to be interesting to all who would become familiar with the great lawyers and statesmen of England. His character is not unfairly drawn by Wood:—"He was an observing person through all changes, being guided more by policy than conscience. He was an excellent common lawyer, as well read in books as men, well versed in the oriental languages, and much beloved by Selden and the virtuosi of his time."[2] We must not, from the disgust excited by his uniform submission to dominant power, forget that he had valuable qualities, and that he not only resisted usurpation as far as he

[1] This was a considerable exaggeration; for in a "Dedication to the King" of a legal work, the fruit of his retirement, he says that the royal clemency had bestowed upon him his small fortune, liberty, and life, and restored him to "a wife and SIXTEEN children—a number exceeded by legal dignitaries of the present day.

[2] Wood's Ath. Ox. Selden's last letter was addressed to him:—

"I am a most humble suitor to your Lordship, that you would be pleased that I might have your presence for a little time to-morrow or next day. This wearies the most weak hand of

"Your Lordship's most humble Servant,
"J. SELDEN."

Whitelock, though then immersed in public business, went to his dying friend, assisted him in making his will and consented to become one of his executors.

safely could during the struggle, but that he continued to strive to mitigate its evils. In many instances he successfully contended for the extension of clemency towards state offenders, and for protection to oppressed communities. He was ever an advocate of a tolerant and humane administration of the executive authority, and he has a right to a considerable share of the praise justly appropriated to those from whose mild disposition the English revolution in the seventeeth century contrasts so favorably with the French Revolution, a century and a half later, when knowledge and civilization were supposed to have made such progress in Europe. He ought, above all, to be honored as a most zealous and enlightened law reformer.

In his character and conduct he has often been compared to Clarendon; but he bears a much closer resemblance to the Lord Keeper who lingered so long in the parliament at Westminster, and then joined the King with the Great Seal at York. Both Whitelock and Littleton were inclined to do good when it was consistent with their interest; both were irresolute and dastardly, and they both acted from time to time with such duplicity as to induce a suspicion that their want of courage was want of principle.

As a contributor to English history, Whitelock does not enjoy the full measure of credit which he deserves. For his "Memorials from the Accession of Charles I. till the Restoration of Charles II.," he justly takes as a motto,

————"Quæque ipse miserrima vidi.
Et quorum pars magna fui;"

and his work has the unspeakable advantage of having been composed almost from day to day, while there dwelt on his mind a lively and accurate impression of the events which he relates; whereas the more popular "History of the Rebellion," by Clarendon was written from a faded recollection, and, besides purposed suppressions and misrepresentations, abounds with mistakes of dates and facts unconsciously introduced. The "Memorialist" is uniformly fair and candid; and although the form of a Diary, which he generally adopts, makes it rather a book of reference than for continuous perusal, we find in it passages of reasoning and eloquence, showing that the author was qualified to reach a high degree of literary excellence.

He compiled also "An Abridgment of the History of England down to the end of the Reign of James I.;" and besides many speeches, and several forgotten Law treatises which he published in his lifetime, there are, in the British Museum, six MS. volumes compiled by him on the Law of Elections, and other subjects.[1]

James, his eldest son, was knighted by Oliver, gained distinction as a Colonel in the parliamentary army, and represented the county of Oxford in parliament. William, his second son, rose to great eminence at the bar, and was knighted by Charles II. I do not find any thing more respecting his descendants.

And now I must proceed to relate the last days of the Great Seal of the parliament. Lady Whitelock having carried it to Lenthal, according to the instructions she had received, he presented it to the House, who immediately made an order "that it be delivered to the Speaker, as Keeper, and remain in his custody till the House should further order."[2]

A committee was named to consider of fit persons to be intrusted with the custody of the Great Seal. They made a report in favor of Sir THOMAS WIDDRINGTON and Sergeants TERRYLL and FOUNTAIN, who were appointed accordingly; and the Great Seal was delivered to them, with much solemnity, by the Speaker in the name of the parliament.[3]

The royal cause having made such progress in public opinion, we may wonder that men were not selected whose principles were more favorable to it; but we must remember that the excluded members had not yet been re-admitted; that a great majority of the members now sitting were republicans in their hearts; that Monk still

---

[1] Ayscough's Cat. 4749-4754.

[2] Mem. 693. At the same time, Lady Whitelock, from apprehension for her husband's safety, burnt many of his papers, which he considered a great loss to the history of these times.

[3] It would appear that they had considerably altered their tone, and were now professed royalists. Fountain was obnoxious to some as a great law reformer.—*Ludlow*, 343. At the same time it was ordained that Newdigate should be Chief Justice; Hill and Nicholas, Judges of the Upper Bench; St. John, Chief Justice; Wyndham and Archer, Judges of the Common Pleas; Wilde, Chief Baron; Thorpe and Parker, Barons of the Exchequer; —who had all been republicans.—*Mem.* 693.

found it convenient to dissemble ; and that a considerable time elapsed before any one ventured openly to propose the King's recall.[1]

No judicial business was done in Hilary or Easter terms, and the functions of the new Lords Commissioners of the Great Seal were chiefly ministerial,—the parliament having ordered " that the Speaker, in execution of their votes, should sign a doquet for patents and other instruments to pass the Great Seal, and that the Lords Commissioners do pass such patents and instruments under the Great Seal, accordingly."[2]

In obedience to an order they received, they sealed a commission authorizing the Master of the Rolls and certain Judges to hear causes in Chancery; but the administration of justice in all the Courts was suspended till Trinity term following, when the King was again on the throne.

It was only on the 13th of March that the resolution passed doing away with the declaration hitherto required from all members and public functionaries, to " be faithful to the Commonwealth as now established, without a King or House of Lords."

Three days after, the ordinance passed for dissolving the Long Parliament, which, being carried by the sole authority of the Commons, the more scrupulous pronounced a nullity, for want of the assent of the King and the Lords; and, in strict theory, there is certainly great difficulty in saying when the existence of this famous legislature, which had continued twenty years, legally terminated, the Convention Parliament that ratified its dissolution being itself illegal, and incapable of giving itself power by its own act.

However, the Lords Commissioners Widdrington, Terryll, and Fountain immediately issued under the Great Seal, a proclamation and writs, in name of " the Keepers of the Liberties of England," for a new election of representatives of the people, to meet on the 25th of April,—not

---

[1] Even after the re-admission of the excluded members, although there was a majority for royalty, a resolution was passed that the Westminster Confession of Faith, framed by the Presbyterian divines, should be the basis of the national religion ; and Baxter acted as chaplain to the House of Commons down to the King's return, when he was made a royal chaplain.

[2] Com. Jour. vii. 814.

sending any summonses to Peers, nor taking any measures for having an Upper House.

On the day appointed both Houses met, without the appearance of royalty, and the Lords without even the form of a summons. None of Cromwell's Peers claimed to sit in the Upper House, and it was, in the first instance, composed of the Presbyterian Lords who sat there in the year 1648. They re-elected their old Speaker, the Earl of Manchester, who had long been a moderate royalist, but was still very hostile to Episcopacy as well as arbitrary government. In a few days the old cavalier Peers joined, asserting their right as *conciliarii nati,* and they formed a great majority, although, to avoid cavil, the Peers who sat in the King's parliament at Oxford, as well as those whose patents bore date after the commencement of the civil war, abstained for the present from demanding admission. All concurred in continuing the Earl of Manchester as Speaker, out of respect to his personal character and his great parliamentary experience.

The Lords, with a view to their authority and independence, were very uneasy at the thought of the Great Seal being still held exclusively under a vote of the House of Commons by the Commissioners Widdrington, Terryll, and Fountain; and their first act was to appoint their Speaker, the Earl of Manchester, a joint Keeper. Messengers were sent down to the Commons, who (to the great horror of some old republicans returned to the Convention) were admitted, and said, "Mr. Speaker, we are commanded by the Lords to wait upon you with a vote of the Lords, whereby they have nominated and appointed the Earl of Manchester to be one of the Commissioners for the Great Seal of England, and their desire is that the House of Commons will concur with them therein."

After several days taken for deliberation, a resolution was passed "that this House doth agree with the Lords that the Earl of Manchester, Speaker of the House of Peers, be, and he is hereby nominated and appointed, one of the Commissioners of the Great Seal, and added to those who have the present custody thereof till further order." The King's letter, by Sir John Grenville, had been received, and it was resolved that all proceedings under the Great Seal should henceforth run in the King's name;

but a dread perplexity arose from the consideration that the Great Seal now in use, instead of having upon it the name of CHARLES II., with his titles "of Great Britain, France, and Ireland, King, Defender of the Faith," &c., represented the House of Commons with the Speaker in the chair, and bore the inscription, "The Great Seal of England, 1651, in the third year of freedom, by God's blessing restored." A select committee being appointed to consider this knotty affair, submitted to the House "whether for the carrying on and present expediting of the justice of the kingdom, the House shall think fit that the Great Seal now in the possession of the Earl of Manchester and the other Commissioners be made use of until further order?" The House agreed in this recommendation, and sent a message to pray the concurrence of the Lords. But their Lordships were very much shocked by the notion of the authoritative use of the republican Seal, and, by way of a gentle refusal, said "they would return an answer by messengers of their own." No answer coming down, the Commons asked and obtained a conference on the subject, when they urged that there were many inconveniences the kingdom suffered for want of the use of the Great Seal,—that the administration of justice was suspended, and all writs, fines and assurances were stopped,—that three terms had been lost already, and there was danger of having no assizes,—that orders for the collection of the revenue were not obeyed, and for want of pay the army would be obliged to live at free quarters,—that while the Great Seal was not used, the House of Commons could not fill up their numbers,—that preparations could not be made for the King's reception, and this punctilious regard for his image might be fatal to his authority,—that the representations and inscriptions on Seals were immaterial as to their efficacy,—and that in former times Great Seals had been used without the name or insignia of the reigning sovereign, as King James used for some time the Seal of Queen Elizabeth, and Charles I. that of King James.

Still the Lords would not come to a formal vote of concurrence, but they connived at the use of the republican Seal till Charles had actually set foot on English ground, and, amidst the enthusiastic plaudits of his subjects, was on his journey from Dover to London to mount the throne.

Being then accompanied by Sir EDWARD HYDE, whom he had constituted his Chancellor while in exile, and to whom he had delivered a Great Seal which he had caused to be made, bearing his name, style, and arms, the Commonwealth Seal was no more wanted, and it was dealt with as the royal Great Seal had been in the year 1646, after the surrender of Oxford. On the 28th of May, the Commons resolved " that the Great Seal in the custody of Sir Thomas Widdrington, and the rest of the late Commissioners of the Great Seal, be brought into this House this forenoon, to be here defaced."

Accordingly, it was forthwith delivered to Sir Harbottle Grimston, the Speaker. "Being laid upon the clerk's table, a smith was sent for, who broke it in pieces, while the House was sitting," and the pieces were delivered to the Lords Commissioners for their fees.[1] This was the final end of the Great Seal of the Commonwealth, —which the King himself, in the treaty at Newport, had agreed to acknowledge,—and under which justice had long been administered,—commissions had been granted to victorious generals and admirals,—and treaties, dictated by England, had been entered into with the most powerful nations in Europe.

The following day the two Houses of Parliament threw themselves on their knees before the King at Whitehall, and Lord Chancellor Hyde was seen carrying the true Great Seal before him, in its red velvet purse adorned with a representation of a royal crown, and all the heraldic bearings of an English monarch.

I must now take a short review of the changes in the frame of the law, and the administration of justice during the Commonwealth and the Protectorate. There were then very wild notions afloat respecting law reform. A party was for utterly abolishing the whole of the common and statute law of England, and substituting the Mosaic law in its place. A very strong prejudice existed against lawyers, who were quaintly denounced as "a purse-milking generation," and were accused of always "bleeding their clients in the *purse vein*." Cromwell him-

[1] Com. Jour.

self was by no means above such absurd and vulgar notions, and was more inclined on those subjects, to listen to such a fanatical buffoon as Hugh Peters than to eminent jurists like Whitelock or Hale. It is because his preposterous schemes for simple and cheap law were properly opposed as impracticable and mischievous, that he complained so bitterly of being worsted by "the sons of Zeruiah." He would not, like Napoleon in a subsequent age, be contented with the glory to be gained by collecting, systematizing, and improving existing laws;—of framing a code adapted to the circumstances and habits of a civilized nation;—but he thought that the controverted rights of property were to be decided by an English Judge in Westminster Hall like disputes in an Eastern bazar by the Kadi. "We can not mention the reform of the law," said he, "but the lawyers presently cry out, *You design to destroy property;* whereas, the law, as it is now constituted, serves only to maintain the lawyers, and to encourage the rich to oppress the poor. Coke, late solicitor for the people of England, at the trial of Charles Stuart, when I sent him, with full powers as Chief Justice to Ireland, determined more causes in a week than all Westminster Hall in a year. The English people will take Ireland for a precedent, and when they see at how easy and cheap a rate property is there preserved, they will never permit themselves to be so cheated and abused as now they are."[1]

But notwithstanding these crude notions, there were men in England in the middle of the seventeenth century

[1] Ludlow's Memoirs, 123. Even General Ludlow himself, though freer from prejudice and with a more cultivated mind than any other officer in the service of the parliament—from keeping bad company had imbibed these notions. "In the meantime," says he, "the reformation of the law went on but slowly, it being the interest of the lawyers to preserve the lives, liberties and estates of the whole nation in their own hands." So that upon the debate of "registering deeds in each county, for want of which within a certain time after the sale, such sales shall be void, and being so registered, that land should not be subject to any incumbrance;" this word "incumbrance," was so managed by the lawyers that it took up three months' time before it could be ascertained by the committee.—*Ludlow,* 165. I make no doubt that, very properly, there was much deliberation on such a difficult subject; but all the liberal, enlightened, and influential lawyers, then as now, were much before the majority of the legislature in disinterestedly recommending practicable and beneficial legal reform; and this very Committee, so jeered at, strongly recommended a registry of deeds which, being still withheld, I several times, while I was a representative of the people, in vain strove to induce the House of Commons to adopt.

as liberal, zealous, and enlightened friends of law reform, as Romilly, Mackintosh, and Brougham in the beginning of the nineteenth,—men who were for adapting ancient laws and institutions to the altered circumstances of society,—who were fully competent to the important task they had undertaken,—and who, if they had been properly appreciated and supported, would have conferred unspeakable benefits on the country, anticipating and going beyond most of the salutary amendments which have been adopted in the reigns of William IV. and Queen Victoria.

They began their labors, as we have seen,[1] before the dissolution of the Long Parliament.[2] Their efforts were greatly obstructed, not only by the violent end of the Long Parliament, but still more by the folly and fanaticism of Barebones' Parliament, and by the abrupt dissolution of the two parliaments which followed: but they procured the actual enactment of some most important laws, and the *projects* of many others which have at last been adopted in the present age. Ordinances passed "for changing tenure in chivalry to common soccage," by which a great portion of the land of the kingdom was freed from wardship, reliefs, and other oppressive burdens;—" for abolishing purveyance," a perpetual grievance to all classes of society;—" for allowing marriage to be entered into according to the religious persuasion of the parties, or as a civil contract at their option," the model of the recent Marriage Act;—" for the registration of births, marriages, and deaths," which we have likewise copied;—" for paying Judges and other officers by salaries instead of fees," the most effectual mode of preventing corruption and correcting abuses in courts of justice;—and " for having all legal records in the language of the country,"—so

---

[1] Ante, p. 353.
[2] The chief credit of these reforms is undoubtedly to be ascribed to Sir Matthew Hale, placed at the head of the non-parliamentary committee. I do not find the name of Coke, the eminent lawyer, who acted as Solicitor for the people of England on the trial of Charles I., in the list of either committee, or that he publicly took any part in these proceedings; but when he came to the scaffold, he took credit for having earnestly supported them, and "declared that he had used the utmost of his endeavors that the practice of the law might be regulated, and that the public justice might be administered with as much expedition and as little expense as possible."—*Ludlow*, 368. According to his practice, when he went Chief Justice to Ireland, he seems to have had notions of jurisprudence quite unsuited to a nation that has reached wealth and civility.

that a knowledge of the laws might be communicated to those who were to obey them.'

I must likewise point out the parliamentary reform introduced by "the Instrument of Government,"—under which the rotten boroughs were disfranchised, and the counties and great towns in England, Scotland, and Ireland chose representatives according to population and property,—the qualification of the electors being well framed to secure independent constituencies,—which Clarendon is obliged to confess "was generally looked upon as an alteration fit to be more warrantably made and in better times."[2] Most of these improvements were lost for many years by the Restoration, except the abolition of the military tenures, which the country gentlemen would not again submit to, and ingeniously contrived to barter against an excise duty to be paid by the whole community, instead of a land tax to be paid by themselves. I have now to mention other "Ordinances," not passed, but of which draughts are extant: "For taking away exorbitant fees on original writs, declarations, and other law proceedings,"—"for abolishing fines and common recoveries,"—"for ascertaining arbitrary fines on pescent and alienation of copyholds,"—"for the more easy recovery of small debts,"—"for the preventing of raudulent contracts and conveyances,"—"for making

---

[1] The proposition for conducting all law proceedings in English was most strenuously opposed, and seemed to many a more dangerous innovation than the abolition of the House of Lords or the regal office. Whitelock, in introducing it, was obliged to fortify himself with the example of Moses and a host of other legislators who had expounded their laws in the vernacular tongue. The reporters, who delighted in the Norman French, were particularly obstreperous. "I have made these reports speak English." says Styles, in his preface, "not that I believe they will be thereby more generally useful, for I have been always and yet am of opinion, that that part of the common law which is in English hath only occasioned the making of unquiet spirits contentiously knowing, and more apt to offend others than to defend themselves; but I have done it in obedience to authority, and to stop the mouths of such of this English age, who, though they be confessedly different in their minds and judgments as the builders of Babel were in their language, yet do think it vain, if not impious, to speak or understand more than their own mother tongue." So Bulstrode, in the preface to the second part of his Reports, says, "that he had many years since perfected the work in French, in which language he had desired it might have seen the light, being most proper for it, and most convenient for the professors of the law." But the Restoration brought back Norman French to the reports, and barbarous Latin to the law records, which continued till the reign of George II.

[2] Instrument of Government, Arts. xi. xix., xxiv. Hist. Reb. book xiv. See some admirable reasoning on this subject, *Ludlow*, 166.

debts assignable,"—and "for establishing a register for all deeds affecting real property." Almost the whole of the other Commonwealth law reforms have been gradually introduced into our system; but this last measure the greatest and most beneficial of all, still remains to confer glory upon the honest and vigorous administration that shall carry it through, notwithstanding the interested clamors of country attorneys and the foolish fears of country squires.

The common-law bench was exceedingly well filled during the Commonwealth and Protectorate, and the law was ably administered through them, except when Cromwell was occasionally driven to supersede them by his Major-Generals and his High Courts of Justice. From the embarrassments produced by the political functions of the Keepers of the Great Seal, "Equity" did not equally prosper although they worked hard,—sometimes sitting from five in the morning till five in the afternoon. Yet one common cry of reproach pursued their labors. In a petition presented to parliament for regulating the Court of Chancery, the prevailing opinion is thus expressed; "as long as the bar is more able than the bench, *as of late it hath been*, the business of the Court can never be well dispatched."

"The Chancery," says a contemporary pamphlet, "is a great grievance, one of the greatest in the nation. It is confidently affirmed by knowing gentlemen of worth, that there are depending in that Court 23,000 causes; that some of them have been depending five, some ten, some twenty, some thirty years and more; there have been spent in causes many hundred, nay thousands of pounds, to the undoing of many families; what is ordered one day is contradicted the next, so as in some cases there have been 500 orders."

Lay Peers, like Manchester, Kent, and Gray, must have made but a bad figure in giving their opinions on nice questions of conveyancing, or the common practice of the Court. Whitelock, sitting by himself, would have proved a good Equity Judge, but he was thwarted and embarrassed by his colleagues. "The burden of the business," says he, "lay heavy on me, being ancient [senior] in commission, and my brother Keble of little experience, and my brother Lisle less, but very opinionative. The business of the Chancery was full of trouble this Michaelmas term, and no man's cause came to a determination, how just soever, without the clamor of the party against whom judgment was given; they being stark blind in their own causes, and resolved not to be convinced by reason or law." When Whitelock had resigned, Lisle, who was grossly ignorant of his profession, "bore himself very highly and superciliously." The chief weight of the Equity business lay on the shoulders of Lenthal, the Master of the Rolls; but his time was much occupied with politics till after the dissolution of the Long Parliament, and he lost character greatly in the year 1654,—when, after boasting that "he would sooner suffer himself to be hanged over the Rolls gate than submit to Cromwell's absurd and illegal ordinance to regulate the Chancery," and seeing two Lords Commissioners dismissed for denying its validity,—he agreed to acknowledge it sooner than lose his place,[2]—and he made himself the laughing-stock of the bar, by trying, along with Fiennes and Lisle, to put a reasonable construction upon nonsense.

He further lowered himself by his childish anxiety to get one of Cromwell's peerages. The House of Lords being to be restored, it was then thought that, being an attendant on that House as Master of the Rolls, he could not sit in the House of Commons, and "he complained that he, who had been for some years the first man of the nation, was now denied to be a member of either House of Parliament." This complaint coming to the ears of Cromwell, he sent him a writ—which so elevated the poor man, that, riding in his coach through the Strand and meeting a friend of Sir Arthur Hazelrig, who had received a similar writ, and was disposed to treat it with contempt, he said with great earnestness, "I pray write to him and desire him by no means to omit taking his place in the House of Lords, and assure him from me that all that do so shall, themselves and their heirs, be for ever Peers of England."[3] The Lords Commissioners,

[1] Mem. 548.
[2] "Lenthal, who seemed most earnest against the execution of this ordinance, and protested *that he would be hanged at the Rolls gate before he would execute it*, yet now, when he saw Widdrington and me put out of our places for refusing to do it, he wheeled about, and was as forward as any to act in the execution of it, and thereby restored himself to favor "—*Whit. Mem.* 627.
[3] Lud. Mem. 227. "When Cromwell had dissolved this parliament, he

while they resisted the preposterous plans of Cromwell and his officers for reforming the Court of Chancery, from time to time issued very sensible orders for remedying abuses, and under their auspices an ordinance was passed in 1654, abolishing the sixty clerks, introducing many excellent regulations for the conducting of suits, and enacting a table of fees to be received by the Master of the Rolls, the Masters in Chancery, the counsel,[1] and the solicitors.

Although no such monument of juridical improvement as the "Code Napoléon" was transmitted to us by the English Commonwealth, we ought to be grateful to the enlightened men who then flourished, for they accomplished much, and a comparison between them and the leaders of the French Revolution would turn out greatly to the advantage of our countrymen, who not only showed a much greater regard for justice, humanity, and religion, but a sounder knowledge of the principles of government, —not changing merely for the sake of change, but only where they thought they could improve. The French copied the most exceptionable measures of the English Revolution—such as the execution of the King, the commencement of a new era from "the first year of liberty," and the appointment of "a Committee of Public Safety," which disposed, in an arbitrary manner, of the lives and fortunes of the citizens. But they wholly neglected the wise lesson set before them, to preserve what is good—to amend what is defective—to adapt ancient institutions to altered times—and to show some respect for the habits, the feelings, and the prejudices of the people to be governed. It is difficult for us to separate the men who suggested and supported the wise civil measures of the Commonwealth parliaments from the excesses and absurdities of the Puritans; and the Cavalier party having gained a complete victory over them, we take our impressions of them from their enemies; but I believe that many of them were of the same principles, and actuated by the same spirit, as Lord Somers and the authors of the

assured his Lords, that, notwithstanding the practices that had been used against them, they should continue to be Lords." —*Whit. Mem.* 226.

[1] The fee to a barrister with a stuff gown, on the hearing of a cause, was only £1, and to a Lord Protector's counsel, or serjeant-at-law, £2.—*Ordinance*, anno 1654, c. 44; *Scobell's Acts*, p. 324. See also, 1654, c. 25; 1656, c. 10; *Whit. Mem.* 421, 562, 608, 621, 622.

Revolution of 1688,—whom we are all taught to admire and venerate. If the Restoration had not been conducted with so much precipitation, if the proposition of the virtuous Lord Hale had been acceded to, "that before recalling Charles II. they should consider what reasonable restrictions on the abuse of prerogative the late King had consented to, and what good laws had been passed in his absence as the basis of a happy settlement," the nation might have escaped much of the misgovernment. dissoluteness of manners, and political convulsions, which marked the history of England during the remainder of this century, and we should have been taught habitually to do honor to the memory of those by whose wisdom and patriotism such blessings had been achieved.

CHAPTER LXXIII.

LIFE OF LORD KEEPER HERBERT.

I SHOULD now naturally proceed to the life of the Earl of Clarendon, who executed the duties of Chancellor in England upon the Restoration; but as Sir EDWARD HERBERT actually held the Great Seal for a considerable time, with the title of Lord Keeper, although *in partibus* only, and as his name is always introduced into the list of Lord Chancellors and Lord Keepers, some account of him may be expected in this work. He acted a prominent part in one of the most memorable passages of English History.

On the execution of Charles I., the Prince, being in Holland, took upon himself the royal title, and had a Great Seal engraved; but he did not deliver it to any one, although he immediately swore in some of his fellow-exiles Privy Councillors. He carried this Seal with him into Scotland when he was crowned King there, having subscribed the "Covenant," and he still kept it in his own custody when he advanced at the head of the Scottish army into England. After the fatal battle of Worcester, this Great Seal was lost. It would rather have been an incumbrance to Charles, sheltered by the royal oak, and in his marvelous adventures with the Penderells, the

Mortons, and the Lanes.—It was probably thrown into the Severn, that it might not be sent to the parliament as a trophy of Cromwell's victory.

When Charles was again in safety under the protection of the King of France, he caused another Great Seal of England to be engraved in Paris, chiefly as a bauble to be kept by himself, till, upon a fortunate turn in his affairs, it might be handed over to a Lord Chancellor or Lord Keeper, to be used for actual business within his recovered realm. But it became an object of ambition and contention among his courtiers, who amused the tedium of their banishment by intrigues for the titles of offices of state and offices of the royal household, although no power or profit for the present belonged to them.

Charles himself favored the pretensions of Hyde to the Great Seal; but this minister was most particularly obnoxious to the Queen Dowager, Henrietta Maria, on whom her son chiefly depended for a subsistence; and out of spite to the man she hated, she warmly supported the cause of his rival, Sir Edward Herbert, about whom she was indifferent. Her importunity succeeded: the Great Seal was delivered by the King, with all due solemnity, to her candidate, as Lord Keeper: he took the oaths of allegiance and supremacy, and the oath of office, before a meeting of the pretended Privy Council; and thenceforward, on all occasions of mock state, when the King of England was supposed to be attended by his high functionaries,—the envied exile strutted about bearing the purse with the Great Seal in his hand,—and he was addressed as "Lord Keeper Herbert."

This gentleman, whose professional honors brought him so little comfort or advantage, was nobly descended, being the son of Charles Herbert, of Aston, in the county of Montgomery, of the family of Lord Herbert of Cherbury. After leaving the University, he was entered of Lincoln's Inn, that he might be qualified for the profession of the law. He applied himself very diligently to his studies, and on being called to the bar,—from his connections and his own industry he rose into good practice, without gaining any distinction. In the famous masque given by the Inns of Courts to the Queen, in 1633, he was one of the managers for Lincoln's Inn, and assisted Mr. Attorney General Noy in exposing to ridicule the projectors who, about this time, anticipated some of the discoveries of the philosophers of Laputa.

He likewise assisted him and Banks, his successor, in the scheme for taxing the people without authority of parliament, under the name of "ship-money,"—an invention as impracticable as many of those which were ridiculed. He actually abetted all the measures of the Court, and was one of those who hoped that parliament would never more meet in England. Their wish would very likely have been fulfilled, had it not been for the Scottish insurrection, caused by the attempt to force Episcopacy upon that nation but money to pay the army being indispensable, and a parliament being called,—to be dismissed as soon as a supply was granted,—he was returned by family interest a member of the House of Commons, and testified his determination to defend every abuse which had been practiced during the preceding eleven years. For this earnest of his services he was made Solicitor General on the promotion in the law which took place in consequence of the death of Lord Keeper Coventry. Clarendon, who always mentions him ill-naturedly, says, that he was remarkable in the House "for pride and peevishness;" that "his parts were most prevalent in puzzling and perplexing;"—accuses him of speaking very indiscreetly on the question of the subsidy, whereby it was lost;—and imputes to him the fatal advice by which the King was induced suddenly to dissolve the parliament because "he found he was like to be of less authority there than he looked to be."[1]

When the Long Parliament met in the end of the same year, Herbert was exposed to the pelting of a most pitiless storm, for he was posted in the House of Commons to defend the Government, and the task of excusing or palliating ship-money, and the monopolies, and the cruel sentences of the Star Chamber and High Commission, fell exclusively upon him; for Mr. Attorney General Banks, who was much more implicated in these grievances, was quietly reposing on the Judge's woolsack in the House of Lords,—availing himself of the old opinion that the Attorney General, being summoned as an attendant of the Peers, could not sit as a Member of the House of Commons. Awed and terrified by the proceed-

[1] Hist. Reb. book ii.

ings taken against Strafford, Finch and other ministers, Herbert apprehended that he might himself be impeached. Under these circumstances, without venturing boldly to meet Hampden and the other parliamentary leaders, he tried by private applications to them to soften them towards him, but with little effect, and he repented that he had ever taken office.

"Longing infinitely to be out of that fire," he was snatched from it at a moment when he least expected relief."[1] Lord Keeper Finch having fled the country, and Littleton, the Chief Justice of the Common Pleas, having succeeded him, Banks was made Chief Justice, and Herbert Attorney General. With infinite satisfaction he vacated his seat in the House of Commons, and, in obedience to his writ of summons, took his place on the woolsack in the House of Lords, at the back of the Judges.

His joy must have been a little abated by having soon for his colleague the famous republican lawyer, Oliver St. John, who, agreeing at this juncture with two or three of his party to take office in the momentary prospect of an accommodation, became Solicitor General.[2] It is impossible that there could have been any cordiality between them, for St. John, though continuing down to the King's death to be called "Mr. Solicitor," soon ceased to have any intercourse with the Government, still pressed on the impeachments with unmitigated rigor, and was in reality the chief legal adviser of those who who were preparing for civil war.

Herbert, as Attorney General, passed a year in anxious inactivity, during which Strafford was attainted and executed, and a revolution was making rapid progress, which he deeply deplored, but was unable to oppose. As assistant to the Lords, he remained during this time in the place assigned him in the House, a silent witness of the proceedings against his colleagues,—of the passing of the acts to abolish the Star Chamber and High Commission, —and of the debates upon the bills for excluding the Bishops from parliament, and for transferring to the two Houses the power over the militia.

At last, he was suddenly called into action by the King sending for him to Whitehall,—personally delivering to him articles of impeachment ready engrossed on parch-

[1] Hist. Reb. book iii.   [2] Clarendon, Ibid. book iii.

ment, which charged Lord Kimbolton and the five principal popular leaders in the House of Commons with high treason,—and commanding him to proceed instantly to the House of Lords that he might there exhibit the articles and take the necessary steps for having the accused persons committed to prison, and brought to condign punishment. If any faith can be given either to the King or the Attorney General, the latter had not before been in the slightest degree privy to this illegal and insane scheme. It appears to us that Herbert should have strenuously, though respectfully, resisted it, and pointing out how it violated the law, and the fatal consequences which it must necessarily produce, have resigned his office into the King's hands rather than have assisted in carrying it on.[1] But we must judge him by the notions of right and wrong prevailing in his own age,—and Lord Clarendon, a constitutional lawyer of great candor, who not unfrequently censures violations of law to extend the prerogative, seems to have thought that the Attorney General was as little at liberty to disobey or question the instructions he then received,—as if he had been an officer in the field of battle ordered by his General to open a fire upon the enemy. Herbert readily and promptly obeyed, and from that hour civil war became inevitable. "The court was reduced to a lower condition and to more disesteem and neglect than ever it had undergone. All that had formerly been said of plots and conspiracies against the parliament, which had before been laughed at, was now thought true and real, and all their fears and jealousies looked upon as the effects of their great wisdom and foresight."[2]

In the Life of Lord Keeper Littleton, who was more deeply implicated in this transaction, I have described the manner in which the charge was brought forward in the House of Lords, and the proceedings to which it directly gave rise.[3] I have now to relate how it recoiled upon the Attorney General himself.

The House of Commons, having insured the safety of the five members, forthwith began to act upon the offens-

---

[1] As my most honored friend, Sir Charles Wetherell, in 1829, nobly resigned the same office when required to prepare the Roman Catholic Relief Bill, which he conscientiously disapproved of.
[2] Hist. Reb. b. iv.   [3] Ante, Ch. LXV.

ive, and required the Attorney General publicly to answer interrogatories: "Whether he did contrive, frame, or advise the articles of impeachment? Whether he knew the truth of them upon his own knowledge, or by information? Whether he would undertake to make them good when he should be thereunto called? From whom he received them, and by whose direction or advice he did exhibit them?" And having received his answer, "that he had neither framed nor advised them, nor knew anything of the truth of them, nor could undertake to justify them, but that he had received them from the King, and was by him commanded to exhibit them;" they resolved "that he had broken the privilege of parliament in preferring those articles, and that a charge should be sent to the Lords in the name of the House of Commons against him, to have satisfaction for the great scandal and injury to the members thereof."[1]

Accordingly, on the very day the royal assent was given to the Act for excluding the Bishops from parliament, an impeachment was brought up against the Attorney General, and the articles being read to him while he stood up in his place he required a copy of them. Eight days were given to him to put in his answer; and being required to give bail for his appearance, the Earl of Monmouth became his surety to the amount of £5,000.[2]

In his formal plea, he repeated the facts he had before stated,—concluding with the observation that "he did not conceive that there could be any offense in what was done by him in obedience to his Majesty's commands."

The King then very irregularly sent a letter to the Lord Keeper to be read in the House, in which, after reciting the articles of impeachment, which he had with his own hand delivered to the Attorney General, he thus proceeds: "We further declare that our said Attorney did not advise or contrive the said articles, nor had any thing to do with or in advising any breach of privilege that followed; and for what he did in obedience to our commands we conceive he was bound by his oath, and the duty of his place, and by the trust by us reposed in him so to do; and had he refused to obey us therein, we would have questioned him for the breach of his oath, duty, and trust."

[1] 2 Parl. Hist. 1089   [2] Ibid. 1090. 4 St. Tr. 120.

But the Lords were highly incensed by this letter, considering it "a prelimiting of their judgment;" and, having communicated it to the House of Commons, intimated that they were ready to proceed with the trial. This case being taken up by the Commons as "a breach of privilege," they intrusted the management of the impeachment to Sergeant Wilde, who opened it at the bar of the House of Lords, at prodigious length, and with great learning. Having examined all the precedents which could throw light upon the subject, he came to the defendant's plea. "But for the excuse under which he seeks to shelter himself, *that it is the King's command*, this adds more to his offense; a foul aspersion on his Majesty, and wrong to his gracious Majesty; for he could not but know that the King's command in things illegal is utterly frustrate and of no effect; his patents and grants, if against the Crown in matter of interest, are merely void *quia in deceptione Regis;* if against the weal public, they are *ipso jure vacua;* much more his command in matters criminal, because no action lies against him." The Sergeant then said that many aggravating circumstances might be added, "as the Attorney's profession and knowledge of the law,—his long experience in the course and privileges of parliament, having been so often and of late a member of the House of Commons, and obliged to them by many favors, and now an assistant or attendant in the House of Lords."[1]

Sir Thomas Beddingfield, Sir Thomas Gardiner, and some juniors, had been assigned by the House as counsel for the defendant, and he now prayed to be heard by them,—which he claimed as a right, being only charged with a misdemeanor; but Sergeant Wilde exclaimed, "We are a committee representing the House of Commons, and it doth not stand with the dignity of our House to have counsel come to confront us." He further alleged that this offense of Mr. Attorney's had been voted a high breach of the privileges of parliament, "which no counsel can, neither ought they, to judge of."[2]

It must be confessed that Sergeant Wilde, a meritorious and useful member of the Lower House, did sometimes push his privilege notions to a most extravagant length. On this occasion the Lords very properly decided, "that

---

[1] 4 St. Tr. 123.   [2] 2 Parl. Hist. 1125. 4 St. Tr. 124.

Mr. Attorney should have the benefit of counsel." It being late, the House then adjourned.

Next morning a scene took place at the bar, to be recorded by me with pain, as being little creditable to my profession, which with very few exceptions, has shown great independence and spirit, entitling itself to the respect and gratitude of the nation.

Sergeant Wilde, in the name of the Commons, intimated that, notwithstanding the erroneous decision of the Lords, " counsel would appear and plead for the defendant at their own peril," and very intelligibly threatened them with the vengeance of the House of Commons. Beddingfield and Gardiner, instead of boldly and manfully doing their duty to their client, and rejoicing in the dangers they had to encounter in braving the Commons, —when they were called upon to proceed, in a sneaking and paltry manner pretended that they were not prepared, as " a question of privilege " had been unexpectedly started upon them,—and they prayed for delay. The Lords construed this into a refusal to plead, and contempt of the authority of the House, and very properly committed them both to the Tower, there to remain during pleasure.[1]

On the petition of the defendant, the House assigned him two other leading counsel, Sergeant Green and Sergeant Pheasant; but they being sent for, pitifully excused themselves on the ground that, having been so suddenly called in, they could not do justice to the defense. The defendant's junior counsel, Hearne and Chute, who, to their honor, had been willing from the beginning to do their best for their client, whatever might befall themselves, were now heard, and spoke for him with great ability.

Finally, he was himself heard as to the right of the Attorney General to originate such a prosecution without a grand jury; and he showed several instances of charges of treason, originated by the Attorney General, *ex officio*, before the Lords, as that against the Earl of Bristol at the commencement of the present reign; but these were all against Peers, and no instance could be found since

---

[1] Having lain in prison six days, on their humble petition they were released.—4 St. Tr. 124.

MAGNA CHARTA of an attempt to convict a Commoner in this manner, without the intervention of a jury.[1]

The Lords found the defendant guilty; but, as far as he was concerned, considered it rather a venial case, and he had nearly escaped with a nominal punishment. The sentence finally agreed upon was,—" That he was disabled and made incapable of being a member, assistant, or pleader in either House of Parliament, and all offices, save that of Attorney General, which he now holds, and that he should be forthwith committed to the Fleet."[2]

He thus retained his office of Attorney General, to the great annoyance of those wished to have seen it conferred upon St. John.

He was liberated from gaol just about the time when the King left London. He joined his Royal Master at York, and remained faithful to him amidst all the vicissitudes of the civil war. He did not, like some other lawyers, both royalists and republican, throw aside his gown and put on harness; but he assisted as a civilian with his advice and his pen, and was generally respected by the cavaliers, although much disliked by Sir Edward Hyde, who, from jealousy, tried to keep him at a distance from the King, and to depress him as much as possible. He stationed himself during the war at Oxford and acted as assistant to the House of Lords in the rival parliament held there in 1644.

Among the doquets of the patents of Letters Patent, and other instruments which passed under the Great Seal at Oxford in the time of Charles I., is the entry of "a discharge for Sir Edward Herbert, Knight, continuing no longer in the office of his Majesty's Attorney General;" and another of "a patent to Sir Thomas Gardiner, Knight, of the office of his Majesty's Attorney General, with all fees, profits, rewards, and privileges thereto belonging;" but Dugdale takes no notice of this change, and Clarendon continues to designate Herbert by the title of Attorney General till the time when he was made Lord Keeper.

He never would acknowledge the authority of the parliment; and when the royal cause was desperate, he went abroad and joined the Prince in Holland. Here he was much favored by Prince Rupert; but in all the intrigues of the little Court he was crossed by his old personal

[1] 4 St. Tr. 129. [2] Ibid. 130.

enemy, Hyde, who, under the title of Chancellor of the Exchequer, wished to guide every thing by his own single opinion, and who says that at this time " the Attorney-General, Herbert, of all men living, was most disposed to make discord and disagreement between men, all his faculties being resolved into a spirit of contradicting, disputing, and wrangling upon anything that was proposed. He having no title or pretense to interpose in councils, found it easy to infuse into Prince Rupert, who totally resigned himself to his advice. such arguments as might disturb any resolution.¹ This chiefly refers to the employment of the small naval force under Rupert's command, with which he for some time carried on a buccaneering warfare against English commerce.

Clarendon, for once, was softened towards his rival by kindness shown him in distress. After relating the dangerous adventures which he and Lord Cottington had encountered when taken by freebooters, and carried into Ostend, on their way to join Charles in Holland, he says, " They had not been an hour at the Hague when Herbert, the Attorney General, came to them and congratulated their arrival, and told them how much they had been wanted, and how much Prince Rupert longed for their company." But the merit of this courtesy he lessens by the observation, " The Prince of Wales's Court was full of faction and animosity against each other, so that the new-comers were not only very well received by the Prince, but very welcome to every body, who being angry with the other Councillors there, believed that matters would be better carried now they were come."

The noble historian's inextinguishable spleen soon after again breaks out in his narration of a fracas in which Lord Colepeper received a black eye from Sir John Walsh. This he ascribes to a breach of confidence on the part of the Attorney General, who had been told of a dicussion in council respecting Walsh's character, and "who was the unfittest man living to be trusted with such a secret, having always about him store of oil to throw upon such a fire."²

The next notice we have of the subject of this memoir is in Clarendon's account of the Declaration in the name of the new Sovereign, which he himself prepared, on the

¹ Hist. Reb. b. xi. ² Ibid.

news arriving of the death of Charles I. The Prince of Orange insisted that this should be communicated to Herbert, "as one who was like to make a judgment how far anything of that nature was like to be acceptable and agreeable to the people;" and the author was very indignant that his composition should be submitted to such criticism, but was obliged to adopt several alterations which were suggested to make it less unpalatable to the Presbyterians.[1]

When Charles went into Scotland, and for a time became a "covenanted King" under the Marquis of Argyle, Herbert remained on the Continent in the suite of the Duke of York,—attended him to the Court of the Duke of Lorraine, and is accused by Clarendon, without proof or probability, of having there tried to marry him to the natural daughter of that Prince. He gave entire satisfaction to the royal family, and particularly to the Queen Mother, who would have shrunk with horror from the notion of a *mésalliance*, as Clarendon himself afterwards found—from her disdainful refusal to acknowledge his own daughter as her daughter-in-law.

Herbert joined the young King at Paris on his arrival there, after the battle of Worcester, and was kindly received by him. I have already related how he was afterwards invested with the dignity of Lord Keeper of the Great Seal.[2] Clarendon in vain attempted to conceal his extreme mortification at this appointment; and tries to comfort himself by saying that "the King knew the man very well, and had neither esteem nor kindness for him, and was only influenced by the Queen to make the Attorney General Lord Keeper, which was a promotion very natural, men ordinarily rising from the one office to the other. So his Majesty called him to his Council, and made him Lord Keeper of the Great Seal, with which he seemed wonderfully delighted, and for some time lived well towards every body; though to anything of business he appeared only in his old excellent faculty of raising doubts, and objecting against any thing that was proposed, and proposing nothing himself; which was a temper of understanding he could not rectify."[3]

I shall not be expected to give an account of Lord Keeper Herbert's speeches in opening parliaments,—of

[1] Hist. Reb. b. xii. [2] Ante, p. 395. [3] Hist. Reb. b. xiv.

the manner in which he dispatched business in the Court of Chancery,—or of legal reforms introduced by him. He held the Great Seal rather more than a year, during all which time he was resident at Paris; and if we are to credit his historiographer, he was employed in stirring up rather than in composing strifes. The implacable enmity between him and Hyde kept the Court in a state of constant agitation. The account we have of his conduct places him uniformly in the wrong, but this coming from such a quarter, and being entirely *ex parte*, must be received with many grains of allowance.

We are told that Herbert excited Long, the Secretary of State, to bring a false charge against "the Chancellor," (for this is the pompous title by which Hyde always designates himself at this time, that he might not appear of inferior rank to his rival, the "Lord Keeper,"[1]) of having gone over to England and had a secret interview with Cromwell, and that, when this was shown to be ridiculous, Herbert himself charged "the Chancellor" with having slandered the King. The witness in support of this charge was Lord Gerard, who swore that "Sir Edward Hyde had lamented to him *that the King was so fond of pleasure, and so adverse to business.*" The accused party answered, "that he did not recollect exactly what had passed in a private conversation supposed to have taken place a year ago, but if the Lord Gerard would positively affirm he had used such language, he would rather confess it, and submit himself to his Majesty's judgment, whether such words could be thought to proceed from any malice of his heart towards him, than, by denying it, continue the debate." The "CHANCELLOR" then offered to retire, but the King forbade him, upon which the "KEEPER" was very angry, and said "the words amounted to an offense of a high nature; and that he was sorry his Majesty was no more sensible of them; that for any man, especially a Councillor, and a man in so near a trust, to accuse his Master of not loving his business, and being inclined to pleasures, was to do all he could to persuade all men to forsake him." While he was proceeding, with great warmth and positiveness, the King interrupted him, and said, "I do really believe, that the faithful Councillor now blamed has used those very words, because he has often

---

[1] He was nominally Chancellor of the Exchequer.

said that and much more to myself; which I have never taken ill; and I do really believe I am myself in fault, and do not enough delight in business, which I must own is not very pleasant to me." But he declared "that he was well satisfied with *the Chancellor's* affection towards him, and took nothing ill that he had said;" and directed an entry to that effect to be entered in the books of the Council.[1]

At this time there was a considerable chance that Herbert might have continued in office and in favor till the restoration of the King; and then as Lord Chancellor and Prime Minister, he might have guided the destinies of the country; but after a hard struggle his rival triumphed, the Lord Keeper was dismissed, and he died in exile of a broken heart.

Prince Rupert, his great patron, having left the Court in disgust, had now retired into Germany, and Hyde, by unwearied assiduity, had for a time softened the dislike to him felt by the Queen mother. Charles was often told, that all the disputes among his followers arose from the ill temper of Lord Keeper Herbert, and in the hope of a more quiet life, determined to sacrifice him. He took the opportunity of effecting his purpose, when, in consequence of the strict alliance between Cardinal Mazarine and Cromwell, he was about to remove from France into the Low Countries. "He could not forget," says Clarendon, "the vexation the Lord Keeper had always given him, and how impossible it was for him to live easily with any body, and so in making the list of those who were to go with him, he left his name out, and, thereupon, this coming to the knowledge of the Keeper, he sought the King, and asked him, *if he did not intend that he should wait upon him*. His Majesty told him, *No! for that he resolved to make no use of his Great Seal; and therefore, that he should stay at Paris, and not put himself to the trouble of such a journey which he himself intended to make, without the ease and benefit of a coach.*[2] The Keeper expostulated with him in vain upon the dishonor that it

---

[1] Hist. Reb. 786. This anecdote is at all events very creditable to Charles, and deserves to be more generally known.

[2] Charles was too poor to keep a carriage for some years after, and in this journey yoked two old coach-horses which he had to a wagon, to carry his bed and his clothes.

would be to him to be left behind, and the next day brought the Great Seal and delivered it to him, and desired *that he would sign a paper in which his Majesty acknowledged that he had received again his Great Seal from him*, which the King very willingly signed."[1]

On whatever terms they parted, they never met more. Stung by what he considered the ingratitude of that family for whom he had renounced his profession, his family, and his country, he gave up all intercourse with them, and as they would forget nothing and learn nothing, he considered that they were irredeemably doomed to destruction. However, he would by no means attempt to make his peace with the Cromwellians, whom he held in unabated abhorrence. When Charles, attended by Hyde, Cottington, and Colepeper, proceeded to the Low Countries, Herbert took an obscure lodging in one of the fauxbourgs of Paris, and there he languished for three years, neglecting all the world, and neglected by it. Had he, according to the example of his rival, employed this time in recording the eventful scenes through which he passed, he might have thrown a very different light upon them from that in which we view them; he might have achieved a considerable name in history for himself, and his chance of being remembered as an English lawyer and statesman would not have depended on this imperfect memoir. Having lived in entire seclusion and idleness,—his mind a prey to discontent and despair,—he expired at Paris, in the autumn of the year 1657, at a time when Cromwell was courted by all the powers of Europe, and the star of the Stuarts seemed to have set for ever.

There are no sufficient materials to judge fairly of his character beyond pronouncing him a man of high principle, whose conduct was ever consistent and honorable. There is reason to think that, though a sincere Protestant, he was more tolerant on religious matters than his successful rival, and that, if he had remained in office till the King's return, the settlement of the Church might have been more comprehensive, and more in accordance with the expectations held out to the Presbyterian party, by whose efforts the monarchy was re-established. Yet, not only in literature, but in a knowledge of mankind and aptitude

[1] Hist. Reb. b. xiv.

for affairs, he must be allowed to be greatly inferior to the man by whom he was supplanted.

Upon the Restoration, his services were remembered and his family was patronized. His eldest son rose to a high command in the army, and was slain fighting for King William at the battle of Aghrim. His second son was the distinguished naval officer who fought at Beachy Head, and was created Earl of Torrington. His third son became Chief Justice of the King's Bench under James II., followed him into exile, was made by that Sovereign Lord Keeper of the Great Seal *in partibus*, and if there had been another restoration of the Stuarts might have stood in the list of " Lord Chancellors," whose lives I have to record.[1]

CHAPTER LXXIV.

LIFE OF LORD CHANCELLOR CLARENDON FROM HIS BIRTH TILL THE EXECUTION OF LORD STRAFFORD.

I NOW enter upon a task of great difficulty—embarrassed not by the scantiness, but by the superfluity of my materials.

"Inopem me copia fecit."

The subject of this memoir was personally concerned in many of the most important events which marked the thirty most interesting years to be found in our annals; by his own voluminous writings, and those of his contemporaries, we are amply informed of all he did, and said, and thought; and more praise and censure have been unduly lavished upon him than perhaps on any other public man who ever appeared in England. But striving to condense, and keeping in view the just boundaries of biography and history, I must not omit any statement or observations which I may deem necessary to convey an adequate notion of his career and of his character.

EDWARD HYDE was of a respectable gentleman's family, which for centuries had been settled in the county of Chester, and, in Scottish phrase, had been "Hydes of

[1] L. L. C. 131.

that ilk," being possessed of an estate by the name of which they were designated when surnames came into fashion. Lawrence, his grandfather, a cadet of this family, migrated into the West, and established himself at Dinton, in the county of Wilts. Henry, the Chancellor's father, studied the law in the Middle Temple, but marrying a Wiltshire lady "of a good fortune, in the account of that age," he became a country squire, after having traveled through Germany and Italy. He sat in several parliaments; but having neither hope of Court preferment, nor ambition to complain of grievances, he resolved to devote the remainder of his days to country pursuits and pleasures. "From the death of Queen Elizabeth he never was in London, though he lived above thirty years after; and his wife, who was married to him above forty years, never was in London in her life; the wisdom and frugality of that time being such, that few gentlemen made journeys to London, or any other expensive journeys, but upon important business, and their wives never; by which they enjoyed and improved their estates in the country, and kept great hospitality in their houses, brought up their children well, and were beloved by their neighbors."[1]

The Chancellor was born at Dinton, on the 18th of February, 1609. He received his early classical education under the paternal roof from the vicar of the parish, who, "though of very indifferent parts, had bred good scholars;" but he was chiefly grateful to "the superintending care and conversation of his father, who was an excellent scholar, and took pleasure in conferring with him."

In his fourteenth year he was sent to the University of Oxford, and admitted of Magdalen Hall. Being then a younger son, he was intended for holy orders; but he did not make much progress in theological studies, and having taken his Bachelor's degrees in February, 1626, he quitted the University "rather with the opinion of a young man of parts and pregnancy of wit, than that he had improved it much by industry."[2]

About this time his elder brother died, and he was entered a student of law in the Middle Temple, under the care of his uncle, Sir Nicholas, afterwards Chief Justice of the King's Bench, then Treasurer of that Society.

[1] Life of Clarendon, i. 5.   [2] Ibid. 8.

But his studies were seriously interrupted, first, by the plague which raged for some months in London, and then by a lingering attack of ague when he had retreated into the country. It was Michaelmas term, 1626, before he was able to establish himself regularly in chambers. He confesses that he had contracted a habit of idleness and of desultory reading, and that, when he returned, "it was without great application to the study of the law for some years." He now spent most of his time with "swash bucklers" and discharged military officers who had fought in Germany and the Low Countries, accompanying them to fencing-schools, ordinaries, and theaters. But he assures us that his morals were not contaminated by these dangerous associates; and this being so, he seems rather to have reflected with satisfaction on the opportunity he then improved of acquiring a knowledge of men and manners. He says, "that since it pleased God to preserve him whilst he did keep that company, and to withdraw him so soon from it, he was not sorry he had some experience in the conversation of such men, and of the license of those times,"—adding, with considerable felicity, "that he had more cause to be terrified upon the reflection than the man who had viewed Rochester Bridge in the morning that it was broken, and which he had galloped over in the night."[1] He was fond of literature, and he employed several hours each day in reading; but he would utterly have neglected Plowden and Coke, which then showed the newest fashions of the law, if it had not been for his uncle, Sir Nicholas, who questioned him about the "moots" he attended, and often "put cases" for his opinion. But natural disposition, or the prospect of succeeding to a comfortable patrimony, still made him affect the company of the gay and the dissolute.

In the summer of 1628, the old Chief Justice, with a view of compelling him to mix with lawyers, appointed him to "ride" the Norfolk circuit as his Marshal. Unfortunately, at Cambridge, the first assize town, he was attacked by the smallpox, and he was so ill that his life was despaired of; but at the end of a month he was able to proceed to his father's in Wiltshire.

[1] Life, i. 10. In his old age he bestows this qualified commendation on this passage of his youth, that "he was desirous to preserve himself from any notable scandal of any kind, and to live *caute*, if not *caste*."—*Life* iii. 974.

Soon after the recovery of his health, a circumstance occurred which gave a new turn to his views and his character. He fell desperately in love with a Wiltshire beauty, the daughter of Sir George Ayliffe, a young lady with no fortune, though of good family and high connections. His indulgent father consented to their union.

He thus became allied to the Marquis of Hamilton, and " was introduced into another way of conversation than he had formerly been accustomed to, and which, in truth, by the acquaintance, by the friends and enemies he then made, had an influence upon the whole course of his life afterwards."[1] But his domestic happiness came to a sudden termination. In little more than six months after his marriage, his young wife, in a journey from London into Wiltshire, caught the malignant smallpox and died. When he was sensible of the loss he had sustained, he was so overwhelmed with grief that he could hardly be restrained by his father from resigning his profession, and seeking seclusion in a foreign land.

He remained a widower near three years, the greater part of which time he devoted to books, but neither then, nor at any period of his life, did he attend very seriously to the study of the law,—with the technicalities of which he was never familiar. He continued to cultivate the high-born relatives of his late wife, and he made acquaintance with Ben Jonson,[2] Cotton, Isaac Walton, May, Carew, Edmund Waller, Sir Kenelm Digby, and Chillingworth. His manners were more polished and agreeable than those of most lawyers, and he was kindly noticed, not only by Lord Keeper Coventry, but by the Earl of Manchester, Lord Privy Seal, the Earl of Pembroke, Lord Chamberlain, the Earls of Holland, Hereford and Essex, and others of great consequence about the Court. His regard for the members of his own profession he chiefly confined to Lane, Attorney General to the Prince, and afterwards Lord Keeper, Sir Jeffrey Palmer, then a rising conveyancer, afterwards Attorney General to Charles II., and Bulstrode Whitelock, then getting into the lead on the

[1] Life, i. 18.
[2] " He (Ben Jonson) had for many years an extraordinary kindness for Mr. Hyde, till he found he betook himself to business, which he believed ought never to be preferred before his company."—*Life*, i. 30. Hyde preferred Ben to all poets, living or dead, except Cowley, but does not seem to have been at all acquainted with the writings of Shakespeare.

Oxford Circuit, afterwards Lord Keeper to the Commonwealth,—with all whom he was at this time on a footing of the most friendly intercourse, although their courses were afterwards so devious.[1] But the man with whom, he tells us, he had the most entire friendship, and of whom he speaks in terms of the warmest admiration and affection, was Lucius Carey, Lord Falkland,—in all whose sentiments he continued ever heartily to concur, till this bright ornament of his country fell in the battle of Newbury.

Hyde having recovered his spirits, again entered the married state, and formed a most auspicious union, which proved the great solace of his life. The lady was Frances, daughter of Sir Thomas Aylesbury, Master of the Mint. Having been his companion in all the vicissitudes of his fortune,—having lived with him in exile, sharing in his dangers and privations, and with difficulty providing food and raiment for their children,—she was preserved to see him Earl of Clarendon, Lord Chancellor, and Prime Minister of England.

His happiness was in a few months interrupted by the sudden death of his father. Burnet relates that, walking in the fields together, the old gentleman warned him of the disposition then observable among lawyers to stretch law and prerogative to the prejudice of the subject; charged him if he ever grew to any eminence in his profession, that he should never sacrifice the laws and liberties of his country to his own interests, or to the will of a Prince; and that, having repeated this twice, he immediately fell into a fit of apoplexy, of which he died in a few hours.[2] Clarendon himself wrote thus to a friend:—"Without one minute's warning or fear, I have lost the best father in the world, the sense of which hath been so terrible to me, that I was enough inclined to think I had nothing to do but to follow him."

The shock being over, he resolved instead of renouncing the world and living in retirement on his small estate, to continue to cultivate his profession, in the hope of rising to eminence, and with the resolution to observe the dying

---

[1] In Whitelock's Memorials we have an amusing extract of a letter addressed to him in the country, from Hyde in the Temple:—"Our best news is that we have good wine abundantly come over; and the worst, that the plague is in town, *and no Judges die.*" [2] Burn. Times, i. 270.

injunction of his father. " He put on his gown as soon as
he was called to the bar, and, by the countenance of persons in place and authority, as soon engaged himself in the
business of the profession as he put on his gown, and to
that degree in practice that gave little time for study
that he had too much neglected before."[1] He would not
submit to the drudgery of "riding a circuit,"—which he
afterwards lamented, "both because it would have improved his acquaintance with various classes of his countrymen, and because there is a very good and necessary
part of learning in the law which is not so easily got any
other way;"[2] but he regularly attended the Courts at
Westminster, and diligently devoted himself to the business of any clients who employed him. Though not
much of a lawyer compared with the black-letter men of
those days, he could, by his books and his friends, get up
a respectable argument, even against Selden or Noy,
and having a much better delivery, he was sometimes
thought by the by-standers to be superior to them in
learning as well as eloquence. He lived handsomely in
London, and exercised a distinguished hospitality at his
house in Wiltshire; but, though he was rather fond of
talking of wines and dishes, he was very temperate, and
generally abstained from supper, the meal at which those
who were fond of good living most indulged.

His growing eminence appears from the fact that at the
grand masque given by the Inns of Court to the Queen,
which we have several times had occasion to allude to,
the task was allotted to him, along with Whitelock, of
conferring with the Lord Chamberlain and the Comptroller of the household, and taking order about the
scenery and preparations in the banqueting house, and he
was deputed by the Middle Temple to the office of returning thanks in the name of the four Inns of Court to
the King and Queen, "for their gracious acceptance of the
tender of their services in the late masque."[3]

[1] Life, iii. 974. 975.
[2] Ibid. i. 32. He regretted the want of this practice so much, that he meant to have joined a circuit, when the troubles broke out.
[3] As this is, I trust, my last notice of this performance, I may be permitted to say I am sorry, for the credit of the Inns of Court, that they were obliged to apply to Shirley the poet, to write them "The Trumpet of Peace," the masque then exhibited to show their detestation of the *Histriomastix*, and of the coarse words supposed to be applied to the Queen for her love of theatricals; but they escape the disgrace of Shirley's ironical dedication of

In this mixture of business and pleasure some years rolled on, by far the happiest period of the life of Clarendon. "With an excellent wife, who perfectly resigned herself to him, and who then had brought him, before any troubles in the kingdom, three sons and a daughter, which he then and ever looked upon as his greatest blessing and consolation,"[1] his practice steadily increased, particularly before the Privy Council; he was respected by his own profession; he kept up an intercourse with men eminent in literature; he was countenanced by powerful courtiers; and he had before him a fair prospect of reaching the highest honors of his profession.

The system of ruling by prerogative alone having been pursued ever since he was of age, he had no opportunity of acquiring parliamentary reputation. In his heart he highly disapproved of "ship-money," and the arbitrary proceedings of the Star Chamber; but he was moderate in his principles and cautious in his conversation, and trying to live well with both parties. I do not find that he was employed in any of the celebrated political cases which then attracted the attention of the nation. However, in a dispute which the merchants of London had with the Treasury as to their being compelled to unload their goods at a particular quay, Hyde was their counsel, and he here displayed what was considered great courage against the government. This introduced him to Archbishop Laud, then chief Commissioner of the Treasury, who wished to see the young lawyer who was not afraid to plead the cause of the merchants, "when all men of name durst not appear for them." Hyde consequently went to the Archbishop, whom he found alone in his garden at Lambeth, was received very civilly, and was afterwards treated by him with condescension and kindness.[2] Those who regret the strong high church bias which he afterwards displayed, impute it to the impres-

the " Bird in a Cage " to Prynne, then in gaol under the inhuman sentence of the Star Chamber—congratulating him on his "*happy retirement.*"

[1] Life, i. 75.

[2] I am glad to say a good word for LAUD when it is in my power, and he certainly deserves credit for his patronage of merit. He brought into notice JEREMY TAYLOR; and though the fantasy must be condemned of making Bishop-JUXON Lord High Treasurer, it should be recollected that this prelate not only kept the best appointed pack of foxhounds in England, but was a most kind-hearted, pious man, and so inoffensive that even faction could not find fault with him.

sion now made upon him by his visits to Lambeth, and
think it might have been better for the cause of religion
in England if he had been thrown into the company of
Bishop Williams, Ex-Keeper of the Great Seal, who was
then leading the opposition against ceremonies and doctrines which he contended led directly to Romanism.

At last Charles was driven to call a Parliament, and
Hyde was in such good repute in his own country that he
was returned both by Shaftesbury and Wootton Basset.
He made his election to serve for the latter town, which
had likewise the honor of first sending to the House of
Commons, Twiss, the eminent lawyer, and the biographer of
Lord Eldon. Hyde's public career now begins, and he
certainly started with most enlightened and praiseworthy
views. A friend to the monarchy, he deeply regretted the
abuses which had been practiced in the name of prerogative,
and was eager to correct them. For this purpose he associated himself with Pym, Rudyard, Whitelock, and the
most experienced statesmen and lawyers, who, during this
"short parliament," co-operated with him in the same
cause.

He had the honor of striking the first blow in the
House at a specific grievance. This was by a motion for
papers respecting the Court of Honor, or Earl Marshal's
Court, which, under pretense of guarding heraldic distinctions, had become a powerful engine of oppression. He
mentioned several instances with decisive effect. A citizen was ruinously fined by this Court, because, in an
altercation with an insolent waterman who wished to
impose upon him, he deridingly called the *swan* on his
badge "a goose." The case was brought within the jurisdiction of the Court by showing that the waterman was an
earl's servant, and that the swan was the earl's crest.
The citizen was severely punished for "dishonoring" this
crest.—Again, a tailor who had often very submissively
asked payment of his bill from a customer of *gentle blood*,
whose pedigree was duly registered at the Heralds' College, on a threat of personal violence for his importunity,
was provoked into saying that "he was as good a man as
his debtor." For this offense, which was alleged to be a
leveling attack upon the aristocracy, he was summoned
before the Earl Marshal's Court, and mercifully dismissed
with a reprimand—*on releasing the debt.* While the

House was thus amused and excited, Hyde successfully concluded his maiden speech by telling them that not only was this Court oppressive to the humbler classes, but that its exactions were onerous to the nobility themselves, and to the whole body of the gentry of England.'

So active was he, that his name is to be found in seven of the twenty-one select committees which were appointed during the sixteen days the commons sat, including "the committee of privileges and elections," "the committee on ship-money," and "the committee to inquire into the proceedings of the convocation and innovations in matters of religion."

Very soon after he showed his moderation by supporting the Court on the grand question of supply. An indiscreet message had been brought down from the King, demanding twelve subsidies to be paid in three years, and making the abolition of ship-money depend upon this specific grant. Hampden, described as being now "the most popular man in the House," dexterously demanded that the question to be put might be, "Whether the House would consent to the proposition made by the King *as it was contained in the message?*"—so as to insure the rejection of the King's proposition.

Hyde, not dreading the collusion into which he was brought, nor the misconstruction to which he might be liable, with great moral courage desired that the question, as proposed by Mr. Hampden, might not be put. He argued that "it was a captious question, to which only one sort of men could clearly give their vote, which were they for rejecting the King's proposition and no more resuming the debate upon that subject; but that they who desired to give the King a supply, as he believed most did, though not in such a proportion, nor it may be in that manner, could receive no satisfaction from that question; and therefore he proposed, to the end that every man might frankly give his *yea* or his *no*, that the question might be put only upon the giving the King a supply."[2]

There were loud cries for Mr. Hyde's question, when old Sir Harry Vane, the Treasurer of the household (as

---

[1] Com. Jour. April 18, 1640. The business only began on the 16th of April, after the choice of the Speaker.

[2] Hist. Reb. b. i. This is the mode in which the question is now put, the motion being "that a supply be granted to her Majesty."

some thought treacherously), declared that there would
be no use in that question, for he had authority to say
that a supply would not be accepted by his Majesty if it
were not granted in the proportion and manner proposed
in his message. Hyde therefore no longer pressed his
amendment, and the debate on the general question was
adjourned till the following day, the courtiers threatening
an immediate dissolution.

Hyde, foreseeing the fatal consequences of such a step,
instantly repaired to Laud, on whose advice, in the ab
sence of Strafford, it was supposed the King would act,
and finding him in his garden at Lambeth, told him he
feared a dissolution was meditated, and that "he came
only to beseech him to use all his credit to prevent such a
desperate counsel, which would produce great mischief to
the King and to the Church, assuring him that the House
was as well constituted and disposed as ever House of
Commons was or would be." The Archbishop heard him
patiently, but differed from him entirely as to the disposition of the House, and affected to say that he would
not advise a dissolution, but neither would he counsel the
King against it.

On returning to the House from this interview, Hyde
was more grieved than surprised by the Black Rod's summons for the Commons forthwith to attend his Majesty
in the House of Lords, and by there hearing him, with
expressions of high displeasure, dissolve the parliament.

All were struck with consternation, except a few hot-
headed courtiers and some deep designing men, who did
not wish to obtain redress by temperate means, and were
desirous of aggravating dissensions between the parliament and the Crown, with a view to important organic
changes in the constitution. One of these was Oliver St.
John, who, with an air of unusual cheerfulness, met Hyde
an hour after the dissolution, and hearing him deplore the
unseasonable dismissal of "so wise a parliament," answered
with warmth—"All is well: it must be worse before it
can better: this parliament would never have done what
must be done before it is merry in England."

"No man can show me," wrote Clarendon, when, after
the lapse of many years, he recalled this scene to his
memory, "a source from whence these waters of bitterness
we now taste have more probably flowed than from these

unseasonable, unskillful, and precipitate dissolutions of parliament."[1]

To his unspeakable grief, this dissolution was immediately followed by measures which indicated a determination that parliament should never meet again,—popular leaders being committed to the Fleet for refusing to disclose what had passed in the House,—ship-money being exacted more rigorously than before,—a new tax being levied on the counties under the name of " Coat and Conduct Money,"—and four aldermen of London being being sent to gaol for declining to contribute to a forced loan in the City.

But before the end of the same year it was found, that if the King had attempted to trust longer to mere prerogative he would have ceased to reign.

Hyde sat in the Long Parliament for the borough of Saltash. His conduct in the first session of it entitles him to be placed in the first rank of English Reformers. He began by sacrificing his lucrative profession to the discharge of his public duties. Without office, or any immediate prospect of political preferment, he left the bar, reserving to himself the right to return to it in quieter times, and he bent the whole energies of his mind to the constitutional correction of existing abuses. While he zealously supported the great measures brought forward by others for abolishing the Star Chamber and High Commission, for determining the boundaries of the royal forests, for preventing the arbitrary levy of customs upon merchandise, and for insuring the frequent meeting of parliaments, he himself originated and carried through several very important reforms.

He began with his old subject, the Earl Marshal's Court, and moved for a select committee to inquire into its oppressions. This obnoxious tribunal had not relaxed in its mischievous activity since its recent exposure, and Hyde, who now "spake smartly and ingeniously,"[2] said, that for words of supposed defamation, of which the law took no notice, more damages had been given by the sole judgment of the Earl Marshal in two days, than by juries in all the actions tried in all the Courts in Westminster Hall during a whole term. He further proved, that the

---

[1] Hist. Reb. b. i. Charles had little regarded the dying advice of Lord Keeper Coventry, *ante*, Vol. III. Ch. LXII. [2] Whit. Mem. 50.

supposed Court was a mere usurpation during the present reign, the earliest precedent of its having entertained a suit for words being in the year 1633. The committee reported, "that the Constable's and Earl Marshal's Court has no jurisdiction to hold plea of words, that the Earl Marshal can make no Court without the Constable, and that the Earl Marshal's Court is a grievance." The report was adopted by the house; and so palpable was the usurpation which, unchecked, might have been confirmed by usage, that the Earl Marshal begged pardon for what he had done, throwing the blame upon his advisers, and, without any bill to abolish it, " the Court never presumed to sit afterwards."

Hyde was a member of the committee for inquiring into the illegal conduct of the Judges respecting ship-money, and assisted Lord Falkland in preparing the charges against Lord Keeper Finch. He presented from this committee a report which so deeply implicated Mr. Justice Berkely, that the learned Judge, while sitting in the Court of King's Bench in his robes, was arrested, and brought away prisoner through Westminster Hall, then full of people. But his unmeasured exposure of "judicial delinquency" was at a conference with the Lords respecting the Barons of the Exchequer, which he thus began: " My Lords, there can not be a greater instance of a sick and languishing commonwealth than the business of this day. Good God! how have the guilty these late years been punished, when the Judges themselves have been such delinquents? It is no marvel that an irregular, extravagant, arbitrary power, like a torrent, hath broken in upon us, when our banks and our bulwarks, the laws, were in the custody of such persons. Men who had lost their innocence could not preserve their courage; nor could we look that they who had so visibly undone us, themselves should have the virtue or credit to rescue us from the oppression of other men. It was said by one who always spoke excellently, *that the twelve Judges were like the twelve lions under the throne of Solomon,*—under the throne in obedience, but yet lions. Your Lordships shall this day hear of six, who (be they what they will be else) were no lions; who upon vulgar fears delivered up the precious forts they were trusted with almost without assault, and in a tame and easy trance of flattery and servitude, lost and forfeited (shamefully forfeited) that reputation, awe, and reverence which the wisdom, courage, and gravity of their venerable predecessors had contracted and fastened to the places they now hold; and even rendered that study and profession, which in all ages hath been, and I hope now shall be, of an honorable estimation, so contemptible and vile, that had not this blessed day come, all men would have had this quarrel to the law itself, which Marius had to the Greek tongue, who thought it a mockery to learn that language, the masters whereof lived in bondage under others. But it is in your Lordships' power (and I am sure it is in your Lordships' will) to restore the dejected, broken people of this island to their former joy and security, the successors of these men to their own privilege and veneration, *et sepultas prope leges revocare.*"[1] Having dwelt upon the resolution in favor of ship-money, which he denounced as "a prodigy of crime," he came to the misconduct of the Barons, in going so far as to deny the subject the opportunity of being heard against the illegal increase of duties on importations, by refusing replevies, and in sanctioning the levy of tonnage and poundage without authority of parliament.—If we do not altogether approve his rhetorical figures, we can not but admire his sentiments, and the boldness and vehemence with which he urged them. The known moderation of his character gave additional weight to his efforts against the Judges, and he was mainly instrumental in bringing down punishment upon them, and in procuring the condemnation of the slavish doctrines which they had inculcated.

The next subject which he took up was "the Council of the North," which had been established by Henry VIII. after an insurrection, and being continued without any regard to the rules of the common law, had become, —particularly under the presidency of the Earl of Strafford,—a scourge to the northern counties. He clearly showed its illegality and its mischiefs,—and after a conference with the Lords, in which he made another long speech against it, he procured its suppression.

He testified his sincere desire of a peaceable settlement by earnestly joining in the negotiations with the merchants in the city to raise money for paying the arrears

[1] Rushw. iv. 333.

due to the Scottish army, and enabling them to return to their own country, although the more violent party wished them to remain as a check upon the King; and Strode said publicly in the House, "We can not yet spare the Scotch; the sons of Zeruiah are too strong for us."

A controversy has arisen respecting the part taken by Hyde in the prosecution of the Earl of Strafford. In his account of it in the History of the Rebellion, he never once introduces his own name, and he censures those who conducted it. But though he thought fit thus to write long after the event, there can not be a doubt that he, as well as Lord Falkland, at the meeting of the Long Parliament, looked with abhorrence upon the apostate who had systematically attempted to establish despotism in England and in Ireland—that they both thought he deserved death, or reconciled it to their consciences that he ought to die, on the ground that his existence was incompatible with the public safety,—and that they both were instrumental in bringing him to the scaffold.

Hyde, when denouncing that unconstitutional tribunal, the Council of the North, inveighed bitterly against the tyranny of the Earl of Strafford as its President. When, in the course of the impeachment, a difficulty arose as to the attendance of members of the House of Commons as witnesses in the House of Lords, he was one of the committee of seven by whose assistance the difficulty was removed. He was originally a member of the committee to prepare the charge against Strafford (morally speaking, the blackest of all)—for his illegal judgment of death by a court-martial on Lord Mountnorris, and he was added to the committee of impeachment for the examination of the serious charge brought forward by the petition of Lord Langdale. He acted as chief manager in a conference with the Lords, with the view of sequestrating Strafford from his offices while the prosecution was pending,—and he was added to a committee for expediting the trial. But what shows even personal animosity and vindictiveness is, that Hyde took an active part in discovering and counteracting the plan that was formed to enable Strafford, like Lord Keeper Finch and Secretary Windebank, to escape beyond the seas. He communicated the name of a suspected ship, in consequence of which an examination took place before the House of the master of the

CHAPTER LXXV.

CONTINUATION OF THE LIFE OF LORD CLARENDON TILL HE WAS SENT TO BRISTOL WITH THE CHARGE OF PRINCE CHARLES.

IN the "History of the Rebellion" there is strong, and I think just, censure thrown upon the bill which was next brought forward "for the perpetual parliament," as it was afterwards called; but there is as little doubt that "the noble Historian" not only acquiesced in it, but applauded it. He says, "it is not credible what an universal reception and concurrence it met with, although it was to remove the landmarks and to destroy the foundation of the kingdom." The truth is, that he and others saw the mischiefs which arise from abrupt dissolutions, but were blind to the dangers of an irresponsible oligarchy uncontrollable by constitutional means—to be overthrown only by military despotism. It is deeply to be regretted that the reasonable amendment, carried in the Lords, was rejected by the Lower House,—limiting the operation of the bill to two years,—within which time it might have been reasonably expected that all grievances might be redressed, and all constitutional controversies adjusted,—so that the power of dissolving the parliament might be safely restored to the Crown.

But although Hyde was carried away by the general impulse—when the bill had passed, he soon saw "that the Commons now that they could not be dissolved without their own consent (the apprehension and fear whereof had always before kept them within some bounds of modesty), they called any power they pleased to assume to themselves a branch of their privileges of which they were the only proper judges."[1] He now changed his party, but (I must say), without being at all liable to the imputation of a change from mercenary motives, which

---

[1] Hist. Reb. b. i. The House resolved, on the motion of Sergeant Wilde, "that when they had declared what was the law of the land, it was a breach of their privileges that it should not be obeyed;" and this doctrine they applied even to their right to issue orders to raise troops in the King's name to fight against his person.

is conveyed by the modern word "*ratting*." He did not, like Wentworth, barter his principles for preferment and power. He thought, very plausibly, that enough had been done to redress grievances, and that the danger now was from popular usurpation, much more than from an extension of prerogative. Whatever opinion might be entertained of the King's sincerity or secret inclinations, the royal assent had been given to statutes which, in some measure, adapted the constitution to the actual circumstances of the country. And although there was a pestilent set of lawyers, who contended that acts of parliament limiting the prerogative were not binding, the same national energy which had extorted these acts would have been ready to defend them. Hyde threw his weight into the royal scale, that it might not kick the beam. He says that his resolution was much strengthened by conversations he had about this time with some of the popular leaders who betrayed their anti-monarchical views. "I do not think one man wise enough to govern us all," said Henry Martin,—and Fiennes, at this time a furious presbyterian, told him "that there were many who would encounter the worst extremities of civil war if the King should resist the abolition of episcopacy, for that there was a great number of good men who wished to lose their lives before they would ever submit to that government." [1]

It was upon a church question that he split with his old friends. After the failure of the first attempt to exclude the Bishops from parliament, a Select Committee had reported, "That the legislative and judicial power of Bishops in the House of Peers is a great hindrance to the discharge of their spiritual functions, prejudicial to the Commonwealth, and fit to be taken away." Against a bill founded on this resolution, Hyde made an earnest speech, arguing that it went to change the whole frame and constitution of the kingdom, and of the parliament itself.

Lord Falkland defended it—according to Hyde—as the only expedient to save the church,—but dealt by no means tenderly with the arguments of his friend against it, and boldly insisted that both on spiritual and civil considerations the Bishops ought to be excluded.

[1] Life, i. 92.

This encounter in debate did not interrupt their friendship. After the difference of opinion between them had for a short time extended to some matters of minor importance, it entirely vanished, and they continued ever after politically, as well as personally, united,—for there was now manifested a clear intention to upset the Church and the Monarchy.

The bill for excluding the Bishops from parliament having passed the Commons, it was followed by a bill "for the utter abolishing and taking away of all Archbishops, Bishops, their Chancellors and Commissioners, Deans and Chapters, Archdeacons, Prebendaries, Choristers, and Canons, and other under Officers, out of the Church of England."[1] This Hyde strenuously opposed, but the second reading was carried by a majority of 139 to 108. When it got into a committee of the whole House,—by way of a manœuvre, that he might be silenced, he was placed in the chair; but he, considering counter-manœuvring pious in such a cause, tells us, that by dexterous management as Chairman, he was enabled greatly to obstruct it, and as it contained clauses for the new government of the Church, about which few were agreed, it had made but little progress when parliamentary proceedings were suspended by the King's journey into Scotland.[2]

Before then an event had taken place which had a powerful influence on the destiny of Hyde. He had held no intercourse with the Court, and there, till very lately, he had been regarded with bitter aversion. But one day, while the "Episcopacy Abolition Bill" was in Committee, he was informed by Mr. Percy, brother of the Earl of Northumberland, that the King desired to speak with him. He went, and the following is his account of the interview,—written, however, many years after. Charles told him "that he heard from all hands how much he was beholden to him, and that when all his servants in the

---

[1] 2 Parl. Hist. 725, 792, 814, 916.

[2] While this committee was sitting, he continued on terms of great courtesy with the promoters of the bill. He says, "the House keeping those disorderly hours, and seldom rising till after four of the clock in the afternoon, they frequently importuned him to dine with them at Mr. Pym's lodging, which was at Sir Richard Manby's house, in a little court behind Westminster Hall, where he and Mr. Hampden, Sir Arthur Hazelrig, and two or three more, upon a stock kept a table where they transacted much business, and invited thither those of whose conversion they had any hope."—It appears that Hyde often accepted the invitation.—*Life*, i. 80.

House of Commons either neglected his service or could not appear usefully in it, he took all occasion to do him service; for which he thought fit to give him his own thanks, and to assure him that he would remember it to his advantage. The King took notice of his affection for the Church, for which he said he thanked him more than all the rest, which the other acknowledged with all the duty that became him, and said that he was very happy that his Majesty was pleased with what he did; *but if he had commanded him to have withdrawn his affection and reverence for the Church, he would not have obeyed him, which, his Majesty said, made him love him the better.* Then he discoursed of the passion of the House, and of the bill then brought in against Episcopacy, and asked him whether he thought they would be able to carry it? To which he answered, that he believed they could not; at least, that it would be very long first. 'Nay,' replied the King, 'if you will look to it, that they do not carry it before I go for Scotland, which will be when the armies are disbanded, I will undertake for the Church after that time.' 'Why, then,' said the other, 'by the grace of God, it will not be in much danger.' With which the King was well pleased, and dismissed him with very gracious expressions."[1]

Hyde was now a regular adherent to the royal cause, and if we forget the insincerity of Charles and the supposed necessity of imposing harder conditions for securing what had been obtained, we should be disposed severely to blame those who wished still further to humble the Crown: but Hampden and Whitelock, who were attached to the constitution, and who, at the opening of the parliament, had hardly differed from any sentiment of Hyde and Falkland, remained unsatisfied; and as they well knew the character of the King and the circumstances of the times, we must be slow to blame the course which they adopted. It led in the result to civil war; but if Charles had been allowed quietly to carry into effect his plans in Scotland, and with a well supplied treasury to support an army in England,—all the bills to which he had recently assented might have been treated like the Petition of Right; he might have wreaked the vengeance which he certainly meditated upon the popular leaders; and he

[1] Life, i. 93.

might finally have triumphed over the liberties of this country.

With a view to check the reaction which was very perceptible in the King's favor on his return from Scotland, the famous "Remonstrance" was moved,—recapitulating in harsh language all the errors of his reign, and all the grievances under which the people had labored. This Hyde strenuously opposed as unnecessary and insulting, and it was carried only by a small majority.[1] A question then arose as to whether it should be published before it was communicated to the Lords; and he was in great danger of being sent to the Tower for having proposed, after the fashion of the Lords, to enter a protest against a resolution to that effect.

He now wrote his maiden state paper in the royal cause, which was a manifesto in the King's name, in answer to the "Remonstrance." He says, that he first sketched it as an exercise without any thought of its being used; but showing it to some friends, it was carried to the King, who was highly pleased with it, and adopted it. The tone of it is certainly excellent, and if the composition be not quite pure, it is at any rate in better taste than the addresses of the parliament.

Falkland and Colepeper were now introduced into office as Secretary of State and Chancellor of the Exchequer, and the King again sending for Hyde told him, in the presence of the Queen, "that he was much beholden to him for many good services; and that now he had preferred two of his friends, it was time to give him some testimony of his favor, and therefore he had sent for him to tell him that he intended to make him his Solicitor General in the place of him who had served him so ill."[3] *Hyde.* "God forbid." *King.* "Why, God forbid?"—*Hyde.* "Sire, it is my duty to advise your Majesty that it is by no means fit that at this time the other should be removed, and to assure your Majesty that if he were removed, I am in no degree fit to succeed him."

The Queen then, in a very complimentary manner, insisted on Hyde's high qualifications for the office; but he besought them to believe, "that although the present Solicitor General will never do much service, he will be able to do much more mischief if he be removed." They then

[1] 159 to 148. [2] Parl. Hist. 937, 942. [3] Oliver St. John.

proposed another opening to him; but he tells us he assured them "he should be able to do much more service in the condition he was in."[1]

Hyde thus for the present remained without any office; but a sort of *inner cabinet* was constituted, consisting of him, Falkland, and Colepeper,—whom the King desired to meet frequently to consult on his affairs,—to conduct them in parliament,—and to give him constant advice what he was to do,—solemnly pledging himself "*that without their consent, he would take no step in parliament whatever.*"[2]

The three associates met nightly at Hyde's house, conferring on the events of the by-gone day, and concerting measures for the morrow. To him was assigned the drawing of all papers which were to appear before the world against the proceedings of the parliament, and he likewise carried on a private correspondence with the King to inform him of their sentiments, and to keep him steady to his purpose.

Under this arrangement the royal cause visibly prospered; and the people, according to their natural levity and ingratitude, already forgetting the reforms which the parliament had achieved for them, were beginning to regard the leaders as men merely actuated by personal ambition,—when the King, being told by foolish courtiers and bed-chamber women that the moment had arrived for victory and vengeance, ordered Herbert, the Attorney General, forthwith to go to the House of Lords, and to impeach Lord Kimbolton, and the five members for high treason,—and he himself, in his own proper person, entered the House of Commons to arrest them with his own hand.

We may judge of Hyde's consternation at the news of these proceedings, from his statement written years after, when indignation at the treachery of Charles, and contempt for his weakness, had been almost absorbed in pity for his misfortunes. "The three persons before named, without whose privity the King had promised that he would enter upon no counsel, were so much displeased and dejected, that they were inclined never more to take upon them the care of any thing to be transacted in the House, finding already that they could not avoid being

[1] Life, i. 101. [2] Ibid. i. 102.

looked upon as the authors of those counsels, to which they were so absolute strangers, and which they so perfectly detested; and, in truth, they had then withdrawn themselves from appearing often in the House but upon the abstracted consideration of their duty and conscience, and the present ill condition the King was in."[1]

It is creditable to Hyde that, without office or emolument, he continued, on public grounds, to serve a Sovereign in whom he could no longer place private confidence, at a time when difficulties were so rapidly accumulating round him. The parliament now openly assumed the functions of the executive government, by ordering out the train-bands, and issuing commands to the governors of fortresses. They even interfered with the management of the King's children; and Hyde was ordered, along with another member of the House of Commons and a Peer, to attend his Majesty and inform him of their wishes, that Prince Charles should not be removed from Hampton Court. The deputation found the King at Canterbury on his return from Dover, where the Queen had embarked—after persuading him to assent to the "Bishops' Exclusion Bill." They were ordered "to attend him after he had supped, and they should receive their answer." Accordingly they were admitted at nine o'clock, and a sharp rebuke was read to them for their impertinence. In public, Hyde could only act and be treated as one of the deputies; but he contrived to have a private interview when the King was undressing for bed, and, with great difficulty, prevailed upon him to recall the answer, "which could produce no good, and might do hurt," and to desire the deputation to wait upon him at Greenwich to receive his final reply, although Charles still "enlarged, with much sharpness, upon the insolence of the message."

In the meantime Hyde, with the sanction of Falkland and Colepeper, framed a more moderate answer, which was adopted. Henceforward he was entirely in the King's confidence, and drew all the papers which were supposed, by the Council even, to be the King's own composition,—on a promise that the real authorship of them should be kept a profound secret. "His Majesty continued so firm in this resolution, that though the declarations from the

[1] Hist. Reb. b. ii.

Houses shortly after grew so voluminous, that the answers frequently contained five or six sheets of paper closely writ, his Majesty always transcribed them with his own hand, which sometimes took him up two or three days and a good part of the night, before he produced them to the Council, where they were first read, and then he burned the originals."[1]

Charles now withdrew from Whitehall, which he never again entered except as a prisoner, and traveling towards the north, prepared for war. Hyde seems to have thought that he would have done better to have trusted to the general disgust which must soon have been produced by the violent encroachment of the parliament, if he had appeared to place confidence in the returning good sense and loyalty of the people. In a letter to Charles, he solemnly warned him against the counsels of violent men. Having mentioned the reports respecting his Majesty's "designs of immediate force," he decently says, "to none of which your servants give the least credit, assuring themselves that, however your affairs and conveniences have invited you to York, you intend to sit as quietly there as if you were at Whitehall. For your Majesty well knows that your greatest strength is in the hearts and affections of those persons who have been the severest assertors of the public liberties; and so, besides their duty and loyalty to your person, are in love with your inclinations to peace and justice, and value their own interests upon the preservation of your rights. These your Majesty will not lose by any act which may beget just fears in them. Neither can there be so cunning a way found out to assist those who wish not well to your Majesty (if any such there be), as by giving the least hint to your people that you rely upon anything but the strength of your laws and their obedience."[2]

The parliament saw the advantage which the King might have drawn from delay, and they hurried on their Ordinance about the militia, to which he could not consent,—as, in violation of the first principles of the constitution, it transferred to them the power of the sword, and it virtually dethroned him. The King's declaration, drawn by Hyde, on rejecting this measure, is a masterly per-

---

[1] Life, i. 119–125.   [2] Clar. State Pap. ii. 139.

formance, and must have produced a considerable effect upon the public mind.[1]

Notwithstanding all the precautions which were used, there was a strong suspicion that the member for Saltash carried on a secret correspondence with the King, and a motion was planned for an inquiry " upon whose advice the King acted,"—to be followed up by an order for sending the offender to the Tower; but before this intention could be carried into effect, Hyde finally withdrew from the parliament. He received a letter from the King expressing a wish that he should repair to York, "there being now urgent occasions for his immediate advice." Having come to an explanation with the Lord Keeper Littleton,[2] he obtained leave of absence for a few days upon a physician's written recommendation " that he should take the air of the country for his health."[3] He first went to the house of a friend near Oxford, and there hearing of the escape of the Lord Keeper, he prosecuted his journey accompanied by Chillingworth. Traveling by unfrequented roads he safely reached Nastall, the residence of Sir John Worstenholme, about twenty miles from York. Here, where he had been expected, the King sent him the parliament's famous proclamation of the 26th of May, and required him to furnish a prompt reply, " that the poison might not work too long upon the minds of the people." Having performed this task, he kissed the King's hand at York, and thenceforth remained constantly near his person, till the disasters of the war caused their final separation.

Then came " the nineteen propositions"—more rigorous than those imposed by the Barons on Edward II. or on Richard II., by which were to be subjected to the control of parliament the appointment of all privy councillors and ministers of state, the keeping of all forts and castles, the command of the militia, and the government, education, and marriage of the King's children;—the King was to consent to such a reformation of the church-government and liturgy as both Houses shall advise ;—every member of either House dismissed from office during the present parliament, was to be restored on the petition of the House of which he was a member;—the justice of parlia-

[1] Rushworth, iv. 578–599. [2] Parl. Hist. 1201.
[2] Ante, Vol. III. Chap. LXVI. [3] Life, i. 136.

ment was to pass on all delinquents, notwithstanding the royal pardon;—Papist Peers were disqualified,—and no Peers made thereafter were to sit or vote in parliament till admitted thereunto with the consent to both Houses.[1] The King's answer, prepared by the three friends, powerful in reasoning and touching in sentiment, thus concluded:—"These being passed, we may be waited upon bare-headed, we may have our hand kissed, the style of Majesty continued to us, and the King's authority declared by both Houses of parliament may be still the style of your commands; we may have swords and maces carried before us, and please ourself with the sight of a crown and a scepter; but as to true and real power, we should remain but the outside, but the picture, but the sign of a King."[2]

Hyde now heartily concurred in the issuing of the Commissions of array,—in the declaration signed by a majority of the Peers and many of the northern gentry, binding themselves to defend the King's person, crown, and dignity,—and in the proclamation requiring the aid of all the King's subjects north of Trent and within twenty miles southward thereof, for suppressing the rebels now marching against him. He was present, not disapproving, though with an aching heart, at the scene of erecting the royal standard at Nottingham, of which he has left us such a graphic description:—"The standard was erected at six of the clock in the evening of a very stormy and tempestuous day. The King himself, with a small train, rode to the top of the Castle hill, Varney, the Knight Marshal, who was standard-bearer, carrying the standard, which was then erected in that place with little other ceremony than the sound of drums and trumpets. Melancholy men observed many ill presages about that time. There was not one regiment of foot yet brought thither, so that the train-bands which the sheriff had drawn together, were all the strength the King had for his person and the guard of the standard. There appeared no conflux of men in obedience to the proclamation. The arms and ammunition were not yet come from York, and a general sadness covered the whole town. The standard was blown down the same night it had been set up, by a very strong and unruly wind, and could

[1] 2 Parl. Hist. 1389.   [2] Rush. iv. 728.

not be fixed again in a day or two till the tempest was allayed."[1]

To gain time, a pacific message, prepared by Hyde, was sent by the King to the two Houses, and their intemperate rejection of it operated powerfully in his favor, and "levies of men and all other preparations for the war incredibly advanced." I do not find that any gentleman of the long robe took arms on the King's side in this memorable struggle, with the exception of Lord Keeper Littleton's volunteer corps at Oxford, and they probably would have met with little countenance from Prince Rupert and the cavalier officers. Hyde made himself useful by obtaining large supplies of plate to be coined into money from the two Universities, by raising loans for the King from persons of wealth in the midland counties, and, preceding the march of the army, by trying to induce the mayors of towns and other civil authorities to espouse the royal cause.

He was present at the battle of Edge Hill, but placed in the rear among the non-combatants,—the King's two sons, the Prince of Wales and the Duke of York, then boys of twelve and nine years of age, being intrusted to his care. It is said that the day after the fight, when the King, notwithstanding his severe losses, might have marched to London, both Falkland and Hyde dissuaded him from this step, "not desiring to obtain that by a pure victory which they wished to be got by a dutiful submission upon modest, speedy, and peaceable terms."[2] But his approach to the metropolis would have roused a a dangerous resistance to him there, while the Earl of Essex would have hung upon his rear,—and he probably followed prudent advice in marching to Oxford, "the only city that he could say was certainly at his devotion."[3] Here he established and retained the seat of his civil government till the termination of the war.

Through the instrumentality of Hyde a negotiation was now opened with the parliament, and there was a very favorable prospect of a settlement; but it was suddenly terminated by the treacherous march of the King to Brentford,—after which "all thoughts of treaty were dashed; they who most desired it did not desire to be in the King's mercy; and they now believed, by his Majesty making

[1] Hist. Reb. b. v.   [2] Sir P. Warwick's Mem.   [3] Hist. Reb. b. vi.

so much haste towards them after their offer of a treaty, that he meant to have surprised and taken vengeance of them without distinction."[1]

The attempt at negotiation was resumed ineffectually during the winter, and in the spring both parties prepared actively for operations in the field. Now at last, Hyde was installed in a responsible office. A letter from the King to the Queen had been intercepted and published by the Parliament, in which, after expressing an intention to make Secretary Nicholas Master of the Wards, he adds, "And then I must make Ned Hyde Secretary of State, for the truth is I can trust nobody else." The King having procured a printed copy of this letter, himself showed it to Hyde, and proposed immediately to carry the plan into effect. Hyde refused, unless with the full consent of Nicholas, who represented that the change would be disadvantageous to him. Luckily at this time the office of Master of the Rolls, which Colepeper greatly coveted, became vacant by the death of Sir Charles Cæsar. Colepeper willingly gave up his office of Chancellor of the Exchequer for the Rolls, of which he never enjoyed but the title, Speaker Lenthal being soon in possession of its jurisdiction and emoluments,—and Hyde was made Chancellor of the Exchequer, was sworn of the Privy Council, and received the honor of knighthood.

He exerted himself with great energy in his office, and was in hopes of a favorable issue to the contest—when the battle of Newbury was fought, in which fell Lord Falkland, "a loss," he says, "which no time will suffer to be forgotten, and no success of fortune could repair."[2]

The office of Secretary of State, now vacant by the untimely death of this distinguished man, was offered to Hyde, but he declined it in favor of Lord Digby, who, it was thought, might be more competent to conduct negotiations then pending with Harcourt, the French ambassador.

The Chancellor of the Exchequer was soon overwhelmed with grief by the decline of the royal cause—

[1] Hist. Reb. Passage suppressed in 1st edition.
[2] Hist. Reb. iv. There is nothing in the writings of Clarendon which gives us so high an opinion of his head and his heart, as his character of Lord Falkland. The writer must have had high qualities himself who could so enthusiastically admire, so delicately discriminate, and so beautifully delineate the high qualities of another.—*Life*, i. 42-50

which he mainly ascribed to the misconduct of the royalists, both in the military and civil departments. "Those under the King's command grew insensibly unto all the havoc, disorder, and impiety with which they had reproached the rebels, and *they* into great discipline, diligence, and sobriety. Thus one side seemed to fight for monarchy with the weapons of confusion, and the other to destroy the King with all the principles of monarchy." Hyde himself, notwithstanding his talents and services, was regarded with envy by ignorant, profligate, high-born cavaliers as an upstart. The recollections of the slights and indignities which he now suffered afterwards drew from him these cutting observations:—"It were to be wished that persons of the greatest birth and fortune would take that care of themselves, by education, industry, literature, and a love of virtue, to surpass all other men in knowledge, and all other qualifications necessary for great actions, as far as they do in qualities and titles; that Princes, out of them, might always choose men fit for all employments and high trusts; which would exceedingly advance their service, where the reputation and respect of the person carries somewhat with it that facilitates the business. And it can not well be expressed or comprehended by any who have not felt the weight and burden of the envy which naturally attends upon these promotions which seem to be *per saltum*, how great straits and difficulties such ministers are forced to wrestle with."[1]

About this time Hyde had to resist a bold measure, which the King, at the suggestion of some hot-headed courtiers, strongly urged,—to issue a proclamation for dissolving the parliament. His Majesty said, "that he thought there was too much honor done to those rebels at Westminster in all his declarations, therefore he knew no reason why he should not forbid them to sit, or meet any more there; he knew learned men of an opinion, that the act for the continuance of the parliament was void from the beginning, and that it is not in the power of the King to bar himself from dissolving it." The Chancellor of the Exchequer answered with irresistible force, "that not only the people in general, but those of his own party, and even of his Council, would take more umbrage upon

---

[1] Hist. Reb. b. iv.

such a step than upon any one particular that had happened since the beginning of the war; that his forbidding them to meet at Westminster, would not make one man the less meet there; and that if he had the power to dissolve this parliament on such grounds, he might likewise repeal all other acts made by this parliament, whereof some were very precious to the people; and that such a proclamation would confirm all the fears and jealousies which had been infused into them, and would trouble many of his own true subjects."

The noble historian insinuates, that this advice came from Herbert, the Attorney General, against whom he ever shows his grudge. After some conferences with Mr. Attorney, the scheme was abandoned.[1]

Hyde continued to struggle vigorously amidst all difficulties and discouragements, and in the hope of producing a scene where talent and merit might have the ascendency, he prevailed on the King to call a parliament at Oxford, as a rival to that at Westminster. He was now for a time in the important position of leader of the House of Commons, being decidedly the first in eloquence and a knowledge of parliamentary business of the 120 Commoners who assembled in Christ Church Hall. As Chancellor of the Exchequer he opened his budget, detailing the mischiefs which arose from raising money by unlawful means, and under the plea of warlike license; and showing the necessity for finding more regular methods for raising supplies to carry on the war. He did not, however, venture to propose that any tax should be formally imposed,—which might have speedily raised an awkward question as to the regularity and powers of this Oxford parliament, while another was sitting under a law to which the King had given his assent. He proposed, therefore, that, under the authority of the two Houses, as testified by letters to be signed by their respective Speakers, a contribution should be levied on the wealthy, with their own consent, in the nature of a property tax; and that the royalists should imitate the tax lately imposed by an ordinance of the two Westminster Houses, on wine, beer, and other articles of household consumption,—the origin of our excise.[2] These "ways and

[1] Life of Clarendon, i. 169.
[2] Both parliaments declared that this tax should only continue to the end

means" were agreed to, and produced a considerable supply.

The other great measure attempted by this Convention,—the opening a negotiation for peace, proved abortive,—the two Houses at Westminster refusing to receive any communication till they were recognized as a parliament,—and when they had been so recognized, complaining that "the persons now assembled at Oxford, who, contrary to their duty, had deserted the parliament, were put on an equal footing with the two Houses convened according to the known and fundamental laws of the kingdom." This "little Senate," to which Hyde gave laws, concluded its session by a resolution, "that the Lords and Commons remaining at Westminster have rejected all offers of peace and treaty; and that for having made war against the King, counterfeited the King's Great Seal, and abetted the Scotch invasion, they are guilty of high treason, and ought to be proceeded against as traitors to the King and kingdom."[1] The desire for peace and the jealousy about religion, manifested by some of the members, had given much uneasiness, and the prorogation was a great relief to the King, and still more to the Queen, who hated the very name of parliament.

During the campaign which followed, in which Prince Rupert once more, at Marston Moor, lost a great battle by his blind impetuosity, Hyde remained at Oxford trying in vain to establish some order and regularity in the administration of the King's affairs. He received a flattering mark of his importance, in being specially exempted from pardon in some new demands made by the parliament at Westminster, in the autumn of 1644.

In the beginning of the following year, Hyde was the leading commissioner on the part of the King at the treaty of Uxbridge, the last time the two parties negotiated on any thing like equal terms,—subsequent events soon placing the King as a prisoner in the hands of his subjects. Seeing that there never would be another chance of pacification on the basis of preserving a limited monarchy, his exertions were now stupendous. "They that had been most inured to business had not in their lives ever undergone so great fatigue for twenty days to-

of the war, and then be utterly abolished—"which," adds Clarendon, "few wise men believed it would ever be." [1] Rush. v. 565. Ante.

gether as at that treaty. The Commissioners seldom parted during that whole time till two or three o'clock in the morning. Besides, they were obliged to sit up later who were to prepare such papers as were directed for the next day, and to write letters to Oxford," [1] a task which fell chiefly on Hyde himself. He was particularly charged with the church question, and peremptorily refusing the entire abolition of episcopacy, he expressed a willingness to modify the church establishment, and disallow pluralities with cure of souls,—that the Bishop should keep constant residence in his diocese, and preach in some church within it every Sunday,—and that £100,000 should be raised out of Bishops' lands for the public service.[2]

On this and every other point the parliamentary Commissioners were inflexible, so that a constitutional settlement was impossible, and another trial of strength in the field was to determine whether England should fall under the sway of an absolute monarch or of a republic.

CHAPTER LXXVI.

CONTINUATION OF THE LIFE OF LORD CLARENDON TILL HIS RETURN FROM THE EMBASSY TO MADRID.

BEFORE the expected crisis arrived, Hyde's position was entirely altered. The King wished to remove Prince Charles, now a spoiled youth of fourteen, from the Court (as he said), "to unboy him," and the presence of some person of exalted rank was greatly wanted in the west of England, where Goring, Granville, and other royal generals were quarreling for the command, and exposing themselves to loss and discredit. An association of the gentry and yeomanry of the four western counties had petitioned that the Prince should be placed at their head, and notwithstanding his tender years he was invested with two commissions, one as General of all the King's forces in England, and another as Commander of the western association. But he was to be guided in every thing by a mixed council of military officers and civilians, and among the latter was Sir Edward Hyde, on

[1] Hist. Reb. b. v. [2] Ibid. b. v. Rush. v. 892.

whose prudence and attachment the King placed such reliance. Although he was still to retain his office of Chancellor of the Exchequer, he very little relished this new appointment, but he deemed it his duty to submit. I suspect that the real cause of his removal was the dislike entertained for him by the more violent cavaliers, and by the Queen, who considered him little better than a Roundhead. From this time he had no influence whatever in the general direction of the King's affairs.

On the 5th of March, 1645, the Prince and his adviser took leave of Charles, now fated to destruction, and neither of them ever saw him more. They journeyed on to Bristol, then a royal garrison, where they stayed a considerable time, while efforts were vainly made to allay the jealousies of the rival Generals. The Council, at the suggestion of Hyde, wrote to the King, proposing that the Prince should be recalled; but before an answer was received, news arrived of the disastrous defeat at Naseby, and there was no safety for the royal family in the center of England. Fairfax advanced towards Bristol, and it was necessary to conduct the Prince further to the west. Had he remained, he must have been taken prisoner on the shameful surrender of that city by Prince Rupert.

The King, who had retreated into South Wales, now anxious for the safety of his son, summoned Hyde and Colepeper, who was likewise of the Prince's Council, to repair to him. The former was confined to his bed by illness, but the latter joined Charles at Brecknock, and brought back from him a mandate addressed to the Prince in these words: "My pleasure is, whensoever you find yourself in apparent danger of falling into the rebels' hands, that you convey yourself into France, and there to be under your mother's care, who is to have the absolute full power of your education in all things except religion." Hyde, who was always at enmity, either openly or secretly, with the Queen, and who, on public grounds, dreaded the consequences of her influence over her son, prevailed upon the Council to write a letter of expostulation, in which, while assuring the King that nothing should be omitted to save the Prince from falling into the hands of the Parliament, they besought that a place of refuge might be left to their discretion, and that at all events, Ireland or Scotland might be preferred to France.

In the meantime, under color of giving some directions as Chancellor of the Exchequer respecting the duty of customs, he went to Falmouth, and there secured a vessel to be ready at any moment for the escape of the Prince and his attendants.

The King wrote back a peremptory order that the Prince "should quit the kingdom; that he should not go to Scotland or Ireland; that he should go, if possible, to Denmark, and if not thither, rather to France or Holland." There were no means of reaching Denmark, and from Holland the Prince would have been sure to be transferred to France, and placed under the dominion of his mother, whereby a settlement of the nation would become impossible. Hyde and his colleagues, who now had the Prince in their care at Tavistock, addressed another remonstrance to the King, assuring him "that nothing but his commands should put the Prince in the power of the Parliament, but also telling him how strongly the followers of the Prince were disinclined that he should quit the kingdom; that many who were faithful would rather see him in the hands of the enemy than in France; and that the Council must advise that he continue still within the King's dominions, but if occasion required they would transport him to Scilly or to Jersey." At Truro they received an answer by which Charles acquiesced in their views, but reiterated the command that the Prince should leave England whenever there was serious hazard of his being captured by the parliamentary forces.

The victorious Fairfax was now on the borders of Cornwall, and intelligence was received by the Council of a design to seize the Prince's person, "to which they had reason to believe that some of his own servants were not strangers."[1] They withdrew him to Pendennis Castle, but that was no safe asylum; for, on the 2nd of March, they learned from fugitives that Fairfax had taken possession of Bodmin. That night, about ten o'clock, the Prince attended by Hyde and others of his suite, embarked in the vessel that had been prepared for his escape, and in the afternoon of the second day arrived safely in Scilly. Here they found nothing but misery and destitution, and "Colepeper was sent into France to acquaint the Queen with his Highness being at Scilly

[1] Hist. Reb. b. v.

with the wants and incommodities of the place, and to desire supply of men and moneys for the defense thereof, and the support of his own person."[1]

The Prince and his attendants remained in Scilly till the 16th of April, sometimes almost in a state of starvation, for they had only a scanty supply of provisions from Cornwall and from Normandy. They were likewise again in great danger of captivity. Lord Hopton, the King's brave but unfortunate general, who commanded the remnant of the royal army in the west, having been obliged to capitulate, an expedition was fitted out to pursue the Prince; a summons to surrender to the Parliament was sent in; and a hostile fleet of above twenty sail was seen hovering round the island. Happily, a violent storm arose, during which no ship could keep the sea, and the immediate danger was over. As soon as the storm had subsided, the Prince and Hyde set sail for Jersey, where they arrived in safety.

The great struggle now was, whether the Prince should remain at Jersey, or cross over to France. The Queen resorted to every artifice to get him into her power: and knowing that Hyde would never consent to this, she sent him by Colepeper a crafty letter directed to him at Scilly, intimating the friendly disposition of the French Court, "if the Prince, in his way to Jersey, should be necessitated by the contrary winds or the danger of the Parliament shipping, to touch in France." Hyde caused representations to be made to her of the injury likely to arise to the King's affairs from the Prince going to reside in France,—assuring her that he was in perfect safety at Jersey; but she contrived to get from the uxurious King a written authority, signed with his own hand, empowering her to join his "positive commands" to hers that the Prince should repair to her immediately.[2]

After the King's flight from Oxford, and while between him, now a prisoner, and the victorious Parliament, negotiations were pending which might possibly have led to a settlement, if confidence had been placed in his sincerity (for higher terms were not asked than at Uxbridge),—Henrietta, with a certainty of offending every party in the state, and at the risk of raising the suspicion of a plot between the royalists and Cardinal Mazarine, sent over Lord Jermyn,

[1] 1 Hist. Reb. b. v.   [2] Clar. Pap. ii. 230.

her favorite, as the bearer of positive orders in her own name and the King's, that the Prince should forthwith join her at Paris. Hyde could detain him no longer, but refused to accompany him,—seeing that in France he himself must be utterly without power, or influence, or the capacity to render any service to the King, or the Royal family, or his country. He prevailed on Lord Capel and Lord Hopton, two other members of the Council, who concurred in his views, to join him in a respectful letter to the King, justifying their conduct.

Now comes that period of Clarendon's life which, to the vulgar eye, appears disastrous, but to which chiefly he owes his celebrity. Had he flourished in quiet and prosperous times, had he been regularly promoted from being Attorney General to the woolsack, and held the Great Seal till he died,—he might have been surrounded with luxury and flattery while he lived, he might have left titles and fortune to his family, and he might have been quoted in the Court of Chancery as a great Equity Judge,—but he would only have been high in the vulgar line of professional lawyers. Who would exchange the reputation of Clarendon for that of Guilford, or even of Nottingham or of Hardwick?

He remained in this sequestered island above two years,—having entirely sacrificed his profession,—without office or employment,—without the occupation and excitement now afforded by parliamentary opposition to the leaders of a discomfited party,—even without the comforts and solaces of domestic life. But instead of indulging in despondence, or in idleness, or in frivolous amusements, he employed his time with well-directed industry and vigor, and he rendered his name immortal. Seeing the struggle in which he had been engaged was the most important that ever had occurred in English history, and knowing that it must be interesting to all future generations of Englishmen, he had long resolved, for his own fair fame and for the benefit of his country, to become its historian. This purpose was strengthened as he saw the royal cause decline, from the apprehension that the domination of the opposite faction would taint the sources of historic truth. So intent had he become on his object that he began his great work the moment he set his foot on the rock of Scilly, and he seriously applied himself to it amidst the distractions and difficulties of his short and anxious sojourn there,—in danger if taken prisoner by the forces of the Parliament of being brought to trial as a malignant,—and deeply occupied in counteracting the selfish plans of Queen Henrietta Maria, by which she was injuring the royal cause, and cutting off all hope of a happy settlement. Now released from other engrossing duties, he earnestly and devotedly applied himself to his literary undertaking,—of which we can distinctly trace the progress as well as the commencement. He had with him original papers and memoranda which he had been some time collecting, and he anxiously taxed his memory respecting events which had come under his own observation. He endeavored, by application in various quarters, to supply his deficiency of materials with respect to military operations and distant transactions. He wrote to Lord Witherington, the friend of the Marquis of Newcastle, entreating from both of them a narration of those affairs in which they had borne a part. From Lord Bristol he asked information respecting the treaty of Berwick, the Great Council of the Peers at York, and that nobleman's own commitment by the Parliament. To Lord Digby he wrote:—" I pray let your secretaries collect all material passages concerning Ireland you may think fit to impart to me. I would be glad you would yourself collect as many particulars of Count Harcourt's negotiation in England, of Duke Hamilton's commitment, and of the Marquess of Montrose's managing in Scotland, and any other things you imagine conducing to my work." He placed great reliance on Secretary Nicholas, to whom he says, " you will by all your diligence, intercourse, and dexterity, procure me such materials for my History as you know necessary,—which I take to be so much your work that if I fail in it, I will put marginal notes in History that shall reproach you for want of contribution. By your care I must be supplied with all the acts of countenance and confederacy which have passed from France, Holland, and Spain."

His application to Colepeper is particularly interesting, from the allusion to Falkland, and the confidence which the writer displays in his own powers. After asking him for his recollections of Edge Hill, he says, " The like care I expect from you concerning the siege of Gloucester, the raysing y⁰ siege and retriete, the oversight there, the quick march after, and y⁰ first battle of Newbury, where wee lost deare Falkland, *whom y⁰ next age shall be taught to valew more than y⁰ present did.*"

He thus communicated his intention to Charles I., now in the power of the Parliament, but allowed considerable liberty of correspondence and still treated with respect. "I flatter myself with an opinion that I am doing your Majesty some service in this island whilst I am preparing the story of your sufferings, that posterity may tremble at the reading of what the present age blushes not to execute." The King took the most lively interest in the work, and co. tributed a narrative of all important matters between the time when Hyde quitted Oxford to attend the Prince in the west, and his own escape to the Scottish camp. The expectation of further assistance from the same quarter was disappointed, as we learn from a letter written by Hyde, in December, 1647, in which he says,— "Your Majesty's sudden remove from Hampton Court hath for the present taken away the opportunity of de riving those materials which your Majesty graciously intimated by Mr. Secretary Nicholas you intended for me, which renewed my courage when I was even ready to faint for want of some supply." But from Prince Charles he unexpectedly received useful memorials of the campaigns of Prince Rupert.

He devoted not less than ten hours a day to his work, being generally employed three hours a day in writing, and the rest of his time in examining authorities and collating materials. From the unspeakable advantage of having a great and worthy object to pursue, he not only escaped the tedium which must otherwise have devoured him; but, with much to mortify and alarm him, he preserved equanimity and even cheerfulness. He thus describes his course of life at Jersey, till he was left in entire solitude: " Whilst the Lords Capel and Hopton stayed there, they lived and kept house together in St. Hilary's, which is the chief town of the island, where, having a chaplain of their own, they had prayers every day in the church at 11 of the clock in the morning; till which hour they enjoyed themselves in their chambers, according as they thought fit, the CHANCELLOR [1] betaking him-

[1] Our historian shows his fondness for pompous appellations (for which he

self to the continuance of the history which he had begun in Scilly, and spending most of his time at that exercise. The other two walked or rode abroad or read, as they were disposed; but at the hour of prayers they always met, and then dined together at the Lord Hopton's lodgings, which was the best house, they being lodged at several houses with convenience enough. Their table was maintained at their joint expense—only for dinners, they never using to sup, but met always upon the sands in the evening to walk, after going to the castle to Sir George Carteret, who treated them with extraordinary kindness and civility."[1]

After a few months he was deprived of the society of his friends,—Lord Capel leaving Jersey for Holland, and Lord Hopton for Normandy, with a view to their return to England. He was too obnoxious to the Parliament to venture to put himself in its power, and he was too poor to send for his wife and children, who were sheltered by relations in Wiltshire. Speaking of Lady Hyde at this time, he says, "She bears her part with miraculous constancy and courage, which truly is an unspeakable comfort to me."[2]

He now left the town of St. Hilary's, and under the protection of Carteret, constructed for himself some convenient rooms among the ruins of an old castle, and over his door he set up his arms, with this inscription, "Bene vixit qui be, e latuit."

Like most authors, he was occasionally discouraged by the difficulties he met with, saying that he wished he had never begun the work, and that he was determined to lay it aside,—but it made steady progress, and in seven months he got as far as the erecting of the royal standard at Nottingham. To tune his mind to historical composition, and to improve his taste, he read over Livy and Tacitus, and almost all the works of Cicero. He likewise availed himself of the opportunity of improving himself in the French language, which he had hitherto neglected.

His studies were interrupted, first by a report that Lord Jermyn, the Queen's favorite, had engaged to de-

---

was ridiculed) by thus always designating himself when he was in exile in Jersey, because he had been once Chancellor of the Exchequer to Charles I., when there was no revenue to look after.

[1] Life, i. 239.   [2] Clar. Pap. ii. 310.

liver up Jersey and Guernsey to the French for a sum of money, rather than submit to which he patriotically agreed with Carteret that they would call in the assistance of the Parliament,—and afterwards by the preparations of the Parliament forcibly to reduce these islands to subjection; which alarmed him so much for his personal safety that he made his will, wrote a most tender letter to his wife, to be delivered to her when he should be no more, and gave directions respecting his papers and the publication of his " History of the Rebellion."

But all these dangers passed over, and he remained unmolested in his retreat at Jersey till the month of June, 1648. Early in that year he had received the King's commands by Lord Capel that he should attend the Prince, whenever required by the Queen, and the King had directed the Queen to summon him as soon as the Prince, according to a plan agreed upon, was to quit France. In May, a letter came to him from the Queen, requiring him to wait upon the Prince at Paris on a day then gone by. He immediately looked out for the means of a safe transport, and bidding adieu to the island where he had spent his time so creditably, so usefully, and so agreeably, he crossed over to Dieppe, and proceeding to Rouen, he there found his old colleagues, Lord Bristol, Lord Cottington, and Secretary Nicholas who had received similar orders.

A little before this, seventeen sail of English ships of war, lying in the Thames, under a fit of returning loyalty, had declared against the Parliament, and, displacing their Admiral, had sailed to Holland; and the Prince of Wales posting to Calais, had embarked there to join them, and had been acknowledged as their commander. Hyde and Cottington, receiving this intelligence, hastened back to Dieppe. Here they found a French frigate, which conducted them to Dunkirk, where they heard that the Prince with the fleet had entered the river Thames, in h pes of exciting a popular movement in favor of his family. They were eager to participate in this enterprise, and Marshal Ranzau, the Spanish Governor of Dunkirk, furnished them with a vessel to carry them across to the coast of England. Unluckily, they were becalmed and boarded by pirates from Ostend, who, though pretending to have a commission from the King of Spain, " observed no rules or laws of nations." They stripped and rifled the passengers, taking from Lord Cottington to the value of £1,000, and from Hyde £200 in money, and all his clothes and linen, and then carried them prisoners to Ostend.

The two Englishmen, being set at liberty, complained to the law for redress, and they were surprised as well as irritated to find that no effectual steps were taken to arrest the malefactors or restore their stolen property,—till they heard that the piratical ships were the private property of the Governor and magistrates of Ostend, who had divided the spoil. They were obliged to be satisfied with 100 pistoles to discharge the debts they had contracted in the town, and to carry them on their journey. The Prince's naval expedition had failed, and being obliged to retire before the fleet of the Parliament, commanded by the Earl of Warwick, he was then in Holland. Hyde rejoined him at the Hague.

Now arose those bickerings in the exiled Court, to which we have referred in the life of Lord Keeper Herbert, who is so strongly charged by Hyde with having fomented and continued them.[1] A temporary calm was produced by the astounding intelligence of the execution of Charles I., by the exiles formally acknowledging Charles II. as his successor, and by the ceremony of swearing in the old Councillors, with the addition of Secretary Long, of the Privy Council to the new Sovereign. But Hyde soon after had great difficulty in preventing a duel between Lord Cottington and Prince Rupert. He himself had a violent altercation with the Earl of Lauderdale, who would only agree to receive Charles as King of Scotland, on condition of all enemies to the Covenant being left behind,—and he was rendered unhappy by the apprehension of the Great Seal being given to Herbert, whose abilities and services he justly considered much inferior to his own, but whose pretensions were supported by Prince Rupert and others, on the ground of his high birth,—of his having filled the office of Attorney General,—and of his great professional practice and experience. The heartburning on this subject was allayed for a time by an injunction from the Queen mother, to which her son promised obedience, that no new appointment to any state office should

---

[1] Ante, vol. iii. p. 402 *et seq.*

take place for the present, nor till she should give her consent.

The murder of Dorislaus, the ambassador of the Parliament at the Hague, having greatly alienated the States of Holland from the cavalier cause, and Cardinal Mazarine beginning to fear and to court Cromwell,—the only foreign country from which aid could now be expected was Spain. Lord Cottington had been ambassador there before he was made Lord High Treasurer, and from his knowledge of the Court of Madrid, where republican principles were held in great abhorrence, he held out a hope of powerful assistance from that quarter to effect the King's restoration,—particularly through the instrumentality of the Irish Roman Catholics, of whom there was a large number in the Spanish service. He offered himself to undertake the mission, if Hyde would accompany him as his colleague. Little could rationally be expected in such a service except mortification and danger; but Hyde did not feel that he was at liberty to decline it, and he could not be more wretched, or more useless, than in his attendance upon Charles in his wanderings. "In the end he told the Lord Cottington that he would only be passive in this point, and refer it entirely to him, if he thought fit, to dispose the King to like it; and if the King approved it, and commended it as a thing he thought for his service, he would submit to his command."

Charles approving, "soon afterwards publicly declared his resolution to send the Lord Cottington and the Chancellor of the Exchequer his ambassadors extraordinary into Spain, and commanded them to prepare their own commission and instructions, and to begin their journey as soon as was possible."

Their secret instructions were to press for the recognition of Charles as the legitimate King of England; to try to effect a league offensive and defensive between him and the King of Spain; to raise a loan, for which security was to be given under the Great Seal of England, in any fashion that might be desired; and that, by way of concession, they should give assurances of the King's resolutions of grace and favor towards his Catholic subjects, and that they should offer all manner of civilities to the Pope's nuncio at Madrid.

Hyde left the Hague in the end of May, and spent

nearly two years in this mission, which turned out to be the most harassing and unprofitable portion of his life. After settling his wife and family at Antwerp, visiting the Archduke and the Duke of Lorraine at Brussels, and with difficulty raising a small supply of money to defray the necessary expense of his journey, he visited Charles at St. Germain's, and his mother at Paris, and tried to make peace between them. At last he reached St. Sebastian's, on the Spanish frontier. Here Cottington and he met with their first rebuff, for the Corregidor showed them a letter from the Secretary of State at Madrid, ordering that when the ambassadors of the Prince of Wales should arrive there, they should be received with all respect; but they should be instructed not to proceed till the King of Spain's further pleasure was made known to them,—and in the passports handed to them they were designated as "ambassadors of the Prince of Wales." They dispatched a remonstrance to Don Luis de Haro, the Spanish minister—desiring to know if their coming was unacceptable to his Catholic Majesty,—in which case they would immediately return,—and desiring that if they were received, it might be in such a manner as was due to the King they represented. An answer was sent imputing the designed insult to the negligence of a Secretary, and assuring them of a good welcome from the Spanish King. But on their arrival at Alcavendas, three leagues from Madrid, they found that no preparations were made for their reception, and that the Spanish Court wished them heartily at a distance—beginning to entertain apprehensions of the displeasure of the English parliament. To avoid proclaiming to all Europe the ill usage they experienced by now retreating they privately entered Madrid, and, preserving their *incognito*, took up their residence at the house of an English merchant well affected to their cause. On a fresh representation to the minister, a formal reception was promised, and in the mean time they were invited to tournaments and bull-fights, where places of honor were assigned to them.

Intelligence arrived at Madrid that the Parliament was becoming unpopular and weak, and the promised reception was accorded to the royalist ambassadors. "The King[1] slightly moved his hat and bid them cover." Their

[1] Philip IV.

credentials being delivered, " he expressed," says Clarendon, "a very tender sense of our King's condition, and acknowledged that it concerned all Kings to join together for the punishment of such an impious rebellion and parricide ; and, if his own affairs would permit, he would be the first to undertake it ; but that they could not but know how full his hands were, and whilst he had so powerful an enemy to contend with he could hardly defend himself; but that when there should be a peace with France (which he desired), the King, his *sobrino* (for so he called the King his nephew), should find all he could expect from him ; in the mean time he would be ready to do all that was in his power towards his assistance and maintenance."[1]

But the dread of Cromwell, to whom Europe now began to look, as the person who would terminate the troubles in England by military despotism, prevented any further notice being taken of them—till Rupert, with his fleet, appeared upon the coast of Spain, and dispatched a letter to Hyde, desiring him to obtain from the Court of Madrid " good reception for his vessels in any Spanish port they might have occasion to enter." The character of this unscrupulous warrior indicated immediate danger, and letters were dispatched that very night conveying the required directions to the Governors of all Spanish ports on the ocean and within the straits, " with as many friendly clauses as could have been inserted if the King had been in possession of his whole empire ;—so great an influence a little appearance of power had upon their spirits : and the ambassadors found they lived in another kind of air than they had done; and received every day visits from the Court and from those in authority."

But Hyde and his colleague, before long, found themselves again neglected, by reason of a storm which did great damage to the fleet bearing the royal flag of England, and the arrival on the coast of Spain of a more powerful fleet equipped by the Parliament, the commander of which menacingly warned the Spanish government, "that he knew well how to do himself right for any injury or discourtesy they might sanction." Not only were orders issued to entertain his ships with all hospitality, but he received a valuable ring from the King as a propitiatory offering.

[1] Hist. Reb. b. vi.

Hyde and Cottington soon after got into still greater disgrace by the assassination at Madrid of Ascham, the diplomatic agent of the Commonwealth. "They immediately sent a letter to Don Luis de Haro to express the sense they had of this unfortunate, rash action, of which they hoped he did believe if they had any notice or suspicion they would have prevented."[1]

Although Don Luis disclaimed a belief so injurious, suspicion fell upon them, as they had warmly protested against Ascham's reception, and one of his assassins was in their service. However, there seems no reason to believe that Hyde was at all privy to the affair. In a letter to Secretary Nicholas he said, " This accident hath been very unfortunate to our business, concerning which we were promised to have positive resolutions within a few days, but we must now sit still, without pressing them, till this matter be concluded; there having not wanted some malicious spirits here, which would beget an opinion that we were privy to this mad action, when God knows, we knew not of the man's being come to the town till we heard that he was dead."[2]

They were again courted, and feted, and fed with fine promises on news arriving that Charles II. had been received and recognized as King of Scotland,—the Spaniards not being aware of the insecurity of his tenure of power there, and not understanding what was meant by his having been obliged to deplore the wickedness of his father, and to declare that, "detesting prelacy, he would henceforth have neither friends nor enemies but such as were the friends or enemies of the COVENANT." But a dispatch from Cardenas, the Spanish resident in London, announcing to his government the decisive victory gained by Cromwell at Dunbar, by which Scotland was conquered, proved the final ruin of all the hopes of Hyde and Cottington at Madrid. They had received instructions from Charles to protract their stay, and they tried to make it appear that this defeat would advance his cause in England; but the Spanish govern-

---

[1] Hist. Reb. b. vi.
[2] Clar. Pap. iii. 21. It is curious to consider that during the heat of the civil war, there was not a single assassination in England; but that when it was over, the recollection of it caused several assassinations on the Continent by Englishmen of the cavalier party, as that of Dorislaus in Holland, of Ascham in Spain, of Lisle in Switzerland, &c.

ment placed no faith in this explanation, and after many hints that their continued attendance was unwelcome and fruitless, they at last received a formal message in the name of King Philip " that they had received answers to all they had proposed, and were at liberty to depart, which his Catholic Majesty desired they would do, since their presence in the Court would be prejudicial to his affairs." They demanded and obtained an interview with Don Luis de Haro, but instead of being swayed by their remonstrances, " he pressed them very plainly, and without any regard to the season of the year, it being toward the end of January, to use all possible expedition for their departure, as a thing that even in that respect did exceedingly concern the service of the King." A day even was fixed by the Spanish government for their audience of leave.

It is a striking fact, that at no Court in Europe was much sympathy exhibited for the Stuarts, and in the middle of the 17th century there was no such coalition of Sovereigns in support of royalty as was witnessed at the conclusion of the 18th century, when a republic was about to be estabished in France. On the Continent, the contagion of republican principles does not seem to have been at all dreaded, and the English nation, being left to the entire management of their own affairs,—first the parliament, and then Cromwell, were cordially admitted into the community of European governments.

Thus terminated Hyde's most irksome residence of fifteen months at Madrid. Besides the diplomatic disappointments he encountered, his pecuniary resources were so low, that he often found the greatest difficulty in providing for the personal wants of himself, and his wife and children left destitute in a distant land. " All our money is gone," he writes, " and let me never prosper if I know or can imagine how we can get bread a month longer." [1] Again, " Greater necessities are hardly felt by any men than we for the present undergo,—such as have almost made me foolish ; I have not for my life been able to supply the miserable distresses of my poor wife." [2]

Hyde found consolation in that love of study which was his best friend throughout his chequered life. His History was suspended for want of materials, but he now assiduously cultivated the Spanish language, initiated

[1] Jan. 6, 1650.   [2] Aug. 16, 1650.

himself in Spanish literature, and made himself familiar with Spanish laws and customs.[1] He also here composed a devotional work, entitled "Contemplations and Reflections upon the Psalms of David, applied to the Troubles of this Time."

He had soon the affliction of losing the society of his colleague, Lord Cottington, who having no wife or children to return to, being worn down by age and infirmity, being reconciled to the Roman Catholic Church in which he had been educated, and sickening at the thought of being again plunged into the civil and religious distractions of his native country, resolved to spend the remainder of his days in Spain, and obtained permission from the Spanish government to reside in a private capacity at Valladolid.[2]

Hyde accordingly had his audience of leave as sole ambassador. He had conducted himself during his residence at Madrid so decorously, so inoffensively, and, notwithstanding his narrow circumstances, with so much dignity, that he had made a very favorable impression upon the Spaniards, which now showed itself in spite of the usual selfish and timid policy of the Court. "Hearing that he intended to repair to his family at Antwerp, and stay there till he received other orders from the King his master, they gave him all dispatches thither that might be of use to him in those parts. The King of Spain himself used many gracious expressions to him at his last audience, and sent afterwards to him a letter for the Archduke Leopold, in which he expressed the good opinion he had of the ambassador, and commanded that whilst he should choose to reside in those parts under his government, he should receive all respect and enjoy all privileges as an ambassador; all which ceremonies, though they cost him nothing, were of real benefit and advantage to him, for besides the treatment he received from the Archduke himself in Brussels, as ambassador, such directions or recommendations were sent to the magistrates

---

[1] He must surely now have read Don Quixote in the original, but he says only that "he made a collection of and read many of the best books which are extant in that language, especially the histories of their civil and ecclesiastical polity," and I do not trace in his writings any allusion to Cervantes. He does not appear to have had any taste for what we call *light reading;* if he had, his History might have been a little less *weighty.*

[2] He died there in 1652, in his 77th year.

of Antwerp, that he enjoyed the privilege of his chapel, and all the English, who were numerous in that city, repaired thither with all freedom for their devotion; which liberty had never before been granted to any man there."[1]

CHAPTER LXXVII.

CONTINUATION OF THE LIFE OF CLARENDON TILL THE GREAT SEAL WAS DELIVERED TO HIM AT BRUGES.

HYDE left Madrid in March, 1651, and after a fatiguing journey, performed chiefly on mules, reached Paris. Here he was received more graciously than usual by Queen Henrietta, who was in a state of great anxiety from the perils to which her son was exposed in Scotland. The ex-ambassador then traveled on to Antwerp, where he had, for some months, the exquisite enjoyment of living quietly in the bosom of his family, although disturbed by the sad news of the battle of Worcester, and under long suspense respecting the fate of his young Sovereign. At last, news came of Charles's miraculous escape and safe arrival in Normandy. Hyde soon received a summons to repair to Paris, and on Christmas-day, 1651, again took up his residence there as a member of the exiled Court. All the former enmities, and jealousies, and rivalries between the titular ministers now broke out with fresh violence, the Queen recklessly inflaming and exasperating them in her efforts to gain an ascendency for herself. She was at the head of one party, and Hyde of another. To strengthen herself, she tried to introduce Sir John Berkeley into the Council, and to have him appointed "Master of the Wards," an office depending upon the oppressive military tenures which the parliament had abolished, and to the abolition of which the late King, at several conferences had readily agreed. Hyde urged "that the King could not, at the time, do a more ungracious thing, that would lose him more the hearts and affections of the nobility and gentry of England, than in making a *Master of the Wards* in a time when it would not be the least advantage to his Majesty

[1] Hist. Reb. b. vi.

or the officer; to declare that he resolved to insist upon that part of his prerogative which his father had consented to part with." This opposition succeeded, but rendered the Queen still more hostile to Hyde.

In the next controversy between them, I must say it seems to me that he was decidedly wrong, and that he displayed those narrow-minded and bigoted principles, as an ultra-high-church Episcopalian, which subsequently betrayed him into serious errors, and even a sacrifice of good faith. The French government becoming more and more intolerant, would not suffer any English strangers to have a place of worship in Paris according to the rites and ceremonies of the Church of England; but at Charenton, in the suburbs, there was a Huguenot chapel, where, the Edict of Nantes not being yet repealed, the Protestant service was celebrated according to law, and a very pious and learned divine ministered to a most respectable congregation. The Queen declaring that, notwithstanding her zeal for her own religion, she respected the dying injunctions of her late husband, and was contented that her son should remain a Protestant, consented to his going to this chapel, as he could not be present at the celebration of mass, and there was no other place of public worship for him to attend. In answer to Hyde's opposition, she observed "that Queen Elizabeth had greatly favored the Huguenots; that they were recognized as a reformed church; and that their pastors had been admitted into the Church of England without fresh ordination." But Hyde, who heartily disliked the Roman Catholics, but much more any Protestant church that did not rigidly adhere to the "Apostolic succession," declared with much earnestness, "that whatever countenance or favor the Crown or Church of England had heretofore shown to these congregations, it was in a time when they carried themselves with modesty towards both; but that, of late, some of their preachers had countenanced the doctrine that it might be lawful to resist a King by arms, and had even inveighed against Episcopacy; that the Queen, whose ulterior object was the conversion of her son to Popery, intended to unsettle his faith, and weaken his attachment to the only true reformed church; when he would be more accessible to her persuasions; and that, from the King's going to Charenton, it would be concluded everywhere that he thought the Episcopalian profession and Presbyterian profession were indifferent, which would be one of the most deadly wounds to the Church of England which it had yet suffered."

This matter being debated in Council, Charles, who was delighted to be entirely exempted from the restraint of attending public worship said with affected gravity (having probably first cast a sly look at Buckingham), "that upon the whole he thought the arguments of the Chancellor of the Exchequer preponderated, and that, out of respect for that true Apostolical church, to the safety of which his blessed father died a martyr, he would not frequent the heretical conventicle at Charenton."[1] He was thus at liberty, without any interruption, to devote himself on Sundays to Miss Lucy Walters and other ladies of the same stamp, in whose society he now spent almost the whole of his time.[2]

Plunged in the gayeties of Paris, he forgot the misfortunes of his family, and lost sight of his three kingdoms, content if, from any source, he could be supplied with money to defray his personal expenses. Hyde often gave him excellent general advice, which he received with good humor, and neglected, — and all that he would promise with regard to business was, "that a part of every Friday (*a day of penance*) he would employ in reading and answering letters on public affairs." But the number and publicity of his amours at last caused general scandal among his followers, and was reported to his disadvantage in England. His character particularly suffered from the utter worthlessness of Lucy Walters, who by her arts had won his affections, who by her influence continued to exercise a powerful control over his easy temper, and who was now the mother of a child she called his,—afterwards

---

[1] Hist. Reb. b. vi. Life of Clarendon (L. C.) 94.
[2] A sincere friend to the Church of England, I can not conceal my disapprobation of this horror of entering a Presbyterian place of worship, which we still occasionally meet with in the High Church party—which induced Hyde to advise that Charles should rather live like a heathen, than attend public worship in a French Protestant chapel—and made Dr. Johnson say, when in Scotland, that he would not go to hear Principal Robertson preach, unless he should take a tree for his pulpit. The only arguments to support such intolerance place those who use them at the mercy of the Romanists, to whom, perhaps, they would be glad to be re-united. Very different is the conduct of our beloved sovereign, Queen Victoria, who, when in Scotland, attends divine service in the church of the parish in which for the time she is residing.

the celebrated Duke of Monmouth. Hyde, assisted by Ormond, interfered to dissolve this disgraceful connection, and representing to Charles the injury which it did to the royal cause at home, where the appearances, at least, of morality were so highly respected, they prevailed upon him to separate from her, and as he still renewed his intercourse with her, they induced her, by an annuity of £400, to repair with the child to her native country. When she arrived there she called herself Charles's wife, and Cromwell, after keeping her some time in the Tower, sent her back to Paris. But Hyde had little more trouble with her, for her open lewdness was such as to forfeit the royal favor, and she soon after died disgracefully. Her son had been taken from her and placed under the care of the *Oratoriens* at Paris [1]

A plan was now brought forward by a party in the exiled Court, to marry the King and the Duke of York to Mademoiselle d'Orléans and Mademoiselle de Longueville,—alliances which, from the ladies being Roman Catholics, would have caused extreme dissatisfaction in England, and might seriously have obstructed the restoration of the royal family. This was successfully opposed by Hyde; but he wisely supported the proposal, that the younger brother should serve in the French army, and honorably employ himself in seeking military experience under the great Turenne.

In proportion as Cromwell gained an ascendency in the Continental Courts as well as at home, and the royal party was isolated in the apartments of the Louvre assigned to them, Hyde's difficulties increased—from their want of real business. "It is hard," he says, in a spirit of good-natured sarcasm, "for people who have nothing to do, to forbear doing something which they ought not to do. Whilst there are Courts in the world, emulation and ambition will be inseparable from them; and Kings who have nothing to give shall be pressed to promise. Men who would not have had the presumption to have asked the same thing if the King had been in England, thought it very justifiable to demand it because he was not there, since there were so many hazards that they should never live to enjoy what he promised."[2] Upon Hyde was thrown the unpopular task of refusing these solicitations, for in the

[1] 2 Clar. Pap. iii. 180. Thurloe, v. 163, 173. [2] Hist. Reb. b. vi.

illness and absence of Secretary Nicholas, he was now considered the acting and sole Secretary of State.

As Chancellor of the Exchequer devolved upon him the duty of attending to the scanty finances of the impoverished King. A handsome revenue had been expected from the prizes to be made by the fleet under the orders of Prince Rupert; but he returned from his buccaneering expedition to the West Indies, bringing in an account by which he made the King his debtor, and nothing was now to be expected from this quarter except a trifle by the sale of the decayed ships and their guns and stores.

In a letter written to Sir Richard Brown, in August, 1652, Hyde says, "A sum lately received at Paris for the King is all he hath received since he came hither, and doth not enable his cooks and back-stairs men to go on in providing his diet, but they protest they can undertake it no longer." The deficit increased. In the end of this year, the Finance Minister writes, "the King is reduced to greater distress than you can believe or imagine;" and in the summer of the following year, he thus describes the state of the treasury:—"I do not know that any man is yet dead for want of bread, which really I wonder at. I am sure the King himself owes for all he has eaten since April; and I am not acquainted with one servant of his who hath a pistole in his pocket. Five or six of us eat together one meal a day for a pistole a week; but all of us owe for God knows how many weeks to the poor woman that feeds us."[1]

This may seem the language of *badinage*; but to other correspondents he writes in a strain which proves that his own personal sufferings from poverty were most severe. "At this time I have neither clothes nor fire to preserve me from the sharpness of the season."[2] "I am so cold, that I am scarce able to hold my pen, and have not three sous in the world to buy a faggot."[3] "I have not been master of a crown these many months, am cold for want of clothes and fire, and owe for all the meat I have eaten these three months, and to a poor woman who is no longer able to trust; and my poor family at Antwerp (which breaks my heart) is in as sad a state as I am."[4] "I

[1] Clar. Pap. iii. 174.
[2] Nov. 9, 1652.
[3] Clar. Pap. iii. 126.
[4] Ibid. 114.

owe so much money here to all sorts of people, that I would not wonder if I were cast into prison to-morrow; and if the King should remove, as I hope he will shortly have occasion to do, and not enable me to pay the debt I have contracted for his service, I must look for that portion, and starve there."[1]

His new honor of "Foreign Secretary" added greatly to his embarrassments, as the letters for his Government were all directed to him. "I can not," he says, "avoid the constant expense of seven or eight livres the week for postage of letters, which I borrow scandalously out of my friends' pockets, or else my letters must more scandalously remain still at the post-house: and I am sure that all those which concern my own private affairs would be received for ten sous a week; so that all the rest are for the King, from whom I have not received one penny since I came hither."[2]

He bore up nobly amidst all these embarrassments. In a frame of mind firm, cheerful, and resigned, he thus writes to Nicholas:—"Keep up your spirits, and take heed of sinking under that burden you never kneeled to take up. Our innocence begets our cheerfulness; and that again will be a means to secure the other. Whoever grows too weary and impatient of the condition he is in, will too impatiently project to get out of it; and that, by degrees, will shake, or baffle, or delude his innocence. We have no reason to blush for the poverty which is not brought upon us by our own faults. As long as it pleases God to give me health, (which, I thank him, I have in a very great measure,) I shall think he intends I shall outlive all these sufferings; and when he sends sickness I shall (I hope with the same submission) believe, that he intends to remove me from greater calamities."[3]

But all these sufferings were light compared to the tortures which he felt from the promotion of Herbert, the late Attorney General, to be Lord Keeper. This individual, as we have before explained in his Life, was made an instrument in the hands of Hyde's enemies to mortify

---

[1] Clar. Pap. iii. 164.
[2] The Queen could not be blamed for not assisting her son with money; for it is related that about this time she was obliged to keep her daughter Henrietta all day in bed during a severe frost, because she had not money to buy fuel to light a fire to warm her.   [3] Clar. Pap. ii. 310.

and depress him.¹ "The Queen's displeasure grew so notorious against him, that after he found, by degrees, that she would not speak to him, nor take any notice of him when she saw him, he forbore at last coming into her presence, and for many months did not see her face, though he had the honor to lodge in the same house, the Palace Royal,² where their Majesties kept their Courts."³ But she had ample vengeance when she had prevailed upon her son, on specious pretexts, to deliver the Great Seal to Herbert,—which Hyde, notwithstanding all his awkward attempts at seeming indifference evidently considered the heaviest misfortune which had ever befallen him.

The new Lord Keeper by no means bore his faculties meekly; and, not contented with parading his rank and precedence, he entered into cabals for the utter ruin of his rival. But these terminated in his own discomfiture, and after holding the Great Seal little more than a year, he was deprived of it, and consigned to a premature grave.⁴

Hyde cleared himself satisfactorily of the charge of having had an interview in England with Cromwell, and of having received a pension from him for secret information, as well as having spoken slanderous words of the King, and he wrote pleasantly to his friends: "I hope you think it strange to hear that I have been in England, and have had private conference with Cromwell." "It seems I was in England at the time you were at Antwerp, and I believe upon examination you will be found to have been there with me. Of the pension I heard not till lately. My comfort is, that I do not know that any such little stratagems do make impression upon any worthy person."⁵

From the powerful influence of the Queen, and the ill offices of other enemies, and the levity of the King, Hyde had been in serious danger of being discarded, and of being driven either to sue for pardon to Cromwell, or to die of chagrin and misery in exile. The year ending in June, 1654, was the most unhappy he had ever passed. But he was recompensed by seeing the Great Seal again in the King's own custody, and certainly knowing that

---

¹ Ante, vol. iii. p. 404.   ² Palais Royal.   ³ Hist. Reb. b. vii.
⁴ See Life of Lord Keeper Herbert, *ante*, vol. iii. p. 406.
⁵ Clar. Pap. iii. 188.

when the Court moved into the Low Countries, "Ex-Lord Keeper Herbert" was to be left behind at Paris.

While Charles was making this journey, Hyde had leave of absence to visit his family, now stationed at Breda. Before quitting Paris,—on the suggestion of Charles, he asked and he obtained an audience of leave from his old enemy the Queen. She charged him with disrespect, saying, "that all men took notice that he never came where she was, though he lodged under her roof." He replied,—" Madam, your Majesty mentions my punishment, not my fault. Duty apart, which I hope I shall ever feel, I am not so devoid of sense as needlessly by my own act to render it notorious that I am not favorably regarded by the widow of my deceased Master and the mother of my present Sovereign. But unfortunately for me, Madam, it has been sufficiently evident that my presence was unwelcome, and for this reason alone have I abstained from obtruding myself upon your Majesty's notice; but now I do most humbly pray that your Majesty will dismiss me with the knowledge of what has been taken amiss, that I may be able to make mine innocence and integrity appear." "But," says he, speaking historically of himself in the third person, "all this prevailed not with her Majesty, who, after she had, with her former passion, objected his credit with the King, and his endeavor to lessen that credit which she ought to have, —concluded that she should be glad to see reason to change her opinion; and so carelessly extended her hand towards him—which he kissing, her Majesty departed to her chamber."[1]

While Charles was sojourning at Spa, in the society of his sister, the Princess of Orange, Hyde spent his time most happily with his wife and children at Breda; but the Court being fixed at Cologne, in the month of November, he was obliged to repair thither, and to resume the irksome duties of prime minister to an exiled monarch.

An event of a domestic nature now occurred to him

---

[1] Hist. Reb. b. vii. The noble historian is sure to put his opponent in the wrong in relating any controversy in which he was personally concerned, and we must always remember the enmity between him and Henrietta when we read his remarks upon her—particularly in judging of the dark insinuations he throws out against her, while pretending to excuse her, for discouraging the escape of her husband into France, where she was then living, attended by Lord Jermyn.

which afterwards led to important consequences. The Princess of Orange had been very kind to his family, had provided a house for them rent free at Breda, and taken much notice of his daughter, Anne, now a sprightly girl reaching woman's estate. By the sudden death of a maid of honor, of the smallpox, this situation became vacant in the establishment of the Princess, and Hyde, in his narrow circumstances, was advised to ask it for his daughter. But he declined,—saying, "that he had but one daughter, who was all the company and comfort her mother had in her melancholy retirement, and therefore he was resolved not to separate them, nor to dispose his daughter to a court life." This, however, was only coyness, and the matter was managed indirectly. The appointment was suggested to the Princess and to the King, who both approved of it, and they, though a little afraid of the reproaches of their mother, proposed it to Hyde. He still affected to dislike it, but agreed to leave the decision to Lady Hyde. She, well knowing what would please her husband, accepted the offer, and the future Duchess of York, and mother of Queen Mary and Queen Anne, was established in the household of the Princess.

With a short interval, during which Charles removed to the sea-coast to favor a rising in England, he remained at Cologne above two years, and Hyde attended him almost as his only minister. The royal exile now saw near the lowest ebb of his fortunes, and was obliged to live like a distressed private gentleman, the whole expense of his establishment not exceeding 600 pistoles a month.

Hyde at this time wisely trusted to general discontent in England rather than to open insurrection or to military assistance from foreign powers. He thus reasons in a letter to Secretary Nicholas: "I am confident there are many officers who will always believe that they have done as much for the Commonwealth as Cromwell himself, and therefore will not be content that he should carry away the reward; and if I did not assuredly think that in that method of destruction, and from that fountain of pride and madness, they will at last determine the confusion, and be each other's executioners, I should be very melancholick; for I have really more hope from that than from all the armies and fleets you and your enterprising friends will be able to draw together." [1]

The tranquillity of the little Court at Cologne was much troubled by the discovery of the treachery of Manning, a young Roman Catholic, who, pretending to be an ardent royalist, had been admitted into their inmost confidence, and who, being detected in a correspondence with Secretary Thurloe, confessed that he had been Cromwell's paid spy for three years, transmitting to him, in consideration of £100 a month, all the plans of the royalists. By a stretch of power, which we can not understand how Hyde, who possessed a smattering of municipal law and of the law of nations, could sanction,—the English shot him as a traitor;—pretty much in the same way as Queen Christina of Sweden soon after, when she had ceased to wear a crown, thought fit to execute her chamberlain at Fontainebleau. Cromwell was advised to retaliate, but he would not recognize his spy.[2]

The former charges against Hyde for being himself in correspondence with Cromwell were certainly ridiculous; but many believe that seeing the splendid success of the Protector's foreign policy, the regularity of his internal government, notwithstanding the mutinous disposition of his parliaments, and the power now conferred upon him of naming a successor, the expectant Chancellor regarded him as the founder of a new dynasty, and despairing of the recall of the ancient royal line, and sick of the evils of exile, wished to be reconciled to him. The story goes, that shortly before the removal of the Court from Cologne, he wrote a confidential letter to Secretary Thurloe, with whom he had formerly been on terms of friendship, praying that he might be allowed to return with his family to his native land,—that the letter being shown to Cromwell, he readily gave his assent, thinking that such a defection would be highly detrimental to the royal cause,—that a favorable answer was returned,—but that while difficulties arose as to the mode of executing the plan, a ray of hope broke in from the offered support of Spain;—that Hyde therefore resolved to prefer the chance of a Restoration;—that his letter was carefully preserved

---

[1] Nov. 1655.
[2] "The wretch soon after received the reward due to his treason." This is the whole of Clarendon's account of Manning's execution.—*Hist. Reb.* b. xiv.

by Thurloe;—that when the Restoration did take place, Thurloe, whose head was very insecure, adventured to the house of the Lord High Chancellor, and saying he had a present to make him, delivered the letter into his hand,—and that his Lordship having perused it in some confusion, gave him thanks, bade him go and live quietly in his chambers, and promised that he should be in nowise molested.[1] No strong proof is brought forward to support this charge; but I must say that it is not by any means improbable, and we ought not to discredit it merely from Hyde's own professions, for he did not hesitate to practice duplicity, even with his friends. Upon this very subject while at Madrid he thus writes to Secretary Nicholas: "I know no other counsel to give you than by the grace of God I mean to follow myself, which is to submit to God's pleasure and judgment upon me, and to starve, really and literally, with the comfort of having endeavored to avoid it by all honest means, and rather to bear it than do anything contrary to my duty. Compounding is a thing I do not understand, or how a man can do it to save one's life. We must play out the game with that courage as becomes gamesters who were first engaged by conscience against all motives and temptations of interest, and be glad to let the world know that we were carried on only by conscience. Indeed, all discourse of submitting or compounding with those rogues in England hath so little of sense or excuse in it, that there needs no reply to it. You and I must die in the streets first of hunger."[2] Yet at the same time he thus discloses his secret thoughts in a letter to his intimate friend, Sir Toby Matthew: "And now, sir, let me tell you in your ear (as one whom I dare trust with my want of judgment), that after all my travel through the Low Countries, and, I think, the length of France, and little less than 400 miles in the King's dominions, England is a very convenient place; and the people were once as good company as any of their neighbors; and if they can be yet reduced to half the honesty they had, if you please I will meet you there; and if we ever come again willingly out of it, let us be banished London. But I

---

[1] See Life of Clarendon, by an impartial hand. 2nd ed. 1712, p. 110.
[2] Clar. Pap. iii. 24, 25.

will take no peremptory resolution till I know how far I may depend upon your conscience." [1]

If he did sometimes vacillate in the trying circumstances in which he was placed, we must not condemn him with too much severity. There is no reason to suppose he ever would have compromised the personal safety of the expatriated King, or betrayed any confidence reposed in him; and like Prince Talleyrand, in other revolutionary times, he might have honorably served opposite parties and dynasties as they successively gained the ascendency.

In April, 1656, Charles proceeded suddenly from Cologne to Bruges, in consequence of a negotiation opened with him when Cromwell engaged in hostilities against Spain. Hyde was, for a time, left behind to settle the King's financial affairs,—which he found no easy task. This was the first dispatch to his Britannic Majesty: "Your family here is in an ill condition and your debts great; much owing by you and by those to whom you are indebted; and yet, that the state may not appear more dismal and irreparable to you than in truth it is, give me leave to tell you that 4,000 pistoles will dischrge the whole seven months' board wages which are due, pay all you owe here, supply those acts of bounty you will for the present think necessary, to those who receive not in wages, and honestly remove and bring your family to you." [2]

Small as the required *supply* was, the Chancellor of the Exchequer could not find *ways and means* to raise it, and four months after, still remaining himself in pawn, he thus addresses the King: "I do confess I do think that the payment of what is due at Cologne is of the most importance to you, and is to be such an ingredient in the establishing your future credit, of which you have so much use, that it ought to be compassed, even with some hazard to your Majesty of future inconvenience." [3]

By receipt of the arrears of small pensions allowed him by the Elector of Cologne and other German Princes, Hyde was at last able to clear off these demands and to join his Master at Bruges. [4] There he entered into a nego-

---

[1] Clar. Pap. March 18, 1650.   [2] Ibid. iii. 293.   [3] Ibid. iii. 302.
[4] These distresses probably furnished the hint for one of the chapters of Addison's "Annals of the Reign of the Pretender," the son of James II. "Anno Regni 4º. He ordered the Lord High Treasurer to pay off the debts

tiation with his Holiness the Pope for his aid, upon principles sufficiently liberal; for, discouraging the hope of the King's conversion he intimated his desire to put the Roman Catholics in the same condition with his other subjects; and thus concluded: "You know well, that though the King hath in himself power to pardon and dispense with the execution of laws, yet that to the Repeal of them there must be the consent of others, and therefore the less discourse there is of it the more easily it will be done; and it is no small prejudice the passion and unskillfulness of some Catholics bring to their own hopes, which must be compassed with gravity and order." [1]

But the negotiation least creditable to Hyde, was that which he carried on with Sexby, the enthusiast who had published the famous pamphlet, entitled "Killing no Murder;" and who, though he required a dispensation from the ceremony of *kneeling* to Charles when he came over to Bruges, had made no secret of his intention to assassinate Cromwell, as an act for which he expected to be applauded by men and rewarded by Heaven.

After Hyde had been some months at Bruges, an occurrence took place which materially altered his nominal rank and precedence. It was suggested in council, that as Charles was now formally recognized as King of England by Spain, and was entering into a regular treaty, offensive and defensive, with that country, it would be proper that his own Court should assume more the aspect of royalty, and that he should have a Lord High Chancellor. There was only one person that could be named for this distinction. Clarendon very affectedly and hypocritically pretends that he urgently declined the office when it was offered to him, "giving many reasons besides his own unfitness, when there was no need of such an officer, or, indeed, any use of the Great Seal, till the King should come into England; and that his Majesty found some ease in being without such an officer; that he was not troubled with those suits which he would be if the Seal were in the hands of a proper officer to be used, since every body would be then importuning the King for the grant of offices, honors, and lands, which would give him

of the Crown, which had been contracted since his accession to the throne; particularly a milk score of three years' standing."—*Freeholder*, No. 36.

[1] Clar. Pap. iii. 291.

great vexation to refuse, and do him as great mischief by granting." We are asked to believe that the King not only initiated, but vigorously carried through the measure, and now said, "*he would deal truly and freely with him; that the principal reason which he had alleged against receiving the Seal, was the greatest reason that disposed him to confer it upon him.* Thereupon he pulled letters out of his pocket, which he received lately from Paris, for the grant of several reversions in England of offices and lands; one whereof was of the Queen's house and lands of Oaklands, to the same man who had purchased it from the State; who would willingly have paid a good sum of money to that person who was to procure such a confirmation of his title; the draught whereof was prepared at London, upon confidence that it would have the Seal presently put to it; which being in the King's hand, none need, as they thought, to be privy to the secret. His Majesty told him also of many other importunities with which he was every day disgusted, and that he saw no other remedy to give himself ease, than to put the Seal out of his own keeping into such hands as would not be importuned, and would h l> him to deny. And, therefore, he conjured the Chancellor to receive that trust, with many gracious promises of his favor and protection. Whereupon the Earl of Bristol and Secretary Nicholas using likewise their persuasion, he submitted to the King's pleasure; who delivered the Seal to him in the Christmas time in the year 1657."

I must, nevertheless, be permitted to doubt whether, in the absence of all other lawyers, the King, or any human being about the Court of Bruges, would have ever thought of the office of Chancellor, or recollected that there was in existence such a bauble as the Great Seal, which had lain neglected in the bottom of an old trunk ever since it was taken from Lord Keeper Herbert at Paris,—if Hyde himself, now beginning to see a better prospect of the King's recall, and anxious that, when that event arrived, he should have no competitor for the office of Chancellor, had not deemed this a convenient opportunity for securing it, and had not indirectly contrived that it should be offered to him.[1]

---

[1] He evidently assigns a reason that could have no real connection with the transaction—"Sir Edward Herbert, who was the last Lord Keeper of the

The exact day of the appointment is fixed by the following entry in the register in the Council office:—

"Att the Court att Bruges, the 13th day of Jany. 1658, st. n.

    "Present, His Majestie.
      "Duke of York.
      "Lord Lieut. of Ireland (Ormond).
      "Mr. Secretary Nicholas.
      "Mr. Chancellor of the Exchequer.

"His Majestie declared his resolution to leave his Greate Seale in custody of an officer, and therefore had made choice of Sir Edward Hyde, Chancellor of the Exchequer, to be Lord Chancellor of England, unto whom he forthwith delivered the Greate Seale, and commanded him to be sworn; who took the oath of supremacy and allegiance upon his knee at the board, and Mr. Secretary Nicholas gave him the oath of Lord Chancellor of England, and then he took his place by his Majestie's command."

Great Seal, being lately dead at Paris." The Great Seal had been taken from Herbert on the removal of the Court from Paris in 1654. But this statement has misled almost all writers who have noticed the subject, to state that Herbert continued Lord Keeper as long as he lived, and that it was on the vacancy occasioned by his death that Hyde was appointed.

www.ingramcontent.com/pod-product-compliance
Lightning Source LLC
Chambersburg PA
CBHW032028150426
43194CB00006B/194